LAWYER GAMES

AFTER MIDNIGHT IN THE GARDEN OF GOOD AND EVIL

Dep Kirkland

First published by Dog Ear Publishing
4011 Vincennes Rd
Indianapolis, IN 46268
www.dogearpublishing.net

ISBN: 978-1-4575-3945-9

This book is printed on acid-free paper.

Printed in the United States of America

ACKNOWLEDGEMENTS

I would like to recognize the following, who aided this ridiculously difficult effort in ways both grand and small, even if some of them don't know it.

Two miraculous young women, Maggie and Emily, who happen to be my daughters, who stuck with me through some radical turns in my life that, in turn, flipped theirs upside down, but who never doubted me, at least not to my face. Their mother, Lisa, who survived that upheaval with dignity and grace, who raised these incredible young women with little help from me, and who lived through much of what is described in the following pages, beginning with a phone ringing in the dark.

My dear friend, Rick Andosca, consummate actor, director, teacher, and tireless reader of this manuscript, without whose support none of this would have been possible.

Legendary acting teacher, mentor, and friend Fred Kareman, who gave me the gift of self.

Anne Reingold, who finally convinced me to write this thing. Roger Williams, who helped hone it. And the delightful Megan Weedle, Adrienne Miller, Amber Ortner, and their sidekicks at Dog Ear Publishing, who made it real. For many and varied reasons: D. Everette Ragan, J. D. Smith, Priscilla Russell, David T. Lock, R. Eugene (Gene) Roy, Donna K. Stevens, Michele Schiro, Dr. Richard M. Draffin, Barbara Wright, Ann Woolner, Meg Daly Heap, John S. Strickland, Ricky E. Becker, Linda Kaapa, Daniel Massey, and Greg McConnell.

Spencer Lawton Jr., who allowed me access to his personal archives, files and records related to the Williams matter without any restriction or qualification.

Dear friends and family who have always supported what some have thought was the life path of a lunatic: Jo Louisa Tebeau, Jim Epting, Janie Belcher, J.C. Epting, Bob Epting, Lee Ellen Hanberry, Dave Brantley, Gen. (Ret.) Steven Westgate, Fritz Rumpel, Steven Hyam, Paul Burks, Jo Ann Miles-Miller, and Bray Patrick-Lake.

To Dr. Larry B. Howard: You were right.

And finally, in memory of my mother, Mertice Kieffer Kirkland, who should have gone to law school herself instead of suggesting it to me. She would have made a good one.

PROLOGUE

He did it.

In the early morning hours of May 2, 1981, in the antique-filled study of a mansion in historic downtown Savannah, fifty-year-old James Arthur Williams killed twenty-one-year-old Danny Lewis Hansford with three 9mm slugs from a vintage WWII German Luger. According to Williams, he shot young Hansford in self-defense—because Hansford had tried to kill him with another vintage WWII German Luger.

Over the ensuing eight and a half years, following four murder trials, a record-setting best seller and a major motion picture, a perception arose that Williams was right, that he had shot and killed Danny Hansford only to save his own life.

I was there the night it happened, standing in the study of Mercer House with detectives and a Crime Scene Unit ID officer, surrounded by a wealth of damning physical evidence. I was the person who advised detectives to arrest Williams for murder. The truth is that James Williams's defense of himself did not begin until after Danny Hansford was dead.

During preparation of the case for presentation to a grand jury, District Attorney's Office Chief Investigator J. D. Smith and I traveled to Atlanta to consult with Dr. Larry B. Howard, Director of the Forensic Services Division of the Georgia Bureau of Investigation (more generally known as the State Crime Lab). Dr. Howard was past vice president of the American Academy of Forensic Scientists, president of the American Society of Crime Laboratory Directors, charter member of the American Board of Forensic Toxicology, and past vice president of the Forensic Science Foundation (research arm of the American Academy of Forensic Sciences). Georgia's Crime Lab was the second largest in the nation, and Dr. Howard was a legend in forensic criminalistics, having dissected thousands of crime scenes and performed more than six thousand forensic autopsies.

We told Dr. Howard the version of events according to Williams, handed over crime scene photos, and headed off to find some lunch. Upon our return, I asked Dr. Howard what he thought, anticipating detailed questions about the scene. Dr. Howard simply handed the photos back and said, "The son of a bitch is lying."

A few pitch-dark minutes before 4 a.m. on May 2, 1981, the phone rang in the upstairs bedroom of a Trustees' Garden townhouse in downtown Savannah.

Even though I was the Chief Assistant District Attorney, being called in the middle of the night to come to the scene of a shooting was unusual.

Savannah was not a sleepy Southern hamlet and shootings were not rare events, yet my labeling as merely *unusual* the call that would precede the criminal prosecution of James Williams for the murder of Danny Hansford would prove to be the understatement of a lifetime. The *Williams* criminal case would continue for more than eight years and produce a trail of bloody legal battles of legendary proportion, quite aside from its four murder trials.

The residence where the killing took place—a stately brick mansion at 429 Bull Street known as Mercer House—was originally designed for General Hugh Weedon Mercer, great-grandfather of the songwriter Johnny Mercer. In May of 1981, Mercer House was the residence of James A. Williams and the location of his antique business, with a refinishing shop in the basement and the commercial enterprise operated from the carriage house at the rear of the property, fronting on Whitaker Street. The site was bounded on the front (east) by Bull Street and Monterey Square, on the north by W. Wayne Street, on the west by Whitaker Street, and on the south by W. Gordon Street.

There is something about being at a live crime scene before it's processed. Many investigators believe they gain special insight from physically walking a scene, being present as soon after the event as possible. I would not purport to have those kinds of instincts, but I was there while the scene remained a pristine snapshot of its final moment—the moment Danny Hansford fell dead to the study floor. Being there matters.

If you have an issue with crime scene photographs, put the book down now. If you want to know what happened in the study of the mansion on Monterey Square, keep reading.

From the moment he fell dead, Danny Hansford became an item of evidence—a critical item of evidence. This might sound callous, but there is no choice. To understand what caused the victim's death, you have to consider the victim. When you see the way a victim can be treated after death by a defense team—as in this case—you might conclude that being shot was the least of the violations perpetrated upon them.

When you have finished this book, you will know more than any jury ever knew about the *Williams* murder case. You will also be privy to an explanation that no jury ever heard of what happened in that room and why.

As in any similar case, everything begins and ends with the crime scene. To quote myself, from my closing argument in the first trial of Williams:

I would suggest to you that there is ... another voice in this courtroom, that's been here the whole time, that we've had a hard time hearing. ... Danny Hansford is here somewhere with us. ... He's here

in these photographs, and I think if it's quiet enough ... if you'll con-
centrate ... you can almost hear him screaming, "Please listen to me."
Perhaps he is screaming still. There's an adage that claims, "Dead men tell no
tales." It isn't true. If it were, very few homicides would ever be solved. Danny
Hansford was speaking loudly on that May 2 morning, less than two hours dead
when I entered the study.

Thus began the case that would become known as *State of Georgia vs. James
A. Williams*. The four *Williams* murder trials are referred to herein as *Williams I*,
Williams II, Williams III, and *Williams IV.* Trial testimony quotations are verbatim. Occasionally, words are set in italics for emphasis. The emphasis is mine.
Trial transcript excerpts do not include volume and page citations, in the interest
of length. The transcripts are public records, and anyone who wants to check the
citations is welcome to do so. Source material quoted verbatim might contain
typographical or grammatical errors but is included as it appears in the original
material, without correction or notation other than by the occasional use of (sic)
for clarity.

One final note on the use of italics: The criminal case is referenced as
Williams in italics. Otherwise, Williams refers to the individual.

In the end, this book is not about a single, though fascinating, criminal
case. This book is about the underbelly of the criminal legal system. It's not a
pretty sight.

Seldom is a murder case tried four times. Only occasionally does a murder
case involve a defendant with virtually unlimited financial resources. These forces
came together in this case, presenting a rare opportunity to observe the criminal
system operating at its best and at its worst. The great advantage of seeing multiple trials of the same defendant on the same facts is the ability to see changes in
strategy, approach, and, unfortunately, even testimony when there are plentiful
Benjamins to fund the battle and very little in the way of ethics to restrain the
combatants.

Thus, there are two stories within the following pages. One is the story of
the case: the facts, the evidence, the trials, and the result. The other is a deeper
story that is, in many respects, more disturbing: the story of an eight-year campaign of a defendant and his lawyers to beat a murder rap—no matter what it
took—and what that campaign says about the criminal justice system and those
who ply their trade therein.

We will cover witnesses, evidence, and tactics from all four trials, but with
a focus on the larger war. When we cover a witness, for example, we will look
under the surface. Why was a question asked in a particular way? How was a witness's answer crafted to convey an impression rather than a fact? When is a lawyer
"testifying" through a question rather than asking one? We will go beyond the

game on the playing field, to the game within the game. I expect that you will never look at a criminal trial quite the same way again. In my opinion, that's a good thing.

We will follow the timeline, taking the path the case took, allowing the evidence and the prosecution to unfold as they did at the time, peeking ahead only on rare occasion when it's essential. We have an enormous advantage on this journey: the luxury of reflection. I will repeat a phrase several times: Hindsight has excellent vision.

I would not try the same case today. I even disagree with myself from the first trial on occasion. Noticing things after the fact that might have been done in a trial is extraordinarily easy compared to thinking on the fly, while in the line of fire. Hindsight has excellent vision, but it is not always fair to those who were in the battle.

It is also important to understand some differences between criminal and civil trials at the time of *Williams*. In a civil setting, each side knew the other side's case. Discovery was conducted, documents exchanged, interrogatories answered, and any number of tools employed to avoid surprise. Not so in a criminal setting. There was very little discovery in criminal cases and it ran almost entirely in one direction. The prosecution was not entitled to any information from the defense, other than a witness list. And if a witness wouldn't talk to you before trial, that was their privilege. You did the best you could.

Nonetheless, despite these caveats about hindsight, there are places in this narrative where I note that something was not done by the prosecution. If it was related to the first trial, I was there and am as accountable as anyone else involved for any omission. When and if I point out things not done, I leave to the reasonable judgment of the reader whether something *not* done rises to the level of something that *should have been* done, with only a couple of exceptions. It is very difficult after the fact to replicate the conditions in a courtroom at the time of the event.

No, I wasn't personally present for the second, third, or fourth trial, but I followed each vicariously as I went on to Atlanta and then to Alexandria, Virginia. Despite the distance, I did not remain far removed from the criminal investigative field. For example, in Alexandria, I designed and directed a task force of several dozen former FBI agents with a team that included the former director of the FBI National Academy, the former unit chief of the Behavioral Science Unit, and an FBI Capitol Hill Legislative Counsel.

Ultimately, I did leave the law, without regret, to follow a different path, but *Williams* is that case you never let go. I have no basis to claim that *Williams* was "my case." It went on for so long after I left Savannah and went through so many bloody battles that it was the district attorney's case, he being the only person, other than Williams himself, who was there for every minute of its unique life.

But on a personal level, I have always felt that *Williams* was my case in that I was there at its inception and was instrumental in shaping its original course. I was there when Danny Hansford was still lying in a pool of his own blood. I later personally looked through his wallet and personal effects seized as evidence. As I said earlier, being there matters. And it stays with you. Call it more a sense of responsibility than ownership.

For that reason, this journey has been something of a personal coroner's inquest, dissecting this case and laying it all out before me, going through it one step at a time, retracing its long and often twisting path. Along the way, I have discovered many things, shared herein. It is an astounding, and confounding, story.

Immersing myself once again in *Williams*, I was reminded of the facet of the criminal law that I relished: reconstructing an event from the faint imprint left in the ether. I have reviewed every scrap of evidence, witness statement, affidavit, laboratory report, photograph, and word of testimony (except that which was destroyed, which we will cover). I even found my own handwritten notes from *Williams I* within the district attorney's office archives.

And with the kind assistance of some dedicated current and former law enforcement officers and court personnel, I even managed to stir up a mystery. It remains unsolved, but the fact that it remains unsolved tells us something we did not know about a major chapter in the *Williams* case. Something not being where it should be is often as important as what is there.

There are some aspects of the criminal law that I do not miss. It can be a dirty business, when the lust for the win overwhelms all else. Prepare yourself to know as much about one unique murder case as anyone currently living, and more about the dark side of criminal law than you might want to know.

PART ONE

THE BEGINNING

CHAPTER I

"I SHOT HIM"

At 2:58 a.m. on May 2, 1981, Corporal M. J. Anderson and Patrolman M. A. White received a radio dispatch of a shooting at 429 Bull Street (Figures 1, 2). Approximately ninety seconds later, Anderson and White pulled up to a brick mansion facing Monterey Square—one of the remaining garden-like squares laid out in the original Savannah city plan in 1733 by General James E. Oglethorpe. Corporal J. J. Chesler and Patrolman Gibbons arrived just behind Anderson and White. At the same time, one Joseph Goodman and girlfriend Nancy Rushing drove up, parked, and followed Anderson and White through the iron gate and up the stone steps, immediately in front of Chesler and Gibbons.

Cpl. Anderson and Ptl. White were met at the open front door by a fifty-year-old male, James A. Williams, who said, "I shot him; he's in the other room."[1] Williams led the officers down the wide entrance hall to his study entrance on the left. Just beyond the study entrance, a grandfather clock and chair appeared to have been turned over (Figure 3).

The study is referred to variously, in reports and testimony, as Williams's study and office. Both terms refer to this room (Figure 4), referenced herein as "study" to avoid confusion. To the left as one entered the study was a Louis XV bureau plat[2] that Williams used as a desk. In front of the desk, facedown in a pool of blood on the antique Turkish Oushak[3] carpet, was twenty-one-year-old Danny Lewis Hansford (Figure 5).

Cpl. Anderson asked Cpl. Chesler to escort Williams out of the study and stationed Ptl. White at the door. Anderson's visual examination of the room revealed two WWII vintage German Luger pistols, spent 9mm shell casings, live rounds of 9mm ammunition (apparently ejected from one or more of the pistols), bullet fragments, and a chair situated over the body, as well as an apparent ricochet mark high on the north wall.

Cpl. Anderson radioed for detectives, EMS, ID (what television viewers might recognize as CSI), the county coroner, and the shift supervisor. While awaiting the arrival of ID and detectives, Cpl. Anderson exited the study and observed Williams talking with Cpl. Chesler. Approaching, he heard Williams state, "He was shooting at me and I shot him."[4] Cpl. Anderson interrupted this conversation and advised Williams of the standard *Miranda* warnings. Williams informed officers that he had two lawyers on the way.

ID Officer Donna K. Stevens arrived at approximately 3:05, took custody of the scene from Cpl. Anderson, and began photographing the scene. At 3:30, Homicide Detectives D. E. Ragan and J. P. Jordan arrived.

Joseph E. Goodman, the thirty-two-year-old male who had entered the residence with officers, explained to Detective Ragan that he had been called and told to "come quickly," that Williams "had to shoot Danny Hansford."[5] According to Goodman, Williams first called between 2:00 and 2:05, at which time Goodman spoke to both Williams and Hansford. Williams told Goodman that a planned antique-buying trip to Europe was canceled. Hansford asked if Goodman was disappointed about not going on the trip and told Goodman that he was "playing a game and talking."[6]

Goodman told Det. Ragan that he received a second phone call from Williams at 2:22, during which call Williams told Goodman that he had shot Danny and to come quickly. This meant Williams had shot Hansford somewhere between 2:00 and 2:22, or anywhere from thirty-six to fifty-eight minutes before he called the police (at 2:58).

SPD headquarters was only a dozen blocks from Mercer House, and officers had responded within ninety seconds. There was a substantial time gap between the time Hansford was killed and the time Williams called for help—other than for himself.

Williams's two attorneys, Robert J. Duffy and Robert Shearouse, arrived. Detective Ragan was faced with a puzzle in Williams's study that had pieces out of place and two defense lawyers already at the scene. Considering the circumstances, Det. Ragan decided to call in the district attorney's office. Unable to reach District Attorney Spencer Lawton directly, he called me.

Past the collection of patrol cars out front, through the iron gate, and up the stone steps, I entered Mercer House and was directed to the study door on the left. On the way, I observed a trim, angular, mustached man sitting on a sofa in the rear of the adjacent parlor with one of his attorneys. The gentleman was identified to me as one James A. Williams. I didn't know Williams. I did know his attorney, Robert J. Duffy, Esq.

Entering the study, I found the skeptical homicide detective who had called me, an ID officer, and a young man facedown in a pool of his own blood—a young man whom I was told had been shot by the angular, mustached man on the sofa. Williams had told responding officers that the dead young man on the rug—Danny Lewis Hansford—had attacked him, firing a shot at him from the Luger under Hansford's hand, and that he had managed to return fire and kill his attacker. A self-defense case.

So why was I there? Two reasons.

First, pause the film and split the screen. This split screen is what homicide detectives were viewing: two movies running side-by-side. On one screen was the story told by Williams. On the other screen was the story being told by the scene. The movies did not match. This is a gross understatement. Not only did some items of evidence contradict Williams's story; virtually *every* item of evidence contradicted Williams's story.

There was a second reason I was there that night. This was not merely another Savannah shooting. James Williams was a prominent member of the Savannah community, a pioneer in the historic restoration movement, a wealthy man, and a fixture within the Savannah social stratosphere. In other words, he was a very well known somebody. Personally, I had no idea who he was. Had this shooting taken place in another part of town, considering the obvious disconnect between the survivor's story and the evidence, I believe homicide detectives would have merely followed their own excellent instincts and hauled Williams in.

In this case, in an abundance of caution, and considering that Williams already had two lawyers at the scene, detectives decided to call for a second opinion. This was a smart move on their part and would be a good idea in any case, if there were enough prosecutors to go around.

It was readily apparent why Det. Ragan had called me. The scene was screaming "setup" at operatic levels. It had obviously been contrived, and in the history of crime, there is no known case of a suspect tampering with a scene to make themselves look *more* guilty. Suspects often do some stupid things, but not on purpose. It is safe to assume that a suspect doctoring the scene is trying to help themselves, not the police or prosecutors.

Williams's defense lawyers would later suggest that the crime scene was like a teen party with the parents out of town, with cops playing tag in party hats, tripping over the body. This is a common defense allegation in a physical evidence case and seldom based in fact. A crime scene—particularly a murder scene—is more often treated with the care of a shrine by experienced investigators. Call it a shrine to the crime if you like. That was the level of reverence and seriousness of purpose that I felt when entering the study at Mercer House. You will see what I saw and what Det. Ragan and Ofc. Stevens saw, collected, measured, and photographed over the ensuing five and a half hours.

Homicide detectives aren't Wild West trackers in buckskin, kneeling by the dusty trail through the Sierra Nevadas, but in many ways, they approach a scene the same way. The *Atlanta Constitution* would have this to say about the *Williams* case: "Homicide detectives are skeptical by nature and by training, and they are especially cautious when survivors of gunfights claim self-defense. One prerequisite to such a claim is that the crime scene must present no unexplained puzzles."[7] The unexplained puzzle in the study was why I had found myself passing through the iron gate and up the stone steps of Mercer House that early morning.

Inside the study, I was shown a series of items that immediately started my head shaking with an unspoken "You've got to be kidding." Danny Hansford's right arm was extended from his body and his hand was perched on top of a handgun, a WWII 9mm Luger semiautomatic (Figure 6).[8] There was blood caked on the hand but no blood on the rug underneath. The only source of blood was under the body. The thumb was tucked under, against the palm of the hand, and the fingers were squeezed together and slightly curled.

The Luger was aligned perfectly under Hansford's hand but wasn't in his hand. The hand was simply laid on top of the grip, with the thumb still tucked against the palm. The blood on the wrist was smeared. The head was facing away from the weapon. Hansford was supposed to have reached for a gun that he couldn't see. Somebody had obviously pulled the hand out from under the body and laid it on top of a carefully placed weapon.

The second screaming clue was not readily visible. A chair was so far up over the body that it couldn't possibly have gotten there on its own (Figure 7). The most shocking proof of all that the scene had been rearranged was the chair's right rear leg, squarely atop Hansford's pant leg (Figure 8). There was only one explanation: The chair had to have been placed on top of the body after the fact. And because Williams had been the only one there at the time, he had done it.

The dead man's hand indicated that Williams had staged the scene. The chair removed any doubt. Williams was not telling the truth about what had happened in that room—other than the fact that he had shot the dead man three times with the Luger on Williams's desk (Figure 9). It was time to arrest James Williams.

I left the study and walked across the entrance hall to where Williams and Mr. Duffy were sitting. I advised Duffy that Williams was to be arrested. This led to one of the more bizarre events of the entire *Williams* case for me personally. I offer no suggestion as to what it meant, because it wasn't clear at the time and has become no more clear over the ensuing years.

When I informed Bob Duffy that Williams was to be arrested, Williams himself responded. Completely calm and controlled, he looked up at me and said, "If I'd wanted to, I could have shot you; there's another pistol in this table." He meant the side table next to the sofa where he was seated. Obviously, someone had forgotten to secure the suspect and "the area within his immediate control" to quote the standard phrase, but that was understandable. Williams's attorney was sitting with him, this was supposed to be a self-defense case, and both weapons from the alleged shootout were accounted for. After all, how many loaded handguns does one person have lying around the house? The answer in Williams's case would be five, three of them WWII vintage Lugers.

I have never understood the relevance of Williams's remark or how shooting me could have helped his case. In any event, Williams did not shoot me and was arrested for the murder of Danny Hansford. Mr. Duffy managed to wake a judge, the Hon. Eugene H. Gadsden, to hear an ad hoc bond application. The hearing was held at Judge Gadsden's house. I do not recall whether Judge Gadsden wore a judicial robe or a bathrobe.

Bail was set at $25,000. Williams called his friend, Joseph Goodman, who was standing by at Mercer House. Goodman brought $25,000 in cash to the jail in a paper bag and Williams was released.

The search continued at the scene. Detective Ragan and ID Ofc. Stevens would spend almost six hours combing through the study, the living room, and the upstairs at Mercer House, collecting and logging evidence.

An autopsy on the body of Danny Hansford was performed later the same day. We will not be viewing photos of the autopsy for two reasons. One reason is benign—there simply is no advantage to the reader that outweighs their graphic nature. The second reason is not so benign—the photos and the original negatives don't exist. More accurately, they do not exist among the files of the Savannah Police Department (now the consolidated Savannah-Chatham Metropolitan Police Department) or any other law enforcement or judicial agency.

Multiple searches have been conducted by a number of police officers, including the original ID officer who took the autopsy photographs. We will revisit this subject. For now, know only that the negatives are not where they should be and have not (yet) been found.

As to the photographs of the crime scene used here, they are digitally produced from original negatives. None have been altered other than, in some instances, being cropped and magnified for better viewing. We will also be using State Crime Lab test results and diagrams illustrating relationships between items of evidence seized in an attempt to fit the evidence from the Mercer House study into the puzzle provided by Williams. As will be demonstrated shortly, that task is impossible.

The grand jury agreed. A true bill of indictment was returned on June 12, 1981, charging James A. Williams with murder in that Williams "did unlawfully and with malice aforethought cause the death of Danny Lewis Hansford, a human being, by shooting the said Danny Lewis Hansford with a pistol."

CHAPTER 2

THE MEN

W ho were these two men, James Williams and Danny Hansford? They were a culturally mismatched pair whose relationship made little sense—on the surface.

James Arthur Williams was born on December 11, 1930, in Gordon, Georgia, a small town east of Macon in Wilkinson County. His father was a barber and his mother was a bookkeeper at a local kaolin mine. James had one sibling, his sister Dorothy.

By the time of the Hansford killing in 1981, Williams had gone from country boy to interior decorator, then to wealthy antique dealer and prominent resident of Savannah (Figure 46).[9] He was a leader in the historic preservation movement and a patron of the arts. James Williams traversed the highest levels of Savannah society, but, like most urban cities, Savannah had a far different underbelly and Williams knew it well.

Williams's annual holiday party was one of the biggest social events of the season. It was sumptuous, joyous, filled with laughter and song, attended by the social elite and political poo-bahs, and topped off by Williams playing the pipe organ on the second floor, windows open and house lights ablaze. But there were two parties. The later—unofficial—party the following evening was also sumptuous and joyous, but different in one key aspect—it was men-only: well-dressed men with manners befitting the setting and occasion. Williams had yet a third type of acquaintance, not on either holiday-party guest list: young men from other walks of a much different life, young men like Danny Lewis Hansford.

In times past, Savannah has been referred to as a beautiful woman with a dirty face. Her face might have been scrubbed pink and fresh. But if one waited until dark and melted into the shadows, one might have bumped into Williams, just as Williams had bumped into Danny, buyer and seller coming to a mutual bargain and Danny ending up at Mercer House.

Danny Lewis Hansford was born in Savannah on March 1, 1960. To say that he had a difficult childhood would be laughable. Danny Hansford had a hell of time of it, right from the start. Danny's mother, originally Emily A. McGehee, came from a family of five children. She left school after the ninth grade and was married in 1955, at the tender age of fifteen, to Danny's father, Charles Hansford. The two were separated frequently and finally divorced in 1961 when Danny was one year old. In 1963, Emily married again, to Edward Banister. Emily and Banister were divorced in 1970. Charles Hansford committed suicide in 1967.

Danny had two brothers and a sister. Brother John was born in 1957, when his mother was 17. Brother Billy was born in 1958. Then came Danny in 1960. A sister, Tracy, was born in 1966.

Danny's father had barely been around. His step-father had nothing to do with the boys, and the boys didn't like him. None of the boys finished high school. Danny made it through seventh grade, failed eighth grade and gave up. In 1971, all three boys were placed in Savannah's historic and excellent Bethesda Orphanage.[10] Bethesda recommended they stay, but Emily refused and pulled them out.

On three other occasions, Danny was placed in Gould Cottage—established by New York philanthropist Edwin Gould in 1933 for children from troubled or broken homes—but Danny's mother didn't "agree with their rules" and took him home. Much of Danny's disruption growing up seemed to stem from clashes with his mother.

When he was fifteen, he was briefly admitted to Georgia Regional Hospital, a regional mental health facility in Savannah. He was admitted by his mother. He was there for two days and was signed out by his mother. Georgia Regional tried to work out a treatment plan for the family, but Emily failed to show up for any appointments or to communicate further with the hospital.

Danny was admitted to Georgia Regional Hospital again when he was nineteen, after having been seen at Memorial Medical Center where he received sutures for lacerations suffered when his landlord reportedly struck him with a stick during an altercation. Danny checked himself out of Georgia Regional two days later.

An observation of the staff at Georgia Regional who interviewed Danny's mother may be a candidate for the top understatement related to this case: "Care and supervision of adolescent boys seems to be a problem for the mother."[11] The staff went on to note that Emily was in need of supportive help but was "not willing to take the time, or accept responsibility for working out a plan."[12]

It is no surprise that a girl married at fifteen, frequently separated from her husband, and left with three small boys by the age of twenty-one, might develop some issues with the "care and supervision of adolescent boys." Danny believed that his mother hated him.[13]

Danny's girlfriend, Debra Lynn (Debbie) Blevins, had some insights into Danny's relationship with his mother. Debbie told the prosecution that Danny's life growing up had been hard, in large part because "his mother didn't want him and his dad had killed himself."[14]

Danny Hansford had a *girlfriend*? Yes.

Danny took a nice mug shot, as evidenced by his arrest in April of 1981 (Figure 48). The county jail apparently served as Danny's substitute for the photo booth at the mall (Figure 49). But if Danny Hansford had a girlfriend, what was James Williams doing with him? Williams would claim he was trying to save Danny from himself. Somebody should have saved him from Williams.

CHAPTER 3

THE SAINT AND THE ORPHAN

Danny Hansford was a hustler. He was a male hooker. You wouldn't call him an escort, because it wasn't likely that a man in Williams's position would allow Hansford to escort him anywhere that polite people gathered. You wouldn't find Danny at the opera. You would find him on the street and in the parks where a far less public business was conducted.

I described that world in my closing argument in *Williams I*:

All children don't come from fine homes; some of them come from broken homes where there's only one parent. Some of those children and young men, particularly in this city, as we heard, have an opportunity to become involved in a culture that probably none of you—I hope none of you—have ever seen, and probably ninety-nine percent of the people in this community have never seen. They would be surprised to know it exists, only on television. Maybe it happens in New York, but not here. It goes on at two o'clock in the morning, three o'clock in the morning, four o'clock in the morning, somewhere out there in those streets, and there are some young men who get caught up in it. Danny Hansford was one of them.

You didn't take Danny Hansford home to sip champagne and discuss Proust. Danny's friend George Hill believed Williams met Danny like other men met Danny, in "the parks" turning tricks. Yet Williams telegraphed, very early, that he would claim Danny Hansford was only a young man in whom he had taken a benevolent interest.

In a wide-ranging interview Williams conducted with a newspaper, the *Georgia Gazette*, Williams told a lovely story that might have been titled "Father James and the Orphan."[15] Add a cold, snowy night, a fire made from the last of Danny's belongings, and the benevolent millionaire who takes Poor Orphan Danny home for a bowl of hot soup and a hug. It should come as no surprise that investigators and prosecutors did not queue up for tickets to that movie.

The Williams–Hansford relationship did not look anything like a nurturing benefactor saving a troubled young man, and Mercer House did not resemble a home where a troubled youth might find redemption. It appeared to be a home where a troubled youth might find a bed, car, clothes, and cash.

Even so, it wasn't clear why Williams was so fearful of the truth about his relationship with Hansford. Williams's sexual preference was not a secret. His rise to prominence in Savannah society had hardly been held back because he was an articulate, sophisticated gay man.

Joseph Goodman, the friend Williams called before anyone else the night of the killing, hinted at the reason for Williams's attempt to paint himself as Hansford's benefactor rather than something more personal. In a formal, recorded statement, Goodman said, "I know what they gonna try to do. They gonna try to say it was a lovers' quarrel or something like that."[16] When the suspect's confidant offers up a defense to a claim the prosecution hasn't even made yet, it's a bright red flag.

Williams was going to try to redefine the relationship. It appeared that he was going to try confessing to an "error in judgment" for bringing home an emotionally damaged madman, in an effort to avoid being convicted of killing his boy toy in a lovers' quarrel. Not a bad deal if you can get it.

But the truth was radically different from the postcard. This was no remake of *Oliver Twist*. The challenge would be to show a jury the right movie, the one playing in the underground theatre. Despite the strength of the physical evidence, with such a prominent, well-respected defendant, it would be essential to answer the unspoken question: "Why would a man such as James Williams kill somebody like that Danny Hansford person?"

CHAPTER 4

MOTIVE DOESN'T MATTER—BUT IT DOES

M otive is not an essential element of a criminal offense. Motive is often confused with intent. They are not the same thing.

In New York City in 2013, a man was walking along West 58th Street between 7th Avenue and Broadway at 2:00 in the afternoon when another individual, seen on surveillance footage, stepped up behind the man and shot him in the back of the head. The shooter hopped into a getaway car and sped off. This was an execution. It doesn't matter whether the shooter had been paid for the hit or the guy he killed had insulted his sister. The shooter had the intent to kill (also known as "malice aforethought"). His reasons were his own.

In the *Williams* case, proof of criminal intent was provided by Williams. He said he "intended" to kill Danny Hansford, but with justification. If he was lying, the *intentional* killing was *not* justified.

So, motive was not a legal component of the *Williams* case, but it wasn't that simple. Motive was going to be injected into the case by the defense. "Why in the world would a fine man like Jim shoot a low-life thing like that Danny person unless the boy tried to kill him; the whole thing is just absurd." That's bad writing from a *Gone with the Wind* sequel, but that's the idea. What reason in the world (motive) would Williams have to kill a piece of trash like Hansford?

This was tricky ground for Williams, because this was a self-defense case. Williams claimed Hansford had tried to kill him. But, at least on the surface, Hansford also had no conceivable "motive" for trying to kill Williams, his personal golden goose. So motive can work both ways.

We will cover the tortured reasoning this quandary forced on the defense but, for now, know only that the case would involve the question of motive—in the form of an alleged *lack* of motive injected by the defense on behalf of Williams. This was the impetus for Williams's efforts to avoid any hint of an emotional link to Hansford. Why?

Assume a relationship between lovers, whether male, female, or one of each. What is the immediate reaction to a story about one of them killing the other? Ho hum, happens every day. The reason (call it motive if you like) for the killing, if known, can be laughable. "He wouldn't put down the toilet seat" or "She hid the remote control" sound perfectly reasonable in that setting. People accept that the emotions involved in an intimate relationship can lead to acts of sudden violence. So Williams and his lawyers needed to repackage the Williams-Hansford relationship and sell the sanitized version to a jury. It is much easier to defend a benefactor than a lover or—another possibility—a sexual predator.

Conveying the true nature of the relationship might even affect a jury's view of the physical evidence. One example: the sequence of the three shots fired by Williams and the position from which he fired them. A benefactor has no reason to round his desk in a fury and deliver a message to a protégé with a final shot through the back. An enraged lover does.

So, ignoring the "why in the world" question would have been foolish. Was this the story of a battered pit bull who turned on his rescuer? Was Williams a naive man who tried to do a good deed only to be rewarded by a psychopath trying to kill him? Or was this Joseph Goodman's "lovers' quarrel"? It was important that we answer what should have been two simple questions: who were these men, and what was their relationship?

Rather than Father James defending himself against a raging pit bull, this might be the story of a hot-tempered James Williams who had finally had enough. A man who had been tweaked, teased, and tormented once too often. A man who was sick and tired of the damn dog.

CHAPTER 5

REMOVING THE MASK

Although the case evidence would eventually reveal Williams's true relationship with Danny Hansford, Williams was busy telling a different story. He was holding a mask in front of his face like an actor in an ancient Greek play, playing the mentor of troubled youth rather than an older man having a taste for young men with rough edges. Which was it? Had Father James taken Poor Orphan Danny home out of the snow, or had a man with a sweet tooth taken some candy home one night and gotten hooked? If so, what was a man like James Williams doing shopping for cheap candy on the street?

How did someone like Danny Hansford—an eighth-grade dropout—end up with his own room in one of the finest residences in historic Savannah, keeping intimate company with a wealthy, sophisticated older man? The best person to tell us is Danny himself.

Among Danny's belongings was a sketch he drew, possibly of Williams (Figure 47). What is most telling about the sketch, other than the fact that Danny could draw a little, was what he scribbled on the back. He wrote the word "school" eleven times, some large, some small, some underlined. He also wrote this: "What have I done. I'm 20 years old. I suck dicks and get fucked by different people for money."

Chilling, and heartbreaking. Danny's friend George Hill also confirmed the nature of Danny's relationship with Williams in his interview with Investigator J. D. Smith: "Danny was doing sexual favors for the man in exchange for money and for his car and stuff. That's the relationship they had, basically."[17]

George said he had asked Danny several times what he was doing with Williams. According to Hill, Danny told him, "If the guy wants to jack me off and give me money for it what's the big deal. You know I ain't having to work for it."[18] No matter what we think of what Danny was doing or his reasons for doing it, we know why he was in the relationship with Williams. It might have bothered him and it might bother us, but that's what it was, a way to survive.

How did they meet? We didn't know for sure, but Danny's friend had an idea. In those days, men would cruise the parks—a lesser known benefit of the garden squares dotting the historic downtown landscape. This is how George Hill described it to J. D. Smith:

GH: [T]hey motion over to the car and they strike up a deal with them and then leave with them. Whatever they agree to do.

JD: Do you think this is the way Danny ...

GH: I think that's how Danny met Williams because that's what he was doing, you know. And you don't make a whole lot of money doing that anywhere from $7 to $30 depending on what you're doing and then all of a sudden Danny started hanging around with this Williams and ended up making all kind of money.[19]

Danny said it on the back of his sketch. He was having sex with Williams for money. If James Williams was a mentor to Hansford, he was one of the strangest mentors imaginable. I also believe, with hindsight, that Danny's wildness—in the tradition of Tennessee Williams and the ribald, decadent characters who inhabited some of his tales and his personal life—was a turn-on for James Williams. In that way, a disturbed Danny Hansford was a human mirror, reflecting Williams's own character.

CHAPTER 6

TRIANGLES AND TRAGEDY

I f Williams's mask dropped, what would people see? A wealthy gay man who liked young men? Sex between what might be deemed age-inappropriate partners is not a new phenomenon. Those people don't all shoot each other. Williams's and Hansford's sexual preferences simply didn't matter, not to the district attorney, not to me, and not to anyone else on the prosecution team. All that mattered was the emotional nature of Williams's relationship with the man he killed.

To understand that aspect of the relationship, it was necessary to understand another relationship. There was an additional element present in the *Williams* case, one that can and often does lead to violence: a triangle. Danny had a girlfriend. Williams didn't like it. That's something anyone who's been through puberty and high school can appreciate.

Straight people kill people. Gay people kill people. Jealous people kill people with unfortunate frequency. The third category was the only category of interest in the *Williams* prosecution. This was what Williams feared—not the label of gay man, but the label of jealous gay man. This may sound facetious, but it isn't; as any veteran homicide investigator can confirm, there are few more fearful organisms on earth.

Joseph Goodman told investigators a story probably designed to show that Williams was bisexual, in an effort to reduce the likelihood that investigators might see the killing as the result of a lovers' quarrel, but the effort was far too familiar, a tired cliché for a gay man looking for cover or for a straight man trying to prove he's got game with women.

This was Goodman's version: "I'd say he's bisexual. ... he says 'see that one right there,' he'd say 'I've been to bed with her two or three times.'"[20] Any male in the world—straight, gay, or otherwise—knows that such a statement is a virtual guarantee that it never happened. Goodman had known Williams for over twenty years but didn't recount having seen Williams with an actual female companion; he had to resort to a caricature.

Enter the third side of the triangle, Debra Lynn Blevins, Danny's girlfriend. Debbie was also twenty-one years old in 1981 (a month and fifteen days younger than Danny). She and Danny started dating at the beginning of 1980 and were still dating when Danny was killed. This had been a source of extreme irritation to Williams and, according to George Hill, Williams had prohibited Danny from continuing to see her.[21]

Debbie didn't take the relationship with Danny as seriously as Danny did and complained that he wouldn't stop asking her to marry him—literally every day. She also had no idea about the sexual favors Danny was selling to Williams until Hill told her, after Danny had been killed.[22]

We were on the threshold of trial by the time Debbie Blevins was interviewed by investigators. We already knew that Debbie was Danny's girlfriend and that she was at the center of a controversy over a necklace, but it simply wasn't a centerpiece of the prosecution, because it didn't matter. As in the case of the midday shooting in Manhattan, killers kill for many reasons, and the reasons might never be known or might be as strange as an argument over a slice of pizza.

As for Debbie's role, it did prove that Hansford was a terrible student of human nature. Williams had given Danny a gold necklace purchased at a cost of approximately $400 (over $1,000 in current dollars). George Hill told us that Williams gave Danny the necklace as a condition of breaking up with Debbie.[23] What did Danny do? He gave the necklace to Debbie.[24]

Williams noticed that Danny was not wearing the necklace and asked him where it was. Danny told him. Williams exploded. Two days later, Danny was dead.[25] Jealousy, provocation, emotions cranked beyond the breaking point? It fits. The fact that Danny had a girlfriend and that Williams didn't like it were illuminating facts with respect to the relationship.

But what happened on May 2 in Williams's study? Was there a hint about the final straw, the straw that snapped and triggered Williams to grab his Luger and fire three 9mm slugs into Danny Hansford? Only through dissecting the scene itself would the final moments of Danny Hansford's life come into focus.

PART TWO

THE PUZZLE

CHAPTER 7

THE SELF-DEFENSE GAMBLE

Criminal cases are like puzzles, with one difference—you almost never have all the pieces. With an ordinary puzzle, you fit every piece into its proper spot. Only then can you congratulate yourself as the lighthouse from the puzzle box stares back at you.

In a criminal case, you don't need every piece. You need only enough to solve the puzzle. Among them, you need some special pieces, the elements of the crime. And the pieces you have must fit "to the exclusion of all reasonable doubt" (a terrific definition borrowed from the late Vincent Bugliosi), but once it's clear that the lighthouse is a lighthouse, you're good to go, even with some pieces missing.

In a self-defense case—such as *Williams*—the defendant actually proves the elements of the crime. For murder, the elements are, generally: (a) that the defendant did *act*, (b) with *malice aforethought* (meaning—to risk a translation—the defendant intended the act, whether it was to shoot, stab, poison, or push from a train), (c) so as to *cause the death* of the victim.

You could call self-defense the "I did it ... but" defense. If the pieces don't fit—to paraphrase the late Johnnie Cochran in a way he would not have appreciated—you do not acquit. If "the son of a bitch is lying," as Dr. Larry Howard suggested, the son of a bitch goes to prison. If you make a claim of "justifiable homicide" and the justification disappears, the homicide remains and you've essentially confessed to murder.

What about the scene? It's going to tell its own story. If you're the accused and the story told by the evidence at the scene doesn't match yours, you have to fix it. But staging a crime scene is hard. Criminals prove that every day. And the difficulty isn't restricted to the fools in "stupid crook" videos. No matter how brilliant the person, he or she will invariably miss something. Another reason that mistakes are made, aside from the difficulty, is time.

If you legitimately have to defend yourself, you would be expected to seek help for your attacker. Even if you're lying and couldn't care less, you need to do it anyway, and do it quickly, because it would look unnatural for an innocent person to do otherwise. This adds a time element to the difficulty factor. You have to rush, not really knowing what you're doing, trying to recall some *CSI* episode.

There are two other challenges to a self-defense claim: (1) the type of evidence usually involved, and (2) the tendency of a person claiming self-defense to talk, to explain exactly how it all happened. Both of these would come into play in Williams's case.

First, the evidence against you is often physical or scientific. Such evidence is circumstantial by definition. But that's good for the bad guy, right? Everybody knows circumstantial evidence is terrible evidence. Lawyers say that all the time, so it must be true.

CHAPTER 8

ROCK, PAPER, SCISSORS, SCIENCE

Contrary to popular myth, circumstantial evidence is not weak evidence. In fact, circumstantial evidence can be the strongest evidence known to mankind, while some direct evidence—such as eyewitness testimony—can be so unreliable as to be worthless.

I could argue that all evidence is circumstantial: Someone claiming they saw an event involves circumstances that require scrutiny: the claimant's ability to see clearly what they claim to have seen, possible motivation to lie about what they claim to have seen, or whether they were actually present at the time and place. Even a confession involves a set of circumstances that must be evaluated. The distinction between "direct" and "circumstantial" evidence causes more trouble than it's worth, in my view.

Particularly in self-defense cases, such as in *Williams,* the suspect is often the only witness. There is no third party to cry fair or foul. The deceased will never speak again. Where is reliable direct evidence supposed to come from?

It doesn't matter. The scene is a witness—and can be the most reliable witness of all. The scene speaks through physical evidence—blood, shell casings, bullet fragments, angles and positions of entry and exit wounds, something misplaced, something overlooked—and such evidence is *unimpeachable* for bias. Collection procedures and laboratory analysis can be challenged, but the evidence itself is completely neutral to the outcome. It's nonsensical to argue that gravity has suddenly suspended its effect because it doesn't like the defendant's cologne.

The knee-jerk claim of every defense lawyer in a case involving physical scientific evidence—that the case "relies" on circumstantial evidence and is therefore weak by definition—is a professional lie, nothing more or less. Yet it's a lie told so routinely that the public has come to believe it. It's nonsense.

To quote an attorney for a former NFL football player, speaking after the player's arrest for murder in July of 2013, "It is at bottom a circumstantial case. It is not a strong case."[26] He might or might not have continued to make that point after his client's conviction. The "circumstantial = weak" fallacy has been proved wrong so often that it should be banned.

From later in the life of the *Williams* case, as reported in the *Atlanta Journal Constitution,* one of Williams's lawyers was quoted as saying, "They offer circumstantial evidence, and that's all there is in this case."[27] Where was the direct evidence he seemed to prefer going to come from? Testimony from Williams—

which fits the definition of direct evidence—might have been helpful, if Williams had told the truth. Absent that, there could be nothing *but* circumstantial evidence in the *Williams* case. It's a straw man, and a tired old straw man at that.

Assume a killer was injured in the victim's fight for life, that the victim's blood and other blood is found on the murder weapon, along with fingerprints, and human tissue is found under the victim's fingernails. If DNA analysis proves that's your tissue, the other blood on the murder weapon is your blood, your fingerprints are all over the weapon, and your blood is all over the victim, you can yell "circumstantial evidence" at the moon if you have a cell with a view.

What is the lesson for someone like Williams at the moment they are standing over a body while gripping a smoking gun? If you're going to stage the scene, you'd better get it right.

CHAPTER 9

THE CHATTY SUSPECT

Though a suspect has the "right to remain silent," as any television viewer knows, in a self-defense case there is pressure to talk. If you're innocent, wouldn't you act innocent? That's the reasoning. When a suspect talks, however, his or her version of events can then be checked against the evidence. Investigators know what the puzzle should look like and can match the evidence to the suspect's story, or prove it doesn't match. Game over.

Even in this respect the *Williams* case was unusual. Not only did James Williams talk, he talked at length. And he didn't stop. He actually gave an exclusive interview to the *Georgia Gazette* laying out his version of events in detail. In doing so, he provided us with a virtual blueprint against which to set the physical evidence. He also reduced the ability of his defense to shape the story to better suit the facts—not that I'm suggesting a defense attorney would ever consciously change a story to better fit the facts of a case.

Simply put, it's always a really good idea for a defendant to shut up. Sitting down for an interview with a newspaper when you're charged with murder is unheard of, but Williams seemed to have an expectation that the commoners would simply let him go, thank him for straightening out the whole affair, and apologize for any inconvenience he might have been caused. Instead, we began to try fitting the puzzle pieces from the study into the puzzle picture that Williams had provided. It would not go well.

CHAPTER 10

THE STORY THAT WOULDN'T STAND STILL

The first problem Williams faced was himself. His story began to change as soon as he started telling it. His changing versions conflicted with each other like bickering children. Williams's first statement at the front door of Mercer House was "I shot him; he's in the other room."[28] The next statement was "He was shooting at me and I shot him." Williams should have stopped there.

Later that night, he made a statement to Cpl. M. J. Anderson:

I was sitting in my office and Danny was at the TV with a Superman game. He came in and wanted me to join him and I refused. He got angry and we argued. Talked also about the London trip. Danny went wild going around breaking things. He came back into the room with a gun and shot at me three times, almost hitting me. I got my gun and shot him.[29]

After entering Mercer House, Joseph Goodman and Nancy Rushing had been escorted into the rear of the residence. Later in the evening, Williams appeared and spoke to them. Goodman later related what Williams said:

"I always keep my composure," he said. "I went in my desk and I sit down." And he always keeps a lot of little notebooks and all, he likes to doodle, you know make little squares and all. "I just went in my office and sit down and started doodling." He said in a couple of minutes the boy came in with a gun.[30]

Already, radical differences were emerging. It would be reasonable to expect a story to hold together for the few minutes it takes for the suspect's lawyers to show up and shut him up.

Next came one of the few newspaper interviews ever given by an accused killer in a murder case. The May 6, 1981, edition of the *Georgia Gazette* carried the interview with Williams.[31] Typically, the image of a defense lawyer and defendant in front of the media is a clear sign that the defendant is in trouble. It can also indicate that the individual has ego problems. To be clear, this refers to the defendant, not defense counsel. All good criminal defense lawyers have egos; it's part of their enduring charm.

Williams might have thought he was being clever, sitting down for an interview, but all he succeeded in doing was laying out yet another version of his story that we could test against the evidence. Regis Philbin could have helped by asking Williams, "Is that your final version?"

Williams didn't only tell several different stories, he also exaggerated elements of every one of them. The following are segments of Williams's interview:

- Williams said that they had attended a movie earlier in the evening at a local drive-in theater.
- Williams said that by the time they returned to his home at 429 Bull Street, Hansford had smoked nine marijuana cigarettes and had drunk a half-pint of whiskey.
- "I thought what he had consumed was far better than all the pills he used to take. He had come a long way in the two years I had been working with him."

Only nine marijuana cigarettes and a half-pint of whiskey? During one movie? This was a testament to Williams's skill as a mentor of troubled youth?

- The two played a game on a new computer he had recently bought Hansford. Then, as he rose to leave the room, Hansford accused him of not enjoying the game. "He grabbed me by the throat and said, 'You've been ill. Why don't you just go off someplace and die?'"
- Hansford then stomped the keyboard of the computer "to death" and began breaking furniture in the living room. ... Williams found his way into a room he used as his office and sat down at his desk.
- "He came into the room where I was sitting and said, 'I'm leaving tomorrow.' I said, 'That's fine,' and he left the room. Then he came back and said, 'You're leaving tonight.'"
- Hansford pointed a German Luger pistol in his direction and fired, "I don't know how many times," Williams said, "maybe once, twice, three times."

A sidebar ran a news story entitled "Claims Victim Shot First." Here are excerpts:

- ... a German Luger Williams said the young man had used to fire three shots at him during the incident.
- Williams said he called his attorney, police and a longtime friend just after the shooting.

They were either playing a game (in the *Gazette*) or Danny wanted Williams to play but Williams refused (in his statement to the police). Williams went to his office and sat at his desk, either doodling or not doodling. There was no sign that anyone had fired three shots at him; if they had, he'd have been dead. And finally, he had not called his attorney, police, and friend "just after the shooting." We knew that wasn't true but it was also obvious: The police arrived in less than two minutes and Goodman lived on Savannah's southside, several miles away, yet they arrived at the same time. Nagging inconsistencies and outright conflicts—a feature that would be shared by Williams's statements and testimony throughout the *Williams* case history.

In the *Georgia Gazette* interview, something else popped up for the first time: a nearly identical incident a month earlier involving Hansford, the police, damaged furniture, and shots fired from a Luger.[32] The resemblance to the killing was unsettling. Ironically, four of the same officers—Anderson, White, Chesler, and Gibbons—responded to the call, at 3:45 a.m. on April 3, 1981.

Williams's various descriptions of the April event also suffered from glaring inconsistencies. According to Cpl. M. J. Anderson's April report, "[A]t approximately 0200 hrs. this date the suspect *came home* and appeared to be heavily under the influence. A verbal argument arose and Hansford went into a rage, breaking several antiques about the house."[33] Williams told them Danny Hansford was a "guest staying with him," that Hansford had threatened to "do bodily harm to the complainant and himself," threatening "to kill himself and the complainant."[34] He had "discharged a pistol inside and outside the house." He "allegedly fired two rounds into the floor, then went outside and discharged the weapon."[35]

This April incident had also been described by Williams to Goodman and others on the night of the killing. In that version, as Goodman related it, "[H]e said Danny got screwed up ... threatened my life, shot *at me* two or three times."[36] In the April police report, it was two shots into the floor, but now, on the night Williams claimed Danny had shot *at him* one, two or three times, he told his friend Danny had shot *at him* two or three times back in April.

This new version of April had two major flaws: If Danny had shot at Williams two or three times in April, trying to kill him, why was Williams still alive, and why had Hansford only been charged with Criminal Damage to Property and Reckless Conduct?

There were now *three* versions of the April story: (1) the version contained in the April police report, (2) the version Williams told the night of the killing, and (3) the version contained in Williams's *Gazette* interview.

There was another brief mention of April in a story appearing in the May 3, 1981, edition of the *Savannah News-Press*. The April and May events were now a matched set—too well matched. According to this article, "During the earlier dispute, Williams alleged that Hansford destroyed *thousands of dollars'* worth of antiques during an argument."[37] In the *Gazette*, it was a marble-topped table, a turned-over lamp, and a silver tray overturned "with glassware on it."[38] In the police report, Williams set the damages at $600, just enough to cross the $500 misdemeanor-felony damage cutoff.

We had all of this information within days of the killing. It was obvious that the puzzle wasn't going to stand still long enough for us to nail down the details, but there was a general outline. There was also a secondary benefit. The statements were a clear indication of the arguments that Williams and his lawyers were going to adopt at trial. First, Danny Hansford was a madman who, only a month earlier, had done the *same thing,* only this time Williams shot back, saving his own life. Second, Williams was going to distance himself as far as possible from the implications of an emotional attachment—emotion that might raise a gun in anger, perhaps?

In the *Gazette* interview, referring to April, Williams's response to Hansford firing the Luger was "That's fine, Danny. If you can get it out of your system that way, that's fine. Now, let's put the guns away." Williams was talking to Danny as if Danny was a naughty child playing with daddy's gun. These stories about April contained stark inconsistencies impossible to reconcile, which led to only one conclusion: Williams was changing them to fit his version of the relationship. In April, Williams had told the police that Danny "came home" at 2:00 a.m. In the *Georgia Gazette* version, Danny had "dropped by to pick up a few dollars for a date."[39]

Even the language of the *Gazette* version rang false. Williams told the *Gazette* that "[Hansford] said, 'I'm alone in this world. No one cares about me, I don't have anything to live for.'"[40] Danny Hansford only completed the seventh grade. Goodman had told us Danny "couldn't hardly talk,"[41] yet now he was spouting B-movie dialog. It was impossible to believe Hansford had uttered those words.

But the most obvious "sanitizing" effort was still the claim in the *Gazette* that Danny "dropped by to pick up a few dollars for a date." Danny "came home" at 2:00 a.m. and the police arrived at 3:45 a.m. A very odd time for a date. Who was Danny's "date" and where were they going? There was no twenty-four-hour Del Taco in 1981.[42]

If Danny Hansford was only an employee, why would he assume that his employer would be up at two o'clock in the morning and ready to loan him a few bucks? The most telling aspect of the various versions of Williams's sanitized story was that Danny never left on his mystery date. Williams was clearly pedaling as fast as he could away from any suggestion of a relationship with Danny Hansford. His problem was that other evidence told a different story.

The *Savannah News-Press* coverage of the killing reported that Hansford had lived in the house "for more than two years."[43] Hansford's home address on the April police report: 429 Bull Street. Danny didn't "drop by" in April. To "come home" means exactly what it says.

Williams's stories about April were so obviously doctored that there was a chance we had missed something—or the answer was simple: Williams was spinning the tale of *The Prince and The Psychopath* and either couldn't keep his scripts straight or didn't care enough to try.

I don't believe Williams expected himself or anyone else to be seriously interrogated about the killing. Assuming he had set up the scene and was satisfied with the job he'd done, he likely expected his staging to receive rave reviews. The police would believe him this time, just like they had in April, and Danny wasn't around to tell them any different.

So where were we at this point? We had inconsistent statements about the killing and a "carbon copy" a month earlier. We had a timeline with a half hour or more between the killing and the call to the police. We knew that Williams was going to cast himself as a kindly benefactor with his only motive being to help his young furniture-sanding employee. And the rating was going to be PG.

Williams had his work cut out for him. The scene was shouting the things he wasn't saying. It was clear what had occurred, though not why. We knew we had the trigger man, but we didn't have the trigger—what had set him off.

But trials can bring surprises. Maybe Williams would testify and explain why none of the evidence in the case fit his self-defense claim. Maybe, while he was at it, he would explain the ground speed at which pigs rise in flight. Neither seemed very likely.

PART THREE

WILLIAMS I

CHAPTER 11

THE CAST

The *Williams* case was assigned to the senior judge of the superior court, the Hon. George E. Oliver. Judge Oliver was a veteran jurist with over twenty-five years on the bench, the previous eleven in the superior court.

The district attorney, Spencer Lawton, was a descendant of a distinguished Savannah family and had been a long-time Savannah attorney at the time of his election in 1980. Mr. Lawton would be lead counsel (called "first chair" in some jurisdictions) for all four of the *Williams* trials as well as all other legal proceedings over the life of the case.

I was a third-generation Savannahian who had returned to the district attorney's office with Mr. Lawton's election to serve as his appointed Chief Assistant District Attorney. From an organizational standpoint, I was responsible for supervising the office's trial teams while also trying major felony cases.

The third member of the prosecution team was Robert (Bob) Sparks, a former Assistant Attorney General, Assistant U.S. Attorney, and Assistant Solicitor General. Bob was then working with the Prosecuting Attorneys' Council of Georgia and was loaned out to our office for the *Williams* trial. Bob had prior experience dealing with the internationally renowned Bobby Lee Cook.

Any doubt that the *Williams* case would be unique dissolved with the appearance of Bobby Lee Cook for the defense. Cook was one of the most famous trial lawyers in the United States. In the March 2009 edition of the *ABA Journal*, the magazine of the American Bar Association, the cover story, "Lions of the Trial Bar," featured profiles of seven defense lawyers, including Cook.

Cook had tried cases in forty states and several foreign countries. He had represented the Rockefellers and the Carnegies but was best known for his work in murder trials dating back to the 1940s. The long-running television show *Matlock* was rumored to have been based on Cook's law practice.[44]

Bobby Lee Cook is credited with many quotable quotes about the defense of a murder case. One quote attributed to him counsels that, if the trial of your client is not appearing auspicious, don't let them try your client—try the dead man instead. Here is how it was related in the *ABA Journal* profile:

> Cook ... says there are two things a lawyer must prove to a jury in
> order to win a murder case: That the victim was a bad person who

deserved to be killed, and that your client was just the man for the job.

"If you prove those two things, nine times out of 10, your client walks," he says.[45]

Coincidentally, I had recounted something remarkably similar in my closing argument in *Williams I*, which I am certain Bobby Lee committed to memory because of my eloquence:

If you're faced with a murder trial and you're defending someone, you've got two questions you've got to answer. First, you've got to figure out whether your man killed the victim and whether they can prove it. If you can't fight that, and they can prove it, the thing you've got to try to prove is, he needed killing.

It can work. Also in 1981, in Skidmore, Missouri, a brutal town bully named Ken Rex McElroy, was shot dead while sitting in his pickup truck in the middle of town in broad daylight. Dozens of citizens reportedly watched as bullets from two different weapons hit McElroy.

Miraculously, no one saw the killers. Despite the best efforts of law enforcement agencies, including the state police and FBI, no one in the town of Skidmore saw a thing. According to the dead man's long-time attorney, "The town got away with murder."[46] The town might see it differently, but the point is someone thought Ken Rex McElroy was, to quote Bobby Lee Cook, "a bad person who deserved to be killed."

The notion that Danny Hansford wasn't worth being missed and probably needed killing had been previewed even before Cook had entered the case. Joseph Goodman offered up the following description of Hansford in his formal statement in October 1981:

[T]he boy was nasty looking. Because the first thing Nancy [Rushing] said when she met him [was], who the hell is that guy. You know he had like a fifth or sixth grade education. He couldn't hardly talk. He was on drugs. He was always nasty. He had tattoos, dirty fingernails, didn't bathe regularly, smelled horrible, had green teeth. You know everybody in Savannah knows Jim. ... everybody knows, nobody hides it. You can accept that. But I know what they gonna try to do. They gonna try to say it was a lovers' quarrel or something like that. ... And the boy was violent, he was bright (sic) on drugs when he was 13 or 14 years old.[47]

Goodman didn't mention that neither he nor Williams knew Danny Hansford existed when Danny was 13 or 14 years old, but it didn't matter. It was obvious where this was headed: The abused pit bull had turned on the man who had rescued it from the pound.

If this was the plan, it held some risk for Williams. The more despicable the defense made Hansford, the more irrational Williams might look for his apparent obsession with "the boy" as Goodman called him. The more garbage Williams heaped on Danny Hansford, the more a jury might start to look at Williams's own pathology.

Another danger was that, if the defense overdid the attack on Hansford, it could come across as exaggeration, and exaggeration is a form of lying. For example, considering Goodman's description of the creature with "green teeth" also known as Danny Hansford, it might seem odd that Goodman had been trying to get Danny a job where Goodman worked—the local plant of American Cyanamid.[48]

Regardless of the challenges the defense strategy presented, the strategy was clear: They were going to kill the dead man twice.

The second lawyer on the defense team in *Williams I*, chosen as local counsel, was John Wright Jones. John Wright was one of the top criminal defense attorneys in Savannah. There certainly were none considered any better. I knew and respected him.

CHAPTER 12

THE GIANT PANDA

James A. Williams appeared in the Superior Court of Chatham County on August 12, 1981, for arraignment on Indictment No. 34,982 charging him with murder. Williams was represented at the arraignment by John Wright Jones. I appeared for the State. Through his attorney, Williams waived the reading of the indictment and entered a plea of not guilty.

Thus the gears of the criminal justice system began to turn in what should have been a simple murder case. This observation would rank fairly high in the Understatement Hall of Fame, because this simple murder case was going to collide with the *Really Big Case Syndrome*, the tendency of a simple case to grow beyond all reasonable proportion when a defendant has problems with the evidence and wheelbarrows full of cash.

Just as a "magic sponge" might start as a speck and grow into a giant panda when dipped in water, a criminal case can do the same thing when dipped in money—except the result is not nearly as cute as a giant panda.

There is a popular fiction that wealthy defendants can buy themselves a super-lawyer with superpowers and beat the rap, regardless of the charge or the facts. Wealthy defendants do occasionally beat the rap, but such outcomes are seldom the function of the courtroom nimbleness of a legal Houdini. Yes, money can buy the best lawyer money can buy, as the saying goes, but more importantly, money can buy tag teams of expert witnesses with impeccable credentials and remarkable imaginations, expert jury consultants, the finest courtroom posters, photographic blow-ups, diagrams, and charts—all manner of accoutrement common to the high-profile trial of a well-funded defendant. In some cases, it might buy a witness or two.

But if the facts are simple, why spend mountains of money on a defense? Because the simple facts might result in a simple, quick conviction and a ride on a bus with bars on the windows, to go meet your future playmates. If you can afford to continue hammering a chisel against the wall of evidence and can afford the fees of the chisel and the hammer, you keep hammering as long as possible.

But money can only help a defendant make a case when there is a case worth making. To quote a paradigm related to me by a noted jurist: "I'll let you pick your lawyer if you let me pick my facts." Personally, I'd prefer a high-definition movie filmed by a nun, coupled with a tearful confession by a defendant who happens to be Catholic and can't help but spill the beans upon spotting the nun as he leaves the scene while carrying marked bills from the bank vault.

What does this have to do with the trials of James A. Williams? If facts should trump lawyers in the rock-paper-scissors-science legal world, what happens to cases involving wealthy defendants with serious fact problems? The defense will push the case as far away from the facts as possible, in search of a way around, over, or under them. Or they will try to turn the case into a marathon, hoping delay and time can deliver a break.

At his retirement ceremony from the FBI, a former colleague and friend told a story about his father, who was still practicing law back home in Crofton, Nebraska. His dad would occasionally still handle an indigent criminal client at the request of the court. His dad's idea of representing the accused was to go to the jail, ask them if they did it and, if they said yes, go over to the courthouse and plead them guilty. I think that was probably a joke—maybe not, but it doesn't work that way these days. It certainly wasn't going to work that way in *Williams*.

There is an oft-quoted paradigm of trial law: "If the facts are against you, argue the law. If the law is against you, argue the facts. If both are against you, yell like hell." Some relate the conclusion as "If both are against you, call the other lawyer names" or "bang your shoe on the podium." Because Williams's story was contradicted by the evidence in the case, even including the very things he contrived to indicate his innocence, the "yell like hell," "call the other lawyer names," and "bang your shoe" tactics—and more—were triggered.

In the past, criminal defense lawyers occasionally felt compelled to address something known as Perry Mason Syndrome. Perry Mason Syndrome was the notion that, in addition to proving the defendant's innocence, the defense attorney was expected to conclude the case by dramatically revealing the identity of the true perpetrator of the crime, as Perry did at the close of each television episode. I explained this phenomenon on more than one occasion when doing criminal defense work. Perry Mason did have superpowers, granted to him by television writers, and his mythology was so embedded in popular culture that attorneys felt the need to remind juries that proving the defendant didn't commit a crime did not carry with it the obligation to prove who did.

In today's practice, there is an upside-down cousin of Perry Mason Syndrome. It could perhaps be named for Johnny Cochran's infamous "If it don't fit, you must acquit" mantra from the O. J. Simpson criminal trial. In this version, defense counsel doesn't prove that the defendant didn't do it, or who did. Rather, defense counsel creates such a fog in the courtroom that the jury is unable to figure out who did what to whom—all in search of that precious commodity known as *reasonable doubt*—anything to make a jury, even one member of a jury, uncertain and hesitant.

Perhaps this concept would read, "If the facts and the law are against you, and you already yelled like hell and called the other lawyer every name you can think of, come up with something else." There would be a lot of something else in the *Williams* case.

CHAPTER 13

THE BRADY FILE

As a part of the criminal pretrial process at the time, the entire State file was copied and delivered to the court in order to address a case known as *Brady v. Maryland* and cases interpreting that US Supreme Court decision. This copy of the State's file, popularly referred to as the Brady file, was given to the presiding judge for review as a safeguard to ensure that nothing "arguably exculpatory" was concealed from the defense. The practice was developed by *prosecutors*, to safeguard themselves against any possible accusation of concealing evidence. The practice was routine, but it would turn out to be anything but routine in the *Williams* case.

On July 8, 1981, Robert J. Duffy, who was still acting as Williams's counsel, filed several motions, among them a standard Motion for Discovery. In Paragraph 3, the motion requested "all copies, records, memoranda or summaries of any confessions, admissions against interest, or statements, either oral or written, attributable to JAMES A. WILLIAMS."

A defendant is always entitled to receive copies of all statements they might have made and this is taken care of routinely as a part of normal pretrial motion practice. This is completely unrelated to "arguably exculpatory" evidence. The concepts are joined here only because they will be joined later.

The accepted practice for giving the defense a record of oral statements, if any were made, was to provide the defense a photocopy of the original transcription of the statement from the responsible officer's report. This was done to avoid any question about whether the statement, as originally given, had been altered in any way. This was considered the best evidence, a photocopy of what the officer had written when the statement was made.

Of course, the same report could also contain investigative information to which the defense was not entitled (under rules at the time), so the practice was to copy the portion of a report that contained a statement and redact the investigative content, leaving the statement. Two pages of Cpl. Anderson's Supplemental Report in May reflected oral statements made by Williams. Those pages, with everything redacted but the statements, were delivered to the defense in the routine course of business on August 8, 1981, almost six months before trial would commence.

There is an aspect of police reports that will become relevant later. Incident Reports, initial reports stemming from police calls, are generally available. This is the "police report" your insurance company might ask for in the case of an auto accident, for example. Supplemental Reports are follow-up reports that normally contain *investigative* information. Supplemental Reports are not public and are not provided to the defense (unless they contain "arguably exculpatory" evidence—which is always to be provided to the defense if uncovered during an investigation, whether or not contained in a report).

Only the first two pages of Cpl. Anderson's Supplemental Report regarding the May call reflected oral statements made by Williams. The other pages of this report were not provided to the defense, as they didn't reflect any statements by Williams. This was the procedure used at the time of *Williams I*. Separately, complete copies of all police reports were contained in the Brady file delivered to Judge Oliver.

Little did we know that delivering a copy of the prosecution's entire case file to the court, a process developed to safeguard prosecutors, would prove useless to safeguard prosecutors.

CHAPTER 14

THE TRIAL

All rise!

Trial in the case of *State of Georgia v. James A. Williams*, Indictment No. 34982, was called into session on January 25, 1982, the Honorable George E. Oliver presiding.

All rose and, following Judge Oliver's entrance and the banging of his gavel, sat back down and the trial of James A. Williams for the killing of Danny Lewis Hansford began. Though Williams's self-defense claim would be the ultimate focus of the trial, the State always has the burden of establishing a prima facie case in any criminal trial. So we went first.

THE STATE'S CASE

We began with the missing minutes—the gap in the timeline. For Williams to have tampered with the crime scene, what did he need? Time. Because officers were at the scene within ninety seconds of dispatch, this meant the time between the killing and Williams's call to the police.

The State's first witness was SPD Officer Patricia V. Slaughter, who confirmed she was on duty in the radio room in the early morning hours of May 2. She took the call and, while on the call, stamped a dispatch card with a date-time machine and handed the card to the radio operator to broadcast the call for units. The dispatch card was stamped 2:58 a.m.

The second witness for the prosecution was Joseph E. Goodman, Williams's dear friend. Remarkably, we were in the position of having to put up the first person Williams called after killing Hansford—as a *prosecution* witness. There was no other choice. Goodman established the unexplained time gap between Williams shooting Hansford and calling the police.

According to Goodman's statements, he had spoken with both Williams and Hansford between 2:00 and 2:05 when Williams woke Goodman to tell him that an antique-buying trip to Europe was off. The conversation had lasted a couple of minutes. Williams had called again at 2:22, saying, according to Goodman, "I just had to shoot Danny" and "come down here quick."[49] Goodman told Det. Ragan at the scene that he knew the times of the phone calls because his microwave had been right in front of him and it had a digital clock.

Goodman and his girlfriend, Nancy Rushing, were living in a garage apartment rented, in an odd coincidence, from the secretary of Judge Oliver. The apartment had only two rooms and only one phone, just inside the main room. To answer it, Goodman had to get out of bed and step through the doorway into the other room. This left him facing his microwave and its illuminated digital clock.

These calls were important enough for us to have Williams's friend lead off the State's case. If the second call was at 2:22 and the call to police was at 2:58, this left anywhere from thirty-six to fifty-eight minutes unaccounted for. Why a range? Because we didn't know exactly when—between the first call (2:00 to 2:05) and the second call (2:22)—the actual shooting had occurred.

Time gaps are antithetical to a self-defense case. Such a lengthy delay before seeking help is completely counter to normal human behavior. Williams's first act after killing Danny Hansford (putting aside, for the moment, staging the scene) wasn't to call the police; it was to call his friend and tell him to "come quick." This is not the act of a distraught man. This is the act of a man in trouble calling for help.

This was important evidence. The problem was, the person with this evidence was Joseph Goodman, and his relationship with Williams was not cause for comfort. According to Goodman's statements, he had known Williams since Goodman was a youngster.[50] Goodman had first met Williams when he (Goodman) was twelve years old and had begun having sex with Williams when Goodman was either sixteen years old—which would constitute statutory rape in some seventeen states—or seventeen years old, which gets Williams down to eleven states. When Goodman was seventeen, Williams would have been thirty-five.

The sex had been an experiment, according to Goodman, who claimed that he hadn't seen what all the fuss was about.[51] Williams had also been the best man at Goodman's first wedding. Goodman described the closeness of their relationship this way: "He's always been real close to me and I guess he'd do anything in this world for me if he could. I haven't ever had to ask him to do anything for me but I guess if he ever needed to he would if he could. We just real close."[52]

A natural deduction was that Goodman might do the same for Williams. But it was Goodman who, probably unwittingly, established the time frame with a huge hole in the middle, in three separate statements: (1) in an oral statement to Det. Ragan at the scene, (2) later the same day in a handwritten, signed statement taken at SPD headquarters, and (3) in a later recorded, transcribed statement to District Attorney's Office Chief Investigator J. D. Smith. We had good reason to believe that Goodman's statements were locked down, so Spencer Lawton called Goodman as the prosecution's second witness.

Goodman testified that he was in bed asleep when Williams first called. When Lawton asked him the time, the first hint of possible trouble appeared. "I'd say shortly after two. If I had to make a definite, I couldn't swear on *exactly the time*, but it was shortly after two." So far, fine, but why couldn't he swear on "exactly the time?" He had a clock; two clocks in fact. In addition to the microwave digital, in his formal statement he had described the "Baby Ben" alarm clock that he kept next to his bed. But, for now, he said "shortly after two" and moved on.

Goodman testified that Williams had called to tell him that an antique-buying trip to Europe was off and that Danny had gotten on the phone to tell Goodman he hoped there were no "bad feelings" about the trip. Danny sounded like normal Danny. Goodman said he told Danny it was no big deal and hung up.

With the second call, Goodman's locked-down statements came unlocked. According to Det. Ragan's handwritten note, Goodman had said the time was exactly 2:22 and that he had known the time exactly because he had been look-ing at the numbers on the digital clock of his microwave (Figure 45). But on the stand at trial, his microwave clock suddenly didn't mean a thing:

> I can think and I can think, but unless you're right up on it and—the
> two's look like eight's sometimes, the four's look like five's sometimes,
> you've got to be dead up on it, but I'd say between the first phone call
> and the second phone call was probably fifteen, twenty, twenty-five,
> thirty minutes.

The vivid image from Goodman's microwave clock—three glowing matched twos in the dark—had disappeared. Or had he been persuaded to un-remember it?

Goodman's new story was nonsensical. If his twos had looked like eights, he should have told Det. Ragan the time was 8:88. And there were no fours any-where to be found. Go fish. This is a current observation. It was not raised with Goodman.

The immediate dilemma was that Goodman was our witness. A lawyer isn't allowed to challenge, or "impeach" the testimony of their own witness. The only way around that rule (for a witness who isn't designated as "hostile" or "adverse" in advance) is to plead surprise at the testimony and request that the court waive the rule. Lawton asserted a claim of surprise and Judge Oliver permitted him to refresh Goodman's memory using Goodman's prior statements, over the defense's vehement objection. The defense appeared to have a stake in Goodman's "newly improved" memory that they did not want to relinquish.

Lawton showed Goodman his original statements. Goodman acknowl-edged the statements and that he had made them, but he wasn't giving up. He still refused to say what time he had received the second phone call. He would not admit even the *possibility* that he had been right about the time when he made his statements on the night in question.

Hopefully, once the jury better understood the relationship between Goodman and Williams, they would figure out why Goodman was now running away from his own statements: to help eliminate the problem he had created for his friend.

There is another way to evaluate the original time statement from Goodman that Det. Ragan noted on his pad (Figure 45). Did Goodman speak to Ragan? Yes. Did Goodman tell Ragan the time he received the phone calls? Yes. Neither of those facts was in dispute. Ragan noted other things from the same conversation: the microwave clock and the time (2:22) of the second phone call. Do we believe that Goodman said those things as well? Or do we believe that Det. Ragan simply wrote additional random items in his notes because he was struck by cosmic brain interference from aliens? The notion is ludicrous.

There was virtually no possibility that Goodman hadn't said exactly what Det. Ragan noted that he had said. And there was no requirement that Goodman remember (or admit remembering) at trial. He had acknowledged making his original statements. The jury was perfectly entitled to believe those original statements were true, accurate and complete, whether or not Goodman wanted to confirm them at trial.

Something said at trial is not somehow "better" than an earlier statement, particularly an earlier statement made at the time of the event, when facts and memories are fresh and other "considerations" haven't occurred to the speaker. Both statements can be weighed by a jury and either (or neither if the circumstances so dictate) can be judged to be true.

This jury could believe Goodman's original statement, or they could believe that the second call had really been made at 8:88 and Goodman had misread his clock. We were willing to live with that choice. But it didn't make Joe Goodman any less troublesome—and this was only the beginning.

On faux cross-examination of the defendant's friend, John Wright Jones attempted to reverse-engineer the entire time frame by throwing out everything Goodman had said in his statements *and* his testimony. Goodman and Nancy Rushing had driven up at 3:00 with the police. Jones's tactic was to suggest that Goodman's previous statements were *all* wrong, allowing Jones to do whatever he wanted with the phone calls.

In a prior statement, Goodman had said he thought he arrived at Mercer House at 2:45.[53] Yet it was undisputed that he and Rushing had driven up with the responding officers. Jones decided that, because Goodman's guess about his arrival time had been wrong, he had been wrong about all the times in all of his statements and Jones could throw it all out and start over. Pretty clever—if the jurors were buying manure for their gardens.

Jones didn't mention, of course, that Goodman had used a clock to establish the time of the two phone calls while his 2:45 arrival time estimate had been a blind guess (Goodman didn't wear a watch). Yet Jones didn't merely give Goodman's guess equal weight with his clock-based references. He gave the guess even *greater* weight, using it to justify throwing out all of Goodman's statements related to the times of Williams's phone calls.

There is another possible explanation of Goodman's 2:45 estimated time of arrival at Mercer House which has a less innocent basis than the lack of a wristwatch. We will return to it, but for now, Goodman is still on pretend cross-examination.

With a clean slate courtesy of himself, Jones started with Goodman's 3:00 arrival time and performed some basic arithmetic. Subtraction was Jones's math of choice. Goodman estimated he lived approximately seven to nine minutes from Mercer House by car. At nine minutes, this wasn't grossly unreasonable—seven minutes would be only half the expected drive time from Goodman's apartment. The route he took (according to his formal statement) measures 4.4 miles and is estimated as a fourteen minute drive, without traffic.[54] Nevertheless, Goodman said seven to nine and that's what Jones used.

But in addition to the inexact (and likely understated) drive time, there was no way to establish with any precision how long it had taken for Goodman to explain to a just-roused Nancy Rushing what was going on and for both of them to get up, get dressed, get out of their apartment on the southside of Savannah, into the car, and on their way. Jones simply subtracted an arbitrary total of ten to fifteen minutes from 3:00 to suggest the second call to Goodman—the "I shot Danny" call—had to have been made at 2:45 or even 2:50, ignoring everything else Goodman had said.

This would have been almost a *half hour* later than Goodman had said he received that second call. Jones would have had Goodman receiving a phone call while in bed in the middle of the night, nine minutes' (or more) driving time from Mercer House, and pulling up to Mercer House as soon as ten minutes later with his girlfriend.

Even though Jones was terrific at subtraction, Jones couldn't testify, and math isn't evidence—60 minus 15 does equal 45, but it proves nothing more than that. It couldn't make Joseph Goodman's microwave and digital clock disappear (even with Goodman's help). Goodman received the phone calls, Goodman made the statements, and Goodman was the witness. Jones might have wanted to ignore Goodman's clock, statements, and testimony, but it would be unlikely that a jury would buy it.

What about this 2:45 arrival-time mistake? Was it simply an estimate by Goodman that was off? Perhaps. But there's another option that was never examined at trial and that wouldn't be for the life of the *Williams* case—for good reason: It couldn't be proved without a confession from Goodman, Rushing, or Williams. But it's an option that I have always found intriguing: *All* of Goodman's times make sense if the 3:00 arrival was *not the first.*

All anyone knew for certain was that Goodman and Rushing drove up when the police arrived, at 3:00 that morning. There was no independent verification of where they had been prior to that moment.

In his statement to Investigator Smith, Goodman had said, "I must have got to Jim's house about twenty minutes to three, fifteen minutes to three."[55] He had estimated to Det. Ragan that he got there around 2:45.[56] Was he simply mistaken? What if he wasn't? Assume that Goodman was called by his dear friend at 2:22 and told to "come quick." Williams wouldn't call the police until 2:58, but he needed Goodman to "come quick." Why?

Was it possible that Goodman grabbed Nancy and flew to Mercer House, putting him there at 2:40 or 2:45 as he said? Could Goodman have arrived, checked over (or helped stage) the scene with his friend, then hopped back in his car and driven around the corner while Williams called the police, waited until he saw police cars rounding the park, then pulled up at the same time, thus establishing his and Rushing's arrival through the police while avoiding being inside the house when the police showed up? I have always suspected this option had validity. The advantage is that it fits the evidence. The disadvantage is that it cannot be proved.

As for Goodman's testimony at trial, his unwillingness to agree with his previous statements wasn't fatal, even if the jury bought his suddenly mushy memory completely. There was no way to reduce the time gap to less than Goodman's *reasonable* travel time plus the time required for Goodman and Nancy to get up, dressed, out of the apartment, into their car, and headed downtown—plenty of time for Williams to do what needed to be done. It's also important to remember that Williams was not likely to have been dialing Goodman as the body was falling. The second phone call didn't tell us when Williams shot Hansford, only when he *told Goodman* about it.

Leaving the time of Williams's phone calls, Goodman also testified to their content. This time, he was not so helpful to his friend. According to Williams's statements, Hansford had morphed into Conan the Destroyer, slammed him into a "pocket door," and chased him into the study, where Williams had tried to call the police but—caught in the act—had called Goodman instead. This was the first phone call. Here's how Goodman described Danny on that call at trial:

A. He was kinda—I guess he was almost his self. He was a little—
slurred words a little bit. I could tell he'd been drinking or—but he
sounded—he sounded like Danny.

Q. There's no question it was Danny?

A. Yeah.

Q. You say his speech was slurred? Is that what you said?

A. Well, he talked kinda slow, but he slurred his words most of the time anyhow.

There was no sign of Williams's raging madman.

Cpl. M. J. Anderson was called and testified that he and Ptl. M. A. White were the first to enter Mercer House. Anderson thus became what is known as the "primary" on the scene, the most senior officer first to arrive.

Williams met Cpl. Anderson and Ptl. White at his front door and told them, "I shot him; he's in the other room." Williams led them inside, down the entrance hall, and into the study, telling Anderson that the "he" in the study was "Danny." Anderson testified that he was familiar with Danny from a prior call to the same residence (the April incident).

Anderson had Cpl. J. J. Chesler take Williams out into the hallway, stationed Ptl. White at the study door and radioed for an ID unit, detectives, EMS, and the coroner, then checked for a pulse and respiration, but did not disturb the body. Williams was "rather cool, calm."

Anderson testified that before exiting the study he did a quick visual inspection. He noted the antique chair over Hansford's body, the two Lugers, the ricochet mark on the wall behind the desk, and several other items. With that, Anderson's direct testimony was completed.

The chair over Hansford's body was disastrous for Williams. This single item of evidence destroyed his self-defense claim. There was *no* explanation for it consistent with Williams's innocence—at least none that I had been able to come up with in the nine months since the event. It seemed that the most logical approach would be to have Williams say he had placed the chair there without thinking, despite the fact that this would create another irreconcilable conflict with his self-defense claim.

Bobby Lee Cook went straight to the chair on cross-examination. Anderson responded:

Both feet were under the chair, practically the entire leg was, both legs were under the chair. The chair was probably located going straight up to his rear-end part; half his body was like under the chair.

From Cook's cross-examination of Anderson, it was obvious that Williams was not going to say he put the chair where it had been found. If not, then how could it have gotten there? If Williams hadn't moved the chair to where it was found, someone else had to have done it—someone like Cpl. Anderson. Despite the ridiculous notion that Anderson's first move upon arriving at a crime scene had been to grab a chair to put over the victim's body—without anyone noticing, including Williams—Cook plowed ahead.

His first gambit was to create some time out of thin air by misstating the arrival time sequence. Cook repeatedly referred to the "thirty minutes" between the time Anderson arrived at the scene (3:00) and the time Detectives Ragan and Jordan arrived (3:30). Cook conveniently omitted ID officer Donna K. Stevens, who had arrived immediately after Anderson and photographed the chair along with the rest of the study.

It looked like Cook was fishing, casting around for an answer. If the defense wasn't going to allow Williams to touch that chair, they had to find another explanation for its position.

The misplaced chair was the single most visually compelling evidence in the entire *Williams* prosecution. It seemed obvious that, in his haste, Williams had reset the chair over the body without noticing that he had set a rear leg squarely on top of Hansford's trouser leg (Figure 8) and that the chair was so far over the body that the feet stuck out the back (Figure 7). It was irrefutable proof that he had tampered with the scene. In time, it would prove much more, including what likely happened in the study that led to Danny Hansford's death.

Actually, Williams made another mistake with the chair that I only discovered during my review of the evidence for this book. Not only had Williams not seen the chair leg on Danny's trouser leg, but he also hadn't realized that he had set the chair significantly off from its normal location. This is *new* information.

Throughout the residence, Williams followed a habit of placing small rugs underneath chairs, likely to protect the larger rugs they sat on. Williams's own desk chair was an example (Figure 38). As to the chair over Hansford's body, note its location in relation to the protective rug underneath (Figures 7, 9, 11). The chair is at least two feet forward of where it should be.

This informs two areas of the case. First, it confirms that Williams altered the scene. Second, returning the chair to its correct position on the smaller rug aligns the chair perfectly with an ashtray containing marijuana joints and a separate joint ground into the top of Williams's antique desk (Figures 12, 21, 22), which suggests the likely series of events that led to Hansford's death that night (which will be explored later).

There was no question that the chair had been placed above Danny's body after he was dead and who had done it. The only remaining question was why.

In the racing minutes following the shooting, Williams was doing only things he had to do. It was not time to tidy up the house. The only conclusion was that the chair had been in a place and position that demanded Williams move it. It would have been a simple matter to have Williams say he picked the chair up without thinking. But, by going after Cpl. Anderson, the defense signaled that they understood the dilemma this choice presented. Williams couldn't admit placing the chair over Hansford's body because it would confirm that it had been somewhere else immediately after the shooting—somewhere that he could not afford to admit that it had been.

Williams fired his first shot at Hansford from behind his desk. This was established by Williams's statements and the location of the physical evidence, so no one but Danny Hansford could have displaced or—to share an advance hint—knocked over that chair. This posed an unsolvable problem for Williams. He couldn't allow Danny Hansford to be anywhere near that chair when shot, because Williams claimed that Danny fired at him from the *other end of the desk*.

This wasn't merely a Williams claim. The physical evidence confirmed the far corner of the desk (the southwest corner) was the origin of the shot that Williams claimed Hansford had fired. Williams couldn't have Hansford at one end of the desk, firing at him, and at the other end of the desk at the same time.

There was no way for Williams to escape this conundrum. He had been faced with two bad choices when standing over Hansford's dead body: either confess or rearrange the evidence, including grabbing the displaced chair and putting it where it was found. The choice at trial was the same: deny staging the scene or confess to murder. This Williams conundrum applied to all of the altered evidence from the study and would launch the merry chase through the magic forest upon which this case was about to embark.

As for the chair, specifically, I had personally spent countless hours trying to imagine an explanation for it that Cook and Jones might construct, and there simply wasn't one. They had the same photographs we had and access to their client. They knew what we knew and more, depending on how much of the truth Williams had told them. They needed another culprit to move the chair if they could create one.

A scale diagram included here shows the items of evidence matched to the Luger that Williams used to shoot Hansford (Figure 13). Note the location of hair and skull fragments toward the southwest corner of the room. They track the direction of fire, from northeast (Williams's desk) to southwest (the fragment locations). The diagram was created for this book. All of the locations and distances are taken from official reports, and the diagram is to scale.

A skull fragment was found sticking to the seat of the antique chair, as shown in the diagram. When upright over Hansford's body, the chair is in the *opposite* direction from the direction of fire and practically across the room from the other fragments. It was impossible for that skull fragment to have flown backward, elevated itself, and found its way onto the chair seat. The only way for that skull fragment to have become stuck to the seat of the chair, consistent with the evidence, was for the chair to have been on its side, with the seat facing Hansford's head.

So we knew the chair had been toppled over. And the only explanation for its position when the police arrived was that Williams stood it back upright, not noticing the rear leg settling onto Hansford's pants leg, the location of the chair relative to its protective rug, or how much of Hansford's body he had covered with it.

Refer to the photo of the body, desk, and chair taken from the west (Figure 14). If the chair is toppled over toward the fireplace (to the right when looking at the photo), the seat is facing Danny Hansford's head.

Also note the small rise or bubble in the rug immediately adjacent to the rear chair leg that is not on Hansford's pants (Figure 8). That small bump is entirely consistent with the chair having been raised up from the floor and snuggled against Hansford's right leg.

This is an example of why even smart people have trouble staging a crime scene. In his haste, Williams had only been concerned with placing the chair back on its feet. He hadn't noticed that the chair was out of position and he hadn't seen the back chair leg pinning Hansford's trouser leg.

After months to come up with an explanation, the defense's answer, beginning with Cook's cross-examination of Anderson, was one of the staples of the defense lawyer arsenal: The cops did it. In this case, that would have to be "the cop," since there was only one cop who'd had even a sliver of an opportunity to grab a chair and put it over the body: Cpl. Mike Anderson.

The defense made no attempt to explain the inanity of the suggestion. But the tradition is to simply accuse and to worry about logic later. Cook didn't discuss with Anderson the fact that, when Anderson entered the study, he was accompanied by three other officers and Williams himself. The chair couldn't have suddenly appeared later, out of the blue. Or so we thought.

Moving on from the chair, Cook had Anderson confirm that EMS technicians had come to the scene to deal with an attack of some sort that Williams had suffered. Anderson agreed that this happened, though he recalled that it was much later. Why did the EMS visit matter? It went to the question of Williams's demeanor.

Corporal Anderson had found Williams to be cool and calm when he arrived at 3:00 a.m. I had also found Williams to be cool and calm when I arrived an hour later. As Williams's situation deteriorated, which might well have been accelerated by my arrival, it would not have been unusual for his stress level to rise, but the defense wanted to counteract the image of a cool, calm killer with evidence that an EMS team had been dispatched to deal with his anxiety.

It was clear that there was confusion about this EMS team, their visit to Mercer House, and Williams's condition. This confusion would not be straightened out for quite some time, and not during the first trial.

Detective D. Everette Ragan, lead detective in the case, was up next. He had been with the SPD for eight years at the time of trial, with more than six years in the Criminal Investigative Division. He had investigated more than a hundred homicides. He was submitted and approved as an expert witness in crime scene investigation.

To offer an opinion on the evidence, a witness must be qualified by the court as an expert witness, a witness having some special education, experience, or training in a particular field. The theoretical basis for having Det. Ragan qualified as an expert was to allow him to pull together the evidence for the jury and to draw conclusions from the evidence that would not be readily apparent to a layperson.

Detective Ragan's direct examination was conducted by Spencer Lawton. Ragan began with his arrival at the scene. Corporal Anderson had told Ragan that Williams had called his attorneys before calling the police and that they were en route. Considering the circumstances, Ragan decided to call in the district attorney's office. When he was unable to reach Mr. Lawton, he had called me.

A common spot for defense lawyers to start looking for a crevice into which to drive a wedge and manufacture some doubt is in the initial moments of an investigation. More units will typically respond to a call than will ultimately be involved in securing and processing the scene. Defense lawyers will talk about "all these people" at the scene—whether or not "these people" did anything or even remained on site.

I call it the "Herd of Elephants" theory. If a police officer is ever present at the scene for any period of time, defense counsel will soon have the officer wandering around, stumbling over the body, kicking the evidence, and generally creating wholesale mischief. Why bring this up? Hindsight is fighting its way onto the stage, and this point will become important later.

In his direct testimony, Det. Ragan mentioned various people present at Mercer House, without being precise about who was where and at what time. Ragan spoke of stepping across the hallway to use a telephone to call me:

Q. I have just one other question, just to clarify. When you went to use the telephone in the other room, whom did you leave in charge of the study?

A. Detective Jordan was there and our policy is when the detective arrives at the scene, he's in charge of the crime scene. Also, Officer Anderson was there, along with Dr. Metts and Officer Stevens.

Q. Okay, who did you actually leave inside the room?

A. I did not—as I left, I did not designate anybody to be in charge of the room. Detective Jordan was there and our policy [is], they're in charge.

Q. Did you leave anybody actually inside that room?
A. Yes, sir. They were still inside.
Q. Who was that?
A. Detective Jordan, Dr. Metts, Officer Stevens and Officer Anderson.

This was relatively minor business, but manufactured confusion is a common tool of the criminal lawyer in search of some fog to help the defense. If this seems overly paranoid, keep it in mind when the defense begins to fill the study with dancing elephants and unearthly spirits.

Unfortunately, as this case would prove throughout its life, lost in the recurring discussion of coming and going was the fact that ID Ofc. Donna K. Stevens, who would testify shortly, photographed the study in its initial state before Ragan, Jordan, or Metts arrived on the scene. Although Stevens *continued* taking photographs as the scene was processed, the more relevant question was when she *began*. Ragan testified that when he arrived at approximately 3:30, Ofc. Stevens started *over* so he could follow along.[57] This was in the age of 35mm film photography. Ofc. Stevens didn't delete photos from her camera—it wasn't possible—she only took *additional* photos of things she'd already photographed.

Ragan continued, describing the location of items of evidence recovered and logged. The measurements described in his testimony were also contained in his Supplemental Report and were used in the preparation of the diagrams showing the two Lugers and the items of evidence matched to each (Figures 13, 20). As noted earlier, these diagrams are *new* to this account. By matching the evidence to each weapon separately, these diagrams are far more useful in tracking movements than is one diagram that includes all evidence items together.

It's also important to view diagrams in conjunction with the photographs. For example, the distance from Hansford's head to the bullet hole made in the rug might appear greater on the diagram (Figure 13) than in a photograph that accounts for another dimension—the thickness of the body and the height of the desk (Figures 14, 15, 16). When viewed with the added dimension, it's readily apparent how little distance there is from the head to the place where the bullet entered the rug.

Because Det. Ragan had supervised the recovery of the physical evidence and had been qualified as an expert witness, he was able to walk the jury logically through the scene and interpret the evidence. One of the first flaws in Williams's story was the path that Hansford had supposedly taken when entering the study in his murderous rampage.

The position from which the alleged "attack" shot had been fired (Figure 20) was established by evidence, even without Williams's statements. At this point, we didn't know if Williams would testify, though we presumed he would.

Q. You're indicating—

A. The right-hand corner of the desk.

Q. The right-hand corner of the desk—the far right-hand corner of the desk from the point of view of a person sitting in it?

A. Sitting behind the desk.

Ragan then described the direct, unobstructed path from the doorway that any murderous madman would have taken (Figure 23).

Q. A person coming in that door would approach from behind a person sitting at the desk; is that correct?

A. That's correct.

We didn't believe Hansford had come into the study to shoot Williams in the first place, but if he had, did it make sense for him to bypass the direct path to his target and circle out to the end of Williams's desk?

The next crack in Williams's defense was that, even had Danny circled out to the corner of the desk to fire at him, Danny was at the wrong end of the desk. The body was upside down (Figure 10). Ragan explained:

Q. Okay, so you are indicating—tell me if I'm correct—is that approximately the spot where the victim's head is indicated on your diagram?

A. That's correct, sir.

Hansford's head was where Williams had claimed Danny was standing when Danny fired at him. Williams had apparently forgotten that a person falls *over* when shot. Note the diagram showing the firing position of the "attack" shot (Figure 20). The shooter is standing on the dead man's head.

If Williams had fired that shot himself, the mistake would be totally understandable. In a hurry and under stress, he might not think to stand Danny up before selecting the point from which to fire a "fake" shot toward his desk chair. But was it possible, somehow, for Hansford to have fallen over so that his head ended up where his feet had been? Considering where his body was found, for Danny Hansford to have fired that shot, he would have had to stand on his head and fire the Luger with his feet.

The position of Hansford's body is only one more inconvenient fact that refuted Williams's story. There's a tee shirt that, had it been available at the time, I would have sent Williams as a gift. It reads, "I'd Be Unstoppable—If Not For Law Enforcement And Physics."

Det. Ragan continued by describing the position of Hansford's right hand on top of the Luger, the blood found on the wrist and hand and in his palm, as well as the lack of blood on the rug or on the Luger grip. Two images demonstrate visually how devastating this evidence was. The first shows both hands (Figure 24). The second shows only the left hand (Figure 25). The fingers of the left hand are squeezed tightly together, clamped down over a thumb tucked against the palm. The third photo is of the right hand alone (Figure 6).

Take the right hand off the gun. Close the fingers back around the thumb. Now imagine that hand sliding back under Hansford's chest and the arm being pulled up to his chest. Both fists are clenched, both arms are up, and the hands are virtually identical. That position is quite common in death. The position of Hansford's right hand and arm when officers entered the study was not merely uncommon, it was laughable. The right hand was on top of the grip, the thumb pressed against the palm and also on top of the grip (Figure 6). Any homicide investigator who saw that hand perched in that position would know immediately that the scene was contrived. That was also Det. Ragan's conclusion, and that's what he told the jury.

Williams might have been convicted with the chair photo alone. The same was true of the position and condition of Danny Hansford's right hand. There was blood on the wrist, on the back of the hand, and soaked into the crevices of the web area between the fingers. The best view of this is from the opposite side (Figure 26). The right hand had been under the body long enough to accumulate a significant quantity of blood.

The hand also had to have remained under the body for a period of time because, as Ragan told the jury, there was no blood on the rug underneath the arm. The blood had to have coagulated or thickened enough for none to have transferred to the rug, and the blood had to have come from underneath Hansford's body because that was the only source of blood in the room.

Still, Ragan wasn't finished. The blood on the wrist and back of the hand was smeared (Figure 6). The only explanation was that the hand had been pulled out from beneath the body. Blood was also found in the palm of Hansford's hand but not on the grip. The only trace detected on the Luger was a single pinhead spot on the trigger guard that Ragan confirmed the State Crime Lab had determined to be blood. Detective Ragan shared with the jury his conclusion from this evidence:

Q. What exactly did that seem to you to indicate had happened?

A. In my opinion, it indicated that the victim was not holding the gun; that the gun was placed under his hand.

Was there another explanation? A lawyer should never grab a theory and stick to it. It should be attacked and tested, from the point of view of the opposition. This was a process we went through many times in the *Williams* case. I personally took our case apart innumerable times, looking for flaws and ways the defense might attack it. Were there other reasonable hypotheses that could explain this evidence?

Assume Hansford had been shot while holding the "attack" Luger. We know he couldn't have continued to hold the Luger or it would have been covered with blood just like his hand. So he would have to have dropped it. Was this possible?

This would be the required sequence of events: Danny is shot and drops the Luger, which falls onto the rug while he falls to the floor. Though shot three times (and undoubtedly dead, with a severed aorta), he waits for enough blood to collect under his chest to soak his hand and to coagulate enough so as to not drip on the rug. He then reaches out—while looking in the *opposite* direction (Figure 24) and still dead—and feels around for his Luger. Meanwhile, the Luger has bounced around into the perfect position for dead Danny to find it and place his hand gently on top of the grip.

Was this feasible? Not so long as physics, physiology, and common sense were components of our universe. Williams botched this segment of his contrivance so badly that he should have been convicted of impersonating a criminal.

What was the *only* conclusion possible? If Danny couldn't have been shot and continued to hold the Luger, and if he couldn't have been shot and dropped the Luger, he had never held the Luger in the first place. There was *no* other conclusion possible. That's what Det. Ragan told the jury.

Under the category of hindsight, what we did not consider or argue at the time was the reasonableness of an action that Williams didn't take, if we assume his story was true. Put him in the study and imagine that Danny Hansford has just tried to kill him. He rounds the desk and sees Danny's hand on the Luger. What would any reasonable person do? Kick the gun out from under his hand, in case he was still alive. Although we thoroughly analyzed whether or not Williams could have put the Luger under Hansford's hand, we didn't consider why, if the Luger had really been under Hansford's hand, Williams would leave it there.

The entrance path into the study, the chair on the pants leg, the tucked thumb, the bloody hand, the curled fingers, the blood smears—on and on—it became an exercise in stacking improbabilities on absurdities. None of the puzzle pieces fit. On the other hand, all of the evidence became clear and unambiguous if Williams was lying.

There is a concept within scientific analysis known as Occam's razor, essentially the principle that the simplest explanation for the data is to be presumed correct until proved otherwise. That's awfully simplistic and there are those who dispute the concept itself, but that's the basic idea.

This is merely another way of stating a preference for simplicity in scientific analysis, a concept that was important to the development of the theory of relativity, quantum mechanics, and any number of scientific principles. It goes back to the ancients. As Aristotle put it, "We may assume the superiority *ceteris paribus* of the demonstration which derives from fewer postulates or hypotheses."[58]

In more pedestrian terms, Aristotle would probably agree that if it looks like a duck, walks like a duck, and talks like a duck, it's probably safe to hypothesize that the organism is a form of waterfowl. Aristotle might also agree that, when the simplest explanation for the *Williams* evidence is that Danny never held the Luger in the first place, having defense experts risk spinal injury trying to create some other hypothesis was a waste of Williams's time and money. But it is amazing what a checkbook will do to Occam's razor and our pal Al Aristotle.

I am convinced that Williams did not expect the scene to be examined as carefully as it was. He overestimated his own cleverness and underestimated the police. It happens every day. Smarter guys than James Williams have made that mistake.

Detective Ragan continued walking the jury through the crime scene. He related the recovery of the two Lugers, the shots fired, the bullet wounds to Hansford (of which there were three: one to the chest, one to the back of the head, and one in the back), and the path of the bullets that passed into and through Hansford's body.

The Luger allegedly fired by Danny Hansford was identified later by the State Crime Laboratory as a "BYF P.08 Caliber 9mm, semi-automatic pistol"[59] (designated as Item 22A in the evidence log and referenced herein as Luger 22A). The Luger used by Williams to shoot Hansford was identified as an "Erfurt[60] Caliber 9mm, semi-automatic pistol"[61] (designated as Item 23A in the evidence log and referenced herein as Luger 23A). (Luger is a popular name taken from the name of the original patent holder, Georg J. Luger.)[62] Our two new diagrams illustrate the recovery location of the shell casings, bullets, and bullet fragments matched to each weapon (Figures 13, 20).

In Williams's upstairs bedroom, a side table contained an empty holster and a box of 9mm ammunition (Figure 28). If the "attack" Luger was retrieved from the upstairs bedroom, this would not fit Williams's story. But then, Williams's story wasn't true. The empty holster and ammunition were evidence and could be given whatever weight the jury chose. Maybe Williams was keeping an empty holster in his bedside table for protection, planning to throw it at an intruder. If this sounds silly, bookmark it for later.

Back to the study. One item that Det. Ragan identified received far less attention than the rest (throughout the life of the case, as we will see). An unfired 9mm round was found between Hansford's head and the fireplace (Figure 13). A Luger has a hinged top that opens when the weapon is either manually cocked or fired (Figure 29). State Crime Lab tests matched the live round on the rug to Luger 22A (the "attack" weapon). A live round is ejected when the slide on the weapon is slid back and released (which places a round in the firing chamber and retracts the hammer, readying the weapon for firing) while a round is already in the chamber. How had this live round—matched to Luger 22A—found its way onto the rug?

To understand the sequence and its importance, we have to trace Hansford's supposed movements. The position from which the "attack" shot had been fired was not disputed: the southwest corner of Williams's desk (the left front facing the desk). A stack of papers on the desk had been penetrated by a bullet. A leather pouch was recovered from the floor next to the desk chair and contained bullet fragments, a grazed belt buckle, and a shattered poker chip (Figures 30, 38). The pouch had been on the desk, underneath the papers, and had been knocked off the desk by the "attack" bullet. None of this evidence would be contested.

That shot was fired with the Luger angled down, pointing at the desk, causing the round to penetrate the papers and pouch, ricochet off the buckle, and continue toward the north wall. The ejected empty shell casing went forward, also toward the north wall, where it was found, as indicated on the Luger 22A diagram (Figure 20).

So what was the explanation for the live round found on the rug? It had to have been ejected manually by someone who racked the slide on Luger 22A with that round already in the chamber, someone standing where the round was found. Williams's self-defense claim already required that Danny bypass the direct line from the door to his intended victim and, instead, walk around to the front corner of Williams's desk. For Hansford to have ejected the live round onto the rug where it was found, this enraged killer would have to have continued *past* the desk where Williams was sitting, almost across the room, then stopped, prepared his weapon for firing, and finally turned to shoot his victim.

The suggestion is logically absurd. Williams could have emptied a clip into Hansford by then. Another diagram illustrates the circuitous route Hansford would have to have taken (Figures 31, 32). Was it likely that this path and these actions were those of a raging madman?

These were the actions of someone thinking through what they were doing while doing it. An enraged killer doesn't do that. Someone calculating the contrivance of a crime scene does. What that person didn't do was pick up the live round that ejected onto the floor. Who knew that ballistics experts could match an unfired bullet to a particular weapon?

That live round would only be explored tangentially throughout the *Williams* case, though that unfired round clearly indicates the path of the individual who handled and fired the "attack" Luger. Whoever that person was, they were not concerned with time, or that someone might be shooting back.

Returning to Ragan's testimony, Hansford had suffered three gunshot wounds: one in the chest, one in the right rear of the head, and one in the right upper portion of his back. The diagram for Williams's Luger shows the items matched to that weapon (Figure 13).

Using these new diagrams, it is actually possible to determine Williams's likely position as he fired all three shots into Hansford's body. For example, a shell casing from Williams's Luger (Luger 23A) was found by the west wall. There was a logical reason for the shell casing to be there, based on entry and exit wounds and the weapon's ejection pattern: Someone facing the west wall stood over the body and fired down into Hansford's back, ejecting the spent casing forward. Occam's razor. It all fits.

It was also possible that a mouse wandered by and decided to take the casing to his mouse house, only dropping it later because it was too heavy and he knew his domestic partner mouse would yell at him for bringing more junk home. But for the purpose of analyzing the diagram related to Luger 23A, it is assumed that things go where they're aimed.

What about the other two shots? Det. Ragan described Hansford's wounds. The first shot was to the chest. A spent shell casing ejected from a level Luger ejects up and slightly forward. As shown in the Luger 23A diagram, a shell casing from Williams's Luger was found behind and to the left of Williams's office chair (Figure 13).

If Hansford was standing at the southwest corner of the desk and Williams returned fire while standing, the shell casing would have ejected up and forward, in the same southwesterly direction. It was found behind the desk, in the opposite direction. What if Williams was sitting down, pointing the weapon up at a standing Hansford? We have other evidence that rules out that option, in addition to the fact that Williams had to rise from his office chair to retrieve the second Luger from the chest next to his desk. But, in addition, according to the autopsy, the chest entrance wound was 33 cm from the top of the head. The bullet was recovered from beneath the skin in the back, 38 cm down from the top of the head.[63] In other words, a slightly downward trajectory. That isn't possible with Williams seated and Hansford standing.

So, is there any way to get that ejected shell casing where it was found without assistance from a junk-collecting mouse? Yes. Move Hansford to Williams's left and seat both men.

This is not Williams's story, and it puts Hansford at the other end of the desk, sitting in the radioactive chair. However, this is what the evidence dictates, and without some other explanation, it's necessary to follow the evidence where it leads.

If Hansford was sitting in the armchair smoking a joint and giving Williams hell when Williams grabbed his Luger and turned it on him, and Danny, seeing what was happening, began to rise from his chair when Williams fired from his chair, the ejected shell casing would be ejected up and back, bouncing onto the floor, behind Williams, where it was found (Figure 13).

What of the downward path of that bullet? Assume Hansford was coming up out of the chair, with his head slightly forward, when Williams fired. This is the only explanation that accounts for both the shell casing position and the first bullet's path through the body.

It was never disputed that the first shot was to Hansford's chest. Since there was no dispute surrounding that shot, it was never explored as carefully as the other two. However, looking now at that shot in relation to ejection patterns and bullet paths, an increasingly clear image of the truth begins to emerge. We will return to it later.

Back to Det. Ragan's testimony. The second shot was to the right rear of Hansford's head and through, penetrating the rug and gouging the floor. This shot to the head would become a recurring point of contention throughout the *Williams* prosecution. What was controversial about the shot? After all, Williams admitted firing it. There were two questions: Where was Williams when he fired the shot, and where was Hansford's head when the shot struck?

Why might either answer matter? If Williams remained behind the desk to fire the second shot, it's not inconsistent with the image of a frightened man defending himself. If, however, Williams came around the desk and finished Danny off, this would suggest the callous act of a vindictive killer and would be one more item in conflict with his defense.

I'm not convinced that the argument over the shot to the head merited the attention it would receive throughout the history of the *Williams* case, considering how confusing it could become, but that's purely a personal opinion—the debate was certainly legitimate. The main reason I care less about the second shot is because of the third shot.

The third shot into Hansford's back was clearly fired from almost directly above the body. The bullet passed through almost vertically, very slightly upward and very slightly right to left (according to the autopsy) and embedded itself almost vertically in the hardwood directly underneath the exit wound (Figure 19).

As we know from the ejected shell casing next to the west wall (in the mouse-free version), Williams had to have delivered that shot facing west, with the Luger pointed down. In the crime scene photograph taken from that position, the ejected casing is near the far wall, between the rose-colored chair and the table (Figure 7).

While it's possible to quibble over the shot to Hansford's head, the origin of the shot in the back is clear, and one "coup de grâce" fired into the back was more than enough to demonstrate Williams's state of mind. It would also explain something else: his failure to call an ambulance.

Detective Ragan next described an item of evidence that, on its own, made Williams's self-defense claim scientifically impossible. There was a stack of papers on Williams's desk, through which the "attack" bullet had passed:

Q. Did anything else appear unusual to you about the crime scene?
A. Yes, sir. In speaking of the bullet passing through the papers on the desk top, you see papers facing this position here, this weapon here being identified in this photograph (the Williams Luger), with the paper fragments *on the weapon itself*.

* * *

Q. All right, and what about that appeared unusual to you?
A. The paper fragments here, here, and here, dust particles and small amounts of paper fragments there on top of the weapon itself.
Q. Are there any paper fragments on the grip of the pistol?
A. There's small fragments here, sir.
Q. What—why would that picture—what's unusual about that?
A. In my opinion, with the bullet passing through the papers on top of the desk, the paper fragmenting as it did fragment, the weapon was in that position on the desk when the papers fragmented.
Q. What papers are you referring to?
A. The papers here that had the bullet hole here.

* * *

Q. So explain again, what is it that's unusual about the paper fragments on the gun?
A. The gun apparently was in this position, laying on top of the desk, when the bullet passed through the paper, fragmenting the paper that we recovered on the floor and the desk.

The gun to which Ragan referred was the Luger that Williams used to kill Hansford (Figure 9). The paper debris created by the alleged "attack" shot from the other Luger was *on top* of Williams's gun (Figure 36), meaning Williams's gun had been put down on the desk *before* the "attack" shot was fired.

In other words, it was impossible for Danny Hansford to have fired the "attack" shot at Williams. Danny Hansford couldn't have fired it, because when that shot was fired, he was *already dead*. Williams's story had run into gravity— and gravity always wins, at least on planet Earth.

The papers are shown in the photograph of the desk as it was when the police arrived (Figure 34). Ragan also described papers hanging out of an open drawer (Figure 35). These two stacks of paper were analyzed by the State Crime Lab, along with nineteen paper fragments. According to the lab test results (which would be introduced later), ten of these fragments were "similar in appearance and/or matching marks" to the papers in the stacks.[64] Another nine blue- and/or pink-lined white paper fragments, some with black ink writing were "not similar" to any of the collected papers.[65]

This proved two things: (1) The fragments were created by the "attack" shot passing through the papers on the desk, and (2) Williams had removed something before calling the police. With a dead body on the floor, whatever he removed must have been important. No evidence would ever be presented as to what Williams removed, simply because he was the only one who knew, and he didn't tell us.

In the prologue of this book, I noted the value of being present at a crime scene. This paper-fragment evidence presents an extreme example of that concept in practice. There is no question in my mind that there were paper fragments on top of Williams's weapon (Figure 36). Because I was the one who first noticed them.

Detective Ragan was showing me the items in the study that had caused alarm bells to go off, and I was following along while being careful not to disturb anything. When he pointed out Williams's Luger on the desk, I saw the paper debris on top of the weapon. I think I said something brilliant like "Hey, look at that."

I couldn't testify at trial and didn't need to, but there was no doubt about the paper debris on top of Williams's Luger—which meant that Williams fired the "attack" shot himself, after he'd shot and killed Danny Hansford. This is an example of why circumstantial evidence can be the most powerful evidence in the world when based in the physical sciences.

In an odd twist, circumstantial evidence can be so irrefutable that it can have a negative impact on the conduct of a trial. If the evidence is so strong that it can't be explained away, the only option is to roll out the standard Lawyer Games grab bag: conspiracy, evidence contamination, police incompetence, clumsiness, dishonesty, obesity, and bad personal hygiene. Nothing is safe. There is a common laundry list of defense-lawyer tactics employed when the forensic evidence begins to resemble a key to the big house. This collection of tactics could be called the Lawyer Games Toolbox.

A final area touched upon by Det. Ragan on direct was intriguing: the presence of a bag of marijuana, an ashtray containing marijuana cigarettes (joints), and a single marijuana joint ground into the leather top of the antique desk (Figure 22).

Detective Ragan did not offer an opinion as to what this evidence might mean. It didn't openly conflict with Williams's story. It wasn't in Williams's story. The marijuana, ashtray, and ground-out joint hadn't been mentioned in any of Williams's statements. The fact that they were left out was significant.

There was no doubt who ground that joint into the leather top of the desk—Danny Hansford. And he obviously did it while sitting in that chair, at the mysterious "other end" of the desk (Figure 12). The question was, if Danny ground the joint into Williams's desk, *when* did he do it?

This evidence wasn't central to the trial in *Williams I* because we weren't assuming the burden of proving what had happened; we were focused only on dismantling Williams's self-defense claim. Here, however, we are going where the evidence leads. Our goal is to understand the case, not merely the trials, so we detour for a moment.

When was that joint ground into Williams's desk? The timing can be determined by the process of elimination. Williams was not a casual antique hobbyist. He was a prominent collector and dealer. Assorted treasures—including, for example, this desk (Figure 9)—filled his residence. I call it an antique desk. A better description is "a Louis XV Bureau Plat with tooled leather top, ormolu acanthus mounts and sabots, serpentine edges, cabriole legs and large drawer hardware, either in the style of J. Dubois or by Dubois and, therefore a period piece circa: 1740–1760."[66] Even the description sounds expensive.

How likely was it that Danny Hansford burned a hole in the "tooled leather top" of this "Louis XV Bureau Plat" and headed out for a fun night with Williams at the drive-in or adjourned to the parlor for a friendly game of backgammon? When Danny jammed the burning joint into the surface of the desk, turning it as it burned into the leather, Williams was certainly watching, since that undoubtedly was the point. This was an act done with the clear intent to provoke.

It could not have happened before the trip to the drive-in. They would never have made it to the drive-in. It could not have happened before game playing in the parlor for the same reason. Why had Williams never mentioned it? Because he couldn't. There was no place for it in his self-defense version of the event, but there was a place for it—after the first phone call to Goodman.

The phone was near that end of the desk (Figure 40). Was Danny sitting in the chair, smoking a joint while Williams called Goodman? Here's where the ground-out joint fits. Danny grabs the phone and talks to Goodman. After the phone is hung up, an argument either ensues or escalates, words are exchanged, Danny grinds the joint into the desk, Williams snaps and grabs his Luger, and as Danny tries to rise from his chair, fires his first shot into Danny's chest.

All the evidence, including the unexplained marijuana and burned hole, meshes perfectly with that scenario. Williams couldn't use it, however, for one very good reason: In that scenario, Hansford didn't have a gun. There is no such thing as self-defense against an attack on a desk. With no other choice, Williams left the joint and burned hole out of his stories. By leaving them out, he indicated how important they were.

John Wright Jones conducted the cross-examination of Det. Ragan. Despite the hundreds of hours I had spent reverse-engineering our case to anticipate the defense, the tack Cook and Jones took was startling. They didn't run from

Williams's lousy job of scene manipulation; they embraced it as evidence of his innocence.

Detective Ragan agreed with Jones that Williams was the one who called the police. Yes, Williams called the police—eventually. Who else was supposed to call them? Besides, his other alternative would have been to dispose of the body and hope nobody noticed. Ragan also agreed with Jones that Williams was cooperative with the police when they arrived. Yes, he was. He was claiming to be an innocent victim. Being open and cooperative went with the part he was playing.

The defense's next move was astonishing. It's difficult to believe, even now, that this was a defense lawyer questioning Ragan. Jones asked Det. Ragan to agree with him that the crime scene couldn't have been altered because the job had been so badly done that it was impossible for a guilty person—in this case Williams—to have been that stupid. It was creative, but probably a bit nuanced—and ridiculous—for a jury. Criminals make glaring mistakes every day, thank goodness. But Jones was attempting to use Williams's own bumbling as a defense to a murder charge.

Q. The body was found, almost the center of the body, or the bottom part of the body, was totally underneath a chair; isn't that right, sir?
A. Yes, sir.
Q. The legs were sticking out behind the chair and then the whole chair was on top of it and then the rest—the front of the body was out in front; is that right, sir?
A. Yes, sir.
Q. Did that appear to you to be something that somebody who was trying to fabricate a justifiable homicide scene would fabricate?
[An objection was sustained.]
Q. Certainly, Officer Ragan, this did not indicate to you that somebody was fabricating a scene, did it?
A. It indicates to me that that chair was moved after the victim was lying prostrate on the floor.
Q. I understand that, but if a person was trying to set up a scene, they sure wouldn't want to put a chair like that on top of a person that couldn't move, would they?
[Another sustained objection.]
Q. All right, come on down here. The body was—the feet were out, the lower part of the body was underneath the seat part of this chair, and the front part was out; is that right?
A. That is correct.
Q. Okay, was this one of the clues that you had that made you think that something unusual—

A. I was wondering how that chair got on the pants leg; yes, sir.

Q. And you were convinced that the deceased didn't do that.

A. I know the deceased didn't do it.

Q. Right. That's what I'm saying. That's *exactly what I'm saying.*

That was also exactly what *we* were saying. If that's what *they* were saying and *we* were saying, why were we having a trial? Williams's own lawyer had just agreed that Hansford couldn't have gotten the chair onto his own pants leg. You may safely presume that no Williams defense lawyer would ever again make that admission.

I don't think this went well for the defense, but it was ingenious. A defendant's own lawyer was suggesting that the defendant had done such a bad job of doctoring the scene that he couldn't possibly have doctored the scene. It was at this point that it struck home how right we were about what had happened that night. The fear of that chair was palpable.

On redirect examination, Spencer Lawton returned to the missing minutes, to clarify:

Q. Referring to Mr. Goodman's statement to you concerning the time when he arrived at the house, Mr. Jones showed you a copy of a report that he (Goodman) made that morning. I will ask you, did he make, in addition to that, any oral statement to you concerning the time sequence of events that morning?

A. Yes, he did.

Q. Did he have occasion to tell you at what time he had received the second call from Mr. Williams, which prompted his coming to the scene?

A. Yes, sir, he did.

Q. What time did Mr. Goodman tell you he had received that call?

A. Two twenty-two, sir.

Q. Did he say how he knew that it was two twenty-two?

A. Yes, sir, he did.

Q. How did he know?

A. He has a microwave oven with a digital clock and he observed the time *on that digital clock* whenever the phone rang, sir.

Q. Two twenty-two.

A. Yes, sir.

That time and image have been stuck vividly in my mind for many years: three bright digital twos in the dark. You would think Joe Goodman could have remembered it as well, especially since Det. Ragan had been kind enough to write it down for him (Figure 45).

ID Officer Donna K. Stevens appeared next. She confirmed that she had been dispatched to 429 Bull Street and had arrived at approximately 3:05 that morning. Stevens touched nothing and moved nothing before beginning to photograph the scene, starting in the entrance hall and continuing into the study. She explained the process, authenticated photographs introduced as State's exhibits, and that was it.

This evidence was vitally important and we will return to it throughout the *Williams* trials. Upon arrival, ID takes authority over the crime scene, until the arrival of detectives—meaning that Cpl. Anderson was in charge of the *Williams* scene for no more than five minutes. More importantly, within moments of ID Ofc. Stevens's arrival, the position of the radioactive chair and the other items of evidence in Williams's hallway and study had been captured by her camera.

Detective J. P. (Joe) Jordan appeared next and testified that Det. Ragan had been the primary detective on this case. One important task that Jordan had performed was to "bag" the victim's hands to protect them for later examination at the autopsy. He went over the process:

Q. Okay, when you returned from the bond hearing, did you do anything to assist in the preparation of the victim's body for removal?

A. Yes, sir. Before the funeral home removed it, I put bags on the hands.

Q. What sort of bags?

A. They were paper bags, evidence bags.

Q. What was the purpose of that?

A. This was to protect the hands until we got to the hospital for the autopsy, to do swabbings to forward to the Crime Lab.

Q. Can you be more specific? What's the purpose of bagging—why do you need to protect the hands with bags?

A. Bags are used on the hands to prevent anyone from touching them or, especially the hospital before an autopsy is performed, in the event they wash the body off, it would damage any residue if there was any.

Q. ...what else, if anything, did you do at the autopsy?

A. I swabbed the hands of the deceased.

Q. Were the hands in bags or had the bags been removed when the victim's body was brought in for the autopsy?

A. I removed the bags myself.

Detective Jordan demonstrated the procedure he used to swab Hansford's hands, using a gunshot residue-testing kit. I recall the demonstration well because Det. Jordan used my hand for his demonstration. He testified that he sent the collected swabs to the State Crime Laboratory in Atlanta where all gunshot residue (trace evidence) analysis was done.

Roger W. Parian was the head of the Savannah branch of the State Crime Laboratory. Qualified by the court as a firearms expert, Parian testified that he performed the analysis of the weapons, shell casings, live rounds, paper fragments, leather pouch, belt buckle, and other items of evidence. He also checked the "attack" Luger, Item 22A, for blood. There was none on the weapon other than the barely visible drop on the trigger guard previously mentioned by Det. Ragan:

> It was a small spot, but that was the only spot on the gun that I saw that looked like it could be tested or looked reasonable to test for blood. Although I did [b]enzidine tests on other spots, I did not see anything that looked or appeared to be blood.

Benzidine testing was by far the most sensitive known test for blood at the time. It isn't used today only because benzidine was found to be extremely carcinogenic. Today, the product commonly used is known by the name luminol. The fact that Parian resorted to benzidine in an effort to find other blood, without success, demonstrated how blood-free that Luger was.

Parian found Luger 22A to have a heavy trigger pull of twenty pounds. Parian suggested that a more normal trigger pull was in the four-to-eight-pound range. A twenty-pound trigger pull is not the same as lifting twenty pounds with your finger but does require more pressure to release the firing mechanism. The issue played no part in the first *Williams* trial. It would later.

Parian reported the results of his tests matching shell casings and rounds to weapons. Those results allowed the preparation of the diagrams included here. He also verified the tests on the paper and paper fragments referenced by Det. Ragan.

The final tests reported by Parian were test firings of Luger 22A. The purpose of test-firing the Luger was to determine to what extent the weapon gave off measurable quantities of trace elements referred to generally as gunshot residue, or GSR. Normally, GSR testing means examining the hands, skin, and/or clothing of a person alleged to have been in the vicinity of a discharged firearm to determine the presence (or absence) of GSR trace elements. Gunshot residue is not *gunpowder* though the terms are often interchanged. Gunshot residue is residue from the ammunition *primer*.

This primer residue is expelled from the barrel and, in the case of a Luger, from the breech at the top (Figure 29). The residue consists of submicroscopic particles of lead styphnate, barium nitrate, and antimony sulfide. These particles are typically one to ten microns in size (for comparison, a human hair is approximately one hundred microns in diameter).

> When a gun is discharged, a mixture of vapors and particulate material are expelled from the muzzle, ejecting port, barrel, cylinder gap or open breech. These products of firearm discharge are collectively called gunshot residues (GSR). ... GSR originating from primer is

unique to the discharge of firearms because of their characteristic elemental composition of lead, antimony, and barium.[67]

GSR tests specifically look for the particular *combination* of antimony and barium because the combination of these two elements is unique to ammunition primer. They are not generally found together in nature.

The *absence* of GSR deposits, standing alone, doesn't prove conclusively that a person was not in the vicinity of a discharged weapon; it only means that the elements were not detected in meaningful (scientifically significant) quantities. Taking an additional step, however, can make a "negative" GSR test highly meaningful: testing the weapon. This was the reason Roger Parian conducted test firings of Luger 22A. Testing both the subject *and* the weapon can go a long way toward proving whether or not someone fired that *particular* weapon.

For the combined results of the weapon tests and hand swab results to *help* Williams, the tests would have to show *both* (1) that this Luger *did* deposit significant quantities of GSR, and (2) that GSR *was present* on Hansford's hands. This would indicate that Hansford's hand had, at a minimum, been in the vicinity of the Luger when it was fired.

For the tests to *hurt* Williams, the two tests would have to show *both* (1) that this Luger, once again, *did* deposit significant quantities of GSR, and (2) that GSR *was not present* on Hansford's hands. This would indicate that Hansford had not fired that particular weapon.

The point of the combined test is to determine if there is a source of GSR (the weapon) and, if so, to see if the GSR showed up where it should have (on the person who had supposedly fired the weapon). When someone makes the offhand comment that a negative GSR test doesn't prove anything, they are referring to the test of the hands without the second step, the weapon test. Without the determination that GSR *should* be found, not finding it doesn't mean anything. That is obvious. But ignoring the second step and making a blanket statement about negative GSR tests is simply deceptive. The tendency to repeat that false maxim has led to a good deal of confusion on the subject.

For the weapon test in this case, Roger Parian testified that he test-fired the "attack" Luger and that Det. Jordan performed the swabbing of Parian's hand, as Jordan had done with Hansford's hand, to ensure consistency. Parian also confirmed that he conducted the tests using ammunition from the clip found in the Luger so that there was also consistency in ammunition.

There were four rounds remaining in the Luger 22A clip.[68] Parian fired six total rounds, firing once and having his hand swabbed, then washing his hands and repeating the process with two shots and, lastly, three shots (adding rounds of identical brand and caliber for the three-shot sequence), because Williams's

statements about the number of shots fired at him weren't consistent. The physical evidence showed only one round had been fired from Luger 22A but the
Crime Lab tested all possibilities previously mentioned by Williams.

Parian also tested the weapon to determine the direction in which a shell
casing was ejected after firing. With a level pistol, ejected casings went up and
slightly forward. He further testified that an ejected chambered round (a live
round already in the firing chamber) went up and back slightly toward the
shooter. This meant that an ejected live round should be found near the person
who ejected it. (Recall our discussion of the live 9mm round on the floor.)

What about the defense? The defense in a criminal case has every right to
look at and test the physical evidence. We presumed that a warrior with the reputation of Bobby Lee Cook had an army of experts behind him. What had the
defense's army been up to? I had Roger Parian share the surprising answer with
the jury.

Parian testified that Douglas Moss, an investigator for the defense, had
dropped by the Crime Lab the previous December but that the defense had not
been heard from again until Mr. Moss showed up with Cook, Jones, and a Dr.
Joseph Burton on the previous Friday—*three days before trial*. I had been shocked
when I first heard this and wondered what we had missed. They had to know
something, some hidden flaw in the case, to be so cavalier about the physical evidence.

We also had some interesting information about Dr. Burton, the only
expert on the defense witness list. Dr. Joseph Burton was the Medical Examiner
for DeKalb and Cobb counties (both adjacent to Fulton County, the home
county of Atlanta). The scuttlebutt was that Burton wanted to be head of the
State Crime Lab. The job, however, wasn't open. The man who held the job, Dr.
Larry Howard, was scheduled to be *our* chief scientific expert.

Although Dr. Howard would go on to run the Division of Forensic Services
for many years, rumors swirling at the time were that Burton was "after Larry
Howard's job." With that background, I was surprised that Dr. Burton would
come to town to testify opposite Dr. Howard with so little preparation. Nevertheless, Roger Parian confirmed that no one with the defense, including Dr. Burton, had performed any independent tests of *any* physical evidence in the case.

The only options I could see were that the members of Williams's defense team
were brilliant, were holding a secret card, or weren't all they were cracked up to be.

Dr. Richard M. Draffin, the Medical Examiner who performed the
autopsy on Danny Hansford, confirmed the contents of his autopsy report. He
also confirmed the path of the shots through the body. As for the shot through
the back, that shot had traveled an "almost horizontal plane" through the body,

entering the right upper back and exiting the right upper chest. With Hansford facedown on the floor, "almost horizontal" translates to "almost vertical."

The defense will always ask if the police fingerprinted everything in sight, and if they didn't, this will invariably show up on the "gotcha" list. But the question is generally legitimate. Fingerprints are first on any list; they can be compelling evidence depending on the circumstances. With that in mind, SPD ID Officer W. J. ("Flash") Gordon was called to testify that he had, indeed, checked both weapons for fingerprints but had not raised any prints from either weapon. Considering the gnarled grips on both, he explained, this result was not unexpected.

Finding fingerprints on firearms is not as common as the general public might suspect. Sometimes you are required to put up evidence solely because of expectations created by television crime shows. Even though it was undisputed that Williams had fired at least one of the Lugers, no fingerprints were raised from either one.

It was then time to pair up Danny Hansford's hand-swab test results with Roger Parian's GSR tests of the purported attack weapon. The hand swabs had been sent to the State Crime Laboratory in Atlanta for testing. The results were explained in testimony by Randall H. Riddell, the microanalyst chemist who performed the tests. I conducted his examination. Riddell explained in more detail the GSR testing that we touched on previously:

> [A] lot of gas and the metals, the trace metals that were present in the primer, along with tiny bits of metal shavings and gunpowder particles—which are usually too small to even be seen with the microscope—surround the gun and, if it is a handgun, will surround the weapon in a momentary cloud. ... These tiny particles can then reside on the hand.

Riddell noted the difference between testing live and dead subjects: Residue can be removed through normal physical activity of a live subject. This is not the case with a deceased subject. Riddell also noted that higher-caliber weapons tended to give off more GSR and that a 9mm pistol was a large-caliber weapon.

Even with a dead subject, Riddell explained, the subject's hands needed to be protected until swabbed. This was typically done by placing either paper or plastic bags over the subject's hands, though paper was preferable. In addition, Riddell testified, it was important to know that (1) the hands had not been cleaned before swabbing, (2) the gun itself would deposit residue, and (3) whoever had done the swabbing and testing had done them correctly.

As to the test results in this case, Riddell testified that Danny Hansford's hands had not only been negative for GSR but had been what he called *significantly* negative:

A. There are relative values, if you will, of negatives, and (in) this particular instance, there were—it was completely negative and I would consider that significant.

This was the first prong of the two-test sequence. The second prong was the weapon tests performed by Roger Parian. Riddell testified that those swabs also produced unusual results.

Q. After one shot being fired from the weapon, did you find those results significant in any way, considering the weapon being used?

A. ... In general, automatics or semi-automatics do not leave as much residue as a revolver and—but in this case it did leave significant levels and, primarily, because it's a large caliber weapon.

I was aware of the unusual nature of these results. In preparation for trial, I had reviewed the report from the Crime Lab. It had merely stated that the test firings of Luger 22A were positive for GSR. To follow up, I had called Mr. Riddell. When asked to confirm that the Luger had given off GSR, his response was "clouds of the stuff."

This result from the second prong of the two GSR tests was why GSR had a significance in *Williams* that it might not have in all cases. In many firearms cases, either (1) the weapon isn't available, or (2) the weapon doesn't discharge GSR in sufficient quantities to allow for a conclusion to be reached.

To lay some groundwork for my cross of Dr. Burton, I had Riddell comment on Dr. Burton's use of the State Crime Laboratory. Riddell noted that Dr. Burton routinely submitted evidence to the laboratory. I reasoned that it would be difficult for Dr. Burton to question the reliability of the lab's work since he routinely used the same lab, but I severely underestimated Dr. Burton's chutzpah.

Riddell also pointed out that, to his knowledge, Dr. Burton had *never* taken the extra step of submitting a firearm for testing in connection with a negative GSR test. That was extremely curious, because Burton was listed as the only defense expert and the defense had been given all of the scientific test results. It was still difficult for me to believe the defense didn't have a hidden division of evidence-blasting artillery just over a nearby hill.

Riddell's testimony concluded with his opinion that, based on the combined test results in this case, it was *very unlikely* that Danny Hansford had fired Luger 22A, or *any* weapon. This was damning evidence from a highly credible source.

There was another Georgia "Williams" case in progress at roughly the same time as our *Williams* case. This was the Wayne Williams case, also known as the "Atlanta Missing and Murdered Children" (AMMC) case. The trace-evidence section of the State Crime Laboratory was the same group that cracked the AMMC case using what was, at the time, revolutionary fiber evidence. Riddell's testimony was not something the defense could take lightly.

With the completion of Riddell's testimony, the foundation of our case against Williams was laid. But as with any jury, it was necessary to place the pieces into the puzzle—or, in this case, explain why they wouldn't fit without scissors and tape. This task fell to the director of the Division of Forensic Services, Dr. Larry Howard.

Dr. Larry B. Howard was the State's final witness. I handled his examination. Dr. Howard outlined his background. He testified that he had been with the Crime Lab for twenty-five years, the last twelve as Director. He noted that the Georgia lab was the second largest state crime laboratory in the nation.

I had Dr. Howard explain that he shared the power of appointment over all medical examiners in the State of Georgia—which included Dr. Burton. I thought it worth noting that our lead expert had to approve the defense expert's appointment.

Dr. Howard had examined several thousand crime scenes and had testified in criminal proceedings, according to his estimate, on an average of twice a week for the previous twenty years, which would amount to something over 2,000 criminal trial appearances. Dr. Howard was qualified by Judge Oliver as an expert witness without objection.

We went immediately to the GSR tests, to follow up on Randall Riddell's testimony while it was fresh in the jury's mind. Dr. Howard firmly disagreed with the popular scientific "slang" claiming that a negative GSR test was meaningless. He recounted his many years of experimentation with GSR testing, first with the nuclear reactor at Georgia Tech and then using the flameless atomic absorption test equipment installed at the State Crime Laboratory.

He testified that he had tested several hundred firearms and that one definitely could "draw a conclusion about the lack of GSR if the collection procedure is correct and if you know the particular characteristics of the gun." Considering the combined test results in the *Williams* case, Dr. Howard concluded, "It would be my opinion that the subject (Hansford) *did not fire that weapon.*" Unless successfully refuted, that single sentence was sufficient to convict James Williams.

Moving on to the scene generally, Dr. Howard concluded that "the scene appears contrived or altered." Much of his explanation for that conclusion will be familiar, with some finer points added. The blood smeared across the back of the hand and thumb meant the hand had been moved from beneath the body. The heavy collection of blood under the body meant the hand had been moved before the collection had become heavy, but after a considerable amount had accumulated. As to the hand position:

[B]oth hands assumed the position assumed by most people, that is, the fingers are partially clinched and the thumb is inside the hand.

The left hand and the right hand are in exactly the same position. This indicates to me that there was nothing in that hand, nothing in that hand, at the time the victim died.

There was blood in the palm with no pattern mark from the Luger grip (Figure 27). Blood had flowed down into the web between the thumb and forefinger, where a weapon would ordinarily be held, yet there was no corresponding blood on the weapon. Dr. Howard also explained why the position of the chair was ridiculous for the reasons we have already examined.

As to the nagging question of Danny Hansford's head position, Dr. Howard suggested strongly that the head was on the floor when the second bullet struck. He also explained something that appeared odd in the photographs. The entrance wound in Hansford's head was *facing the floor* in the photographs. How was that possible?

This wasn't a disputed fact. That shot obviously hadn't been fired through the floor by someone in the basement. Dr. Howard explained: When the rear of the head was struck, the force of the large-caliber 9mm round forced the head to the left, causing it to twist on its axis to the point that the neck muscles were stretched to their limit, causing the head to "rebound" back in the other direction and end up resting on the right cheek.

As to the question of whether the head was on the floor or still in the air when struck, raising the possibility that this was a coup de grâce shot (depending on where Williams was when he fired it), as I've said, my view of the case doesn't require two such shots, but I will share my opinion: The head was on the floor.

Although we won't belabor this subject in the future, there is evidence *not* examined in the trials of Williams that supports the conclusion of Dr. Howard (shared by Det. Ragan in his Supplemental Report) that the head was on the floor.[69] This is a *new* observation. Evidence says what it says until proved otherwise, according to Aristotle's Handbook on Crime Scene Investigation. Examine two photos (Figures 18, 24). There is a distinct collection of blood visible just under the right shoulder (Figure 24), seen again on the rug to the left of Det. Ragan's pen (Figure 18). The pen is pointing to the hole made by the exit wound in the chest from the shot through the back.

This distinct blood pattern is separate and apart from the primary collection of blood, which accumulated underneath the body. If Hansford was aspirating blood from his mouth and nose when he hit the floor, due to the puncture of his lung by the first bullet (confirmed by the autopsy report), before his head was struck by the second bullet and rebounded, it would explain the presence of this unexplained blood pattern.

This additional analysis, added to the trajectory of the shot, its path through the skull, and the entry point in the rug, make it almost certain that Hansford's head was on the floor when struck. Whether this was evidence of another coup de grâce shot, in addition to the shot in the back, would depend on where Williams was when he fired it.

With the completion of Dr. Howard's direct testimony, the prosecution case was laid out clearly for the jury. Because Dr. Howard had essentially presented the summation of the State's case from the witness stand, we were looking forward to the defense cross. It was certain to give us a glimpse of the defense's plan of attack.

Dr. Howard was cross-examined by John Wright Jones, which was surprising. Dr. Howard was the prosecution's lead expert, and I was under the impression that Bobby Lee Cook was a legal Merlin with magical powers. Nevertheless, it was Jones who took on Dr. Howard.

Jones went to the GSR evidence immediately: Why don't you swab at the scene instead of waiting? What about the time lapse? The suggestion was that time would eliminate GSR. To the contrary, as Randall Riddell had touched upon briefly, Dr. Howard explained, the time factor was only relevant in GSR testing when dealing with a *live subject*, not a dead man. And the problem wasn't time but rather the potential for *physical activity* of a live subject:

> In a dead subject, the residue is frozen and if there is no abrasion of
> the hands or washing of the hands, for instance, by the medical exam-
> iner before the material is taken, then the test is virtually—or the
> residue is virtually unaltered.

So the mere passage of time between shooting and autopsy didn't help the defense disappear the GSR. They needed something else. They needed to show that (1) the significant GSR produced by this Luger never made it to Hansford's hand or (2) the GSR had somehow vanished.

Here is one of the first glimpses of criminal defense "inside baseball" in the *Williams* case, also known as Lawyer Games. A common Lawyer Games tool is the statement-question combo. A factually incorrect statement is combined with a question. The hope is that the focus will be on the question while the incorrect statement will stick with the jury. John Wright Jones asked Dr. Howard the following series of questions:

> Q. Would that have affected your decision, if this person had *picked
> up the arm* and checked the pulse?
> A. Not unless he smeared the blood.
> Q. Well, if he had *picked up the hand*, then it's likely that he would
> probably smear the blood.

A. I can't say that. I could certainly touch that hand and we see in the
pulse area that there's a relatively undisturbed bloodstain.

This "person" Jones referred to could only have been Cpl. Anderson. But
Cpl. Anderson had already testified, and he hadn't picked up the arm or the hand.
The *ifs* in Jones's questions were not based on any evidence in the *Williams* case.
Jones might as well have asked Dr. Howard if it would have affected his opinion
if this "person" had danced with Hansford's body. A hypothetical question only
has weight if it's based on evidence.

Moving on, Jones couldn't stop incriminating Williams with the mysterious
chair. His question on the subject sounded like a prosecution question, much like
his questions to Det. Ragan.

Q. And there's no question, of course, that someone had to place this
chair on top of this leg.
A. Absolutely.

Again, we *agreed*. I simply didn't understand a defense lawyer asking these
questions. There had been no *time* for anyone other than Williams to have moved
the chair. There was no *reason* for anyone other than Williams to have moved the
chair. It seemed odd that the point was being emphasized by a lawyer for
Williams—unless this was a secret strategy that defied understanding by mere
mortals.

Jones finished up his cross of Dr. Howard by veering back to the head on
the floor. There was no blood on Hansford's left cheek. If not, how could Hansford's left cheek have ever been resting on the rug? The suggestion was, again, that
the head could not have been on the floor when struck by the second bullet. Dr.
Howard explained that the rug hadn't been bloody when the body hit the floor.
The shot could easily have struck and caused the head to rebound before the
blood pooled underneath the head.

With that, the cross-examination of Dr. Howard was complete, as was the
State's case. The prosecution rested. It was time for the legend, Bobby Lee Cook,
to show us how it was done.

THE *WILLIAMS* DEFENSE

Dr. Joseph L. Burton, the defense's sole expert witness, led off the *Williams*
defense. We had done our research on Dr. Burton. We knew he appeared frequently for the defense, being allowed by his county employers to moonlight, and
that he had done quite well financially through this arrangement. We also knew
a few other bits of information about Dr. Burton.

Within the first two minutes of Burton's examination, the entire prosecution
table might have exhaled. I know I did, since I was to cross-examine Burton. He was
regurgitating generic, canned testimony unrelated to the specific evidence in the case.

First, he dismissed the entire field of GSR testing as if issuing a proclamation. Burton testified to the common misconception that negative GSR tests were meaningless. Did Burton not know that the weapon had been tested? The defense had the test results. Had he not seen them?

When he made his next proclamation, I couldn't believe my ears. He was crashing and had barely told the jury his name. Dr. Burton informed the jury, in a condescending tone I found annoying, why the tests done by the State Crime Laboratory were not up to snuff.

A. The atomic absorption test is the test that's currently used in large laboratories today because it's cheaper to use and easier to use than neutron activation analysis. ... It is not as accurate in some instances as neutron activation analysis, unless the *flameless atomic absorption test* is used, in which case its accuracy parallels that of neutron activation analysis. The lab in the State of Georgia presently uses atomic absorption spectrophotometry.

Gee, if only the Crime Lab had used the "flameless atomic absorption test," the tests would have been as accurate as neutron activation analysis. Burton obviously didn't know much about the State Crime Lab that the rumor mill said he wanted to run, and he obviously wasn't aware of this testimony from Randall Riddell:

A. The technique that we use is actually the name of the analytical instrumentation. Its full name is *flameless atomic absorption spectrophotometry*. We just call it AA for short.

* * *

A. This is the state of the art, essentially.

Unbelievable was the only description for Dr. Burton's shallow level of preparation. Unaware that his suit was on fire, Dr. Burton then demonstrated for the jury how GSR is emitted from a *revolver*, which had nothing to do with the *Williams* case, and followed up by showing the jury a drawing of a generic semi-automatic pistol, not a Luger. As we've seen, a Luger has a very distinctive hinged breech, nothing like a common semi-automatic (Figure 29).

He told the jury that a semiautomatic didn't generally emit as much GSR as a revolver. It seemed he had forgotten that we were dealing with a specific case involving a specific firearm. This was not a luncheon talk to the local Kiwanis Club. Bottom line, Dr. Burton knew nothing about the weapon involved in the *Williams* case. He had never tested the weapon. He hadn't even laid eyes on the weapon until the Friday before trial.

Dr. Burton was reputed to have a hang-up about the fact that Dr. Howard was a PhD and not a medical doctor. Yet being an MD hadn't helped Dr. Burton prepare for *Williams*. Medical schools don't include firearms training. In comparison, Dr. Howard had testified to having personally fired some "500 or 600 weapons" in GSR tests using the nuclear reactor at Georgia Tech, even before the advent of flameless atomic absorption spectrophotometry. Even a board-certified forensic pathologist doesn't receive that level of firearms training.

Interestingly, in outlining his qualifications as a forensic pathologist, Dr. Burton didn't reveal to the jury that he wasn't board certified. Throughout the 1980s, he would claim that he hadn't passed the pathology portion of the exam because of the "press of personal business."[70] Dr. Burton was an off-the-shelf expert. He was probably a competent medical examiner, but in this case he was a salesman selling prepackaged testimony.

Dr. Burton testified that the ammunition used in GSR tests could affect their reliability. According to Burton, "The ammunition would have to be exactly the same ammunition because different types of ammunition at different ages burn differently. Powder may burn cleaner in the newer ammunition than in older ammunition." Apparently, Burton was also unfamiliar with Roger Parian's testimony that he had used the same ammunition, taken from the clip *in the same weapon.*

Burton cited two additional factors that he claimed could explain the lack of GSR on Hansford's hand: humidity and the wind factor. If I didn't nudge Spencer Lawton in the ribs, I should have. Who was this guy? Where was the wind in Williams's study? And I could have told Burton myself that Mercer House was air-conditioned.

Burton's testimony was not only sloppy; it was wrong. With respect to GSR, he claimed that people ordinarily have "these same elements" on their hands. To the contrary, "these same elements" do not appear *together* on anybody's hands. The very basis of GSR testing is that barium and antimony do not appear together on humans.

Was Burton ignorant or telling the jury a carefully crafted lie? Those who know television legal analyst Nancy Grace might be interested to hear about a confrontation she had with Dr. Burton while she was an assistant prosecutor in Atlanta. Nancy had the audacity to question Burton about a nickname, Lyin' Joe, given to him by another prosecutor.[71] To be clear, this is not a comment on his nickname, merely a report that he had it. I do not know how (or if) he had earned it.

In the current case, maybe he was simply ignorant on the subject of GSR, but surely he would have an explanation for the chair. That required only two eyes and some common sense, after all. But he had no explanation. According to Burton, "It seems to be somewhat out of place, sitting on his leg like that." No kidding. Why did he think we were all there, trying Williams for murder? Burton couldn't explain the chair, so he testified that the chair "didn't bother" him. Astounding. The single piece of evidence that most vividly proved Williams was lying "didn't bother" the defense's lone expert.

One benefit of a witness like Burton rambling on is that they can accidentally speak some truth. Burton made something approaching a confession, during a tribute to himself:

A. When I try to reconstruct what happened at a death scene, I try to not take any bit of evidence out of context, because I can take *any one bit of evidence* that we find here and make it say *anything that I want it to say*, but it's much harder to take all of the bits of evidence and make them say what you want them to say.

This was a shocking admission, that he could make a piece of evidence say whatever he wanted. But he wasn't finished. According to Dr. Burton, it also was essential to take *all of the evidence* into account and not look at any one piece of evidence in isolation. Why was this statement astonishing? Burton would repeatedly violate his own rule without any apparent awareness of the contradiction. He couldn't figure out the chair, so he ignored it. The GSR evidence looked bad for his team, so he declared all GSR evidence meaningless.

When he got to the skull fragment stuck to the seat of the chair, he couldn't make sense of it, so he didn't deal with that, either. As to the upside-down body, Burton testified that Hansford was shot first in the left chest and that this shot caused him to spin to his left and fall to the ground "where he was found."

How did his head end up where his feet should have been? Burton didn't say. If I had been Williams and paying Burton's fees, considering how incriminating all this evidence was, I might have wanted Burton to at least take a shot at explaining it to the jury. The most obvious reason Burton didn't explain the upside-down body was that it was inexplicable. If you are shot in the chest, do your feet fly backward and your head land where your feet were? The scenario made no sense, so Burton didn't attempt to make sense of it. He just said Hansford fell down and ended up where he ended up.

Burton and Jones would circle back for the second and third gunshots, but they first took a detour to Danny's hand. I watched with fascination because I had not been able to figure out how Danny's hand, smeared with blood and with blood soaked into the crevices, could have gotten out from under his body other than Williams pulling it out. Burton dealt with the blood and the position of the arm at the same time. Observe and be amazed: (1) The blood could have gotten on Danny's hand as he fell and (2) the hand "sprang" out on its own.

Considering the amount of blood on Hansford's hand (Figure 26), any jury would understand that it was impossible for that amount of blood to have gotten onto his hand and soaked into the crevices of his skin in the two seconds it had likely taken him to fall to the floor. Equally as ridiculous was Burton's decree that the hand "sprang" out when the body hit the floor. Even if the quantity of blood on the hand could have somehow accumulated that fast, that fresh blood would have been on the rug and all over the Luger. His "explanations" not only conflicted with the evidence—they conflicted with each other.

He was also combining two grossly unlikely events, a perfect bounce of the Luger and the dead man's hand "springing" out from under his body—only his right hand, for some reason, not his left—to land perfectly on top of the bouncing Luger. Maybe there's a term to quantify the effect of combining one impossibility with a second, or perhaps a new term needed to be coined for Dr. Burton.

What was Burton doing, despite his own warning? He was making "any bit of evidence say whatever I want it to say." I knew I could take him through these grade-school concoctions on cross, but it was tricky. I didn't want to get distracted by chasing after the chaff he was tossing out. Besides, his explanations were so transparent that it was difficult to imagine a jury of breathing humans giving them any credence. It looked as if Burton had figured he would wing it. To me, it looked like his wings were melting.

It got better. Burton was happy to agree with Jones that he couldn't think of *any* reason why Williams might have wanted to pull Danny's hand out and put it on top of the Luger:

Q. Does that in any way suggest to you from a review of these photographs and of the alleged scene and the physical evidence that you have observed any contrivance?

A. Well, I think that would be something one would consider; however, based on the overall information about this case and the scene itself, I don't think much would have been gained by placing the hand in that position.

In a self-defense case, Dr. Burton couldn't conceive of any incentive for Williams to put a gun under the hand of the man he claimed had fired it. A defendant claiming self-defense had no reason at all to want the scene to look like self-defense. This was a theory previously unheard of in the history of criminal jurisprudence.

It seemed that Burton was sinking while rowing his own boat—but I always reserve the right to be wrong because you never know. Maybe I was being unfair by using logic.

There is no need to go through the entire coup de grâce debate, which Burton took up next. We'll only look at a couple of examples that relate directly to the title of this book. The head issue is not as important as the approach the defense took to fudge it.

Jones asked two questions: (1) Could Hansford have been on the floor when the head *and* back shots struck, and (2) could Williams have walked around the desk and fired those shots? Notice Jones keeps the two shots linked. Why? So he can finesse the issue, manipulate one shot to get the answer he wants and then apply the answer to both. Observe how this works.

Could Williams have hit Hansford from behind the desk if the body was on the floor? Burton said no. Why not? Because Burton had gone to the house with a string. He put one end in the bullet hole from the head shot and, when stringing it toward the desk, kept hitting the desk. End of story.

Not so fast. I could hit the desk with the string, too—especially if I knew that raising the string an inch to miss the desk would cause my fee to evaporate. Obviously, Burton could have missed the desk with his string. The correct question was, where would that put Williams? What was Williams's posture? Was he leaning over the desk?

Burton had only gotten to town on Friday. It had been almost nine months since the shooting. There was no body and no rug. Was the same desk even in the study? Was it in the same position? Burton's string theory (unlike real string theory) wasn't a theory at all. It was pure smoke.

Besides, was the defense trying to prove Williams *couldn't* have fired those shots from behind the desk? No. That would have been the worst possible argument for Williams. They were actually working backward, to get to the result they wanted. Observe and learn some Lawyer Games technique.

If Williams couldn't have been behind his desk, did that mean Williams had come out from behind his desk to fire the last two shots? Remarkably, Burton said no again. But wait—doesn't Williams have to be either behind the desk or not behind the desk? We're getting there, but first, to the Lawyer Game Toolbox and the distorted-demonstration technique.

Burton conducted a demonstration for the jury. He walked counterclockwise around the desk. This placed him directly over Hansford's head. Burton then testified that there was no way to get the shot in the head from there, and he was finished. The shot in the back was still lumped in with that shot. So presto: Walking around the desk to fire *either* shot wasn't possible—in Burton World.

In addition to not breaking up the two shots, what else had Burton done? He had gone around the desk in only one direction, bringing him immediately up on top of the body, standing over the head (Figure 13). The question Jones asked Burton was: "Is there a way for Williams to have fired the shot to the head by walking around the desk?" But Burton didn't answer that question, though the jury was supposed to believe he had. The question he really answered was "Can you come up with an example that doesn't work?"

Assume I was asked, "Could you hit the pie plate on that tree with this gun?" I then close my eyes, stand on one leg, hold the gun in the wrong hand, fire and miss, and answer, "Nope, can't do it." What did Burton do? He went counterclockwise around the desk. This got him to a position from which the head and back shots couldn't have been fired. Except that's not what happened and the evidence proves it.

We need only consult our illustrations (Figures 7, 13). The deception is most transparent when we look at the back shot that Burton insisted on keeping linked with the shot to the head. Burton walked counterclockwise around the desk so he was near Hansford's head—facing *east* and firing down (ejecting the casing forward). The shell casing from that shot was recovered twelve inches from the *west* wall, *behind* him, in the *opposite* direction.

Burton's demonstrated scenario wasn't possible. What if he had gone the other way? He would have approached from the east, facing *west*. He would have been farther from the body. And the shell casing would have been ejected toward the west wall—where it was found.

According to the autopsy, the shot to and through the back took a slightly upward (toward the head) and slightly right to left trajectory, with the body facedown. This means the shot was fired from above the body, slightly to the right (2 cm, 0.79 inches) and slightly below (2 cm, 0.79 inches) the entrance wound. In other words, it was fired by someone positioned over Hansford, slightly toward his feet, not his head—directly opposite the position chosen by Burton.

The shot in the back clearly was not, and could not have been, fired from the west end of the body facing east. Of course Burton testified to the same thing: that the shots (still linked together as one) couldn't have been fired from there. He was right. Because the shots weren't fired from there. They also weren't fired from the backyard but that didn't mean they were fired from behind Williams's desk. Dr. Burton took only one path around the desk—the wrong path—to create a single impossible scenario, leaving the jury with the impression that putting Williams behind his desk was the only other option. This was no more than rank deception.

At various points throughout *Williams* we will see the defense attempt to use Williams's tampering with the scene as evidence in his favor. An early, subtle example is embedded in this rigged demonstration. Viewing the scene as it was found might suggest that the natural path around Williams's desk was counterclockwise, because the antique armchair is in the way and blocking access to the body if you take a clockwise path. But the chair *wasn't there* after Williams shot Hansford. It was placed there after the fact, by Williams. Topple the chair over, toward the fireplace, and the path is clear.

What was the defense doing with this Jones and Burton deception duet? They were working backward. They were trying to eliminate two scenarios, leaving a third—their favorite—as the only choice. If Williams couldn't hit Hansford with the second and third shots from *behind* the desk and couldn't have come *around* the desk, was there another option? Burton provided one: Williams behind the desk and Hansford's body *off the floor*.

Instead of raising Williams's end of Burton's string, he raised Hansford's end—by raising the body into the air. Abracadabra! By process of elimination, all three shots struck Hansford before he hit the floor and all three shots were fired from behind the desk. No coup de grâce scenario in sight, all neat and tidy. The problem with this magic trick was that it was directly contradicted by the evidence. This was high level Lawyer Games physics—allowing the words lawyer and physics to share a sentence only for the sake of this discussion.

Burton should already have forfeited his membership in any reputable scientific organization, but for this trick to work, he would have to shred his physics book, if he owned one. To keep Hansford's body in the air for all three shots, he had to make one slight adjustment: He had to make bullets change direction in midair. This exercise alone would suggest that Dr. Joseph Burton's nickname had been legitimately earned.

Even before he could bend a bullet, he had to flip the order of the shots. He testified that the shot in the back was second and that Hansford's body was still in the air when that shot struck. This was bordering on scientific insanity. The shot in the back had gone straight through Hansford's body and the bullet had been dug out of the floor directly under the exit wound in the chest. How was Williams supposed to fire that shot from behind his desk, with Hansford's body still in the air, and the bullet go straight down and embed itself in the floor?

Burton did what he'd done repeatedly: He took a single piece of evidence in isolation and changed it. He testified that, while Hansford fell to the floor, his back had rotated toward Williams, who was standing behind his desk, and this had allowed the bullet to go straight through the body.

This is when Burton's physics teacher would grab the red pen and mark a giant F on his test paper. Burton turned the body in midair so the back would face Williams (behind his desk). Terrific. But turning the body to rotate the back toward the desk also rotates the chest (and the exit wound) toward the fireplace. How did Burton get the bullet that exited the chest—which no longer faced the floor—to end up buried in the floor directly beneath the exit wound?

He didn't say, for one very obvious reason: The only way to make his example work was to have the bullet change direction in midair. Examine a photo of Danny's body on the floor where the desk is visible (Figure 14). Raising the body off the floor (Figure 43) reveals the simple triangle created between points A (Williams), B (the entrance wound), and C (the bullet in the floor). Bullets don't do triangles.

This is not a complicated concept. Burton couldn't possibly have been unaware that he had to ask a bullet to bend in flight. No, Burton was not clueless. He was merely unscrupulous. Do we need more proof? He quickly supplied it.

Not even Burton could get away with curving a bullet. So what did he do? He used the hole in the rug and floor made by the *head* shot for the shot through the *back*. How could he do that? What did he do about the bullet hole directly under the chest exit wound? Nothing. He ignored it. In effect, Burton used the same bullet hole for two bullets (see Figure 44).

This was such a transparent charade that I wanted to turn to Bobby Lee Cook and ask him what he was doing, putting this fool on the stand. But I still had to cross-examine Burton. Maybe everyone else thought he was brilliant. Maybe the jury's water supply was laced with mind-altering drugs. Mine was not.

The last thing Burton took up before being handed over for cross was— believe it or not—the chair again. This would be the final defense statement regarding the devastating chair. Burton claimed that the chair didn't influence his opinion—because he didn't consider it.

A. [My theory] accounts for everything that I see in the case except the chair. ... The chair doesn't really concern me in this case. Again, like I said, it seems to be out of place no matter what I think about it on top of the back of his body.
Q. Does the chair have anything to do with your opinion one way or the other in this case?
A. No, sir, it does not.

Since Burton didn't consider the chair, it didn't affect his opinion. It's like skipping a step on a math test and telling the teacher, "Since I couldn't figure that part out, it didn't have anything to do with my answer." It would have a lot to do with your grade, however.

It was my privilege to cross-examine Dr. Burton. The first thing I did was flush his testimony. If I went into that house of mirrors, neither the case nor I might ever come out. We moved fairly quickly.

Burton confirmed that he had first viewed the physical evidence—including the photographs of the scene—on the Friday before trial. He also admitted that he had confirmed his opinions and theory of the case with defense counsel *prior* to seeing the evidence.

He told us that the *Williams* case was the second case within the previous two weeks in which he had testified for Bobby Lee Cook. It was also the third criminal case in which he had testified in Savannah, all three for the defense.

Both of the two earlier cases had resulted in convictions. I had a particular interest in the case of Roy Willard Blankenship because I had handled Blankenship's resentencing, which reimposed the death penalty. Blankenship had assaulted seventy-eight-year-old Sarah Mims Bowen in her apartment after spying on her praying, in one of the most horrific, brutal attacks imaginable.

The elderly Ms. Bowen was beaten, scratched, bitten, raped, and defiled. She died during the assault which included, among other things, having her head smashed through the sheetrock of the wall above her bed. Dr. Joseph Burton had testified for the defendant. Burton hadn't considered the victim's injuries to be severe. I will spare you the details of what Blankenship did to the elderly Ms. Bowen. Blankenship was executed by lethal injection on June 23, 2011.

The other case, ironically, had a Mercer connection. In 1980, Michael Harper was convicted of the kidnapping and murder of George A. Mercer IV, the great-grandnephew of Johnny Mercer.

Dr. Burton had again testified for the defense. Mercer's extensively decomposed body had been found on April 26, 1980. His manually wound wristwatch was stopped at 29 on the date calendar. Mercer had last been seen alive on January 29. On February 11, Harper had been arrested in possession of medication prescribed to Mercer and a .22 caliber pistol matched to the slugs removed from Mercer's body.

The State's pathologist had testified that, because of the advanced state of deterioration of the body and clothing and the date on the watch, the date of death had been January 29. He conceded that it was "not impossible" that the date was February 29 but that it was far more likely to have been January 29 in light of the extensive state of decomposition. Considering that Harper was apprehended on February 11, Harper obviously preferred February 29 as a date of death.

Burton had done him one better. He had testified that the death could have been as late as March 29, only four weeks before Mercer's severely decomposed body had been found. This gave Harper a nice margin of error in his favor. Harper had made ransom calls to the victim's parents, had incriminated himself to a friend, and was in possession of the murder weapon and Mercer's prescription. He was clearly the killer. He was picked up on February 11. Mercer was not alive at the end of March.

None of this directly affected the *Williams* case, but it gave me a broader understanding of the witness. The more you know about a witness, the better.

Dr. Burton and I moved through a number of points. He agreed that the particular elements sought in GSR testing are *not* found together in nature, correcting a misconception that he had intentionally created on direct. He admitted that he had never fired either of the Lugers. I asked him to demonstrate his testimony about the action of semiautomatic weapons using one of the Lugers. This was a bit of a hunch, but I was right; Burton had significant trouble even removing the clip from the Luger and didn't seem at all familiar with this type of weapon, yet he was the defense firearms expert.

The defense had used Dr. Burton to introduce a diagram of the study showing various items. That diagram was grossly inaccurate. Dr. Burton agreed that the diagram was not correct. In his own halfhearted defense, he stated that he had not prepared the diagram and that he had first seen it *on the morning of his testimony*. None of that had stopped him from using it in his direct testimony, however.

Regarding his expertise with respect to GSR, Dr. Burton admitted that he had never performed a neutron activation analysis:

Q. Have you ever performed the neutron activation analysis?

A. No, sir. There's nowhere in the State of Georgia that I know you can perform one. I've seen the machinery that did it, but I've never performed one.

Q. Are you familiar with the Georgia Institute of Technology?

A. Yes, sir.

Q. And you know that it's located in Atlanta.

A. Yes, sir, and they do have one. I'm sorry.

The "machinery" would be a nuclear reactor. It had simply slipped his mind that Georgia Tech, across town from his office, had a nuclear reactor.

Burton's next move on cross was clever in the extreme. He claimed that Danny Hansford could not have been sitting in the chair when shot because it didn't fit Williams's defense. Of course it didn't fit Williams's defense. That was the point.

Q. So for that to be true [Williams' claim], the individual [Hansford] could not very well have been seated in this chair, could he?

A. That's why I said in order to satisfy all the evidence it was my opinion that he was standing at that corner of the desk.

Q. If he fired the weapon; correct?

A. If he fired the weapon.

Exactly. *If he fired the weapon.*

Incidentally, because Dr. Burton had formed his opinions before viewing any of the evidence, I asked how he had known where Hansford's body was found. He said he knew because defense counsel had told him. What about the papers on the desk and the paper fragments? Dr. Burton said he had not seen the papers until the prior Friday and did not know *where they had been* on Williams's desk.

Just for fun, I decided to ask Burton a question that Cook had asked Roger Parian. Cook had asked Parian a series of nonsensical questions about tests Parian had not performed. Parian had explained why the tests weren't applicable, but

Cook had persisted, even chiding Parian for referring to bullet fragments as lead when he had not tested the metal to see if it was lead. I asked Dr. Burton the same question, how did he know the bullet fragments were lead. I wish I had a picture of the look he gave me. It was a look I deserved. I admitted it:

Q. It's kind of a silly question, isn't it?

A. Yes, sir, it was.

I couldn't see Cook, but I enjoyed imagining his expression.

Back to serious issues. I used Dr. Burton to reiterate a point about the live round on the floor. Burton agreed that if someone cocked the weapon with a round in the chamber, the round would be ejected close to where the person was standing. That meant whoever had cocked Luger 22A had done it nearer to the fireplace than to Williams's desk.

We went through the junkyard known as Dr. Burton's shot sequence. I took him through it again, allowing him to describe the event again, because it was patently ridiculous and he sounded ridiculous explaining it. This included another demonstration Burton had conducted earlier, using the defense's private investigator, the willing Mr. Moss. Burton had instructed Moss to hold himself twelve inches off the floor and to turn his head in various directions while illustrating being struck by Williams's bullets. Burton had then "demonstrated" the finish by having Moss drop himself to the floor.

Maybe Moss was able to stop himself in midair to wait for both shots to hit him, but Danny Hansford couldn't. Danny also didn't start falling from twelve inches above the floor as Moss did. Danny passed *through* the twelve-inch mark in a blur. The acceleration rate of gravity on earth is approximately 9.80665 m/s^2. Without deciphering the value, it is probably sufficient to agree that a body accelerates as it falls. It certainly doesn't stop a foot from the floor on the way down.

At least some jurors also had to be thinking what I was thinking as Burton explained his theory. Annie Oakley herself would have been hard pressed to twice hit a target moving that fast with a WWII Luger as the body blew through the final twelve inches of its drop to the floor.

Dr. Burton had claimed on direct that it was necessary to account for *all* of the evidence. However, in the *Williams* case, that meant all of the evidence *except* the chair, paper fragments, shell casings, live round, skull fragment, blood smear on the hand, lack of blood pattern in the palm, lack of blood under the hand, lack of blood on the gun, and—as an exclamation point—any of the GSR evidence.

It is not clear, even today, what evidence Burton legitimately addressed, unless it was the shot to the chest. He agreed that this was the first shot and that it entered the chest. Perhaps this was all Williams got with the three-day prep discount plan.

As I approached the completion of my cross-examination of Dr. Burton, most of his testimony seemed to be based on nothing more than his willingness to say it. He was so openly impressed with his own opinion, and his opinion testimony was so dependent on his credibility, that I went into something that I had held in reserve, unsure whether to broach it.

I asked Dr. Burton about a case that had gained some notoriety. A man's vehicle had rolled onto a railroad crossing and been hit by a train. Dr. Burton had signed off on the finding that the death was accidental. Dr. Burton, the medical examiner, had been required to either perform or supervise the autopsy but he hadn't. The autopsy had actually been performed by an unsupervised medical resident.

When questions arose about the death, the body had been exhumed and examined—by Dr. Howard. Dr. Howard discovered the bullet hole behind the dead man's left ear, with a corresponding exit wound in his forehead. Accept as fact that an exit wound is generally the larger hole.

My questions did not go over well. I knew I was tweaking Burton's professional jealousy of Dr. Howard, along with Burton's own ego, but the air of infallibility he had brought with him into the courtroom required a reality adjustment.

With that, my cross-examination of the notoriously fallible Dr. Burton was complete, or so I thought. Then the fun began.

Cook couldn't leave it alone. Judge Oliver allowed Cook to conduct redirect examination and take Burton through a regurgitation of the entire train case. Burton rambled on about what everyone else had done wrong, including secondhand comments consisting of rank hearsay. Oliver still didn't stop him. It also appeared that Burton had recited this defense of the train case before. That was all fine. I didn't really care about the train case. Cook and Burton should have just left bad enough alone.

When finally finished, Cook, with dripping condescension, granted the esteemed doctor this "single mistake" in his many years of practice. It was obvious that Cook thought he had put the young pup—that being me—in my place. As far as I was concerned, my place was representing the people of the state against an accused killer. I had a couple of additional questions for Dr. Burton.

Cook and Burton had just declared that Dr. Burton had made only a single mistake in his entire career, a mistake I had been unkind enough to point out. I asked Burton the following:

Q. All right, are you familiar with one Aaron Wyche?

A. Yes, sir, I am.

Q. Is that not the name of a young man who is listed as one of the Atlanta murdered children cases?

A. He indeed is.

Q. Did you or did you not classify that death as accidental?

A. I did.

MR. KIRKLAND: That's all I have.

Ten-year-old Aaron Wyche had fallen from a train trestle in DeKalb County on June 23, 1980. Dr. Burton had ruled that Aaron died of asphyxiation because of the way he had landed and declared the death accidental. Aaron would later be added to the list of Atlanta Missing and Murdered Children. Dr. Burton had been half right: Aaron had died of asphyxiation—he had been strangled, before being tossed from the trestle.

That was two mistakes for Dr. Burton. I didn't have any more in my pocket, so I was hoping Cook wouldn't take us through the history of the AMMC cases. Thankfully, he didn't.

This led to a moment I shall never forget. As I returned to my seat at counsel table, I found myself face to face with a boiling Bobby Lee Cook. In a whisper not audible to anyone else, Cook said, "You son of a bitch." I took it as a compliment.

The defense then turned its attention to two areas: (1) distancing Williams from any hint of emotional involvement with Danny Hansford, and (2) proving that Danny Hansford was a bad person who deserved to be killed.

The defense called Dr. Joseph W. DeHaven, an endocrinologist. Dr. DeHaven was open and straightforward. He testified that he had been treating Williams since April 24, 1981, for hypoglycemia.

Dr. DeHaven testified that he saw Williams for the first time on April 24 but didn't conclusively diagnose Williams's problem until later, after a series of tests, though he had suspected the cause early on. Dr. DeHaven talked to Williams about diet, eating regularly, and avoiding the sweet alcoholic beverages that Williams liked.

Joseph Goodman had testified earlier that Williams had a blood-sugar problem and needed somebody with him in case he passed out—one reason Goodman was supposed to go with Williams on the Europe trip just after Danny was killed. On cross-examination Lawton asked Dr. DeHaven about it. The doctor agreed that Williams could "possibly" faint but added, "Fainting is not that common in reactive hypoglycemia. It does occur." Regardless, Dr. DeHaven had not advised Williams to have someone with him in case Williams passed out.

It was then time for the main event, the testimony of James A. Williams himself. People had already been taking numbers at the courtroom door to get a seat—literally. Scoring a seat for Williams's testimony might have required arm wrestling in the corridor.

Before the State got a crack at him, Williams was escorted on a beauty-pageant runway walk—also known as self-serving direct examination—on the arm of his lawyer. The only things missing were the smile and parade wave to the jury. Williams certainly didn't carry himself like a country boy from Gordon, Georgia. He looked more like the marquis of Mercer Castle. He appeared dignified, haughty, and arrogant. Dignified is fine. The other two are not preferred qualities in a witness. "How dare you question me" is not generally an effective defense to a murder charge.

Cook took Williams through his humble origins, had him describe Mercer House and authenticate a drawing of the study that Williams had made himself, of which he seemed quite proud. "It's one and a half inch squares (sic) equal one linear foot." It is no exaggeration that Williams looked like he wanted a treat and a pat on the head for his drawing.

Williams took the jury on a tour of his home. There were valuable antiques in the house, several of them worth over $100,000. This was apparently to explain why he had armed himself to the teeth. Williams recounted that he had suffered two burglaries before he had gotten his burglar alarm and he still kept a number of weapons loaded and spread throughout the house.

I found this testimony odd. There are cautious people with valuable things, but not many of them have loaded vintage Lugers and other firearms spread throughout their homes, several with rounds chambered and safeties off. I had found Williams's demeanor and his comment to me at the scene uniquely strange. His testimony did not dissipate that feeling.

We knew the defense was going to tell the jury that Danny Hansford would kill for a doughnut while Williams was genetically incapable of anything beyond grumpy, but I had no doubt that this man would shoot somebody under the right circumstances. The jury's reaction might have been different.

For the moment, we had to sit through Williams's ode to himself, conducted by orchestra leader Bobby Lee Cook. Williams claimed that he had met Danny Hansford in 1979 when Danny rode up on a bicycle and asked about working in the refinishing shop. At some point after that, Danny had started working for Williams part time.

What about the relationship between these two? We knew the importance of understanding the relationship between killer and victim, and yet we hadn't presented any relationship evidence in our direct case. Had we overlooked it? No. Judge Oliver had barred us from even broaching the subject.

To be prohibited from exploring the relationship between the accused and the victim in a homicide case was absurd, in my opinion. That opinion has not changed. The restriction led to a lot of unnecessary game playing. Anybody who couldn't figure out that there was more to this relationship than employer and employee was brain dead. The curtain was too short. Anyone could clearly see two pairs of feet underneath, dancing closer than you'd ever dance with your handyman.

The phrase "the law is an ass" is wrongfully attributed to Charles Dickens because it appeared in *Oliver Twist*. No matter who coined the phrase, however, it can be painfully true at times. The mere *mention* of a sexual relationship between Williams and Hansford was prohibited, so the jury, even on cross-examination, was limited to hearing Williams's fictional account of the relationship. Williams said he had blacked out at a party, that he hadn't been eating right and might have two to three vodka tonics at night "just to relax." After he was diagnosed with hypoglycemia, he needed someone to be with him every minute. This was Williams's explanation for Hansford's seemingly constant presence.

Williams had heard Dr. DeHaven testify that he had never told Williams he needed constant companionship, but that didn't bother Williams at all. He had an answer ready:

A. It was not Dr. DeHaven, by the way ... it was another doctor that advised me to do that. He said, "It's an awful thing," but he said, "if you pass out at the wrong time, your condition could get much worse," and he didn't say fatal, but that was inferred, that I should have somebody with me.

Dr. DeHaven had said fainting in hypoglycemia patients was rare, but now it was life-threatening, according to "another" doctor—a doctor with no name.

There was a glaring hole in this story. Williams claimed that he had scheduled Danny to accompany him to Europe because of the danger of passing out from hypoglycemia, but Williams had booked the tickets to Europe before the condition was diagnosed. A Delta Airlines representative had already testified that Williams made reservations on April 10 for himself and Danny to travel to Europe. Dr. DeHaven didn't see Williams for the first time until April 24. If his condition had been diagnosed by another doctor, why was Dr. DeHaven the witness? Where was this other doctor? Williams didn't even blink at the inconsistency.

Williams's fable about his relationship with Danny Hansford continued to unfold in elaborate detail—which would become a Williams trademark. Who knew if the story sounded as phony to the jury as it did to us. For example, Williams had bought Danny—his part-time employee—a Chevy Camaro. Williams testified that he didn't actually *buy* the car, Danny did. Williams had only paid for it.

Williams testified that his part-time employee had a running account. The car money was money Danny had earned by driving Williams to the country to visit Williams's Aunt Mary in Eastman and by performing other unspecified duties. Williams also made a point to tell the jury that Danny had his own apartment. Most people live somewhere. Why would a jury care where a part-time worker lived? Why bring it up? To avoid a more intimate connection—in this case, the truth.

A jury might still wonder how the part-time employee managed to pay rent and buy gas, food, clothing, and a Camaro. I would love to have asked Williams about Danny's hourly rate—it must have been pretty high. The problem with all of this was that we couldn't do anything about it on our direct case or on cross-examination of Williams. It was a charade for the benefit of the jury. I couldn't imagine that they bought it.

The defense was aware of the same dynamic. They knew Danny had been placed at Williams's house at odd hours and that jurors might not be able to personally relate to rolling out to the drive-in with their bosses on a Friday night, smoking some weed and drinking some whiskey before coming "home" for some wee-hours video games. So, having established Williams's need for constant companionship through a doctor who established no such thing, Cook had Williams explain how this arrangement worked:

A. He would come by, check on me, sometimes spend the night in the guest bedroom. Upstairs over my office is my bedroom, where the kitchen is downstairs, there's a bathroom, where the dining room is downstairs, is a bedroom.

Q. How frequent or infrequent would that be?

A. It was frequent and infrequent, both. It depended on how I was feeling. If he was doing part-time work for me that day, he would say, "How are you shaping up?" and I'd say, "Well, I feel pretty good," and he'd say, "Well, I'll come back and check on you," and sometimes we'd play backgammon. He was a big games player and I liked playing games, and we'd engage in backgammon. Sometimes he would spend the night there if I didn't feel too sharp, sometimes he would go out with his girlfriend and they'd party all night and he'd come back the next day sometime and do part-time work.

Notice what Williams does in this one passage. Danny had *his own* apartment. He was doing only *part-time* work. He *sometimes* slept in the *guest* room. Danny and his *girlfriend* would party all night. All quite innocent.

Williams didn't seem to care that he had told the *Georgia Gazette* that Danny had "first moved in with [him] in late March."[72] Williams was now spinning the tale of Poor Orphan Danny and we could only hope the tale sounded as ridiculous to the jury as it did to us: Danny Hansford, lacking any skills and little education, had ridden up on a bicycle five minutes ago and was now sleeping over, playing backgammon with the aristocrat, buying a car with an "advance" against his "account" and seemingly doing very little furniture sanding.

Cook and Williams moved to the night in question. Williams said he was trying to help Danny and, as proof of his efforts, said he had called a fellow in Hinesville after they got home, to ask the man a question about vocational school for Danny. Take note of this event; it will return, but not as Williams described it.

Cook hadn't gotten the Europe trip in, so they went back to grab that. At one time, Williams said, Danny was going on the trip to take care of him and watch his money, but then he took Danny off the Europe trip because of his marijuana use.

Danny had smoked nine joints at the drive-in, according to Williams's statements. A bag of marijuana was on Williams's desk in the study. There were joints in the ashtray and a joint ground into the desk. Nevertheless, Williams said, "I am very much in opposition" and that he wouldn't take Danny to Europe because Danny insisted on taking marijuana on the trip. Right. They didn't sell pot in Europe. Williams also proved to have a boundless ability to write bad dialog. "I said, 'Well, Danny, I'm sorry, you can't go on this international trip with me and take marijuana with you. I have no idea of putting up with that.'"

To top off the tale, Williams testified it was *Danny* who suggested taking Goodman to Europe and that Danny was the one who asked Goodman. Williams had known Goodman since Goodman was twelve years old while Danny and Goodman were barely acquainted. Goodman had already told us in his statement that the switch had come up with the three of them together at Williams's house and that "Jim" had asked him to go.[73]

It was a pointless lie, unless they were trying to avoid a suggestion that Williams had killed Danny so he could take Goodman to Europe. The tickets had been changed since April 24. Goodman was already going. The small lie never made any sense except for the fact that this seemed to be one very paranoid defendant and/or defense team.

Finally, Cook and Williams got to the actual shooting. Williams testified that he and Danny had been playing games—some backgammon and an electronic game—when Danny started complaining about his woeful life, his mother, his friend George Hill, and his girlfriend Debbie—and then, without warning, morphed into a raging beast worthy of a Marvel comic:

A. [A]ll of a sudden his personality snapped. ... It snapped just exactly like a Dr. Jekyll-Mr. Hyde situation, he turned into a raging madman and he stood up and he said, "Those games" - again laced with profanity - "Those games, those games have caused this whole thing," and he went over, he took his right foot, and he stomped right through this control panel in front of the television set, Atari set or something, just pow.

Note the word "raging" and begin keeping a tally; it will haunt this tale, beginning now.

So according to Williams, Danny was discussing his life's many miseries while playing a video game and backgammon in a mansion with his benefactor, decided it was "those games" that had caused "this whole thing," decided to kill an Atari game, and then Williams. Why? It was simple: Danny Hansford was the evil Edward Hyde, Dr. Jekyll's alter-ego.

Only a few pages earlier in his testimony, Williams had said this about Danny and games:

He loved games. I didn't like that one (the electronic game) very much, but I just sat there and we played it a long time, then we got up and we played backgammon. That's my game, *I like that a lot, he liked it,* and we played games for just a real long time and about halfway through the last game we were playing, he started talking about his personal life.

So which was it? Did Danny love games or did Danny hate games for ruining his life? Either way, Danny Hansford-Hyde appeared. As Williams continued to describe the transmutation, Danny went about turning over a silver tray and a table and Williams decided to go to this study to call the police. Then Williams slipped in a link back to the April incident, adding a parenthetical comment:

A. If he weren't going to leave my house, I was going to call the police, *as I had thirty days before.*

This added comment was not innocent. This was the beginning of the intentional binding together of May and April by the defense. Williams continued weaving his tale. The raging Hansford-Hyde caught up with Williams—who still had done nothing at all—on Williams's way to his study:

A. He came out [of the living room] in a rage, like a wild person, and he—he had never physically touched me in any way before, but he grabbed me right here (by the throat according to Williams's Gazette interview) with the strength of ten men, with a look in his face that would have turned you to stone and scared you to death. And he said, "You are sick" - laced with profanity - "You are sick. Why don't you do everybody a favor and go out in the woods and die?" And he threw me against the interior door here ... "Go out in the woods and die and do everybody a favor," and he threw me with such a force that I bounced back. I had never been so afraid in my entire life, Mr. Cook.

Williams escaped the man with the strength of ten men, fled to his study, and picked up the phone to call the police. He said he had the phone in his hand when "raging" Hansford followed him into the study.

A. ... I went in there, I picked the phone up and I had it in my hand and he came in there and he said again - laced with profanity; he was wild, he was raging ...

Q. Don't lace it.

A. No, sir, I'm not going to, but I want you to imagine the fear I felt from a man who was going crazy and talking to me like that and saying the things he was saying. I mean, he was out of control. He said, "Who are you calling..."

Without going too far into this narration from a bad movie, we will look at just a bit more, to point out a major disconnect in Williams's story:

Q. Now, when he came in, what did he say to you?

A. He said, "Who are you calling?"

Q. And did you have the phone in your hand?

A. Yes, sir. I had not dialed, but I had the telephone in my hand to call the police.

Q. And what did you say?

A. I said - I had to think real quick. I mean, he was acting so erratic. I said - well, he had complained earlier about Joe Goodman and the trip to Europe, something about "you gave my trip to Europe away" - this is when he was going into Debbie and his mother and his friend - and I said, "I'm going to call Joe Goodman and just get this whole thing straightened out right now. I'm just going to tell him that the trip to Europe is off. *He sat down across from me.*"

Williams told the raging madman he was calling Goodman and the raging madman simply sat down while Williams dialed the number.

Recall Goodman's testimony. He spoke to Hansford on this phone call. Danny had told Goodman that he hoped there were no hard feelings about the Europe trip. According to Goodman, Danny had sounded like normal Danny. Why would a "raging," "mad," "wild," "erratic," "out of control" man who was "going crazy" and destroying Williams's house suddenly be talking with Goodman in a normal voice, concerned about Joe Goodman's feelings? If this all sounds nonsensical, that's because it makes no sense.

But why go into this? It's Williams's story so it should be expected to profess his innocence and portray Hansford as a beast intent on destruction and mayhem. One reason is the tone. This will recur throughout the *Williams* trials. When drama spills over into melodrama in a play or film, an audience will tune out. Why? Because it's not real. Williams's stories are outlandish, as if we should hear the scary piano music that played in silent movies when the damsel was tied to the railroad tracks with a train approaching.

But we had missed something. Leaving Williams's testimony for a moment, note the following from Goodman's statement to Det. Ragan:

> At approximately 2:00 a.m. on 5-2-81, he (Goodman) was called by Jim Williams at which time Williams told him the London trip was off. Goodman stated he also talked to Danny Hansford at that time and Hansford asked him if he was all right and if he was disappointed about not going to London. He stated that Hansford told him he was *playing a game and talking*.[74]

This was the first Goodman phone call, the phone call Williams was now telling the jury he had made only because Danny had caught him in the act of calling the police—*after* Danny had snapped, morphed into Hyde, smashed the video game, grabbed Williams by the throat, told him to go out in the woods and die, and slammed Williams into a door. The eruption and destruction had *already occurred*—in Williams's courtroom version of the story.

More later but, for now, simply ask the question: How could Hansford have been "playing a game and talking" at the time of that phone call? How could he possibly have been speaking to Goodman in a slurred but normal voice, asking about Goodman's feelings? The only reasonable answer, as outrageous as it might seem, is that Williams wasn't telling the truth about *any* of the events that night at Mercer House, not merely the shooting itself.

If Goodman was right and what Danny had told him was correct, it would mean that, at the time of this phone call, the game hadn't been smashed and the eruption hadn't occurred. If so, who smashed the Atari console and turned over the silver tray, table, and clock?

Welcome to Williams's motivation for repeatedly linking May back to April, which began with his *Gazette* interview and would continue from this moment in his *Williams I* testimony throughout the *Williams* case history. The question, however, wasn't whether the events were similar—or too similar. The real question was when the similarity had been created, and by whom. Stay tuned. I believe the answer to that question is apparent, but only in hindsight. And the clue is contained in this second phone call to Goodman. We will return to this below.

According to Williams's continuing testimony, the moment Danny hung up the phone, he went "raging" again—without any provocation. Williams said Danny picked up a "tankard" and threatened to throw it through a painting. To stop the miscreant, Williams, who moments before had "never been so frightened in (his) entire life," stood up and:

A. [P]ut my finger straight out and I said, "Danny Hansford, you're not going to tear my house up anymore. Now, you get out."

Williams was talking to the madman as if he was a naughty schoolboy. It conjures images of Ichabod Crane pointing an angry finger at a quivering Danny Hansford. But Danny didn't remain frozen by Williams's stern finger for long. He told Williams, "I'm leaving this town tomorrow," and left the room. There were some loud noises in the hallway, and Danny returned holding one of Williams's Lugers. He walked into the room, turned at the corner of the desk, uttered another bad line from *The Beast and The Benefactor*, "But you're leaving tonight," and fired at Williams—all according to Williams.

Williams made no mention of Danny circling out toward the fireplace, stopping to cock the Luger, or anything of the sort. There was no delay at all; Hansford stopped, raised his Luger, uttered his bad line, and fired. His point-blank shot somehow missed Williams. Williams grabbed his own Luger from the chest next to his desk and fired back. Williams didn't report any acrobatics by the dead man: "Danny fell down on the floor immediately. There wasn't any lots of seconds at all. I saw that. I was in the room."

This brought us to the chair—finally. We would now hear from the one person who could clear up the mystery. Williams had to say he moved the chair, even if he lied about how, why, or from where. He had no choice but to explain it. Or so we thought.

A. Mr. Cook, there's no way in the world I put a chair over Danny Hansford's body. I never went to that end of his body. I stopped right there near his head.

That certainly cleared it up. Facetiousness aside, Williams was having nothing to do with that chair or the other end of the desk. His response to another question from Cook said it all: "I didn't know where the chair was. The chair was *not important* to me."

I had a friend who once repaired the factory air in his parents' old Mercedes by taking it completely out of the dash, fiddling with it, and reinstalling it. It worked. When I asked him about the pieces left on his workbench, his response was, "It must not have needed them." Williams and Burton took the same approach to the evidence in Williams's case: If they couldn't explain it, they declared it unimportant.

How about the missing minutes? The approach was similar:

Q. Do you know what order you called anyone in?

A. Mr. Cook, I barely remember calling anybody. I was so emotionally upset, and I *sat there* and realized I'd called those three people and somebody would be there in a few minutes and I was in the room completely alone with a dead man with blood running out on him over there and I just *sat there* and I thought, "This is tragedy beyond anything I have ever thought I would have to live through."

The words *sat there* are emphasized here only to point them out for later. We will come back to them in *Williams II*. By the way, Williams obviously had not "called these three people" at the same time. The police were ninety seconds away. Goodman and Rushing lived on the southside of Savannah. Williams might not have wanted to remember the time gap in his story but it wasn't going away, no matter how "emotionally upset" he professed to have been.

It's telling that, where it might be damaging—the time of his calls, for example—Williams couldn't remember what he did, yet he was equally positive, when it helped his case—the chair, for example—what he hadn't done. It was also telling that in Williams's view, the tragedy had happened to him, not to the dead man.

The guided tour of his home continued. Williams described the damaged grandfather clock in the entrance hall (Figure 3), changing the story for trial, saying, "[Danny] turned over a $20,000 lacquered clock and smashed it beyond belief." According to *The Georgia Gazette*, "He (Hansford) knocked over a grandfather clock which Williams valued at $10,000 and then smashed it."[75] The clock had doubled in value between May and January. Pretty good business, this antique business.

No doubt we on the prosecution were wearing glasses with a different set of lenses, but it seemed that Williams was describing ways in which Hansford had *provoked* him—to prove that Hansford had *attacked* him. There was a disconnect. Action followed by reaction, provocation followed by response. That's the normal pattern. But in Williams's story, there was action and provocation but no reaction or response at all from the man receiving the pokes in the chest.

The single most provocative act of all was the marijuana cigarette ground into the leather top of Williams's antique desk. Now would be the time for Williams to finally explain how and when it had happened. He didn't. It was never mentioned. It was left there, like a flashing red light.

This was a core problem with Williams's entire tale: Danny raged about other people but decided to kill Williams, who had done nothing. Hansford attacked Williams for no other reason than because attacking people is what a raging beast does.

To prove it, Williams and Cook trotted out the doppelgänger event in April. The obvious suggestion was that Danny tried to kill Williams in May because Danny had shot the floor and a tree in April. Danny Hansford didn't need a reason, only a season—and spring was apparently the season for mindless killing of hardwood floors and benefactors. The defense wouldn't put it that way, but they didn't have to. There was a way to get it in under another theory, if they could: to demonstrate Williams's state of mind based on his knowledge of this prior violent act.

The court allowed Cook to take Williams through the entire April event—over Spencer Lawton's strenuous objection. How was April relevant? No relationship between the two events had been established (or would ever be established throughout the *Williams* case's history). But there was legal authority that allowed prior violent acts against the defendant to be admitted in a self-defense case and, regardless of the true motive of the defense for linking the events in this case, Lawton's objection was overruled and the trial rewound to April. Williams narrated the event, immediately linking it to the May killing with an answer that had nothing to do with his lawyer's question:

I said, "What on earth is wrong with you?" and he went into a *very similar rage* that he went into the morning of May the 2nd. He started talking about everybody in the world but me.

Williams went on to add yet another version of his April tale to his growing collection. This time, he said Danny had needed to borrow money for a date in the middle of the night. But then Williams forgot that he had created the fictitious date and said that Danny was complaining about his friend George Hill and smashing things. When, with no explanation, Danny stopped smashing things and said he was going *back to his apartment.* The "date" was forgotten.

Williams testified that he had gone to brush his teeth when Danny magically reappeared with a Luger and asked if it would shoot through the floor. Williams then testified to a statement that he claimed Danny made. Williams had never mentioned this purported statement and would never mention it again. I wouldn't be surprised if it was deleted on the strong advice of counsel. According to Williams, Danny said, "How damn mad do I have to make you before you'll kill me?"

Ironically, it's highly likely that, if Danny Hansford asked Williams that question in April, he got the answer in May. He found out how mad he had to make Williams for Williams to kill him. It's no wonder that Williams would never again recall this statement in testimony.

Williams finished up his performance with his own arrest in May. He added another lie to the tale, making it a point to explain that he'd had to tell Goodman where to find the $25,000 in cash to bring to the jail for his bail. Perhaps the defense didn't want Goodman and Williams to seem too close, but the statement wasn't true. According to Goodman's recorded, signed statement to investigators:

"[H]e said you know where I keep my money don't you, *I said yeah*, and he said I'll be calling you in about an hour."

The jury didn't know about each of these conflicts within Williams's stories and between his changing stories and the evidence. The conflicts were spread across various statements and interviews, and this was Williams's direct testimony, which the jury was hearing for the first time. The question was what to do about each of Williams's flips and flops on cross-examination, which had finally arrived.

This was the single moment in *Williams I* that might have caused actual fisticuffs over a seat in the gallery: the cross-examination of Williams by District Attorney Spencer Lawton. The winners might have been disappointed. Lawton was a lawman, not a showman. His practice was to understand the points that he wished to make and then go about making them. Entertaining the gallery was of little interest to him.

If there was any doubt regarding how Williams felt about the district attorney who was prosecuting him, it dissipated as soon as Lawton rose from his seat. The disdain Williams had for being questioned by Lawton was overt. This is something that cannot be adequately conveyed with a transcript.

First, Williams restated his staunch opposition to marijuana:

Q. Certainly not in your presence and ...

A. Not in my house, period.

Williams was a "Just Say No" disciple. This rule did not apparently apply to his study or to drive-in movies. Moving on, Williams confirmed that Danny was a lethal beast. Williams's gift for hyperbole was on full display:

Q. But you never struck out at him.

A. No. He would have killed me with his hands. He had the strength of a bull when he was normal. When he was raging, he had the strength of a lot of people.

Recall that Williams testified on direct that Hansford had never touched him prior to the night in question so it's not clear how Williams would have been familiar with Hansford's strength "when he was raging," when normal, or otherwise.

What about Williams, did he have a temper? Williams admitted to the possibility that he might throw something if he got angry, but not "at anyone." He only admitted to one violent act, more strange than violent:

A. One night I played backgammon with a man and beat him seven times straight and the next night he was going to beat me. I watched him cheat two games and the third game he cheated, he got double four's and when he moved the people in all directions, I said, "You cheated" - no, I didn't say cheat; I said, "You moved your men wrong." "Are you accusing me of cheating?" and I said, "No, I'm telling you, you did," and I took the board and hit him on the head with it with all the things and walked off.

I'm not sure if hitting someone on the head with a backgammon board would be characterized as violent, but it was no doubt odd. In what would become a *Williams* case tradition, even this backgammon game would reappear. Make a note.

Lawton took Williams back to the trip to the drive-in. Williams confirmed the fantastical statements he had made to the *Georgia Gazette*:

A. I wasn't watching, but it was at least eight or nine joints.

Q. Eight or nine?

A. That was his standard.

Q. And did he drink anything?

A. He bought two half pints of Wild Turkey bourbon at Johnnie Ganem's before we went out there. He consumed one of those and part of the other one.

Q. While you and he were together at the movie; right?

A. Yes.

Q. You were sitting in the car?

A. I was driving.

Williams didn't mention having an oxygen tank or scuba gear, so who knows, maybe marijuana smoke had no effect on him.

How about the shooting and the live round on the floor? It was such an obvious omission that Lawton wanted to be certain that Williams's story was clear and that there was no back door left open. If Williams wasn't going to bring it up, he would. Lawton asked Williams about the possibility that Danny had stopped and cocked his Luger before firing. Williams said he "assumed Danny didn't have to" since both weapons were cocked and ready. There also was no time: "When I saw his gun, I reached for my weapon." One continuous sequence.

Maybe Williams could at least clear up the discrepancies in his statements about the order of events. Lawton asked Williams about a statement in Cpl. Anderson's report.

Q. Did you tell Cpl. Anderson that he (Hansford) had been playing the Atari game by himself and came in to ask you to join him and that you refused and that that's when he became angry? You did not tell Cpl. Anderson that?

A. I couldn't have, because that's not the way it happened. You see, the police weren't making notes at that moment. They were going around asking questions and if I answered them, they could have written down later anything they wanted to. They could have misremembered it.

Williams's statement was in direct quotation marks in Cpl. Anderson's Supplemental Report.[76] Defendants routinely suggest that the police are always busy trying to convict innocent people but, even if that fantasy were true, what possible reason would an officer have to make up (or as Williams put it, "misremember") a statement that was *favorable* to a defendant?

By the way, how did Williams know whether or not police officers were taking notes? He was so upset, he didn't remember anything about the timing of his phone calls, a chair on the body, or any other inconvenient fact, but he had his eye on all police officers at all times and knew exactly what they were doing?

Lawton asked Williams about the empty holster and box of ammunition recovered from the bedside table in Williams's upstairs bedroom. If this was the origin of the second Luger, someone had to go upstairs to get it, which would not fit Williams's story.

Williams told Lawton there hadn't been any Luger in that holster; it had been a different gun altogether. So where was this different gun? In an amazing coincidence, Williams said that only the night before he had heard a noise and that he had always been concerned that someone might "throw a rope" up to his back balcony and climb up, because there was no alarm upstairs. It was hard to keep a straight face listening to this, but it got worse.

According to Williams, "I heard this noise and I picked the pistol up and went in and just put it on the chest of drawers, in the top drawer." Right. Somebody was breaking in, so Williams's answer was to grab his gun and put it in a different drawer. He was going to defend himself by moving his gun and then, apparently, throwing the empty holster at his intruder. He also didn't explain why, when no intruder appeared, he hadn't returned the mystery gun to its holster.

These are the lies of a four-year-old caught with a face covered in cookie dough. But it's impossible to gauge the effect of such whoppers on a jury. The fact that people lie routinely is so ingrained in the process that those in the system can come to wonder if the oath a witness takes means anything at all.

Yet, for ordinary citizens, there is a countervailing instinct that comes into play in courtrooms and politics. If someone is willing to say something, the inclination of ordinary citizens, being less cynical than those with experience in the system, is to believe what's said until it's proved to be untrue (or sometimes longer, in politics). So although these stories might have reeked of fabrication to some noses in the courtroom, the odor might not have reached the jury box.

Mr. Lawton wrapped up his cross of Williams by trying again to nail down the flow and timing of Danny's alleged attack. Somebody had racked a round into Luger 22A, but Williams had testified he assumed Danny hadn't done it. Did Williams's defense not understand that, if Danny hadn't done it, Williams had done it, meaning he'd faked the shot himself? Had they not read the lab report or listened to Roger Parian's testimony? Lawton came at the question another way:

> Q. Can you give us any indication with respect to the actual shooting itself, how soon after Danny came into the room he fired the weapon?
> A. Immediately. He just walked around the desk and picked it up and said, "I'm leaving town tomorrow, but you're leaving tonight," and with that he fired. It was just that fast.

Williams was still rearranging his story, forgetting that he had separated Danny's two movie lines in the *Gazette* version and in his direct testimony, adding some furniture crashing in between, but most significantly, he had left no time anywhere in his story for Danny to have stopped and ejected the live round onto the rug. But, with that, the cross-examination of James Williams was concluded.

What might be coming next? If the defense wasn't going to explain the conflicts between Williams's story and the evidence, what were they planning to do? The usual Lawyer Game tool to address such an unfortunate circumstance is the ever-popular police conspiracy: The police silently conspired to convict the defendant—shades of the *Simpson* case—and they were the ones who staged the scene. There's an inherent problem with that strategy in a self-defense case, however. In a self-defense case, the scene is staged to make it look *less* likely that the defendant did it, not *more*. Why would the police go to a crime scene and tamper with it so as to make someone look *less* guilty?

Another alternative from the toolkit is to convince the jury to elevate sentiment over science, to prove that (1) Hansford obviously tried to kill Williams because he had sort of almost done it in April; (2) Hansford obviously tried to kill Williams because Hansford was a born killer for whom murder was as natural as breathing; or (3) even if Hansford hadn't tried to kill Williams and Williams just got mad and shot him, Danny Hansford was hardly worth worrying about.

The first element—April equals May—and the third element—that the dead man needed killing—had already been introduced. The defense still needed some born-killer testimony. With that, we enter the psycho phase of the first *Williams* trial.

Dr. Aurel Teodorescu was a physician, originally from Bulgaria. He had no specialty and was not a psychiatrist. In 1979, he had been working at Georgia Regional Hospital, a regional mental health facility in Savannah, part of what is today the Georgia Department of Behavioral Health and Developmental Disabilities.

Dr. Teodorescu was on duty when Danny Hansford was admitted to Georgia Regional on a referral from Memorial Medical Center on June 30, 1979. Danny was "apparently intoxicated" and had come from Memorial, where he had received two sets of sutures for injuries suffered in an argument with his landlord during which Danny said the landlord had hit him multiple times with some sort of stick. Danny was upset and didn't know why he had been taken to Georgia Regional. He probably wondered why the landlord who had beaten him wasn't along for the trip. Dr. Teodorescu had done the intake.

On direct examination, the wily coyote Bobby Lee Cook took the doctor through a narration meant to sound far more damning than it was. Part of the questioning is reproduced here. Some words are highlighted to show the difference between what Cook suggests with his question and what the doctor actually says.

> A. [I]t was not so important, *the diagnosis* at that time, when it was an emergency, psychiatric emergency, and it *doesn't matter* if psychosis or not. The patient had to be subdued and he had to be medicated. I place also an order for seclusion order in case it was necessary to seclude the patient, because this *could be dangerous* toward the staff and also dangerous for himself.
> Q. He was *dangerous* to the staff?
> A. Of course, because—
> Q. *How* was he *dangerous* to the staff?
> A. He *could be* dangerous to the staff because this *kind of patient*, they *could be*—they become combative, hostile, combative and aggressive.
> Q. What is a psychosis?
> A. What is a psychosis?
> Q. Yes, sir. What is—when you say that *someone* is psychotic, what does that medically mean?
> A. Well, it *medically* mean that the patient does not know what he is doing. He lost contact with reality and he lost the contact for complete thinking and—as I said, it's not so important to say he was psychotic or *not*, because as a matter of fact, *was not* at the time a problem for the diagnosis right away. It was an emergency. It was an emergency, psychiatric emergency.

Dr. Teodorescu was a general practitioner, was not a psychiatrist, and had seen Hansford for only a few minutes two and a half years earlier. Regardless, Cook painted Hansford as *dangerous* to the staff and *psychotic*, even though the doctor had said no such thing—he had spoken only of this *type* of patient admission generally. It didn't matter; it was open season on the dead man. Judge Oliver allowed the defense to introduce Danny's entire Georgia Regional record.

Some additional information is buried within those records with regard to this 1979 incident, uncovered during this new review. When Danny left Georgia Regional, two days later, the Discharge Progress Report did not list Danny as either suicidal or combative and examination notes within the records indicate that Danny had been "cooperative, socializing well with other patients."[77]

This testimony from Dr. Teodorescu was only the opening salvo in a defense bombardment of evidence intended to prove that Danny Hansford was a mess. We knew Danny was a mess. He had endured a hellacious child-hood. He was a troubled young man. But the defense wasn't trying to prove that Danny was a troubled young man. They were trying to prove that Danny Hansford was a psychotic killer in 1979 and, therefore, must have tried to kill Williams in 1981.

We knew Danny Hansford had done plenty in his brief life, some of it destructive, but if he had been the beast the defense was describing, the authorities should have launched a search for the corpses left in his wake. Williams had claimed Danny could kill "with his bare hands." Yet for some inexplicable reason, he hadn't ever killed, with his bare hands or otherwise. Danny Hansford was apparently a killer who just wouldn't get with the program.

The assault on Hansford continued with Nina A. Kelly, retired nurse, also testifying about the 1979 Georgia Regional admission. Ms. Kelly testified she had been a nurse at Georgia Regional when Danny was admitted. She had been the first person to interact with him, even before Dr. Teodorescu. Ms. Kelly was a nurse, also not a psychiatrist. Cook asked her what "box" she had checked on the intake form in 1979. She responded, as he knew she would, "homicidal." What a great movie moment, where a word hangs over the courtroom and a few gasps are heard.

Lawton rose to object to this entire exercise. Who was this lady? She had barely laid eyes on someone, had no qualifications to render a psychiatric diag-nosis, but checked a box and Danny Hansford became officially homicidal? Judge Oliver ordered the mention of the box struck from the record. It was struck from the record but not struck from the jury's memory.

Evidence like this is fraught with problems. How did "homicidal" get into an official medical record? After all, Danny was the one with the injuries. Ms. Kelly explained. "What Memorial sends is what we go by."

Here's the sequence: Danny's landlord claimed Danny threatened him. That *allegation* went in the police report, and the officer gave that information to Memorial Hospital. Memorial sutured Danny up and, because he was unruly and extremely intoxicated, referred him to Georgia Regional. Dr. Teodorescu had tes-tified that, "according to the report *of the police officer*, he broke furniture and also he threatened to kill somebody." Nina Kelly saw this information, consisting of layers of hearsay, and checked "homicidal" on a form.

The form then came into court as an official hospital record and—presto—we had a "homicidal" Danny Hansford. This is no more than authentication of hearsay through an "official" record exception to the hearsay rule, much like laundering dirty money. It comes out all clean on the other end, brought to court by a well-scrubbed medical professional. But when you peel it away, the sole source of the "homicidal" description was the man who had beaten Danny.

Danny Hansford was released on his own signature in 1979. Why was Danny able to sign himself out of Georgia Regional? Because there were no grounds to keep him. Spencer Lawton had asked Dr. Teodorescu if there were people at Georgia Regional who were not allowed to leave. Doctor Teodorescu said yes, definitely. Danny Hansford was not one of them.

Again, nobody said Danny Hansford was a saint. If he had been a saint, I seriously doubt that James Williams would have been interested in him.

Judge Oliver did set *some* limits on the defense. Unrelated "violent acts" alleged to have been committed by Danny were not allowed. The defense was limited to putting up evidence of Hansford's "general reputation" for violence. All witnesses could say was whether they were familiar with Hansford's reputation for violence and, if so, whether his reputation was more violent or more peaceful.

None of this evidence was strictly admissible, but not many courts, if any, would ever keep it out in a murder trial. Williams hadn't claimed he shot Danny Hansford because of his reputation for violence. Williams's defense was that Danny shot at him from point-blank range. If it were true, Williams had every right to shoot back.

A defendant's reasonable "apprehension of danger" can be an element in self-defense, but when someone shoots at you, your subjective apprehension isn't an issue. We've covered this concept earlier. If a total stranger tries to shoot you, you have every right to return fire to prevent being killed. Your assailant could have spent all day delivering cookies to orphanages and your apprehension is still reasonable. It didn't matter. The *Williams I* jury was treated to a few witnesses to Danny's "reputation" for violence.

Earl W. LeFevre called Danny's reputation "probably more toward violent than peaceable." Not exactly devastating. Robert Cross testified that Hansford's reputation was "bad." Barry William George Thomas, who took home the prize for the witness with the most names, was a Scotland native who had run Williams's antique shop for the previous six years. Barry didn't have anything to say about Danny's reputation for violence. He only testified that on the evening of May 1, 1981, he had left at about 5:30 p.m. and Danny had been sitting at the desk in Williams's study. All of these witnesses would return in future trials, with their muzzles removed. But, for now, this was the extent of the bad reputation evidence against the dead man.

With that, the defense rested. Judge Oliver asked if the prosecution had any evidence in rebuttal. Indeed we did.

THE STATE'S REBUTTAL

Corporal Anderson returned, to talk about the April incident that was now linked to May.

It is only through reexamining the entire case file and all the evidence that I have changed my mind about these too-well-matched twins. Due to their startling similarity, there was a time when we considered whether Williams might have set up April to justify the May killing but that theory never rang true. May was an eruption, not a calculated killing.

And yet, the similarity was too coincidental to be meaningless. Today, with reflection, I believe that May was tweaked to resemble April, not the other way around—and that it was tweaked by Williams. For now, back to Cpl. Anderson.

Anderson testified that he and others answered the April call at 3:45 a.m. Williams told them Hansford was upstairs, armed, and that they probably wouldn't take him alive. They crept up the stairs, found Hansford lying across a bed, and roused him. Williams showed them a hole in the carpet where a bullet fired by Danny was supposed to have gone through the carpet and into the floor. The officers couldn't find a bullet.

Williams wanted Danny removed from the house but Cpl. Anderson told him they couldn't do that on a domestic dispute, so Williams set the value of his damaged property just above the felony threshold for criminal damage to property and Danny was arrested. That was the extent of Anderson's rebuttal testimony.

John Wright Jones cross-examined Cpl. Anderson. Jones had a copy of Anderson's April report and had Anderson compare their copies to make sure they were the same. Jones then went over the bullet-hole issue with Anderson. There's a reason for my added emphasis in the following:

Q. And you found signs of a *bullet wound* or *bullet hole* in the rug and
in the floor itself on the second floor, did you not, sir?
A. Yes, sir.

And a page later:

Q. And you *confirmed* the hole in the rug and the mark in the floor
and you saw the damaged property; right?
A. Yes, sir.

I don't know any way to read that exchange other than that Anderson had found signs of a bullet "wound" or "hole." There is no sign of equivocation or unwillingness to agree with Jones's characterizations. Why no bullet was found was anybody's guess, but there is no indication that the failure to find a bullet was anything more than a peripheral fact from this unrelated, earlier event. I include this brief exchange here only because the entire *Williams I* prosecution would ultimately hinge on a single word in an innocuous notation about this unrelated event in a later report by Cpl. Anderson. This single word would send out shock waves that would be felt at the highest levels of Georgia politics. I repeat this phrase frequently: stay tuned.

The next rebuttal witness destroyed the *Williams* charade about his relationship with Danny Hansford. How was that possible? Judge Oliver had barred any mention of the subject. The testimony was introduced in rebuttal, in response to the defense's case. Williams had gone to great pains to describe his relationship with Hansford. Under the law, a party can't open the door to an area of inquiry and then prevent the other side from walking through the same door.

In my view, this was all unnecessary. The relationship should have been admissible from the beginning. In the end, it came in during rebuttal, and rebuttal testimony can actually be more effective. It can make your point while also demonstrating that the defendant either lied or was hiding something, and it comes at the close of the case—much like an exclamation point.

George Allen Hill was Danny Hansford's best friend and cut from similar stock. George knew a lot about Danny's relationship with Williams and put it in the simplest terms he knew: "Well, Mr. Williams was giving Danny money when he needed it, bought him a nice car, give him fine clothes, in exchange for him to go to bed with him."

George explained that he had talked with Danny about the arrangement and that George hadn't thought it was a good idea. He explained Danny's reaction: "Danny just told me that he liked the money and everything, that if Mr. Williams wanted to pay him to suck his dick that it was fine with him and we let it go at that."

Finally, the fights for a seat in the courtroom had been worth it. This was graphic testimony, but it accurately and succinctly summed up the relationship. Williams's shadow dance with the truth had been exposed under a thousand-watt spotlight. But there was more to Hill's testimony. George explained how Danny would "work" Williams, pushing his buttons and making him mad on purpose to get what he wanted.

According to George, Danny caused arguments deliberately. Then Danny and George would leave Mercer House and come back later. Williams would feel bad and give Danny what he wanted. Provoking Williams was something Danny did all the time.

Finally, the jury heard the story of the girlfriend and the gold necklace that had been given by Williams to Danny, then by Danny to Debbie, and then worn by Debbie to Williams's house—the very stuff of which rage killings are made.

How was George Hill as a witness? He was rough, but I liked him because he sounded truthful. He was Danny's running buddy, so he was no choir boy. Lawton asked him about his record, because it's always best to bring out negatives about your own witnesses.

George said he was coming off probation in a matter of days, had completed the Chatham Alcohol Clinic program, had his own house, and was getting married. George Hill was no model citizen, but I found him refreshingly candid.

Of course, the renowned Bobby Lee Cook would now take George apart on cross-examination. He tried, but it wasn't that easy. People who have been a mess, know it, and don't have anything to hide can be very effective.

Bobby Lee had done his homework, though, and he started in on Hill. Hadn't George and Danny been in a fight with Mr. LeFevre, who had testified earlier? George admitted it and explained that the fight had been between himself and LeFevre's son. LeFevre and Danny had tried to break it up, which had led to George fighting LeFevre and Danny fighting the son.

When Cook claimed that George and Danny had broken down Mr. LeFevre's front door, George explained that he and Danny had left and that he (George) was the one who went back to the scene, chased David LeFevre into the house, and broke the door when David shut it behind himself. Danny hadn't been a part of that. George told Cook that the fight had been about a hat of his that LeFevre's son had "messed up." When Cook feigned disbelief, Hill offered to go get the hat and show it to him.

For me, George Hill's testimony was one of the few light moments in the entire trial. Cook would accuse George of something and George would agree with him. The funniest exchange came with Cook's cross of Hill about the thing that had finally gotten George in some real trouble: shooting out streetlights. He'd done it with a friend (not Danny) after drinking grain alcohol. Cook got into a pointless argument with George about the exact number of streetlights he had shot out, as if that had anything to do with the *Williams* case.

George eventually agreed that whatever number was on the warrant was right and if it was different from what he was saying, he was probably wrong.

Then George asked Cook a question. I thought this was priceless, but I have an odd sense of humor:

A. Yes, sir, I was drunk. Have you ever drank 190 grain?

Q. Have I ever been what?

A. It will get you pretty drunk.

Q. What?

A. That 190 grain punch.

Q. One night of what?

A. 190 grain. It's pure grain alcohol.

Q. We drink that old corn liquor up where I come from.

A nice comeback by Cook, but he simply didn't know what to do with George Hill. George was a rascal, but this is what I would tell the jury in my closing argument:

> The State takes their witnesses where they find them, folks. We tried
> to arrange for a Catholic priest to come in here and talk to us about
> the relationship between Danny Hansford and Mr. Williams [but] we
> couldn't find one that knew anything about it.

Our final witness in rebuttal was twenty-one-year-old Gregory Charles Kerr. He knew Danny. He knew Williams. He also knew about their relationship.

Kerr testified that he had been at Williams's house, playing backgammon, and that Danny had been there. When Danny went to the bathroom, Kerr had commented that Danny was a nice-looking kid. According to Kerr, Williams had agreed, telling him Danny was good in bed and well endowed.

It was then John Wright Jones's turn to deal with an incorrigible witness. I don't know if it was merely in the air, or if the approaching end of the trial added a touch of levity, but Jones actually cross-examined Greg Kerr about Williams throwing a backgammon board at him. In an eerie coincidence, it apparently had been Kerr to whom Williams had been referring earlier when questioned about his own temper. This is what Kerr told Jones on cross:

Q. He took and broke a board over your head or threw it on your head?

A. No, he didn't actually throw it on my head. Can I explain the game, a little bit about the game first and let the jurors know ...

Q. You'll answer my questions and then you can explain what you want to. He threw a board at you as the result of accusing you of cheating, did he not?

A. Yes, sir, this is true.

Q. He accused you of cheating and he said, "I'm not going to play with a cheat," and he threw the board on you at that occasion; isn't that true?

A. That's very true.

Q. All right, and he did accuse you of cheating.

A. Yes, he did, on *several* occasions.

Much like George Hill, Greg Kerr had no apparent pride. It isn't clear why this was great cross for the defense. Why did it help to call attention to Williams's explosion over a board game and the fact that he associated with people like Kerr? As for Kerr and Hill, however, they were impervious. When confronted about minor scuffles or their scurrilous natures, they readily confessed.

In any event, the nature of Williams's relationship with Danny Hansford was finally out in the open. Was it smart for the defense to tell the jury to not look at the men behind the curtain? If it can be avoided, it's never good to have your client caught lying about anything, because your client not only loses on the issue but is also branded as untruthful, which can infect the entirety of their testimony.

Williams's lawyers didn't ask me, but I think their paranoia about the nature of Williams's relationship with Danny was most likely misplaced. It should have been divulged up front. There was no justification for covering up the relationship in the first place, with due respect to Judge Oliver. The fact that testimony is damaging is not grounds to exclude it. Evidence is often damaging to the defendant. That's why they're on trial.

We should have been finished, but we weren't. April was once again coming back to this trial about a May murder. The defense called Goodman back to the stand for "further cross-examination." The quotes are a reminder; Goodman was really Williams's guy.

The defense asked Goodman about a purported conversation with Danny that had never before been mentioned in trial or in any Goodman statement. The testimony was also clearly irrelevant. Goodman testified that Danny had been remorseful about April, had promised to pay for the damage, and was going to sell his car. It sounded like remorse had been flowing from every pore.

No doubt, Danny had done something in April. Whether he had this conversation with Goodman or not, who knew? Who cared? None of it had the slightest relevance to the murder charge against Williams.

On a side note, because the goal of Goodman's testimony was to lay on the remorse, Goodman made Danny Hansford sound like the most remorseful person who had ever lived. At last report, psychopaths aren't remorseful. (Make a note to recall this when we get to *Williams II* and a particular psychiatrist.)

While Goodman was on the stand, Lawton took the opportunity to point out a few things. Goodman had known Williams since age twelve or thirteen. Williams was the only person other than Nancy who called him JoJo. Yes, he had gone on the Europe trip with Williams. When? Tuesday, May 5. He and Williams had waited an entire three days after the killing to take off for London and Geneva.

All that remained was a largely rote exercise: hearing from Williams's lineup of "character" witnesses. The trial concluded with seven witnesses who testified that they knew Williams, knew his reputation for truth and veracity, and knew it to be good. On cross, they each agreed that they knew nothing about the case.

The witnesses were all well-considered citizens, which was why they were there, to add more weight to the already weighty reputation of James Williams. The witnesses were Hal S. Hoerner, John M. Jones, George Patterson, Carol Freeman, Maryanne Smith, Alice Dowling, and Stella Mantoux. Mr. Hoerner would be heard from again in the future, in another capacity.

With that, the prosecution and defense rested and the case moved to closing arguments of counsel. These arguments are called by different names, but whatever the label, they are the final arguments in the trial of the case. There are three argument segments. The first and last are assigned to the party having the burden of proof in the case—the prosecution in criminal cases. The defense makes the second closing argument.

In this case, Judge Oliver allowed the defense to split its argument between Mr. Jones and Mr. Cook, which, in effect, created four argument segments:

(1)   First Prosecution Closing—Spencer Lawton
(2)   First Defense Closing—John Wright Jones
(3)   Second Defense Closing—Bobby Lee Cook
(4)   Final Prosecution Closing—Myself

I made the final closing argument in the case. The arguments of counsel are not covered here. The court routinely instructs a jury: the arguments of counsel are not evidence. So we don't treat them as evidence.

On a tangential note, the order of argument was clearly misstated in a well-known book that we will discuss later. The author claimed that Cook argued *before* Lawton and was thus unable to answer issues that Lawton raised. That was false. Cook argued *after* Lawton. A quick glance at the trial transcript would have prevented the oversight—if it was an oversight.

Following closing arguments, court was adjourned until the following morning, when Judge Oliver would instruct the jury on the law to be applied to the case and the jury would begin deliberations. Or so we thought.

CHAPTER 15

LAWYER MAGIC

There is no such thing as lawyer magic. The magic of David Copperfield isn't magic, either. It's illusion. This might be a shock to some, but magicians don't really saw those people in half. The lawyer magic in this case wasn't real either, but it was impressive.

This is the point where this narrative begins to shift, from a review solely of the *Williams* case history, to an exploration of the more unsavory aspects of the defense of criminals within the American criminal justice system. Over its eight-year life, the *Williams* case became not only about the facts and the defense's challenge to those facts but also about tactics employed by Williams's lawyers—inside and outside the courtroom—tactics that bulldozed the outer limits of professional conduct in search of the almighty W—the win. It should come as no surprise that a wealthy defendant who has already lied about killing a man would be willing to buy the bulldozers. The sobering and disturbing discovery was how willing some defense lawyers were to drive them.

At 9:45 a.m. on the morning following closing arguments, Bobby Lee Cook made a strange inquiry, taken up by Judge Oliver in chambers. I now know something of how a ship captain feels while cruising a smooth sea, without a clue that the submarine is turning into firing position.

I don't know the magician name for what follows, but Cook would eventually take an off-hand, casual question that morning and transform it into moral outrage and a tale of high crimes before the Supreme Court of Georgia. You could call that magic. You could also call it sandbagging the trial court and prosecution.

There would actually be two feats of magic performed in the first trial of Williams. Somehow, Spencer Lawton and I managed to hide helpful evidence from the defense by putting it in the Brady file: the very file we gave the court to review for helpful evidence. Not the equal of Cook's trick, but pretty darn impressive.

Recall the brief segment of Cpl. Anderson's testimony about the April incident and the cross-examination by John Wright Jones about the event and the hole in the rug and floor—all that seemingly innocuous business. We will now see how the seemingly innocuous can rise up to bite you in a certain body part normally used for sitting down.

As noted earlier, two pages from Anderson's Supplemental Report in May had been supplied to the defense in response to Robert Duffy's discovery motions because those two pages reflected oral statements made by Williams. In addition, SPD protocol required an officer responding to a call to note any prior information the officer had regarding the location or individuals involved, so Anderson included—in his *May* report—a note about having been to Mercer House in April.

In his *April* report about the April incident, Anderson had written, "We found a bullet marking in the floor." This was the report to which John Wright Jones had referred during the cross of Anderson about the mark in the bedroom floor. It certainly seemed that Anderson had agreed with Jones that the mark he had been shown was a "bullet wound" or "bullet hole" despite not having found a bullet.

That was the state of the world on that Tuesday morning. We adjourned to Judge Oliver's chambers, along with Barbara Wright, our court reporter, to find out what Cook wanted. It didn't seem that he knew. The lawyer magic that follows was possible only because a chief assistant DA—that would be me—allowed himself to become distracted at the close of trial and forget that a snake in a suit with a goatee is still a snake. The rattle usually gives it away.

Cook told Judge Oliver he'd been extremely impressed by Mr. Lawton's closing (the first clue that something was up—a compliment from the defense), during which Mr. Lawton had mentioned the April incident. This had made such an impression upon Cook that it had occurred to him that Cpl. Anderson *might* have made some mention of the April incident in his May Incident Report (he meant Supplemental Report—the investigative follow-up report—but would constantly confuse the two). Cook wondered if there was such a mention of the prior incident and, if so, if there was anything in the report that was inconsistent with Anderson's testimony.

This didn't make much sense. Jones had cross-examined Anderson about the April incident and driven a truck back and forth over it, to hammer into the jury's mind that Danny Hansford was a raving lunatic who shot things for no reason. The following transpired in chambers:

> MR. KIRKLAND: Also, I believe, if my impression was correct that I gained from Mr. Jones' cross-examination of Corporal Anderson, I do understand—or I believe that you had an entire copy of his report of the April incident. Is that true?

Note that I am obviously referring to the *April* report of the *April* incident, the same report that Jones had used to cross-examine Anderson.

> MR. COOK: Well, I don't know whether we did, an entire report or not.
> MR. KIRKLAND: The incident report that he was cross-examined ...
> MR. JONES: All we had was two pages.
> MR. KIRKLAND: Excuse me?

MR. JONES: All we had was two pages. All we had was two pages of
April and two pages of May.

If the confusion over what Jones and Cook were talking about isn't apparent, take my word for it. Jones had used Anderson's April report on cross-examination. The May report's reference to the previous event had never come up
before. It was not clear at all that Cook was asking about the May report *mention*
of April, rather than the original April report. Still, the rattles were not register-
ing.

MR. COOK: I would trust that there's nothing else in the May 2 incident report of Corporal Anderson that would take away from the testimony of Corporal Anderson or that would in any way not support
what he had testified to. Is that a fair statement?

This was the moment of truth and I admittedly missed it. Cook's inquiry,
if it could be called an inquiry, was so shrouded in nebulous verbiage that I even
wondered if he was talking about the report pages reflecting Williams's statements.

MR. KIRKLAND: All right, there is not, and in fact this entire report is
included in the sealed material which the Judge has reviewed. This report
on the May 2 incident is excised because it was provided in response to
a request for statements of the defendant. These were statements that are
on the report, which were oral statements made by the defendant at the
time, rather than have them reduced to writing ...

MR. COOK: I hope you don't—that neither one of you gentlemen
take it that I'm questioning your integrity. I am not. Indeed, I am simply trying to get the record straight and, as I understand it, there is
nothing in the May 2, 1981 report about the April incident.

A light bulb came on, even if dimly. So Cook was talking about Cpl. Anderson's *May* report but with regard to the *April* incident? It would have been helpful if he had said so in the first place. Once I understood what he was talking
about, I suggested what seemed to be a reasonable way to answer his question.

MR. KIRKLAND: The best way to do that would be to *look at it*.

MR. COOK: Well, I know, but I'm not ...

THE COURT: I would reiterate again, I don't think that's good law.
For several reasons I don't think it's good.

Judge Oliver and Cook then launched into a discussion of what was wrong
with the US Supreme Court's *Brady* decision. If that had not happened, I have no
doubt that we would have gotten Anderson's May report and straightened this all
out. Unfortunately, Judge Oliver interrupted the exchange with a random comment about *Brady* and that was the end of it. I couldn't recall the wording in

Anderson's May report referring back to April, but I was certainly willing to pull it and see what it said.

It is worth noting here that the secret word Cook would later offer to the supreme court as evidence of prosecutorial chicanery was not on the pages of Anderson's May report to which I was referring above, the two pages containing Williams's statements with the other material redacted. There was never any material "redacted" on the pages of Anderson's May Supplemental to which, we would find out later, Cook was referring.

So what happened to Cook's squirrelly inquiry? Nothing. Before we could pull the report, Cook dismissed the whole thing. We all returned to the courtroom. Judge Oliver charged the jury, and the jury retired to deliberate.

What I didn't know was that we'd been had. Bobby Lee had just earned the fee he surely had not earned during the trial of the case.

It was my job to stop the foolishness and ferret out what Cook was up to. The casualness of Cook was the clue I missed. There should have been ten clowns honking and circling Oliver's chambers on unicycles. Cook had raised an issue, but barely, and quickly dropped it. Later, using lawyer magic, he would transform my offer to check the report into the prosecution having *concealed* evidence. Not bad. Almost ready for Vegas.

But there's another question that sheds a bright light on this event. Why would Cook drop the issue so quickly? What if there *had* been something in the report that conflicted with Anderson's testimony? Shouldn't Cook have pursued it when it could still help his client avoid a murder conviction? He could have called Anderson to the stand and cross-examined him. The jury had not been charged or begun their deliberations. It would have taken less than ten minutes. In fact, we could have dealt with it ourselves. If Cpl. Anderson had gone back on the stand, this is what would have followed (spoiler alert: this example gives away the secret word):

LAWTON: Cpl. Anderson, in your May Supplemental Report regarding the call back in April, you used the word "fresh" in reference to an alleged bullet hole upstairs, correct?
ANDERSON: Yes, sir.
LAWTON: Can you tell us what caused you to write "fresh gunshot"?
ANDERSON: That's what Mr. Williams told me.
LAWTON: I have no further questions.

That would have ended the foolishness. But Cook didn't pursue it. The most reasonable conclusion? He had tried 300 murder cases. He knew his expert had disintegrated on the stand and his client was toast. He'd already lost the trial. He needed something for the appeal, so he kicked some dirt over the seed he had planted and left it for later.

It was a weed seed, as it would turn out. The word "fresh"[78] contained on a page at the back of Anderson's May Supplemental Report, noting his unrelated prior visit to Mercer House.

CHAPTER 16

THE VERDICT

Returning to the courtroom, Judge Oliver charged the jury on the law in the case and on the offenses of murder and voluntary manslaughter. Voluntary manslaughter is often charged as a lesser included offense when there is evidence of an emotional killing. The distinction is overused, in my view. Getting mad is not an excuse for killing someone and premeditation is not the same thing as preplanning, though the two are often equated.

In any event, neither the prosecution nor the defense objected to the inclusion of voluntary manslaughter in the charge by the court.[79] The *Williams I* jury was thus authorized to return a verdict of guilty of murder, guilty of voluntary manslaughter, or not guilty.

It has been stated in some accounts that murder was the only charge given to the *Williams* jury and that the jury did not, therefore, have the option of returning a verdict of guilty on the lesser included offense of voluntary manslaughter. That wasn't the case, as a simple review of the record would have clearly indicated.

After deliberating for only four hours, the jury returned a verdict of guilty against James A. Williams for the murder of Danny Hansford. Williams posted an appeal bond and went home.

CHAPTER 17

THE APPEAL

The first step in an appeal is for the defendant to file a Motion for New Trial, asking the trial court to correct errors in the trial. The theory is that it's more efficient to correct errors at the trial court level if possible, thus avoiding an unnecessary appeal. Seldom are these motions granted, since the defense is effectively telling the trial judge that the judge screwed up and should admit it and start over. The motion is required, nonetheless, as a predicate to filing a direct appeal. And, in further service of efficiency, the defendant is required to include in the motion all allegations of error. You aren't allowed to take alleged errors up on appeal that you didn't offer the trial court an opportunity to address. At least, that's the way it's supposed to work but, remember, this is the *Williams* case.

Williams alleged six areas of error. There was no mention of Cpl. Anderson's May report.[80] Similarly, there was no mention of Anderson's report at the hearing on the motion held before Judge Oliver.[81] Judge Oliver denied the motion on April 23, 1982. The defense filed a Notice Of Appeal to the supreme court on May 14, 1982.[82] Our conspiracy to hide evidence from the defense still didn't show up. It only appeared, for the first time, in the defense's initial *appellate brief* filed on June 30, almost six months after the odd exchange in Judge Oliver's chambers.

Skipping to the punch line, the Georgia Supreme Court would reverse Williams's conviction based on our failure to provide the defense with a page at the back of Cpl. Anderson's Supplemental Report from *May* referring to *April* and containing the word "fresh." The defense had not raised the issue before the trial court, which is normally a waiver of the issue, but the supreme court ignored that requirement. Most incredibly, the reversal related to an event other than the event that was on trial in the case.

The supreme court decision was tortured, at best. The court found that the defense not having the page from Anderson's report would *not* have been likely to have produced a different result in the case: "The April 3 incident is not the incident directly in issue here and it could have been contrived with a 'fresh' bullet hole as well as with an 'old' one."[83] The court also found that there had been no perjury by Cpl. Anderson, and that there had been no specific request for the report in the discovery motions that the defense filed in the case. Nevertheless, the Court decided that we had engaged in prosecutorial evil by not handing over the report when Cook made a "request" for it in chambers.

A request? If Cook had made a request for the report, I think somebody in the room would have noticed. Cook had done everything *but* make a request for the report, sloughing off my offer for the court to look at it. The decision was mind-boggling. According to ADA David Lock, who handled the appeal, the court didn't want to hear about my offer to Cook or much of anything else.

This is the operative portion of the court's decision:

We do so (reverse the conviction) because we cannot and will not approve *corruption of the truth-seeking function of the trial process*.[84]

In other words, the court believed we had concealed something that made no difference but they were reversing the conviction anyway, just because. It would be akin to reversing the conviction because we had suppressed information that Danny Hansford hated asparagus. We will move ahead to deal with other issues from this appeal and avoid further discussion of the inanity of the decision. For now, merely take note of a finding from a future decision of the court (five years later), when the court would revisit the *Williams I* decision:

It is clear that *no* intentional corruption of the truth-seeking function of the trial process by the prosecutor [was] established here.[85]

Yes, eventually the original ruling would be corrected—but not before the first ruling reversed Williams's conviction and unleashed the beast that *Williams* would become.

Back to the appeal. How did the supreme court know what Cook had been talking about in chambers when it hadn't been clear to anyone there at the time? Simple: Cook told them. Bobby Lee Cook told the supreme court that he knew what was in the May report of Anderson and that he had known *at the time he brought it up* in chambers.

But how was Cook allowed to tell the supreme court anything of the sort? He had told the trial court (on the record) something entirely different. This new version hadn't been stated, argued, or even mentioned before Cook threw it into his initial brief. You aren't allowed to add new facts on appeal. But Cook did—and the Court let him.

He continued to add new versions and modifications. At oral argument, Cook stood before the supreme court and "testified," changing his story again. Is that permitted? No. Was it permitted for him? Yes.

The obvious question: Did Cook lie to the superior court, the supreme court, or both? For those who find the word "lie" harsh, consider Cook's evolving statements. The first appearance of his complaint about the Anderson report was in the initial defense brief. Cook added a brand-new "enumeration of error" to the brief:

We felt it was *likely* that in preparing his May 2, 1981 incident report [continuing to mis-characterize a supplemental report] that he [Anderson] might have made some reference to the prior April 3, 1981 incident.[86]

This is not so different from what he said in chambers. The story began its metamorphosis when Cook filed his First Supplemental Brief with the court:

The defense maintains that part of the [May] report refers to the April 3 incident and that *such reference* materially contradicts the testimony of Corporal Anderson.[87]

Had Cook said that in chambers? No. Now he knew what he hadn't even been able to articulate in chambers. That wasn't all. Cook had a *source* for his information:

Counsel's basis for such belief is founded on *statements made to him* concerning the April incident which counsel has no reason to doubt.[88]

Statements? What statements? Had Cook really concealed something from Judge Oliver rather than using it to save his client from a murder conviction?

The appellate court is not a fact-finding body and isn't equipped for it. It would normally be expected to make quick work of Cook's mystery sources and new facts—but once again, *Williams* proved just how *unusual* it was. When the supreme court allowed Bobby Lee Cook to, in effect, testify in oral argument, he went even further than his pleadings had gone. Cook told the court that he knew about the report because he had received an anonymous phone call *the night after closing argument.* This alleged call supposedly came from someone claiming to be on the district attorney's staff.[89]

According to Cook's new story, he had all this information before the conference in chambers. But he had told the trial court an entirely different tale, even including an intentional diversion, claiming his nebulous inquiry was the sole result of having been impressed by the district attorney's closing argument.

The chambers conference had taken place at 9:45 in the morning, before the jury had been given the case. According to Cook's new story, he'd had specific information at the time that could have helped his client. Yet he'd fabricated a reason for his inquiry and had almost run in the other direction when a solution was offered to him. Now, on appeal, he claimed that he had known what was in the report at the time, had had a specific source for his information, and that his source was a member of the district attorney's staff. What possible motivation could Cook have had to conceal this information from Judge Oliver, assuming for the moment that the second of his evolving claims was true?

Someone once told me a story about a longtime US Senator from Georgia, Herman Talmadge, bemoaning the new age of communications. His complaint was that you used to be able to tell people one thing in one part of the state and something else in another part of the state but the new age of communications had totally messed things up. The Talmadge rule is not supposed to apply to the legal profession. You don't get to tell two different courts two different stories and get away with it. At least *I* say you don't. But Bobby Lee Cook did just that. And he wasn't finished.

After oral argument, the parties went away and filed more (supplemental) briefs on the subject. When the State pointed out that Cook had changed his story completely and that, even at oral argument, had made nothing more than a bare assertion about an anonymous phone call the night after closing argument, Cook embellished his claim yet again. In his reply brief to the State's brief, he claimed that he knew even *more* than he'd admitted and that he had known it even *sooner.*

According to Cook's latest dial-a-story, he now recalled that he had received his anonymous information "the night following Corporal Anderson's testimony." Corporal Anderson's testimony had ended on *Friday.* The chambers session was not held until the following *Tuesday* morning. If this new version was true, Cook had used the weekend and all day Monday to figure out how to avoid revealing what he had known, while finessing an appeal point at the same time.

Remarkably, that was still not the full extent of Cook's brazen manipulation of the supreme court and the appeal process. Cook's memory improved every time he re-remembered what he had remembered. In this new version, Cook also told the supreme court that his Deep Throat had specifically told him that "Anderson *knew* the bullet hole ... was a new one, and had purposefully *changed his testimony.*"[90]

It might be time for Lyin' Joe Burton to share his nickname with Bobby Lee Cook. Cook was now churning out manure as fast as he could turn the crank. There was no way for anyone to *know* what Cpl. Anderson knew without him telling them. In essence, Cook's new, improved allegation was that Cpl. Anderson had openly confessed to committing perjury and had confessed his crime to a mystery figure within the district attorney's office.

This allegation was unmitigated garbage. I knew the *Williams* case as well as anyone living. I ran the legal staff of the district attorney's office and was one of only three people—along with Spencer Lawton and Robert Sparks—who knew the details of our trial preparation for the *Williams* case. Cook was alleging that Cpl. Anderson had written something down in an official SPD report, had decided on his own to lie about it (without any suggested motivation), and had then shared his lie with some unknown DA's office employee, but not with the attorneys who were trying the case. And, finally, Anderson was to have done all this over a call to Mercer House in April that was not on trial in the case.

The defense was obviously in love with the April incident but Cook's allegations were laughable and easily disposed of if they were given a moment's examination. In April, Williams showed officers a hole that Hansford was supposed to have made by firing a Luger at the floor (supposedly two shots according to Williams's statement to police at the time but who's quibbling). Fine. That's what Williams told them. Neither Anderson nor the officers with him could find a bullet. Anderson didn't *know*, and couldn't know of his own personal knowledge, what had made a hole in a hardwood floor in Williams's house. (Which also begs the question: Where was the bullet? The bullets fired into the study floor in May didn't disappear. Where did Williams's April bullet go?)

Was Cook on a righteous campaign to uncover a conspiracy? The April report about April—the report that Jones had used to cross-examine Anderson—clearly indicated that Anderson hadn't answered that call alone. There were *five* officers present: Anderson, Ptl. M. A. White, Sgt. G. Spivey, Cpl. J. J. Chesler, and Ptl. Gibbons. If Cook had been so concerned with April and a "fresh" bullet hole conspiracy, why hadn't he pulled all five officers in and put them on the stand, uncovered the entire evil plot?

Why? Because Cook wasn't out to uncover an evil plot. He was only seeking a victory on appeal that he couldn't win at trial. Lastly, what "testimony" was Cpl. Anderson supposed to have "changed"? He had never testified on the subject before this trial.

I had already been appointed by the governor to a position in Atlanta and was not in the district attorney's office when the *Williams I* appeal was heard, but I was close by, on the opposite side of the state capitol. It would have been nice to know the supreme court was accepting testimony, as it had from Cook. I could have walked over and given the panel an earful. But who knew you could stand up at oral argument before the supreme court and say whatever you wanted?

I don't blame Bobby Lee Cook alone. I also blame the supreme court justices for letting him blow smoke up their robes. Some would suggest that Cook was only a defense lawyer representing his client, but what Cook did was to present two separate courts with conflicting factual claims about the same event. I would have merely asked Cook the same question he would have asked of any witness: Which time were you lying?

CHAPTER 18

LAWYER GAMES

Lawyers are officers of the court, meaning they are responsible for speaking the truth to the court about either fact or law, just as if they had raised their hand and taken the formal oath of a witness. Rule 3.3(a)(1) of the *American Bar Association Model Rules of Professional Conduct*, titled "Candor Toward the Tribunal," states: "(a) A lawyer shall not knowingly: (1) make a false statement of fact or law to a tribunal or fail to correct a false statement of material fact or law previously made to the tribunal by the lawyer."

For those concerned that there are too many lawyers, all that would be required to thin the herd would be to enforce ABA Rule 3.3(a)(1). That's an unfiltered opinion, but I don't like the kind of behavior demonstrated during the *Williams I* appeal. And that behavior is going to get much worse before this tale is complete. It's one reason I'm not in that business anymore.

There are honorable lawyers as well as scoundrels on both sides of the criminal law practice, but the pressures and temptations are different on the defense side. You're always trying to "beat the rap" and although it's a fiction that the system is inevitably stacked against a defendant, it's true that the facts often are. That explains the drinks and high fives in the bar. Beating the rap isn't easy, and there's nothing wrong with a hard-fought victory. But if you can't do it the right way, with integrity, you don't get respect points from me, because you didn't earn them.

It's like setting a rushing yardage record in football by running out of bounds, behind the cheerleaders. Real players run between the lines.

Most people in America, including a surprising number of lawyers who don't do criminal work, are not aware that the prosecution *can't appeal a verdict* in a criminal case. There is no appellate remedy whatsoever for errors, no matter how egregious, that might prejudice the public as opposed to the defendant. Criminal cases are called *State* (or *People*) vs. *Defendant,* after all.

The United States is nearly alone among developed nations in providing *no remedy* for errors in a criminal trial—unless those errors are complained of by the defendant. There was a howl of disbelief from talking heads in the media in 2013 when the Italian supreme court overturned the 2011 acquittal of Amanda Knox in a murder case because of errors in the case. Purported experts, even in international law, claimed this was a clear "double jeopardy" violation. No, it wasn't. Not in Italy. And they've been at this a lot longer than we have.

The law is supposed to be fair to the defendant. Should the law not also be fair to the citizens it is designed to protect? This is an intriguing law school or philosophy discussion, but the law here is settled: Only the defendant can appeal a verdict.

The difference leads to a public misperception. Of course, anyone wrongfully convicted should be retried or released; being sent to prison for a crime you didn't commit is abhorrent. When such cases are overturned, the news is reported. There are no reports of acquitted defendants being retried because of serious legal errors by the court or the nefarious behavior of defense counsel—because it isn't possible.

There is no way to settle an argument over which system is best. Different countries, different systems, different viewpoints. The imbalance creates perverse incentives in the criminal trial practice in the United States, however. Because the prosecution can never appeal a verdict, if the defense wins, no matter *what* they did to win, it's over. Any personal repercussions for a lawyer come only through action that the trial judge might take during the trial—or disciplinary action by the Bar Association—which is almost unheard of for courtroom behavior.

I was offered some advice once, while in private practice doing criminal defense work: "Represent your client to the fullest extent of the law, but if somebody is going to jail when the trial is over, make sure it's your client." It's funny, but even jailing a lawyer for contempt doesn't affect the underlying verdict. It can't.

As Vincent Bugliosi noted in his book *Outrage*, Simpson defense attorneys Cochran and Scheck objected to the prosecutor's closing arguments seventy-one times, fifty times in the case of Marcia Clark alone. Of their seventy-one objections, two were upheld as legally valid.[91] Did Cochran and Scheck care that their actions were probably ethical violations in addition to outrageous and intentionally disruptive? No, because they knew nobody would do anything about it (including presiding Judge Ito).

Bobby Lee Cook knew if he could get a reversal of Williams's conviction, there would never be any action taken against him for the way he did it. When you don't care what you have to do to win, this is the kind of lawyer you, too, could become one day.

PART FOUR

WILLIAMS II

CHAPTER 19

NEW PLAYERS—SAME GAME

Bobby Lee Cook had finagled Williams a do-over, but everyone involved—including Williams—knew the reversal had nothing to do with the facts. The supreme court expressly stated that the verdict was supported by the facts and that the "error" it found would not likely have changed the verdict (what's known as "harmless error"). In other words, on the facts, the defense had crashed and burned. So Williams did what a lot of defendants do when things aren't going their way: He changed lawyers.

The new team was headed by Frank W. ("Sonny") Seiler, of Bouhan, Williams & Levy, a white-stocking Savannah law firm. Seiler had extensive experience in civil trial work but virtually no criminal experience. Within the state generally, Seiler is best known as the owner of generations of UGA, the University of Georgia bulldog mascot. Filling the gap in Seiler's criminal résumé were Austin E. Catts and Donald F. Samuel, from the Atlanta firm known simply as The Garland Firm.[92]

The State appearances were by Spencer Lawton and Bob Sparks, joined by Kathryn M. (Kathy) Aldridge, who had succeeded me as Chief Assistant when I left for a gubernatorial appointment in Atlanta.[93]

The trial in *Williams I* had taken seven trial days. The trial in *Williams II* would take nineteen trial days. On the same facts. The giant panda sponge was growing.

CHAPTER 20

NEW JURY—NEW STORY

Williams II commenced on September 19, 1983, with Judge Oliver again presiding. How would *Williams II* be different? Williams's lawyers now had the magic word "fresh" in their arsenal. Not surprisingly, the magic word would never again be mentioned by the defense in a *Williams* trial, including this one.

The evidence against Williams had been untouched, so roughly the same case commenced with a "fresh" set of lawyers. This narrative began its turn with Cook's subterfuge on appeal. With a new defense "dream team" on board, the second trial continued the trend and took on a quality of meanness that would drag the entire undertaking down to an unfortunate level of disrespect, excess, and personal vituperation.

Judge Oliver, charged with presiding over what would turn into a bar fight, was a veteran jurist but also, to use an out-of-date term, a gentleman lawyer. I don't believe Judge Oliver was comfortable dealing with lawyers who simply would not behave. In *Williams II*, there would be arguments over objections that went on interminably because, when Oliver would indicate he might rule against them, Seiler and Catts (who together handled the examination of witnesses during this trial) would simply keep talking. On occasion, by the time they stopped, no one appeared to be sure how Oliver had ruled or to remember the basis for the original objection. This is not to say that George Oliver was a pushover. He simply tried to run a courtroom based on mutual respect among the combatants.

Admiral Ernest (Ernie) King, Commander in Chief of the US Fleet and Chief of Naval Operations during World War II, was reputed to have said when taking the job, "When they get in trouble they send for the sons of bitches." He denied saying it but agreed that he would have—if he had thought of it.

Somebody might have wanted to "send for the sons of bitches" to deal with Seiler and Catts. They were the salesman who's told no but continues talking until the door is physically slammed in their face, only to show up at the back door, still hawking the same snake oil.

With that warning, into the slop we tread.

NEW JURY—NEW STORY

Despite the reversal on appeal, the first trial had not gone well for Williams, because the reversal wasn't based on the evidence. If the launch of a ship is followed by its descent to the bottom in front of the gathered well-wishers, that is not good news. Having the supreme court show up with a rescue tug to haul Williams's sunken dinghy out of the muck was no doubt welcome, but the court's largess didn't make Williams's case any more seaworthy.

The reversal and the do-over did create an opportunity to watch the system in action with an enhanced sense of perspective, however. We can watch the patching, sanding, and repair work performed on Williams's defense from one case to the next. In the process, the story will become as much about the criminal lawyer as about the criminal.

We'll see very quickly that the operating principal of the new defense was "new jury-new story." The fact that the first story and the new story couldn't both be true didn't matter. This jury was only going to hear one of them. This jury had no idea what a witness had said last time. Yes, trusting hearts, people do lie in court every day. And if a witness and counsel are "factually flexible" where the truth is concerned, a "practice trial" can be a great advantage.

THE STATE'S CASE

Williams II led off with the human bundle of surprises known as Joseph E. Goodman. What would he say this time? About the first phone call: "Approximately between 2:04 and 2:05 the phone rang and woke me up."

Different, but close enough. Danny got on the phone, checking on Goodman's feelings. Goodman then smoked a cigarette, put it out, and turned over, and the phone rang again, just as he had said in his recorded formal statement.[94]

The beauty of the cigarette reference was that it required no math. It's a common reference that people can easily visualize. But what about the actual time of the second call? Goodman said the second call came at "2:20, 2:21 or 2:22, somewhere around there." The missing minutes were back.

Was this too good to be true? Yes. The defense was not about to give in on an issue as damning as the time gap in Williams's story. At first blush, it might have looked like Goodman was miraculously back on track, but that would have been much too easy.

After the second call, Goodman added that he and Nancy brushed their teeth in addition to getting up and dressing, but that was the only change. Inside Mercer House, when Goodman approached the study door, Goodman testified that a police officer told him, "No, you can't go in there." Remember that testimony for later.

Once again on faux cross-examination—considering that Goodman was really a defense witness—Seiler took Goodman back through the phone calls but didn't seem concerned about the times. Goodman said he got the first phone call at 2:05, spoke to Danny, and got the second call about ten minutes later. That would be only 2:15, even worse for Williams than 2:22, but

Seiler didn't challenge Goodman. Was the defense making sure the jury understood the times that incriminated Williams? If the prosecution had thought of writing the defense a thank-you note, it would have been premature.

The defense did go after the idea that Williams was cool and calm after killing his friend. They returned to EMS being called to the scene to examine Williams. Goodman repeated that Williams had experienced an episode of some sort and that EMS had come to check on him. But Goodman said that happened at least an hour after he arrived—which was after ID arrived, after detectives arrived, and probably after I arrived. If there was a point to be made, it was that Williams became upset at the course of the investigation, not at having shot his friend.

When Goodman was finished, it appeared that he had returned to his original time frame, restored the missing minutes, and done little, if anything, to help his friend. Lawton and Aldridge were most likely shaking their heads—for good reason, as it would turn out.

By the time of the second trial, former SPD ID Officer Donna K. Stevens had completed studies at Armstrong College[95] and was an ID officer with the police department of Garden City, a municipality bordering Savannah and the Port of Savannah and home to Gulfstream Aerospace. Stevens repeated her testimony from *Williams I* on direct.

The cross-examination of Ofc. Stevens was the point in *Williams II* where it became evident how different this trial would be in tone and professionalism. Seiler launched into a long, argumentative shell game with Ofc. Stevens involving crime scene photographs and heavy doses of sarcasm.

Here's how the game went: He would show Stevens two photos. The first photo showed an item in a certain position. The second photo showed the item in a different position. Stevens explained that some of the apparent moves were only illusions due to changes in photographic perspective but in some cases, yes, an item was in a different position in one photo than in another photo. Seiler didn't ask *why* an item had moved, only *if* it had moved.

There were over a hundred photos taken of the crime scene (today, with digital cameras, it might have been several times that number). The defense had all of them. But to reiterate a point made earlier, the truth is a mere speed bump to some lawyers and the first tool in the stumped defense lawyer's toolbox is: conspiracy.

Using his two photos, Seiler pointed out that one of the photos had not been introduced into evidence by the prosecution. The inference was that, because the photo had not been introduced into evidence, the prosecution was hiding it. Seiler was partially right. The prosecution had not introduced into evidence every photograph taken at the crime scene. If they had, Judge Oliver might have grabbed one of the evidence Lugers and shot the district attorney himself from the bench.

Of course, Seiler didn't point out how he had come to have the second photograph—that it had been given to him, along with *all* of the crime scene photos—by the prosecution. A strange way to hide them. But never underestimate a lawyer's ability to manufacture indignation.

The entire exercise was a sham. Seiler failed to mention one critical fact: The photographs were taken at different times. If we think about it, that's obvious. If you've ever photographed a boy's first birthday party, there is probably one photo of the cake with the happy rascal and another photo of the cake after he's put his face in it. Do you stare at the two photos, scratch your head, and say, "Hm, something's different about this other picture"?

The concept surely wasn't foreign to Seiler, yet not only didn't he share the fact with the jury, he attempted to keep it from them. Officer Stevens pointed out—far more patiently than I would have—that there were frame numbers on the negative contact sheets (this being the era of 35mm film) and that she would be happy to tell Seiler the order in which the photos were taken if he was interested. He wasn't interested. Or, more accurately, he was very interested—in not allowing the jury to hear it.

Excuse my departure from good manners, but there should be a machine in a courtroom that punches a lawyer in the face for pulling this garbage.

Stevens explained: She had photographed everything as it was—first—and then continued to take *additional* photographs as the scene was processed. Yet you would have thought defense counsel was waving proof of a grand conspiracy—a conspiracy the SPD had been kind enough to record in photographs.

There is probably a checklist somewhere that defense lawyers collect at seminars: police evidence tampering, along with police conspiracy, police bungling, and police doughnut jokes. There is no requirement to prove the allegation, only that counsel continue to make the allegation in a bold voice tinged with outrage. Waving something is also a nice touch.

The ever-popular "Herd of Elephants" theory was Seiler's next tactic. Seiler got Stevens to admit that she couldn't see who might have been in the study before she arrived at the scene. That was fortunate, for Williams. If she could have seen through walls and across time, Stevens could have described how Williams had gone about shooting Hansford and contriving the scene that she later photographed.

Seiler then tried the false-statement-in-a-question technique we've already seen, but Stevens didn't let him get away with it:

Q. Now you know, we're having a hard time about this simple thing. If this is the door threshold, and I'm looking in—I'm outside the room—and if I do this I'm inside the room. Now is that hard?

A. What I say is around the doorway.

Q. Around—which side?

A. I mean, I'm not going to draw a line and say if they stepped over that line, they're in or out.

Q. Well. I'm asking you to do that, because it means something to us to know how many people were *meandering around in that room* when you and Detective Ragan were working.

A. No one was *meandering around in the room* when I was working.

Do condescension and behaving like a donkey's rear end work for some lawyers in front of a jury? I don't find it persuasive. All Seiler accomplished was to establish, without a doubt, that there were police officers present at the scene of a homicide. I would like to have heard Ofc. Stevens say, "Yes, sir. That's what happens when you shoot somebody. The cops show up." The best lines always occur to us later.

Seiler wasn't finished. He grilled Stevens on the fact that the police hadn't dusted Williams's furnishings for fingerprints. This is another common tactic: "You could have weighed the defendant's house. But you didn't do that, did you?!" This is similar to what Cook did in *Williams I* by asking Roger Parian why he hadn't tested the bullets to make sure they were made of lead.

The suggestion is that if the police had only done this or that, it would have proved the defendant's innocence. Not surprisingly, there was another simple explanation in this case. On redirect, Stevens explained that this had been considered a *domestic* call and in such cases, when a party has regular access to the scene, fingerprints aren't typically taken.

What if there had been fingerprints? Fingerprints on the furniture didn't necessarily work in Williams's favor. Remember motive? Even if Danny Hansford's fingerprints had been found on the grandfather clock, for example, it would not have proved that Williams acted in self-defense. It would have been evidence of Danny *provoking* Williams. Pushing Williams's clock over would be a reason for Williams to shoot Hansford, not a reason for Hansford to shoot Williams. Damaging a clock and trying to kill Williams were not the same thing. If Williams had told the police, "He hurt my clock and I had to shoot him," there would have been no trial.

On redirect by Mr. Lawton, Stevens addressed the issue of the herd of elephants. If they had lumbered into Mercer House, they would not have been allowed to wander into the study and trample through the crime scene. Officer

Stevens confirmed that Ptl. White was already stationed at the study door when she arrived and that she had told him to "make sure he stayed there."

The notorious Cpl. M. J. Anderson was back on the stand. Corporal Anderson confirmed, on direct examination by Mr. Lawton, that he had stationed Ptl. White at the study door as soon as officers had arrived.

But what about the magic word "fresh" that had reversed the first *Williams* conviction? Lawton asked Anderson about it himself:

Q. And did you describe the bullet hole?

A. I described the bullet hole as being a fresh bullet hole, as what Mr. Williams represented to me, 'cause I was trying to remember every— well, I wasn't gonna put detail[ed] information, but I was just remembering what Mr. Williams described to me.

On cross-examination, even Seiler helped put April into perspective. In my opinion, the prosecution could have asked this question:

Q. ... Isn't this true, too? Nobody had been hurt, nobody had been shot, nobody had been killed. So you weren't really interested in pursuing that any more than what you had seen. Remember telling me that?

A. Right, sir.

This was the *prosecution's* point. April's call had been a domestic call and had resulted in a trip to jail for Danny Hansford. The charges had been dropped. It was not an event burned into Anderson's memory. The "fresh" issue would never again be mentioned. It swam away to wherever red herrings go to die. This portion of the transcript should have been gift wrapped and sent to the members of the supreme court who had voted to overturn Williams's conviction over this nonsense.

Moving down the checklist in the Lawyer Games manual, Seiler rolled out the elephants again with Anderson. There was a major flaw in this argument: Not only was no elephant herd ever placed in the study, but there was no *time* for anyone—other than Williams—to have tampered with the scene. Within *five minutes* of Anderson's arrival, ID Ofc. Donna Stevens arrived, took custody of the scene, and began memorializing its original state with photographs.

The defense effort to create a police party scene to explain away Williams's scene manipulation was another red herring—a red herring that would continue to swim happily through the trial, resurfacing repeatedly.

George D. Siegel was the lead EMS tech on the original call, after Hansford's death. Siegel testified that he checked the victim's carotid artery and listened through the back with a stethoscope. That was it. No, he didn't move anything.

He did begin to clear up the confusion over William's "episode." Before leaving Mercer House, Siegel said he checked to see if anyone present needed anything. This included Williams. They all said no. If Williams was in distress, it was later and did not involve this EMS team.

Detective Ragan was back, with a major difference from the outset. There was a bloodletting over the State's effort to qualify him as an expert witness. Judge Oliver eventually qualified Ragan as an expert police investigator and ruled that Ragan could testify to conclusions he had reached so long as he explained their basis.

Ragan's direct testimony covered the same areas as in *Williams I:* the timeline, his actions, and the collection of the evidence. A bit more attention was focused on skull fragment origins and locations. The evidence is marked on our diagram (Figure 13).

In his cross-examination of Det. Ragan, Austin Catts played the same refrains previewed earlier: There had been a cop convention in the study, and something looked different in one photo compared to another photo.

Significantly, the defense would never relate any movement of any item in any photo to an issue in the case. There was a very good reason that they didn't. They couldn't. The items were moved as a normal component of the processing of a crime scene and the collecting of evidence. That was why Seiler hadn't wanted Stevens to put the photographs in order. The defense focused entirely on the fact that an item had moved and ignored *when* or *why* it had moved.

Let's look at an example of this technique in another case—the trial of music mogul Phil Spector for the shooting death of Laura Clarkson. The weapon, a Colt Cobra revolver belonging to Spector, was found on the foyer floor to the left of the victim's left leg. Spector's defense was that Clarkson had committed suicide with his gun—but there was a problem: Laura was right-handed. The defense's answer? "Someone" might have "kicked or otherwise moved" the gun. If this ubiquitous "someone" is ever identified, he or she is going to have to answer for screwing up a lot of crime scenes.

To create some suspect "someones" in this case, Catts took Det. Ragan through the names of everyone Ragan had seen in the house, no matter their role or their location, or whether they were official or civilian. The inference was—of course—that a sea of people was flowing through the scene. Once again, the *inference* was important, not the facts.

Catts asked Det. Ragan if Stevens was taking photos while Ragan was taking measurements. Why did Catts ask that question? Because he could then suggest that Ragan had disturbed the scene. No, Ragan testified, all of the photography had been done *before* any measurements were taken.

Didn't Ragan leave the study to make phone calls? Yes, he did, Ragan agreed, but no, he hadn't gone off into some *other* (suggesting remote) area of the house. He had made the calls from directly across the hall while facing the study door. He did agree with Catts that he could not see through the door or the walls while on the phone.

Whether Det. Ragan went across the hall, upstairs, or outside to play softball in the park after he arrived was irrelevant; the initial photographs of the scene had been taken before Det. Ragan even arrived at Mercer House. Of course, Catts was doing the job he was there to do: find a crack in the case and drive a wedge into it. This is 20/20 hindsight, but it would have been helpful to have Ofc. Stevens organize the photographs, whether the defense wanted it done or not. It would have stopped and revealed the scam at the same time.

Catts continued trying to get Ragan out of the study so some undefined mischief could take place. Notice the phrasing of Catts's question:

Q. I see. (Pause) Then on another occasion, you went on essentially *a tour of the house* with Officer Stevens. Correct?

A. We basically went right across the hallway to the other room. It really wasn't a tour.

What's going on? Catts was playing a theme. In orchestral music, there might be a theme that appears in the beginning, reappears at times, and returns in full voice at the end. That's what's going on here. To find the theme, we have to look at the lawyer's question as carefully as the witness's answer.

Catts continued to work on getting Ragan out of the study. Ragan said that, yes, at some point *after* the study was photographed, he and Stevens went upstairs. This was when the photo of the empty holster in the bedside table was taken. Ragan estimated this happened two or three *hours* after his arrival.

The defense grasped the trip upstairs like a cold Mountain Dew in a desert. Catts asked Det. Ragan whom Ragan had left guarding the door when he and Stevens went upstairs. Ragan assumed it was Anderson. Aha! Catts pounced. Anderson had testified that he left the scene around 4:30 because his wife was having a baby. Because Ragan estimated that the upstairs photos were taken two or three hours after his 3:30 arrival, Anderson *wasn't* the one Ragan left on the door.

The simple answer was that if Anderson was gone when Ragan went upstairs, someone else had been on the door. What difference did it make? It was 5:30 or 6:30 in the morning by that time.

Patrolman White had been on the door since White and Anderson had arrived. Stevens had told him to make sure he stayed there. There's the first option. And if it wasn't White, it was someone else. The other option was that Ragan, a veteran of more than one hundred homicide investigations, and Stevens, a trained ID officer, had strolled out of the study and left the door open so anybody who felt the urge could wander in and play with the evidence. That should be a fairly easy call.

Even if Anderson and Stevens had done just that, it still wouldn't have made the slightest difference. Why did Ragan and Stevens go *upstairs*? Because they were finished *downstairs*. What should they have done, remained barricaded in the study and called another team to come take a picture of the empty holster in Williams's bedside table?

For a defense faced with fact problems, routine matters such as leaving one room to photograph another room are treated as major flaws in the case. These questions were designed to suggest, through inference and innuendo, what the defense couldn't prove with evidence. It was Lawyer Games 101.

The next "flaw" exposed by the defense was The Great Coffee Caper. In his original statements, Joe Goodman had alleged that police officers had been in Williams's kitchen, making coffee, and to make matters worse, they hadn't offered any to anybody else and had refused to allow Goodman into the kitchen. The fact that the kitchen door opened into the crime scene might have had something to do with that.

If there is any question that the defense did not want to talk about a chair, bloody hand, or paper fragments, this should seal it. The jury was treated to Austin Catts cross-examining Det. Ragan as to whether he'd had any coffee that night. No, Ragan said, nobody had made coffee, though he agreed he could have used a cup. He testified that he did get some, eventually, when Det. Jordan brought him a cup from Krispy Kreme upon Jordan's return from Williams's bond hearing. What would a cop story be without coffee and doughnuts?

This minutiae miasma was a change from the first trial, one reason this version took three times as long to try, but at its core it involved the same strategy: The defense needed an intervening third party to mess up the scene so Williams's responsibility for the mess could be erased.

Catts asked, didn't Ragan move the rug and the pad under it? Yes, Ragan answered, he definitely did that. There were photographs already in evidence of him lifting the rug and pad to show the bullet and bullet markings in the floor from the last two shots Williams fired.

Ragan also agreed that Ofc. Stevens moved Williams's office chair—*after* it had been photographed in its original position. She moved it to get a better angle on the paper fragments and debris on the floor. No, she did not climb on top of Williams's desk. Yes, Catts did actually ask that question.

Continuing, yes, Ragan moved the *TV Guide*. Again, there were photos showing this activity, already in evidence. Ragan *lifted* the *TV Guide* to show the paper fragments created by the bullet from Luger 22A (Figures 34, 37).

One might have concluded that these lawyers didn't know much about processing a crime scene, but that would be incorrect. Mr. Catts's firm was one of the best-known criminal defense firms in the southeast. He knew exactly what he was doing. But, on a substantive level, all the defense was doing was spending a lot of time proving that the police processed the scene. These questions were chaff (a combat countermeasure) released by the defense's submarine to distract the enemy sonar—in this case, the jury's fact finding powers. The practice is commonplace and relatively harmless, though it can unduly complicate an uncomplicated case.

Catts did something else in his cross-examination of Det. Ragan, however, that was beyond the normal bounds of expected defense lawyer obfuscation. This involves The Mysterious Case of the Moving Pouch. It might sound like an Australian kids' book about a kangaroo. It isn't.

Detective Ragan had already testified that Stevens had moved the office chair to photograph the debris on the floor. Ragan agreed that there was no photo of Stevens actually moving the chair, though Catts did not suggest how Stevens was supposed to have photographed herself moving a chair while moving it.

Note that the following questions were not asked of Ofc. Stevens, who took the photos. Why not? For the same reason Seiler didn't have Stevens arrange the photos in sequence: It would have made this sleight of hand impossible. What followed was so smooth that it became obvious to me only on this review, with adequate time and a naturally suspicious mind. This was not noticed at trial.

Catts had the clerk mark a photo as "Defense Exhibit 19" and showed it to Ragan. The photo showed the leather pouch that had been knocked onto the floor next to Williams's chair (Figure 39). Catts then showed Ragan a second photo marked "Defense Exhibit 20." It also showed the chair and pouch (Figure 38). The pouch appears to be in a slightly different position. Ragan did not recall having moved it. Catts didn't suggest what the mysterious movement had to do with the case, but the defense was trying to conjure up confusion wherever they could. How they went about it in this instance proves more about the lawyers than about the case against Williams.

Here's the trick: The first photo was marked Exhibit 19 and the second was marked Exhibit 20 because that was the order in which Catts presented them to the clerk. Marking the photos as Exhibits 19 and 20 suggests that the photos were taken in that order. They weren't. The photos were reversed.

D-Exhibit 20 was taken *first*, when the pouch was next to the leg of the chair (Figure 38), exactly where it was in every other photograph in which it appeared other than D-Exhibit 19 (Figure 39). When was that lone photo taken? *After* Stevens moved the chair to make room to photograph the debris on the floor, when the pouch position was *irrelevant* because it had already been photographed multiple times in its original position.

If Ofc. Stevens had been asked these question, she could have checked the proof sheet and found what I found—that the photos were flipped—but the defense asked Ragan instead of Stevens. Ragan didn't have the proof sheet and didn't know any better.

What did the mystery of the moving pouch have to do with the killing of Danny Hansford? Catts never got to that. But sowing confusion is not a crime, technically; it's what defense lawyers do. And the defense in *Williams* had a challenge: They had a lying client who had killed a man. It isn't okay, however, to join the lying client in the chorus.

What was all this moving business really about? The defense wanted things moved around in the study—however, whatever, and whenever—to infer that if these things had moved, other things could have moved. And if enough things were moving, you couldn't rely on the position of anything at any point in time. Put in those terms, the exercise might sound ridiculous, but reconciling the positions of the physical evidence with Williams's self-defense claim was impossible. The defense didn't have any choice. Actually, they did have a choice, but not one that would have been likely to please the man paying their fee.

Moving on from the photos, Catts asked Ragan if it was unusual to find someone shot while they were holding a weapon to be still gripping the weapon. Ragan agreed that it was unusual; he had seen it only three times in his career. So the defense was going with the theory that Hansford had dropped the Luger when shot, rather than continuing to grip it? The prosecution had never suggested that the Luger should still be gripped in Hansford's hand. The prosecution didn't believe it had ever been in his hand in the first place.

What followed next was an example of a lawyer setting the stage with a generalized, fuzzy hypothetical that he could fill in later with his own witness. Ragan agreed with Catts that if "certain blood" (Catts's phrase) had been found on the Luger 22A grip, Ragan's opinion about whether or not Hansford had been holding the Luger "wouldn't have the same foundation." That was all Catts asked. Notice how general the terms are.

The question was general for a reason: to keep Ragan from disagreeing. A defense witness was no doubt going to show up to testify to finding "certain blood" on the grip of the Luger. Then the defense could remind the jury that the lead detective in the case had already agreed that "certain blood" found would make a difference, even though the detective hadn't been asked what "certain blood" even meant.

What if Catts had been specific with Det. Ragan? Here's a question: "Detective Ragan, if the Luger under Hansford's hand was found to be coated with blood on both sides of the grip, how would that affect your opinion?" There's no evidence of those facts; it's only an example. But that's a real question. Catts's question was no more than a fill-in-the-blank-later placeholder.

The close of Ragan's cross-examination by Catts brought some welcome comic relief. Catts got Ragan to admit that his eyes did not go 360 degrees around his head. When Catts tried to use Ragan to populate Williams's study with elephants once again, Ragan testified that, while he and Stevens were processing the scene, *no one else* was in the room. But Catts persisted. Ragan finally agreed that he couldn't guarantee that there had been nothing behind him in the room because he could not see out of the back of his head. Maybe crime scene investigators should start taking a Ghost Buster team along. Who knows what might be going on behind their backs in empty rooms.

What was the end result of Catts's cross-examination? The jury would have to answer that. Although the tactics and techniques employed by Catts weren't unique, that doesn't mean they can't be effective. Jurors can be distracted if enough chaff is released, and the tactic is difficult to counteract if the defense is willing to manipulate the evidence—such as swapping photos out of sequence. It becomes virtually impossible to anticipate defense counsel's moves because no evidence is safe, no matter how settled. It can become like trying to wage a gun battle in a house of mirrors. But that is the game as it is sometimes played.

On redirect by Spencer Lawton, Ragan went back to Catts's question about the likelihood of finding a hand gripping a weapon after someone is shot. Ragan repeated that it was extremely rare and that he had only seen it three times in his career. Lawton then asked Ragan how many times he had seen a hand on top of the gun and the thumb tucked underneath. Ragan's response: *never.*

Former ID Officer W. J. Gordon was back to confirm that he had not recovered any fingerprints from the Lugers, ammo clips, or individual rounds in the clips. With a fingerprint witness on the stand, the defense revived its complaint that the grandfather clock hadn't been dusted for prints—and received more unwelcome news.

Yes, Gordon told Catts, he was familiar with lacquered finishes and, yes, they could make good surfaces for prints, with one exception: If the furniture had been waxed or polished, it was not at all a good surface for fingerprints. There would be no more mention of the clock and fingerprints.

This had all been fairly low-impact cross-examination. The defense was churning the surface, tilling the ground to prep for its own witnesses, who would try to plant a doubt seed or two, hoping something could grow to "reasonable doubt" size before the case ended.

The exercise of sowing doubt can have a cumulative effect. If you're sitting on a jury in a murder case, you might be justified in assuming that something a lawyer brings up means something, especially if the lawyer brings it up with a tone of indignation. Keeping your eye on the ball is tough not only in major league baseball but also in the games lawyers play in a courtroom. In fact, they're counting on it.

On direct examination, Det. Jordan described his bagging of Hansford's hands at the scene. Repeating this testimony might seem unnecessary, but the reason will become clear later, and there are elements here that bear noting, in particular how specifically Det. Jordan describes his actions.

Q. Okay. Did you participate further in the processing of the crime scene at all?

A. Yes, sir, before the body was moved, I put paper bags on the hands—brown paper bags—I couldn't find any string, so I used evidence tape to secure them at the wrist. The body was then placed on a gurney and carried to the hospital.

At the autopsy later in the day, Jordan said he removed the bags and swabbed the hands. Jordan also repeated that he did the swabbing of Roger Parian's hands for the later GSR weapon tests on Luger 22A.

On cross-examination, Jordan repeated that, yes, he had put the bags on. They were paper bags and he used sticky tape, evidence tape, with "evidence" written on it, to secure them. He took the bags off himself at the autopsy. As to what happened to the bags, he assumed they were thrown out.

Leaving the bag question (it will be back), Jordan testified that, at Mercer House, he didn't go into the study at first but went in later. The people in there were Stevens and Ragan. He did not mention seeing elephants or poltergeists.

Catts then did something that both defense and prosecution lawyers would do throughout the trial. This isn't a trick so much as a technique, and it's used by both sides. The lawyer asks a witness about a subject on which the witness is not the primary witness. Particularly in criminal trials, areas of knowledge can overlap. If a secondary witness isn't fully informed or doesn't know the context of the question, it can be possible to get a "better" answer—meaning more favorable to your side—from the secondary witness. Although this tactic might fall into the category of technique rather than trick, it can also be used to mislead in the hands of someone who believes that misleading is a good thing.

Detective Jordan had already testified that he was not the lead detective on the case. He hadn't processed the scene or participated in the collection of the evidence. Nevertheless, Catts played the moving-items photo game with

Jordan. Jordan wasn't clued in at all to what the defense was up to. He was also surprisingly malleable, in my view. Professional witnesses should be aware of the less-informed-witness technique and should not tread into areas of the case with which they aren't totally familiar.

It would have been appropriate for Jordan to have said, "I really don't know anything about these photos, when or how they were taken—I wasn't involved in the processing of the scene," but he didn't say that. Instead, he looked at Photos A and B and either agreed or didn't agree that an item appeared to be in a different place in one or the other. This didn't require a detective. A spectator from the gallery could have done the same thing.

Jordan was asked about two photos showing papers and an envelope on the east end of the desk (Figures 40, 41). It isn't readily obvious, but the papers and two envelopes at the edge of the desk are slightly moved in the second photo. I have examined every photo taken that shows the papers or envelope. Every photo shows them in the same place, other than this second photo shown to Jordan (Figure 41). It appears from the contact sheets that this photo was not only taken after the first photo but might well have been the *last photo taken* in the study. Was this the Seiler–Catts defense to a murder charge, that an envelope unconnected to anything had moved an inch after the scene was processed?

Catts showed Jordan another two photos, comparing positions of rolled papers on top of a chest next to Williams's desk. Jordan did not agree that these photos showed movement; the appearance of movement was an optical illusion due to differing shot angles. The rolls hadn't moved at all. But a lawyer was willing to employ an optical illusion to suggest that they had. What those rolls of paper might have had to do with Williams's guilt, no one knew.

At least the prosecution knew where the defense was headed—down the same road as the defense in *Simpson*, *Spector*, or any other case in which the physical evidence convicts the defendant if the defendant's lawyers can't either explain it or blame it on somebody else.

The direct examination of Dr. Richard Draffin was uneventful. He repeated his autopsy findings from *Williams I*. But on cross, another clue was dropped. It appeared that the defense had come up with an answer to the burning question of who had put the chair on Danny Hansford's pants leg—Danny Hansford himself.

On cross by Catts, Dr. Draffin agreed that a body could theoretically go through involuntary "contractions" between "the time of being unconscious and the time of death." Catts then took it a step further, or several steps further. Was it possible that a person could *flail* his arms and *flail* his feet after receiving such wounds? Dr. Draffin said it was possible, again theoretically.

Dr. Draffin's choice of words was unfortunate. It is doubtful that the jury even heard the word "theoretically." The term "flail" was also not defined, demonstrated, or related to the *Williams* evidence. It was left general enough for the defense to fill in later. So the defense was going all-in. As outlandish as it might seem, they were going to blame the problem chair on the dead man.

John Wright Jones and Bobby Lee Cook might have been surprised at the tactic, considering they had made the point in the prior trial that such a suggestion was ridiculous. Perhaps they had not considered this new theory because they had been employing logic.

In setting up the "dead man did it" scenario, Catts was far more creative. He persuaded Dr. Draffin to accept a wholly inapplicable analogy. Catts likened a "cadaveric spasm" to "a chicken with its head cut off." A chicken with its head cut off runs around because much of a chicken's basic motor activity is programmed into its *hindbrain* (or *rhombencephalon*), which is left behind when the head leaves. If you shoot a chicken three times with a 9mm Luger, you do not get the same effect. In fairness, Dr. Draffin might not have been current on his chicken physiology. This misrepresentation was not corrected.

How was the defense going to reconcile the headless chicken that was surely flapping toward the courthouse with the testimony of the infallible Dr. Burton? In *Williams I*, he had said Hansford spun, went down and did not move, specifically citing the lack of blood anywhere but under the body to prove that Hansford *couldn't* have been moving around. Dr. Burton was on the witness list for the current trial. What were they going to do about Burton's prior testimony? What about Jones's assertion from *Williams I* that Hansford couldn't possibly have placed the chair on his own pants leg? There is no mechanism for raising a previous lawyer's representations from a prior trial. New jury-new story.

The flailing-chicken strategy was audacious, but the chair wasn't going anywhere—so the defense was getting creative. One fact would be frequently overlooked throughout the *Williams* case: There was an *eyewitness* to the event—Williams. Wouldn't he have mentioned something as remarkable as a dead man dancing the Funky Chicken from the '70s?

On redirect, Dr. Draffin backed up a bit. He cautioned that although "spasmodic cadaveric movement" was possible, he was not qualified to offer an opinion on how it might happen. It would have been better if, at the time Catts asked the question, Dr. Draffin had pointed out that he wasn't qualified to answer it. The notion that jury members disregard something they've heard is one of the grand fictions of trial practice.

Roger Parian's direct testimony replicated his previous testimony, but his cross provided more hints of what was coming. Someone had finally noticed there was a live 9mm round on the floor that needed an explanation.

Q. Okay. And the other round, which doesn't bear markings of damage that you would expect if it had been jammed, but does bear markings that are consistent with it having been chambered ...

A. Yes.

Q. ... could simply have been ejected by someone who wasn't aware that there was a round in the chamber when that person got ready to shoot the gun, correct?

A. That's correct, yes, sir.

While this was correct, it's not clear why the defense wanted to point it out as part of their cross-examination. The someone in the question could only have been Williams or Hansford. In the prior trial, Williams had rejected the possibility that it was Hansford. But new jury-new story, so anything was possible.

The final defense clue from the cross-examination of Roger Parian relates to the coup de grâce issue. The defense was going to attack the issue with another method, not involving Burton's string, shared bullet holes, or rotating bodies. They were going to use estimates of the distance of Williams's Luger from Hansford's body when each shot was fired to try to construct a scenario that would keep Williams behind his desk for all three shots.

At the autopsy, Dr. Draffin had taken tissue samples from the entrance wounds. Lab tests of this tissue for powder residue indicated that there had been no "close contact" between the weapon (Luger 23A) and Hansford's body. Parian testified that, based on these tests, the weapon would have been a minimum of eighteen inches away when the shots were fired. Eighteen inches isn't very far. Williams could easily have rounded his desk and shot Hansford once or twice again without being closer than eighteen inches away. But it was a start. Again, this cross-examination was only designed to lay a foundation for the defense's witness to come later.

Another issue raised by Catts involved a flagrant deception that would never be corrected. The issue wasn't critical but does illustrate how a misconception can be created when a witness doesn't pay attention. Catts had Parian confirm that Hansford's blood-alcohol content (BAC) was 0.09, based on the analysis of Hansford's blood taken at the autopsy. Parian hadn't taken the blood or performed the analysis. He was merely confirming a number on a printout, but this is the witness you ask if you're fishing for an answer you like.

Catts then pointed out, as if it meant something, that Hansford's blood sample had not been taken until twelve hours after the shooting. The inference?

If Danny's BAC was 0.09 twelve hours later, he must have been bloody drunk when the shooting occurred. The problem? Dead people *don't metabolize alcohol.* BAC levels can even *increase* after death, particularly if measured from blood (as in this case) rather than urine. Besides, Williams had testified in the prior trial that Danny was not drunk, but that didn't faze his lawyers. They were happy to mislead the jury. They should have cut it out. They didn't.

Before the next witness was called, there was a sideshow over Seiler's subpoena of a police officer to bring a book about crime scene investigation to court so Seiler could use it. Seiler didn't say why he couldn't buy his own copy of the book. The book was the personal property of SPD Officer Roy Willis, who had no connection to the case. Seiler merely wanted Ofc. Willis's book to use for the cross-examination of Cpl. Anderson.

How did Seiler know about the book? The book had been given to him by former DA Andrew J. Ryan Jr., whom Lawton had defeated in the previous election. Ryan had gotten the book from Willis, who had loaned the book to Ryan on condition that it never show up in a courtroom. Ryan had given the book to Seiler.

Seiler had given the book back when Willis confronted him about it but then had subpoenaed Willis to bring the book to court so he could use it to question Cpl. Anderson. To get to the bottom of what looks like a childish spat, Judge Oliver asked the threshold questions for use of any book, treatise, or article to cross-examine a witness: Was the witness familiar with the work, and did the witness consider it "authoritative" in the field. Anderson told Judge Oliver that he had never heard of the book. Oliver quashed Seiler's subpoena and Willis left with his book.

The prosecution had a new witness of its own in *Williams II*, Dr. George E. Gantner Jr., Chief Medical Examiner for the City of St. Louis and Professor of Forensic Pathology at the St. Louis University School of Medicine. The thinking appeared to be that it couldn't hurt to have more support for the prosecution case, particularly from someone with Dr. Gantner's resume who was not part of the Georgia law enforcement community. Dr. Gantner was qualified as an expert witness without objection.

He testified that he believed the head wound was the second wound and that the head had been on the floor when struck. We won't visit the details, for reasons already shared, but Dr. Gantner made an important point: *All* reference points involved in tracking a gunshot must align.

A. [I]nstead of just having the fixation of the line of fire through the body parts themselves ... we also have a third point of fixation, namely, where the bullet is found and what it strikes after it leaves the body. In both cases (the head and the back), the bullets are found adjacent to and, in one case, immediately beneath the body, as it lay on the floor.

In other words, bending a bullet's path is not allowed. Bullets don't do triangles. What was Dr. Gantner's overall conclusion about the event? Did Danny Hansford fire at Williams before Williams shot him?

A. [T]he shots from the gun on the desk occurred *before* the shot into the desk. In other words, the gun on the floor, in my opinion, was shot *after* the other three shots.

Q. Can you say how it is that you formed that opinion?

A. Based upon the fact that the paper overlies the gun, for one thing. And secondly, the lack of extensive blood on the weapon on the floor, despite extensive blood on the hand.

What about the chair and the flailing dead man notion? On cross-examination, Dr. Gantner agreed that "during the dying episode, I think it's possible to make movements, yes." The term "movements" wasn't defined but, rather, was left general for tactical reasons we've already covered. There was no headless chicken, but the questioning confirmed where the defense was headed.

The remainder of the cross-examination of Dr. Gantner goes to the heart of Lawyer Games. It could serve as a prosecution exhibit—in the prosecution of Seiler, not Williams.

Seiler asked Dr. Gantner if his opinion about the paper fragments would change if he were *shown a picture* with paper fragments *beneath* the gun. Of course, Dr. Gantner agreed. Of course, having asked the setup question, Seiler would now show Dr. Gantner the photo that Seiler was talking about—but he didn't.

Seiler had a photo he would use later (Figure 42), but he *didn't* show it to the witness he had just asked about it. He asked a hypothetical while *concealing* from the witness the evidence upon which the hypothetical was based. Here is Dr. Gantner's testimony:

Q. If you were shown a picture with fragments beneath the picture … beneath the pistol …

A. The weapon, mmm-hmm.

Q. … might that not alter your conclusion that you gave?

A. It would alter that particular issue, *yes*.

A prosecution expert was ready to change his opinion in favor of the defendant. Pull the picture out and present it, with a flourish if you like. Boom. What did Seiler do? Nothing. Why? No defense lawyer in their right mind would consciously set that up and leave it—not without a very good reason. By keeping the photo from Dr. Gantner, Seiler answered any question about what the picture really showed—or, more correctly, what it didn't show. We will return to the mystery photo scam shortly.

With regard to the next portion of this cross-examination, if you want your kids to grow up to be lawyers, you should first study what follows. First, Seiler had Dr. Gantner admit that he hadn't personally seen the infamous chair. Gantner pointed out that he understood the chair to be "no longer available." He was right. Seiler apparently wasn't aware that Gantner knew the truth and was quite willing to rely on an untruth if he could swing it. But that was only the beginning. Second, Seiler had Dr. Gantner admit that he had not visited the scene. Suggesting what? That, if he had, his testimony would have had more validity?

If Seiler was suggesting that being at the scene made testimony more valuable, the testimony of Ragan, Stevens, Anderson, and Jordan should have carried the greatest weight, because they were present while the scene was actually a scene. By 1983, the study was merely a room in a house.

What was Seiler doing? He was attempting to diminish the weight the jury might give to Dr. Gantner's testimony by pointing out that Gantner had not visited the scene of the crime, despite the fact that it was now 1983. Did it work? I don't know; I wasn't on the jury. However, the point here is not what the jury heard but, rather, what they did not hear.

What the jury did not hear was the reason Gantner hadn't visited the scene: defense counsel wouldn't let him. His request to visit the scene had been denied by the same defense team now pointing out that he had not visited the scene. This defense attempt at subterfuge was grossly deceptive. But it shouldn't have mattered. Surely this would be taken care of on redirect. The prosecution would simply ask Dr. Gantner to explain his answer to Seiler's question. The end result might be for the defense team members to begin to resemble a well-known reptile in the eyes of the jury.

Normally, that is exactly what would have happened, and the attempt to flimflam the jury would have been exposed. But it didn't happen. Not only wouldn't Judge Oliver allow Dr. Gantner to explain his answer on redirect, but he also prohibited District Attorney Lawton from even asking the question. As soon as Lawton stood, Seiler and Catts leapt to object to a question Lawton had yet to ask. They requested that the jury be removed from the courtroom—so the jury couldn't hear what they were up to—and then asked Judge Oliver to officially bless their effort to mislead the same jury.

In my personal opinion, if this is what you have to pull to win a case, you should have your license to practice law ripped from your greedy hands.

Judge Oliver would have no part of this, right? Wrong. Judge Oliver ruled with the defense. Dr. Gantner was not allowed to explain his answer, and the prosecution was not allowed to ask him to explain it in the presence of the jury.

What was the legal basis offered by the defense for their objection? The Fifth Amendment to the Constitution, the privilege against self-incrimination—applied to a house. They also threw in the Sixth Amendment right to counsel but anyone who can figure out that portion of the argument advanced by Catts is welcome to try.

Where did the defense come up with the legal authority to cite to the court? There wasn't any with the same factual basis as the current case. That isn't a red flag; it's a rotating beacon complete with fog horn. The lack of other cases on all fours with this one was probably due to the fact that the position they were taking was too ridiculous to have ever been raised by a lawyer with a straight face.

The privilege against self-incrimination applies to *oral statements* of the accused. It does not apply to the suspect's house, particularly when the house is a crime scene. The privilege also doesn't apply to blood, urine, hair, or even DNA, all of which are routinely secured from suspects without violating the Fifth Amendment.

Judge Oliver might well have been justified in issuing a search warrant for the same premises, even in 1983. Seiler had just taken the position, with his questions to Dr. Gantner, that the current condition of the premises was relevant to the case. The only question was relevance, not whether the site might be incriminating. Crime scenes are often incriminating. That's *why they're searched*. Nevertheless, Judge Oliver barred a witness from telling a jury in a murder trial the truth about an issue raised by the defense, not by the prosecution. How did this serve the interests of justice?

Was Dr. Gantner's testimony damaged by this sideshow? It's doubtful. The jury didn't observe this scene from the theatre of the absurd because they'd been removed from the courtroom. Dr. Gantner undoubtedly enhanced the State's case, but he might have returned to St. Louis shaking his head about the way cases were tried in Georgia.

Randall Riddell was back to talk about the topic of GSR. He confirmed that the Crime Lab used "flameless atomic absorption spectroscopy," and reported that, by the time of *Williams II*, he had performed 2,400 GSR tests. He reported the results of his analysis:

> Gunshot residue was deposited, and quite obviously, it's much, much higher than in the hand blank analysis [Parian's hand] or on the Hansford analysis [Danny's hand].

* * *

My conclusion is that it's *very unlikely* that Hansford fired a weapon—
that weapon.

This was the same conclusion that Riddell had reported in *Williams I*, but
was not based on the original 1981 weapon firing tests. The Crime Lab knew that
the defense had finally decided to test-fire the "attack" weapon. Dr. Howard had
flown the weapon to Dallas to the defense's chosen lab. With that knowledge in
hand, the State Crime Lab had also retested the weapon.

There was nothing wrong with the idea, in principle. The goal was to duplicate the new tests being run by the defense. However, *no* new test in 1983 could
duplicate the original conditions. There was no more original ammunition from
the Luger's clip, and the test hands were not swabbed by the same person who had
collected all the swabs in the original tests—Det. Jordan. It was possible that having two labs perform new tests would only produce two sets of less reliable results,
cluttering the GSR landscape. When clutter arrives, confusion follows.

For example, in the new State Crime Lab tests in Atlanta, new ammunition
was used, two different people fired the weapon, and two other people did the
swabbing. Some firings were done into a collection box two feet away, others into
a trap farther away. Eight firings were conducted. All produced "significant" levels of barium, and four of the eight produced "significant" levels of antimony (the
remaining four also produced antimony, but not above the threshold set by the
lab). Confusing?

Even so, these new tests did not alter Riddell's opinion: "Well, my opinion
has not changed. I still feel that it's significant that Hansford's hands are negative,
quite negative, as a matter of fact, and it's still very unlikely that he fired a
weapon." He then explained the difference between "negative" and true zero:

There is absolutely *no antimony* [on Hansford's hand]. This is—
believe it or not, negatives have values of small, medium or large.
There can be traces of metals that can be present, but yet still be negative. There's no antimony at all here, and these levels of barium are
essentially zero from an analyst's point of view, and I think that's significant.

Even though he confirmed his earlier opinion based on the Crime Lab's new
tests, Riddell pointed out that the original tests remained more meaningful and
better represented the conditions of the actual shooting.

The cross-examination of Riddell is confusing to me even today with the
benefit of calm contemplation. For the jury in the courtroom, it must have been
mind-numbing. All of Catts's cross focused on the new tests. Catts first separated
out the hand surfaces (front, back, right, and left), despite Riddell telling him this
was *not appropriate* in GSR test analysis. He did it anyway. Then, with the sur-

faces improperly separated, Catts pointed out that the levels didn't reach the lab's threshold in every test for each surface. Riddell had said the same thing in his direct testimony and had already explained why these results hadn't changed his opinion.

Catts's cross of Riddell did reveal another clue to upcoming testimony. Catts asked Riddell about the possibility that residue could be reduced by the hand rubbing across a "bloody cloth." Riddell said it was possible, in theory. But when had Danny Hansford's hand been rubbed with a bloody cloth? And what did "reduced" mean; reduced by how much? Hansford's hands were virtually free of any GSR trace elements.

Once again, it was only a setup question, using generalized terms, to be filled in later by a defense witness, a now-familiar technique. The question was so general that the only likely effect was to alert the prosecution that a bloody cloth was on its way.

On redirect, Lawton cut directly to the point:

Q. Mr. Riddell, of all the test-firings that you analyzed, the ones from Roger and the ones that were done in Atlanta, did you ever get antimony and barium levels as low as those found on the swabbings of Hansford's hands?

A. I don't believe I did. (Pause to check notes) No.

Spencer Lawton called Det. Ragan back to the stand briefly with respect to a subject Seiler had raised and left unresolved with Dr. Gantner—the question of paper fragments possibly having been beneath Williams's Luger on the desk. Ragan stated, emphatically, that he had removed the Luger from the desk and that there had been *no paper fragments* beneath it.

Despite this testimony, which could hardly have been more conclusive, and despite the lack of any evidence to the contrary, the defense wouldn't stop trying to place paper fragments underneath Williams's Luger. They had no choice. In the simplest terms possible, if there were no paper fragments underneath the Luger on Williams's desk, the attack by Danny Hansford had never happened.

Dr. Larry Howard was again in the anchor position. He was still director of the GBI Forensic Services Division and was up to some 7,000 forensic autopsies.

Based on personal research over many years, Dr. Howard disagreed with the uninformed notion that negative GSR tests didn't mean anything. He testified that it was probably easier to prove that somebody *hadn't* fired a gun than that they *had*, using GSR testing:

To prove they did fire a gun, you would need a certain level of residue. While, to prove they didn't fire a gun, if you had no residue at all and it could be shown that that weapon left residue, then there's no other conclusion except that individual did not fire a weapon.

He applied his reasoning to the *Williams* case:

It's my opinion that, based upon the results [of tests] performed by the Georgia Crime Laboratory, that the gun leaves residue in every case where we test-fired it, and that we found no evidence on Danny Hansford's hands ... he *could not* have fired that weapon.

As to the new 1983 tests, Dr. Howard put the mixed results in perspective:

[I]n every case, we were able—new and old ammunition—we were able to detect both antimony, sometimes in small amounts, but nevertheless detected, and large amounts of barium ... elevated levels of barium, up to 1.3, versus 0.02 on Hansford's hands. That's some *seventy times* the level of the - of Hansford's hands.

The 1983 retests of the Luger hadn't altered Dr. Howard's opinion—Danny Hansford *could not* have fired the weapon Williams claimed Hansford had used to attack him. Williams's defense was developing an unfortunate habit of running into science, and losing. His self-defense story wasn't merely questionable; it was scientifically impossible.

At this point in the *Williams* prosecution, a shift occurred in Dr. Howard's testimony. The temptation to prove what really happened proved difficult to resist. The trap for the prosecution: wanting to prove what really happened can add a burden of proof that you don't have under the law. And if the prosecution ever makes an assertion, whether or not obligated by law to do so, the defense will demand that the prosecution prove it, beyond a reasonable doubt. That is a certainty.

It's possible that the prosecution believed the jury was going to want to know what happened, even if convinced Williams was lying. It's not an unreasonable judgment. It carries the risk, however, that you can divert attention from disproving the defendant's theory to proving your own, and there are enough hurdles in a criminal case without setting more on the track. Nonetheless, at this point in *Williams*, Dr. Howard began to lay out his version of events. The first item was the shot through the back.

Dr. Howard believed the exit wound in the chest was a "shored" wound. A shored wound is an exit wound shored, or supported, by being pressed against some object (a floor or wall, for example). Normally, the issue of shoring relates to distinguishing between entrance and exit wounds. An exit wound that is shored can look similar to an entrance wound and can be mistakenly identified.

In this case, there was no doubt that the wound was an exit wound. A shored exit wound in the chest would only add another factor indicating that the body was on the floor when that wound was created: when Danny was shot in the back.

No other witness was convinced the wound was a shored wound, but Dr. Howard was, and he said so. The shored wound question didn't matter one way or the other, because a body can be on the floor with or without a shored exit wound. (We get to more detail on this point later with a defense witness.)

Dr. Howard's indulgence of the temptation to prove what happened ran into trouble when he decided to describe how the chair got onto its side:

The chair was knocked over backwards ... and the *only way* we can get that chair back and get those legs under the chair is for the chair to be knocked over backwards.

He was doing fine until he said "only." He was under no obligation to prove in which direction the chair fell. And though the chair could conceivably have toppled backward, it was extremely unlikely. I had considered that option at one point, but it doesn't fit with the skull fragment evidence. The seat had to have been facing Danny Hansford's head for the bloody fragment of Hansford's skull to have struck and stuck to the seat, and it would be very difficult to get the chair seat to face the body if the chair went over backward.

However, Dr. Howard had uttered the magic word "only." His testimony could now be discounted by finding *any* other way. This was a mistake, known to tennis fans as an unforced error. The State was under no obligation to prove the particularities of the chair's direction when it fell.

The fact that Williams had replaced the chair above the body was all that mattered to the prosecution of Williams. There was no need for Dr. Howard to pick a specific direction and declare it the only possibility. It was a misstatement with which he would be confronted later, would recognize, and would be forced to correct. This is an illustration of the danger in giving the defense something inconsequential upon which to hang some doubt.

Moving on, Dr. Howard addressed the possibility that the "attack" Luger had been dropped and still ended up with Hansford's hand perched on top of it. He noted *three* components of the required movement. The hand had to (1) come out from under the body, (2) rotate so that the palm was down, and (3) rise into the air.

Q. So would you say then—what likelihood there is in your opinion that the placement of the hand on the weapon there is—was done entirely by the victim himself?

A. I see *no* possibility.

The prosecution had been paying attention to the cross-examination of Randall Riddell. Lawton asked Dr. Howard if the bloody-cloth theory could explain the lack of residue on Hansford's hand. No, Howard said, because the *web area* of the hand is swabbed, not the flat back of the hand. Next up was the Funky Chicken:

> Q. Can you say how long he might have been—he might have had the possibility of involuntary movement during that period?
> A. Not very long, because of the precipitous, very rapid drop of blood pressure in the brain, and this is essential for the operation of the nervous system.
>
> * * *
>
> Q. So is there—will you state what in your opinion is the likelihood that the victim himself ... is responsible for getting his pants leg up under there.
> A. I see *no* possibility.

Next, the skull fragment from the toppled chair made a brief appearance. As we know, the chair had no choice but to be on its side facing Hansford, which would mean the seat would have been vertical. Dr. Howard explained: "Skull fragments are always associated with blood—we see at many crime scenes, skull fragments stuck to vertical walls, so that's no different."

Dr. Howard made another point that was more difficult to follow, regarding the fact that Danny Hansford almost certainly wasn't where Williams said he was when Williams shot him. A diagram we've created makes his point clearer than it sounds from his testimony alone. According to the autopsy, the first shot entered Hansford's chest 3 cm left of center, traveled slightly downward, and lodged beneath the skin in the back, 4 cm right of center. That's a right-to-left difference (facing Hansford) of 7 cm, or approximately 2.76 inches.

Our diagram shows how changing Danny's position along the desk more closely matches the geometry of this bullet's path (Figure 33). For now, refer to the figures at the opposite corners of the desk (the center figure becomes relevant later). If Danny moves to Williams's left, the bullet path is much closer to the actual path the bullet took, according to the autopsy. This was merely another factor proving that Danny Hansford was far more likely to have been at the east end of the desk when Williams shot him, not at the far corner. This diagram is new.

With that, the new defense team got its first crack at the venerable Dr. Howard. When Austin Catts got to the radioactive chair, he went immediately to Dr. Howard's reconstruction. The focus was now on Dr. Howard's scenario rather than on Williams's story.

Catts asked Dr. Howard if he had actually tested his theory of the shooting and the toppling chair. Dr. Howard explained that there was no way to do that without a person shot through the aorta and collapsing to the floor. "It is impossible to perform a valid experiment that teaches us that, or that shows us that, because you can't duplicate the condition of the body."

The defense likely didn't shoot anybody to test their version of the event either, but the focus had now moved to Dr. Howard's theory of the toppled chair, which he had to defend. Catts suggested that the location of the skull fragment on the chair seat was not consistent with a chair knocked over backward. He was right. Of course, there was no explanation at all for the skull fragment if the chair had remained upright, but the defense was happy to talk about Dr. Howard's theory instead—all because Dr. Howard had decided to weigh in with his "only way" pronouncement.

When the cross-examination reached blood on the Luger, Catts broadcast another element of the upcoming defense by trying set it up through Dr. Howard. Dr. Howard acknowledged the small spot of blood on the trigger guard. But when Catts asked about blood on the slide of the gun and on the grip, Dr. Howard cut him off at the pass. Howard was no rookie. He knew this meant the defense was going to put somebody on the stand to say that they had found blood on the slide of the gun and the grip—even though Roger Parian hadn't been able to detect any, even using benzidine.

Anticipating what was coming, Dr. Howard did something a truly experienced witness can do when faced with the setup technique. He used the opportunity to preview for the jury what was coming from the defense and put it into context up front, rather than leaving a blank for a defense witness to fill in however they liked later.

Dr. Howard told Catts that undetected sub-microscopic blood in those locations was entirely consistent with the evidence: Hansford's hand had dried blood all over it, so a microscopic trace wasn't important; the key was the *quantity* of blood. Dr. Howard also had a sense of humor:

Q. Dr. Howard, can you answer the question?
A. I am aware that the benzidine test showed a trace of blood on the
handle and that blood was not visibly present on the handle, and that
the benzidine test further is capable of demonstrating blood on an
Egyptian mummy.

On redirect, Dr. Howard explained his mummy reference. He revealed that Benzidine detects blood in parts per *billion*. A blood trace that might have been detected using Benzidine had nothing to do with the amount of blood that should have been on the Luger under Hansford's hand, if he had gripped it.

With that, the State rested its case in *Williams II*. The defense had revealed a lot about their case. They had also revealed a lot about how the trial would be conducted. The members of the defense in this case resembled legal juvenile delinquents—condescending, abrasive, and not much interested in the truth if it couldn't help them. The profile is not uncommon.

THE *WILLIAMS* DEFENSE, ROUND TWO

Williams himself kicked off his defense in the second trial. Leading with the defendant is bold. Its effectiveness depends on the defendant. Putting Williams up front, unafraid, and sure of himself sounds good in theory. Considering his undisguised arrogance, I might have held him back until the experts had tried to soften up the enemy's case.

Williams said he had been living in Mercer House for twelve years, having bought the "entire city block for fifty-five thousand dollars." He kicked off his testimony with an exaggeration, but the jury didn't know any better and it was wholly irrelevant. But, for trivia buffs, Mercer House sits on what originally was known as a trust lot, two each of which sat on the east and west boundaries of the original squares set out by James Oglethorpe, founder of the colony. It wasn't a city block as we normally understand the term, but who really cared.

This was a habit of Williams. He exaggerated and embellished everything, whether the thing was important or trivial. Over time, the effects of exaggeration and embellishment can seep through to a jury, whether or not each item matters, standing alone.

Williams listed the accessible weapons in the house, five of which were loaded and ready: one in the living room, one in the entrance hall, one in the study, one in the back library (the one he would have used to shoot me, presumably), and one in his bedroom upstairs.

In the first surprising new twist, Williams *admitted* to a sexual relationship with Danny Hansford. Strategically, this was smart. The lie during *Williams I* had been obvious and only resulted in the ruse being exposed on rebuttal. But not so fast. Williams admitted having sex with Hansford, but claimed it was no more than a trifle:

And by, oh, I suppose, November, December '79, he had *his girlfriend*, I had *mine*. But to me, sex is just a natural thing. We'd had sex a few times. Didn't bother me. Didn't bother him. I had *my girlfriend*, he had *his*. It was just an occasional thing that happened.

"He had his girlfriend, I had mine" was a brand-new theme for Williams, and he liked it so much, he said it twice in the same passage. Would a jury find this new story believable? Williams had been having sex with Hansford since 1979 but it was no big deal? How occasional was this sex? Did the "girlfriends" know about this occasional sex? Williams described it as an afterthought, like trying red wine one night rather than white.

The more startling disconnect was that there had never been any sign of a Williams girlfriend anywhere. Was one of them on her way? I would have put at least one of them on the stand to talk about playing games at Mercer House with Danny and Debbie. Without a shred of a doubt, if such a woman existed, the defense would put her up, if only as a character witness.

There's an unspoken promise in trial that claiming a fact in testimony carries an obligation to prove it at some point before your case is completed. This new version of the relationship should have started Williams's nose growing like Pinocchio on steroids—but in accordance with new the jury–new story strategy, Williams admitted to being "half pregnant" and left it at that.

Having described sex with Danny Hansford as unimportant, Williams then described the lower life form—Danny Hansford—with whom he had been having this unimportant sex. Williams claimed that Danny had been on drugs, angel dust (which neither Williams nor anyone else connected to the case had ever mentioned), and marijuana at various times. According to Williams, Danny could be totally charming but then would go off like a "cocked rattlesnake" and "you didn't have to give him a reason for it to happen."

Williams was setting up his defense so obviously that it looked like a child drawing with really big crayons. He repeatedly made the point that you didn't have to give Danny a reason to "go raging." It was critical for the defense that Danny "go raging" without a reason because there was no reason anywhere in Williams's self-defense story for Danny Hansford to have tried to kill him. Thus appeared the first report of a "cocked rattlesnake" in North America.

Continuing the portrait of Hansford as drugged and disturbed, Williams gave a play-by-play of a purported 1980 Hansford suicide attempt. The reason for use of the term "purported" here is that Williams claimed Hansford swallowed a bottle of pills and immediately told Williams what he'd done. Most people trying to commit suicide don't rush to tell somebody that they just swallowed the pills that are supposed to do the job—not if they mean it. Regardless, this event will be called a suicide attempt. Danny swallowed pills in August of 1980. He told Williams. He was taken to Memorial Medical Center, where his stomach was pumped.

Within this story was a glaring fallacy by Williams that would never be resolved. Williams claimed that Danny overdosed on Limbitrol that Dr. DeHaven had prescribed to Williams. Limbitrol is a prescription medication for anxiety and depression, not hypoglycemia, and Williams wasn't being treated by Dr. DeHaven in August of 1980. He didn't see Dr. DeHaven for the first time until eight months later. Where did the Limbitrol come from? Make a note of this for later.

Williams continued with the attempted-suicide tale. After Danny's stomach was pumped at Memorial Medical Center, he was placed in Clark Pavilion, the psych wing. He woke up and went nuts. Williams claimed that Danny "tore up" Clark Pavilion and "beat up three orderlies." No witness from these facilities who testified would ever recall any such thing.

Why did the defense bring up this suicide event? To show that Williams saved Danny's life in 1980. Williams's alternative would have been to call no one and wait for Danny to die or to do whatever a massive dose of Limbitrol might make him do. But the clear suggestion was that, if Williams called EMS in 1980, he couldn't have erupted in anger and shot Danny in 1981.

People erupt in anger and kill friends, family and lovers to whom, at other times, they've sworn oaths of love and devotion, and they do it with alarming frequency. But this testimony was laying a foundation. The talking points were: (1) the relationship was no big deal, even if it involved a little sex, (2) Danny Hansford was a drugged-out psycho, and (3) Williams was unfortunate to have chosen a cocked rattlesnake's life to save.

Continuing with this theme, Williams described Danny's 1979 Georgia Regional admission. He described it slightly differently than he had in *Williams I*: "He told me he had been in there *several times*. He'd get in there for *various reasons*." Again, Williams was unable to tell the simple truth. Danny went to Georgia Regional twice for a total of four days: in 1975 at age fifteen and in 1979 after a drunken beating by his landlord.

Maybe the jury didn't notice the frills that Williams attached to every story, but his lawyers noticed. Some things Williams had said before needed fixing, such as the nine marijuana cigarettes at the drive-in. The Lawyer Games tool is simple: change the answer.

Q. What about marijuana? Did you personally see him use any marijuana that night?

A. Yes, sir, I did. He told me he had been smoking it *all day*. Later that night, he told me that he had consumed nine joints and he still had a bag of *green leafy material* in his possession he hadn't burned up at that point.

Williams changed the story he had told the *Georgia Gazette* and to which he had already testified under oath in the previous trial. He simply took the nine joints and spread them out over the entire day. Also note how Williams describes the bag of pot. He calls it a bag of "green leafy material." That's a law enforcement phrase. It is not used by ordinary people. Any chance that this testimony was rehearsed?

Here's another example involving the simplest of questions eliciting an answer that spun off into Wonderland: Seiler asked Williams what time they left the house and when they got back from the movie. Williams replied, "[W]e left for the late movie around ten-thirty, and I guess we got out of that thing around ten-thirty, eleven-thirty, twelve-thirty or maybe a little later, but not much later."

Is this trivial detail? Should it matter? Detail always matters, often because it's not assigned as much care in the crafting of a story as the larger elements. When a witness is all over the place on insignificant details, it's a red flag. Embellishing everything they say can also indicate something more serious, a psychological imbalance. The *Williams* juries were seeing only one case at a time, however. Something that subtle might be difficult for a jury to pick up from testimony in a single case. But, at a minimum, the testimony can sound odd to the rational mind.

There was another disconnect within the tale Williams told this jury about the Europe trip. He was asked how Danny felt about being kicked off the trip, and he answered that both he and Danny were "as happy as we could be" with the substitution of Goodman on the trip. Here's the conflict: Everyone was as happy as fat clams, but when Danny went "raging" and attacked him, Williams's solution was to call Goodman—about the trip. Why, if the trip had nothing to do with Danny raging?

The prosecution had a choice to make with respect to these recurring inconsistencies. It would require messy and lengthy cross-examination to take Williams step by step through his testimony and highlight every conflict. There was a danger of distracting the jury by chasing Williams into the magic forest. Was it a better idea to stick to the simple evidence that he couldn't refute?

Meanwhile, what was the defense doing with this testimony? In boxing terms, they were bobbing and weaving. It was diversion and obfuscation. The defense couldn't allow a lovers' quarrel, because a lovers' quarrel involves *two* lovers. A raging madman requires only *one* madman. So the quarrel was erased from the security tape.

The problem was, the remaining story still had grotesque inconsistencies. Danny was in a rage. Then Williams called Goodman and canceled the trip, and raging Danny was calm—even though nobody cared about the trip in the first place. The moment the call ended, Danny decided to kill Williams because—we don't know.

That was the fundamental flaw in Williams's self-defense claim: *There was no "because" in this case.* It made no human sense for Danny Hansford to kill Williams without the slightest provocation. If Danny Hansford killed Williams Saturday morning, where was Danny sleeping Saturday night? Quite seriously, I would like to have asked Williams if Danny Hansford was in his will.

Williams testified, "I had not said one word to him … at all. I was just listening. He was just raging." Williams was a mere bystander, not a combatant:

And he kept screaming about these *other* people. He never addressed me, Mr. Seiler, personally at all. He never said, "Williams, you've done this, or you haven't done that." He was talking about three *other* different people.

No trip. No quarrel. Just a sudden decision to kill the source of everything he had: home, booze, pot, car, clothes and cool new video game. In essence, Danny railed about everybody on the cattle drive, then turned around and shot his own horse.

Williams rolled on, saying Danny threw him against the door in the hallway. "I was scared to death. I had never seen anybody in such a rage in my life, and he was screaming and looking crazy." Danny had gotten stronger since the first trial: "[H]e came raging out behind me, screaming obscenities about these people, and he grabbed me by the throat with one hand—he had the strength of ten men—felt like *a hundred men*." Then, as before, Williams was walking into his study.

Having escaped to his study, Williams tried to call the police while Danny was "raging up and down the hall." Had I been at counsel table at this point, I would have been tempted to shout, "We got it already—he was raging, raging, raging—can we all agree he was raging so I don't have to hear that word again!"

But the raging didn't stop. As soon as Williams punched a couple of numbers, Danny raged into the study. Williams thought quickly. He called Goodman.

Williams had "never seen anybody in such a rage." Danny was "screaming and looking crazy." But when Williams got Goodman on the line, Danny grabbed the phone and sounded normal, according to Joe Goodman's testimony.

The reason this testimony sounds disconnected is because it *was* disconnected. Williams and Seiler were going down the list of things they needed to put in the story, but they paid no attention to what was missing: normal human behavior. The madman had Williams by the throat in the hallway and then Williams is in his study. The madman is raging but then he's on the phone talking to Goodman. The phone is hung up and the madman is immediately raging again and decides to kill the man who hadn't done or said a thing to provoke him.

It is important that juries listen to stories like this with their common sense on full alert. When the story sounds like there's something wrong with it, there is something wrong with it. If it sounds out of sync, that's because it is out of sync. It's a good idea for jurors to keep their healthy skeptic cards current. And yes, the theory applies to both sides and all witnesses; testimony is testimony.

The attack story continued: Williams heard "a big crash, and another one," then "several other crashing sounds." How long did this take? "[T]wo seconds, three seconds," because "he was moving like lightning, and he came back in the room." Hansford had the strength of a hundred men and moved like lightning.

If Williams had told a fish story, the jury might have heard about the whale caught with kite string and a safety pin.

One item was still missing. The defense had asked Roger Parian about the live round on the floor. The prosecution had to expect Williams's story to change, to add Danny circling out toward the fireplace, stopping and cocking his Luger before trying to shoot Williams. But here is what Williams said instead:

> He had a pistol in [his hand] that I didn't see until he turned, *right at the end of that desk*. He said, "I'm leaving this town tomorrow, but you're leaving tonight." And he took that gun *right up*, and he started firing.

The live round on the floor was still there. The question to Roger Parian about the origin of that round, asked by the defense, hadn't been asked accidentally. Lawyers at this level don't ask questions by accident. So, had Williams forgotten to add something to his new story for his new jury? Somebody ejected that round onto the rug. According to Williams's own testimony, he was the only one who could have done it.

Another hole in his story that could send him away for a long time was the presence of paper fragments *on top* of the Luger. Recall that in *Williams I,* he had said he looked at the body, went back around, put down his gun, and made his calls. That wasn't good enough, now that the defense realized what the paper fragments meant—one benefit of a practice trial.

Seiler had set up his paper-under-the-gun scam with Dr. Gantner. But there was also debris *on top* of the gun. The defense had to fix this—as well as the paper under the gun—or game over. In the prior trial, Williams had been adamant that he hadn't "intentionally move[d] anything or ... disturb[ed] any evidence." But his memory had improved with age. Now, "[w]hatever it was, if it was in my way, I threw it away. I threw it and moved it." He'd changed his story once again.

But that wasn't yet good enough; he hadn't patched the hole. Seiler needed Williams to do something specific with a specific item. What did Seiler do? He didn't bother with the witness; he simply testified. This was Seiler's next question: "What were you *looking for under the papers*?" Williams hadn't used the words "looking," "under," or "papers," but Seiler didn't waste time; he just supplied the answer that he wanted on his own, by putting it in his question. It's called leading your own witness. Yes, it's a violation of the rules of evidence.[96]

In evaluating testimony, as this jury was charged with doing, it's totally reasonable to put oneself in the position of the witness. Assuming a witness made the statement Williams had made and the lawyer's next question was "What were you looking for under the papers," how might a witness react? "Wait ... what?" or something similar might be a reasonable response.

How did Williams react? He gave Seiler the rehearsed answer without even blinking: "Joe Goodman's phone number." Seiler jumped Williams's line, in the parlance of the professional actor. Just like in a play, Williams gave Seiler the next line in the script, without any sign of a problem.

Does it really matter that Seiler was leading his witness by the nose? It should. But there's more to the tale than the clear indication that it had been rehearsed in advance. It also wasn't true. This too-convenient new version had Williams looking for a number that he didn't need. All in all, there were at least *six* flaws in this orchestrated lie.

First flaw: What bright bulb on the defense team decided the answer would be Joe Goodman's number? Just because Goodman was the first one Williams called after the shooting? Not very smart. Rewind Williams's story to the first call. He'd gotten away from a raging Danny Hansford earlier and retreated into his study. He was dialing the police when Hansford burst in and said, "Who are you calling?" Williams stopped, receiver in hand, said he was calling Joe Goodman, and dialed Goodman's number. Williams didn't need to look up Goodman's number. Why not? He knew Goodman's number.

Second flaw: If, for the sake of argument, Williams actually didn't know Goodman's number and had managed to get away with looking it up after Danny surprised him—this had taken place before the *first* call, not the second. If Williams had needed to look it up, he had already looked it up.

Third flaw: If Williams needed to look up Goodman's number—for a second time—his phone register was right there on the desk (Figure 9). Why would he look under the papers for it? Even if he had looked it up the first time and written it on a piece of paper, had he then *buried* it under the papers on his desk?

Fourth flaw: The "attack" bullet ripped through the stack of papers on the desk twice. Was there a piece of paper from "under the papers" with Joe Goodman's number written on it and a bullet hole through it? No. So if such a paper existed at all, it wasn't in the stack that contained the paper debris.

Fifth flaw: The papers were on the west end of the desk and in the drawer (Figures 34, 35). Aside from the fact that Goodman's phone number wasn't in the stack, the papers weren't near the Luger.

Sixth flaw: Despite creative photo angles and suggestive questions, there still weren't any paper fragments *under* the Luger. Detective Ragan confirmed that (and Seiler's photo scam will be exposed before this trial ends). Therefore, the paper debris cloud was created *after* the Luger was on the desk; there was no other possibility. So Williams looking for Goodman's number, even if nice in theory, clearly wasn't the explanation for the debris on the gun.

With that, it was time for Williams's favorite pastime—being cross-examined by Spencer Lawton. This new jury was new for the prosecution as well. They needed to meet the James Williams not shown in the glossy sales brochure.

Lawton began by making clear to the jury who the "gun man" was. He took Williams through the five loaded pistols that Williams kept around the house, including his carry-out pistol in the hall. Then Lawton took Williams through his 1975 burglary report, in which he had claimed thirteen weapons and 650 rounds of ammunition had been stolen. Williams denied the ammunition number and blamed the police. "The police wrote the report. I didn't write the report." The police were already misremembering things about him back in 1975.

Williams had testified on direct about the infamous April incident and had noted that photos were taken of the damages, for insurance purposes. But no, Williams told Lawton, he never filed a claim for either the April or May damage to his property. That would include his $10,000 (or $20,000) grandfather clock.

So how about the relationship with Danny? Back to the April incident, Williams and Goodman had bailed Danny out after having him arrested. Seiler had covered it on direct, but Williams had done the usual, misremembering his own story to suit himself. Lawton took him back to it. Williams had told Seiler it was no big deal that he had bailed Danny out of jail. According to Williams, he was all the time bailing people out of jail. When asked by Lawton on cross, however, Williams couldn't recall anyone he had ever bailed out of jail—other than Danny Hansford.

What about the Europe trip?

Q. Did Danny ever express any unhappiness at not getting to go on the trip?

A. Mmm-hmm. The night of the shooting, when he was raging about everything else, he referred to it very, very lightly, something about "Goodman has taken my trip away from me."

Goodman took his trip away? Didn't Williams toss Danny off the trip in a blow for a drug-free America? Now Danny was mad at *Goodman*, who'd had nothing to do with it?

As for the April event, there is no point in repeating Williams's rambling narrative. It's on pages 836–841 of the *Williams II* trial transcript. There could be a contest to see who could spot the most whoppers in one story. Williams testified that *Danny* told the police "this is just a domestic dispute." (That was what Cpl. Anderson had told Williams.) Rather than one gun, this time Danny had two guns, and when the police showed up, Danny went upstairs "with the guns in his hands" and the police "hot on him." Upstairs, Hansford "bodily attacked" the police officers—though not according to the police officers, the police report, the charges, or any of Williams's other accounts of the same event.

Williams probably didn't enjoy being on trial for murder, but he reveled in telling his tales. His rambling narration of the April incident goes on for five pages, during which he actually left the stand so he could *address the jury*. Judge Oliver eventually told him to return to the stand and sit down.

Williams's behavior and stream of small lies are deeply revealing. Maybe I find them more troubling than a jury might, but I'm convinced that if Williams's blizzard of fallacies could have been rolled out on a screen like end credits in a movie, it would have been difficult for a jury to believe anything he said.

Spencer Lawton asked Williams about his statement to Cpl. Anderson about refusing to go play a Superman game with Danny.

Q. Are you then denying that you made that statement?
A. Oh, absolutely. Anderson didn't listen to anything. There were so many people in that room, you couldn't move for policemen.

Who had said the statement he *didn't make* was made in the study? Note also, he's thrown in a room so packed with "so many people" that "you couldn't move." He threw in a talking point from the defense checklist, though it was totally unrelated to the question he was asked.

As for his interview with the *Georgia Gazette*, he said, "Newspaper men have been just about as bad as Mr. Anderson, writing things down that I'd have quoted."

A. I wasn't in court at the Gazette. That's the newspaper, and they write just about anything you want to—they want to.
Q. Are you denying—what are you saying? That you didn't tell them that?
A. I'm just saying you can tell newspapers the truth, and it can come out so warped you wouldn't believe what you told them.

It was a recurring problem for Williams—he kept saying one thing and people kept writing down something else.

In his prior trial, Williams had said that he sat in his office chair after the shooting. That would have meant he sat on bullet and paper fragments, which had been pointed out. This time around? He told Lawton he sat on the edge of his desk: new jury-new story.

A danger of changing stories to fix conflicts is that you can create new conflicts. As to Williams's story about where he sat, he couldn't sit in his chair this time, so he claimed he sat on the edge of the desk. The problem was that there was nowhere on the edge of his desk for him to sit (Figure 9). There are so many layers to this soufflé that it can be mind-numbing to track them, but I still contend that the trouble is worth it.

It's also important to remember when parsing these stories that Williams had to change his story to fit his *fictional* account, not the truth. Did he sit in his office chair? Quite possibly. It's what he said the first time through, before he thought about the paper and bullet fragments found in the seat. Sitting in the chair was only a problem in the *contrived* version of what happened. If he fired the fake attack shot himself, the paper and bullet fragments weren't in his chair until later.

Lawton moved to the gold necklace. Williams said Danny had earned it. If the jury still believed Danny was a part-time gofer, it must have looked like a pretty good gig. At his pay rate, if Danny had worked full time, he might have had his own mansion.

Williams gave the jury a glimpse of how sensitive he was on the subject of Danny Hansford when he blurted out, "[H]e was a hustler on Bull Street selling himself to anybody who wanted to pay for it." At least Williams was in the same universe as the truth for once. Danny *had been* a hustler on Bull Street, selling himself to anybody who wanted to pay for it. But by early 1981, he was selling himself only to Williams, who wanted it and paid for it willingly.

The second edition of Spencer Lawton's cross of James Williams complete, it was time to hear from the reinforcements that the new team had brought in to patch the holes in the Good Ship Williams.

Dr. Irving C. Stone took the stand. Dr. Stone testified that he was head of the Physical Evidence section of the Institute of Forensic Sciences in Dallas. The institute was a Dallas County organization and he was a Dallas County employee. He was on leave and was being paid by the defense. Dallas County apparently had a system like DeKalb County, Georgia, which allowed employees to moonlight and make a few extra bucks.

Stone was there to shore up three areas of the defense case. First was the firing position of Williams when he fired the shots. Second was the GSR issue. Third, Stone would attempt to answer a question that had not received much attention—how Hansford could miss a 6'2" target from point-blank range and hit the top of Williams's desk instead.

First up, where was Williams when he shot Hansford? Keep in mind that this goes *only* to the coup de grâce question. If the defense could keep Williams behind his desk, it wouldn't prove that he shot Hansford in self-defense, but at least it wouldn't prove the opposite. Dr. Stone's approach was to establish distances from Williams's Luger muzzle to Hansford's body and then draw conclusions about Williams's position based on those distances. At least, that was the theory.

The jury had heard Roger Parian describe his tests of tissue samples for powder residue and suggest that, based on his analysis, Williams's weapon muzzle could have been as close as eighteen inches from Hansford's skin. Eighteen inches wasn't far enough away for the defense. So, in search of a better answer, Dr. Stone tested Hansford's shirt for gunpowder particulates.

Because Stone's tests dealt with the shirt, his testimony was limited to the shot in Hansford's back. Basically, if Stone could prove Williams's Luger couldn't have been closer than X to Danny's back and Williams coming around the desk would make the shot closer than X, the defense could claim that Williams couldn't have come around the desk. That's the general idea and far more simple than the question will soon become.

Fundamentally, this is similar to the method employed by Dr. Burton in his tricked-up demonstration in *Williams I*. Show that a particular scenario put Williams in the wrong position (or in Stone's variation, distance from the body) for Williams to have come around the desk to fire the shot—the shot to the back in this case. In *Williams I*, Burton circled the desk in the wrong direction to demonstrate that the angles didn't work. This time, Dr. Stone would give the defense numbers to work with, but the theory was the same.

Roger Parian had gotten them eighteen inches away from Hansford's skin. Parian had also discussed cloth, such as the shirt, on cross-examination by Seiler, as Seiler prepared a platform for his own witness. Parian had tested both weapons for their discharge of gunpowder residue (in addition to his tests for GSR). Here is part of his exchange with Seiler:

Q. Which would be consistent with the distance from the muzzle of the firing weapon to the wound being eighteen inches or any distance thereafter.

A. Yes, sir.

Q. Really more likely to be *four feet* in fact, wouldn't it?

A. *No*. I did make some tests with these weapons, and they will throw powder - *two feet will be the limit*, but now with tissue, you'd have to be a little closer for it to adhere. ... *Two feet would be like on material*, cloth or paper. But with this weapon on tissue, I think you'd have to be closer for anything to adhere, so the first statement I think was more correct. Eighteen inches on back ... .

So according to Roger Parian's tests—which had been performed at the time of the event, using ammunition of the same brand and caliber as the ammunition in both weapons—Williams's Luger muzzle only needed to be two feet away to find no powder reside on the shirt. Two feet was still too close, which was why

Seiler tried to throw four feet into his question. It didn't work. Seiler would have to wait for his own, more accommodating, witness. He would also need some more accommodating gunpowder particles, because Luger 23A didn't have a stake in the outcome and wasn't being paid a fee by either side—rock, paper, scissors, science.

Dr. Stone dealt with two questions: (1) were gunpowder particles found on the shirt and, depending on the answer to that question, (2) how far away would the muzzle of Williams's Luger have to have been when Williams shot Hansford in the back? For an extreme example, if there were no particles found and, based on the weapon's characteristics, you should find particles with this Luger anywhere within 200 feet from the shirt, Williams would have to have been outside the house when he fired the shot. The lower the number becomes, the closer Williams could have been. The goal for the defense, if possible, was to keep Williams so far away that he couldn't have fired the shot by coming around his desk.

What might we guess Dr. Stone would say? The weapon and shirt had already been tested. The shirt was collected by Det. Jordan at the autopsy and sent to the Crime Lab. There was no gunpowder or muzzle blast found on the shirt.[97] Would Stone agree with Roger Parian, that two feet was the limit for this Luger to throw and deposit gunpowder residue on material? Dr. Stone didn't come from Dallas just to agree with Roger Parian.

So Stone performed his own tests of Luger 23A. Stone fired the Luger and found "detectable residues" up to three feet—none at all beyond three feet. I wasn't there but I do wonder how there is residue at exactly thirty-six inches but none whatsoever at thirty-six and one half inches. It's difficult to believe that the cut off is that precise, but that was Stone's testimony. (Yes, this same question would apply to Parian's two feet.) Because Dr. Stone found no gunpowder particles on the shirt, he then concluded that Williams's Luger muzzle had to be more than three feet from Hansford's back when that shot was fired: "So effectively, three feet of range is the furthest that that Williams Luger will deposit gunshot residues on cloth." Neat and tidy.

Was three feet far enough to preclude Williams having come around the desk? We can all perform our own re-enactments, circle a desk and point at an imaginary body. I've done it and easily fired that shot with the muzzle of the weapon (in my case, a WWII .45 semiautomatic, not having a Luger handy) thirty-six inches away and I'm three inches shorter than Williams was, but that's hardly scientific. Regardless, we can all agree that three feet is far better than two feet. But it still wasn't up to the four feet that Seiler wanted. So here was Seiler's big finish:

> Q. Would the findings of that test be consistent with Jim Williams firing these shots from behind the desk at a distance of *four to five feet*?

Or more?

A. Yes.

Yes, "four to five feet" is more than three feet. So is five hundred feet. Stone's "findings" were that Williams fired the shot from beyond three feet, not "four to five feet." And Stone's findings said nothing about where Williams was when that shot was fired. But Seiler suggested with his question that Stone had done just that, skipping right past the three feet to which his witness had testified to the four feet—or more—that he was after. It's only a slight exaggeration that Seiler might have testified as much in this trial as some of his witnesses.

Note what else Seiler did. He used "these shots" while Stone's analysis only dealt with the shirt. As we know, the shots to the chest, head and back were all quite distinct.

To caution, we are taking this evidence in isolation. There is ample evidence, from bullet entry and exit points, bullet path, recovered bullet location and ejected cartridge location, that Williams didn't fire the shot to the back from behind his desk. We're examining the defense approach to the case, however, and this exercise is illuminating.

We still have Parian at two feet and Stone at three feet. How do we reconcile these tests? We don't have to. Neither conclusion was valid for the purpose for which the defense was trying to use Stone's test: to establish—to the inch—how far away Williams was when he fired into Hansford's back. The flaw wasn't the test, but rather the shirt.

Looking at Dr. Stone's shirt analysis (Roger Parian was never asked these questions by either side in the case), it ignored the *facts of the case* in which he was testifying. His analysis assumed an *undisturbed* shirt (in his case, a piece of cloth in his lab) tested *immediately* after the weapon was fired (which was what Stone had done in his lab).

This shirt was the shirt Danny Hansford was wearing on May 2, 1981. The shirt had been enclosed in a body bag for transport, traveled with the body through the emergency room, to radiology, back to the morgue, was removed from the body for the autopsy, stuffed into a plastic bag and sent to the Crime Lab. The defense had been adamant that Hansford's hands had to be protected—as they had been by bagging at the scene. Had the shirt been removed from the body at the scene and secured in a paper evidence bag? No. There were no efforts made to preserve and protect the shirt.

By the time Dr. Stone saw the shirt, it had been removed from Crime Lab storage, taken to court for trial in *Williams I*, returned to storage, sent in 1983 to Dr. Howard in Atlanta, taken by Dr. Howard on an airplane to Dallas, and unbagged for examination by Dr. Stone. Yet Dr. Stone never considered or mentioned the shirt's history.

Roger Parian had given Seiler the distance at which gunpowder particulates should be found on a piece of material, such as the shirt, based solely on the weapon's powder throw distance. He was never asked about the handling of the shirt and the effect it might have had. Stone also wasn't asked about the shirt's handling or protection—at least not yet.

The next problem Dr. Stone tackled was one that had to be bothering the jury. From the corner of Williams's desk with his arm extended, Danny Hansford could have almost smacked Williams with the Luger itself; how was it possible that he had missed hitting any part of Williams with a bullet, and by such an astounding margin? Dr. Stone had an answer. More accurately, Dr. Stone allowed the jury to think he had an answer.

Roger Parian had established that the trigger pull on Luger 22A was much heavier than normal. What did Stone say about such a heavy trigger pull? Not much, on his own. Seiler testified again, that heavy trigger pull could affect someone's aim and Stone agreed with him. That was it: heavy trigger pull could affect a person's aim with a weapon.

What's more instructive is what Stone did not say. He didn't say the trigger pull of Luger 22A had made Danny Hansford drop the Luger barrel by well over a foot and hit Williams's desk instead of Williams, who was standing right in front of him. Though Stone wasn't asked that question, his testimony was intended to suggest he had answered it. Note again, this is a defense witness and they are restricted to Williams's version of events. If Williams was lying, why the desk was struck was simple: Williams shot it on purpose, to leave evidence of the attack.

As for Dr. Stone's agreement with witness Seiler, trigger "pull" is a misnomer. A shooter doesn't *pull* a trigger but rather *squeezes* it. But the defense gave the impression that "pull" in a firearm setting means the same thing as it does in common usage. To add weight to the inference, the defense conducted another courtroom "demonstration." Seiler brought a boat anchor to court. Stone had measured the trigger pull at 15 lbs. (rather than Parian's 20 lbs.) so they used a 15 lb. anchor. Seiler was going to let the jury feel his anchor, as if that was relevant to the effort required to pull the trigger on Luger 22A.

The anchor led to an objection by Kathy Aldridge. Her objection, however, wasn't related to the validity of the demonstration; it was related to the fact that the weight of the anchor hadn't been verified. This led to a recess and a comical trip by Dr. Stone to the post office to weigh the anchor. The anchor was a 15 lb. anchor, confirmed by the USPS.

After its weight was confirmed, the anchor was handed to the jurors to feel it—which had nothing to do with how a pistol is fired. The most obvious and truly valid demonstration would have been to hand the Luger itself around and have the jurors pull the trigger. The gun was in court. It would have required some preparation, but what were the chances these jurors weren't going to pull the trigger in the jury room? But instead of squeezing a 15 lb. trigger, the jurors got to heft a 15 lb. boat anchor.

As to the demonstration itself, did it have a valid foundation? Hefting a 15 lb. weight is not the same as pulling a trigger with a 15 lb. trigger pull, though it might seem logical. Accept for now that it will be Dr. Stone who will clear up this misconception, though he will not do it voluntarily, or in this trial. In this trial, the jury was left to believe that an anchor weight and trigger pull were directly related. They were not. Stone knew it but didn't tell anybody.

And he wasn't finished. Dr. Stone testified that the first time he had fired the Luger out in Dallas, he had thought the safety might be on. He claimed it had taken two hands to fire it. What was the inference? The same as the anchor game: that Danny Hansford missed Williams solely because of the Luger's trigger pull.

Stone and Seiler were trying to finesse the jury. They filled the courtroom with inferences but note what Dr. Stone did not say: that he dropped the barrel or missed a target with the Luger, even once.

Dr. Stone appears to have read Dr. Burton's manual. He treated trigger pull in isolation and omitted the fact that the trigger finger is *not the only part of the body* involved in firing a pistol. No firearm has a trigger pull of zero. The shooter squeezes the trigger, with varying amounts of pressure from one firearm to the next, remaining sighted on the target, until the firing mechanism is released. How does the shooter do that without dropping the barrel and shooting their foot? By using other muscles of the body, notably the wrist, forearm, shoulder, and back. Otherwise, nobody would ever hit anything.

There is also reason to doubt part of Dr. Stone's testimony on its own merits: his inability to fire the Luger without two hands. Roger Parian conducted test firings. Randall Riddell conducted test firings. Neither one expressed any difficulty firing Luger 22A. No one reported missing a target. If they had missed by the margin Hansford supposedly missed Williams, they might have taken out a lab assistant.

The failure of Stone to consider the human mechanics of firing a pistol was a glaring omission for a man purporting to be a firearms expert. This is a prime example of looking at evidence in isolation so it benefits your side. And yes, Dr. Stone had a side. He was not on a scientific expedition. He was there to help the defense explain how Hansford had missed Williams by a Savannah mile, and he was being paid well for his trouble.

Dr. Stone was also the source of the defense's bloody-rag experiment. On cross-examination, Chief Assistant Kathy Aldridge would take the bloody-rag theory apart, so we can wait to discuss it until cross.

Stone's other task was to neutralize the GSR evidence. Stone and his staff test-fired the "attack" Luger to check its emission of GSR. As in the case of the State Crime Lab's new tests, Stone's tests weren't comparable to the original tests. He used different ammunition. The swabbing technique and personnel were different. Neither set of 1983 tests was as reliable as the original.

Stone had to do something. Williams had a GSR problem, and Dr. Stone had been hired to take care of it. Defense experts who insist that they "tell it like it is" no matter what should raise their feet to avoid ruining their shoes. We may accept without fear of contradiction that there has never been a paid defense expert put on the stand by a defendant to corroborate the prosecution's case. It has never happened and never will.

In Dr. Stone's case, he concluded that no conclusions could be drawn about GSR because he had found "inconsistent" results from his own tests of the weapon. He didn't claim that the Luger failed to deposit GSR, only that it did so inconsistently, according to his new tests—in 1983. This was a question of fact for a jury to resolve. They could decide if Stone's opinion that the Luger was "inconsistent" in its 1983 GSR emissions outweighed the testimony of Howard and Riddell that the GSR test results—from 1981 and 1983—were so extreme that Hansford had not, and could not, have fired that Luger.

Surprisingly, Stone turned out to be the witness that Seiler tapped to pull his paper-under-the-Luger photo trick. Seiler hadn't showed his special photo to Dr. Gantner, but he had it ready for Dr. Stone (Figure 36). There is no secret why Seiler didn't show Dr. Gantner the photograph—the photo didn't show what Seiler needed someone to say it showed. But why select Dr. Stone to carry this particular pail of water for Williams?

Who else could have been asked about this photo instead of Stone? ID Ofc. Donna Stevens was a trained forensics officer who had actually taken the photo in question. Detective Ragan was the lead detective and had personally removed Williams's Luger from the desk. Dr. Gantner was the Medical Examiner for the City of St. Louis and was qualified across numerous disciplines. Yet Seiler didn't ask Stevens or Ragan about his picture and didn't show it to Dr. Gantner even after asking him about it. Accept that, for the defense in a criminal case, having a prosecution witness admit something is far superior to having your own witness agree with you.

What was Stone's background in photography or in analyzing photographic perspective? None that he shared. Stone was a firearms expert. The only thing Seiler's picture had to do with firearms was that there was a gun in the picture. But there is no doubt why Seiler used Dr. Stone. If Seiler had asked Gantner, Stevens, or Ragan, he wouldn't have been able to control the answer. Surprise:

Seiler handed his secret picture to Stone and Stone said there was a piece of paper that "appeared" to be "partially" under the handle. And there it was, finally unveiled, the dream team's defense to murder.

I am reminded of a two-hour television special that aired on April 21, 1986, during which a reported 30 million people watched Geraldo Rivera open a completely empty vault (supposedly once owned by Al Capone). But Seiler had gotten what he wanted—if he was allowed to get away with it.

Stone still had to undergo cross-examination. And note, with regard to Seiler and photographs, he did not show Dr. Gantner any photos of the gun. Even with Dr. Stone, he chose only one view of the gun on the desk. When it was not to his advantage, he didn't share any other photos of the same item. Stay tuned.

Kathy Aldridge went immediately to the flaw in Stone's shirt analysis. Dr. Stone admitted that he did not know anything about the shirt's history. Yes, he agreed, particles could be shaken off if the shirt was moved around. In other words, his tests hadn't taken into account the evidence in *this* case. There went Dr. Stone's three feet, and Seiler's four feet with it.

For his bloody-rag test, Stone said he fired a weapon he knew deposited GSR—not Luger 22A—and wiped his hand with a rag soaked in human blood. After wiping his hand with the bloody rag, he swabbed his hand and found a "reduction" in GSR levels. Aside from the fact that no information was provided about the consistency with which Stone's Luger deposited GSR and in what amounts (saying he "knew" it deposited GSR was not particularly scientific) or any other details, Dr. Stone agreed with Aldridge: There was no bloody rag in the *Williams* case.

Stone was testifying in a murder case, yet he had brought in a demonstration that wasn't based on the facts of the case, to help the defendant. Did it not matter that his testimony might be irrelevant and misleading, so long as it helped the man paying his fee?

Q. In fact, you don't really know anything about what happened to the hand?

A. That's true. Yes, ma'am.

Aldridge also demonstrated an important point: Dr. Stone did not disagree with Howard and Riddell on the validity of GSR testing. This was striking in light of the *Williams I* testimony of Dr. Burton that GSR tests were meaningless. Burton was on the Williams II witness list.

Q. If you were given figures which you knew to be right, showing that the gun that was test-fired had detectable levels of barium and antimony in a number of firings and that the person whose hands were swabbed—we'll refer to him as Hansford—

A. Mmm-hmm.

Q. —had no antimony and very, very low levels of barium such as we see here, you could conclude that, if a proper collection technique had been used and a proper swabbing technique had been used on that person's hand, that that person would be very unlikely to have fired a weapon.

A. I would agree with that, yes, ma'am.

Dr. Stone was also the defense witness chosen to fill in the blank left about the "certain blood" question to Det. Ragan, the witness who had gotten a benzidine reaction on the Luger 22A grip. Roger Parian had not been able to find any trace of blood, even with benzidine, but Stone said he had managed to get a "reaction" on the outside of the grip with benzidine. There was no photographic or video record of his test or any data provided.

As we know, Dr. Howard had already testified that some trace would be expected from contact between any object and another with blood on it, even if the blood was dried. Recall that benzidine measures in parts per billion and scientists have gotten benzidine reactions from Egyptian mummies, so it wasn't impossible that Dr. Stone had gotten a benzidine reaction on the outside of the grip, even though Roger Parian had not.

On cross-examination, Stone said he had found no blood elsewhere, including at the rear where the weapon would have been gripped in the web or on the left side of the grip. A person gripping a weapon touches both areas. A person with their hand laid on a weapon does not.

Dr. Stone didn't suggest what this testimony proved, other than that Danny Hansford's hand had come into contact with the grip of Luger 22A. Of course it had: Williams had made sure of it.

Though this was not brought up with Stone, his testimony actually proved the extent to which the blood on Hansford's hand had clotted and dried before it was placed on top of the grip. Stone required the use of benzidine to get any reaction whatsoever. There was no visible blood on the grip at all. In other words, the blood on the hand was no longer wet when the hand was placed on top of the gun. That was the *prosecution's* position.

Aldridge wasn't finished with Dr. Stone. Throughout his direct testimony, he had used a diagram of the scene. Stone admitted that the diagram was not to scale and was a "pictorial representation only." In other words, he hadn't told the jury that the diagram he was using was inaccurate. As will be revealed on re-direct of Dr. Howard, Dr. Stone's diagram was far more than inaccurate—it was grossly misleading. It's ironic that the police had been accused of untold evil for photographing an item in two different places while the defense was using a diagram that showed items where they never were.

Dr. Stone also admitted that he had never seen the desk. It was gone. He didn't know where the bullet had hit the desk, only what he had been told—by Williams's lawyers. With the body, rug, desk, and chair gone, how much benefit would Dr. Gantner have derived from a visit if the defense had allowed him into the house?

Finally, Aldridge got to Seiler's blockbuster photograph (Figure 36). Aldridge challenged Stone about his testimony that there were paper fragments *under* the Luger on the desk. Dr. Stone made it clear that he had *not* said that there were paper fragments under the Luger: "Well, I said there was a piece of paper which *appeared* to be partially under the handle of the weapon, yes."

Why hadn't Stone clarified his answer when he gave it? Had he pointed out that the Luger was resting on a black notebook, not flat against the desk, producing a shadow along the edge of the handle, and that the tip of the fragment appeared to end in this *shadow* and not *under the weapon* at all (compare Figures 36 and 42)? No. But there was a reason why Dr. Stone might have been unable to make the distinction: Seiler didn't show him the second photo (Figure 42). Lawyer Photo Games, as played by legal juvenile delinquents.

The sum of Dr. Stone's testimony seemed to include a shirt test unadjusted for the shirt's history, inconclusive GSR test firings that didn't match the original conditions, a bloody-rag experiment unrelated to the facts in the case, a deceptive diagram, trigger-pull testimony that ignored how a weapon is fired, and agreement with whatever Seiler said about a picture that didn't show what it was supposed to show.

On redirect, Seiler tried to bolster Stone's credentials to suggest that the jury should buy his testimony anyway simply because he was working for the defense and wasn't overcharging Williams. Kathy Aldridge had asked Dr. Stone about the fees he was charging for his testimony. Seiler followed up with Dr. Stone about his fees, but Seiler's questions weren't about fees. The fees were only a pretext for conducting some redirect examination. Seiler's purpose was to suggest that a defense hired gun was more *impartial* than State Crime Laboratory scientists.

Q. Now before we get away from Dr. Howard and the other people that professionally testified for the State, let me ask you this. The fees that you have quoted to Ms. Aldridge, would you state whether or not that is consistent with similar fees charged in your profession for consultations in this type work?

A. I think it is, best of my knowledge.

Q. As opposed to people who are on a salary, and they would testify all the time for one side?

So Williams was only paying market rates for his expert, if that was somehow relevant. The second Seiler question—the more important question—is actually a statement, despite being followed by a question mark. And it's a false statement. Maybe Seiler was simply ignorant of the workings of the Forensic Services Division of the GBI because he didn't do criminal work. He would become enlightened later on re-cross of Dr. Howard when Dr. Howard returned for some closing summary testimony and explained, in response to Seiler's questions:

A. I'm salaried by the State to run the Crime Lab, and in so doing, appear in court wherever I'm subpoenaed, do autopsies wherever necessary, take care of personnel problems when they occur, all kinds of things.

Q. For the State.

A. I'm not sure what you mean by for the State. I'm paid by the State. If you're talking about for the prosecution, no, *I appear for the defense* sometimes.

This is a very common scam straight from the Lawyer Games Toolbox. If the head of the State Crime Lab—such as, for instance, the past vice president of the American Academy of Forensic Scientists and president of the American Society of Crime Laboratory Directors—testified that water was wet, it should be viewed with the utmost suspicion. At the same time, a defense hired-gun professional witness—whose ilk are routinely ignored by juries—should be believed under all circumstances, whether or not their testimony made any sense, so long as they weren't overcharging the defendant.

How about Dr. Stone? He was a Dallas County employee testifying for the defense in this case. How would Seiler reconcile that with his contention that no one on a government payroll ever testified for the defense or was worthy of belief? But Seiler couldn't be cross-examined despite doing a lot of the testifying. So Dr. Stone made extra bucks testifying for defense lawyers. Dr. Howard didn't. He was busy running the State Crime Lab. More to the point, who would you rather deal with in a sales situation, someone on salary or someone on commission?

I warned that the arrival of this trial team introduced a new level of criminal trial practice to the *Williams* case—the direction was not up, in case that's in question.

It was somewhat surprising, but Dr. Joseph L. Burton showed up again. While Dr. Stone proved himself willing to work around the edges of the facts while purporting to be as pure as driven snow, he didn't spoon out the junk that Dr. Burton had, at least in *Williams I*. Maybe the Burtons of the world were a specialty within a specialty.

Before getting into the particulars of Burton's testimony, we should put all of this testimony into perspective. Burton, Stone, and their ilk are what might be called Maxwell Smart witnesses, borrowing from an old television series. Maxwell Smart (played by Don Adams) was the secret-agent star of the Mel Brooks television comedy *Get Smart* in the 1960s and the movie version in 2008 (with Steve Carell and Anne Hathaway). Max was known for the line "Would you believe…" which became cultural slang for decades. If one theory didn't fly, he'd offer up another one, wildly unrelated to the first.

A legal restriction applied to circumstantial evidence is that it must eliminate "every other reasonable hypothesis" other than the guilt of the accused. What a Maxwell Smart witness does is offer up a smorgasbord of "other" hypotheses. If one doesn't do the trick, it's "would you believe …" and here comes another one. They don't have to conclusively prove a theory (though it is more persuasive when they do); they only have to raise the *possibility* in a jury's collective mind that there might be some "other reasonable hypothesis" to explain the evidence. Unfortunately, these witnesses often forget that the other hypothesis has to be *reasonable*. "An escaped giraffe ate my homework" doesn't do it.

There is a second legal concept that comes up in these circumstances. We're all familiar with the "hypothetical" question "If I had two tickets to the Oscars, would you want to go with me?" That's a familiar form of hypothetical.

Simply put, a witness is asked to assume certain facts are true for the sake of responding to a question. The facts presumed true in the question might be based on evidence already in the record, evidence to be introduced later by testimony or exhibit, or in other ways.

Hypotheticals are used all the time in trial practice, if only to maintain the flow of a trial. The two sides don't present their cases at the same time, so a lawyer uses a "hypothetical" question, with the understanding that the facts, if not already in the record, will be proved later in the trial.

The courtesy allows evidence supporting the hypothetical to be introduced later, but if it isn't introduced at some point, the jury might well be instructed that they're entitled to give the testimony no weight at all. In the case of expert witness opinions, it's more complicated but the general rule is that the examination of witnesses is to be based on admissible evidence in the case being tried. Otherwise, trials could be bogged down by a lot of questions about escaped giraffes and missing homework.

Here are two questions to keep in mind when an expert offers up a hypothesis: (1) Is the hypothesis reasonable, and (2) Is the hypothesis based on the evidence?

Professional expert witnesses in a circumstantial evidence case—witnesses like Dr. Burton and Dr. Stone—can become the other-hypothesis choir, singing out a medley of other hypotheses, hoping to hit on some alternative explanation for the evidence. But a self-defense case is different and presents special challenges to these witnesses. The State's theory of the crime isn't on trial; the defendant's theory is. It isn't sufficient to attack the State's case by tossing other-hypothesis hand grenades. Somebody has to prove the defendant's self-defense claim if the evidence doesn't do it. Otherwise, the defendant is going on a long vacation with a whole new group of friends.

A witness like Dr. Burton is far less effective in a self-defense case. He didn't test anything; he merely testified. In *Williams II*, the prosecution might have reasonably expected Burton to have used the year since the first trial to develop a passing familiarity with the case evidence, but he hadn't. He regurgitated the same testimony he gave in *Williams I*.

What about GSR tests? They were no good, period. Except that the rest of the world didn't agree with him—not even the previous defense witness. Dr. Stone had no problem with GSR testing, as he had told Kathy Aldridge. But Burton was oblivious to this fact. He still testified as if talking to a high school class on a field trip. Burton was so distracted that he concluded, "So, a negative test in no way implies that someone has fired a gun." That's correct. A *negative* GSR test does not imply that someone *has* fired a gun. Yet he plowed ahead, not having heard what he'd said. Defense counsel apparently hadn't heard it either. It's astounding that Burton was being paid thousands of dollars for this. Dr. Burton was what is called in Dr. Stone's Dallas "all hat and no cattle."

In 2003, a full twenty years after the trial in which Dr. Burton was testifying, Phil Spector told responding officers at his estate in California that the young woman he had killed had fired the gun herself, in a suicide. What did the police do? They immediately called for GSR kits. This despite Dr. Joseph Burton of DeKalb County, Georgia, having declared GSR testing meaningless twenty years earlier.

GSR tests can be performed or not performed. It is also perfectly legitimate to dispute the results. They are only a tool, like any other investigative tool. But to deal with scientific evidence by declaring it meaningless sounds a bit too much like the kid who can't get a date declaring that girls are yucky.

Dr. Burton was asked if he had been allowed to "see and inspect" the physical evidence in the case. Yes, he answered, he had done so in 1982. This was intended to give the impression that Burton had examined the evidence at least a year before trial. What the jury was not told was that his "inspection" of the evidence had taken place on the Friday before trial back in 1982.

In light of this testimony, Dr. Burton might have been asked how often he had testified for a defendant, cashed his check, and headed back to his ranch while the defendant headed to jail. He had lost all three of his cases in Savannah by that time. Did he give defendants refunds? Had he ever been called by the defense and testified that the prosecution was right? Are questions like these asked, or does everybody buy into the fiction that these witnesses are only right-eous searchers for truth and that defendants hire them for their impartiality?

As Mark Fuhrman put it in *Murder in Brentwood*: "Professional witnesses may not alter the truth, but they certainly shade its inference in order to please the client."[98] Dr. Stone said he'd come to Savannah without knowing "what value" he would be to the defense. He could have said, "I didn't know for sure, but I figured I'd find something."

Defense lawyers propping up their opinion-for-hire witnesses with self-serv-ing statements of sanctimony is tired and transparent. The obligatory homage to truth and justice should be retired from criminal practice. Maybe it's in the hand-book "How to Try a Criminal Case." If so, the handbook needs a revision. Why don't these witnesses just show up and testify? If their evidence is compelling, it will speak for itself. Expert-witness declarations of impartiality are about as use-ful as a defendant looking sincerely at the jury and promising that they really, really didn't do it. If Stone, Burton, and those to come weren't of value to the defense, no one in that courtroom would have ever known they existed.

Are all defense experts the same? No. Also from the *Simpson* case, Marc Fuhrman observed of Dr. Michael Baden (a renowned forensic pathologist testifying for the defense), "Baden appears to be a scientist first and an expert witness sec-ond." That is high praise. I would place Dr. Burton at the other end of that spec-trum, possibly off the end of the spectrum and into the ditch.

Dr. Stone and Dr. Petty, who came in later, fall somewhere in the middle. They are "helpful" to the defense but will admit misleading aspects of their testi-monies during cross. They only get half credit for that. Real scientists don't do that. It's akin to reporting the height of the ocean at a certain time on a certain date without mentioning the phenomenon of tides. It's a form of lying, scientif-ically, but is routinely done in courtrooms.

As for Dr. Burton, his direct testimony was not worth the time it would take to go through it again. Reviewing it only served to spark the foregoing polemic on the professional defense expert. With respect to the killing, it was the same: dead-man gymnastics, head and feet swapping places, and other spinal challenges.

Cross-examination of Dr. Burton was handled by Robert Sparks. Burton again swapped Hansford's head and feet, though the description had not improved:

Q. So you think—or it's your reconstruction of the scene, that the deceased did a kind of leap-frog thing. He went down ... and then kicked his legs out behind him?

A. No, sir. That he went down like that, and as he fell on down, his torso came closer and closer to the ground, that his legs simply straightened out behind him.

It's difficult to even visualize what Dr. Burton meant without pulling a muscle. How about the radioactive chair? It still didn't "concern" Dr. Burton. It couldn't be allowed to concern him, because he couldn't figure out a way that it didn't convict Williams.

In sum, there was nothing new from Burton. He should have given Williams a discount for using recycled testimony. To conclude, Bob Sparks asked Burton directly about the State's position. Could the evidence Burton had examined not just as well prove that Williams had shot Hansford three times, then gotten another Luger and fired it off to fake an attack on himself?

SPARKS: Can you eliminate that?

BURTON: No, sir, not from the evidence at the scene.

Dr. Joseph Burton, the lead defense expert, could not exclude the possibility that Williams killed Danny Hansford and doctored the scene.

Fortunately for Williams, he still had a witness left. Batting cleanup was Dr. Charles S. Petty, a forensic pathologist, director of the Dallas lab, and Dr. Stone's boss. No one asked who was watching the store while these two were in Savannah being "helpful" to a murder defendant, but it would have been a good question.

Williams's counsel pointed out that Dr. Petty was one of very few MD pathologists heading up a crime lab. This was apparently to suggest that Dr. Petty was unique, and he might well have been. Despite a popular misconception advanced by medical doctors, there is no need for the head of a crime lab to be an MD. These are scientific positions. Analysis of trace metals, firearms, handwriting, fingerprints, or DNA, or any of the other functions with which followers of *CSI* would be familiar do not require a medical degree. Even forensic autopsies don't require physicians. As Dr. Howard was known for observing, "I don't operate on live subjects." Some might have been surprised to know that Dr. Howard had done post-doctoral work in pathology and served as an assistant professor of pathology at Emory University.

Dr. Howard, Randall Riddell, and Dr. Stone all started out as chemists. Dr. Howard's predecessor as head of the State Crime Laboratory, Dr. Herman D. Jones, was a Columbia PhD physicist. In fact, prior to the mid-1980s, there were *no* medical doctors employed by the Crime Lab even though it was one of the largest and most respected in the country.

No criticism of Dr. Petty is intended. I am simply pointing out that the MD reference, along with the following, were no more than defense counsel blowing bugles for his entrance, in yet another attempt to convey an impression that had no foundation:

Q. Is your consulting in cases such as this case in any way, or is the payment of your consulting fees in any way contingent on the subject of your testimony or the outcome of the litigation in which you're called to testify?

A. Well, it's certainly not contingent upon what the outcome is. Insofar as the subject matter is, I wouldn't be involved in something outside my area of expertise, so as long as it's within the area of expertise, it wouldn't matter.

I suggest that it might not matter to Dr. Petty but it would definitely matter to the defendant who was paying his fee. This is seriously tiring. Defense attorneys don't spend their client's money searching for truth; they spend it to help their client walk. Anybody who tells you otherwise is selling nonsense.

With Dr. Petty's impartiality well established by himself, he testified that he too had examined Hansford's shirt. Dr. Petty took Burton's prize for last-minute scientific analysis. He had looked at the shirt in the witness room *immediately before taking the stand.*

Moving on, Dr. Petty didn't think the exit wound in Hansford's right chest was a shored wound. Neither did Dr. Draffin. Dr. Howard did. It doesn't matter. But watch closely. Dr. Petty pulled one of the slicker moves you will ever see. The defense wanted Danny off the floor when all the shots hit him. This means, for their purposes, no shored wound is better than a shored wound, all other things being equal. We know that.

The scene photographs show Danny facedown on the rug, where he was found. Dr. Petty testified that, if the body had been pressed against the floor *as shown in the photographs* when Hansford was shot through the back, the exit wound should be a shored wound. According to Dr. Petty, the wound was *not* a shored wound, so hooray, they win (this issue). Williams might still be a killer but at least he hadn't come around his desk to rub it in.

But not so fast. What did Dr. Petty just do, something we've mentioned before? Dr. Petty just used Williams's doctoring of the crime scene to boost Williams's case. The photographs show Hansford facedown on the rug with his right arm out to the side. That was the position of the body *after Williams pulled the arm out.* But at the time the shot to the back was fired, the arm was underneath the body, mirroring the position of the left arm.

Observe. Even if Hansford's chest were truly flat against the rug *in the photographs* (which isn't conclusive because of the curve of the pectoral muscle), it was not flat against the rug *when he was shot in the back.* Both arms were still underneath his body, underneath his chest. The defendant doesn't get to alter the scene and then use the alterations as proof of innocence.

Next is a great example of how an expert and a defense lawyer can get in trouble by not thinking all the way through an effort to score a point. Dr. Petty reported that he had discovered two "errors" in Dr. Draffin's autopsy report.

Dr. Petty questioned the blood volumes that Draffin estimated having accumulated in the pleural cavity and elsewhere in the body cavity, but this difference of opinion wasn't related by Dr. Petty to any disputed fact in the case. He seemed to be making what he labeled a correction merely for the sake of making a correction to the State's autopsy report.

The problem arrived with his second "error" related to the position of the entrance wound in Hansford's back. Draffin's transcribed autopsy report had said that the back entrance wound was 19 cm from the midline. That's 7.48 inches, which would be all the way around to Hansford's side. The number was obviously off; Dr. Petty was absolutely correct. I incorporated this correction from the beginning so as to make sense of the angles and trajectories we examined. It was an obvious transcription error and would never be disputed. Rather than waste time talking about an incorrect bullet path, we have used the correct number from the outset.

Now for the twist. Correcting this "error" might have given Dr. Petty and Seiler some momentary satisfaction, but it gutted their effort to avoid the coup de grâce shot to Danny Hansford's back. At 19 cm, the entrance wound was on Hansford's side, where the shot could have struck if Williams was still behind his desk. The correction to the autopsy report (to 11 cm, as was later confirmed by Dr. Draffin) places the entrance wound in Hansford's back directly opposite the exit wound in his chest (only 2 cm or 0.788 inches off from vertical). The shot was now almost straight down, through and into the floor.

As we noted with Dr. Gantner's testimony, lining up the entrance wound, exit wound and embedded bullet in the floor virtually eliminates the possibility that Williams could have put that shot into Hansford's back from behind his desk. This was not argued at the time Dr. Petty brought it up but it might have led to some of the defense's wacky attempts to explain the shot angles, if they were misreading the autopsy report. A quick look at the holes in the front and back of the shirt or the autopsy photos themselves should have cleared that up—if it was a mistake.

Dr. Petty's next trick involved making up autopsy results rather than correcting them. Dr. Petty was going to keep Danny Hansford out of that chair. Since the real evidence didn't help him do that, he had to create some. He simply claimed that the autopsy report said something that it didn't say.

Dr. Petty proclaimed that Hansford's spine was damaged by the first bullet. He didn't refer to any such finding in the autopsy report—there was none. With this proclamation in hand, Dr. Petty made a second: Because of this (fictional) spinal damage, Hansford "unquestionably" had no control over his lower body after the first shot struck. Petty concluded with a third proclamation based on the first two: Danny Hansford *couldn't* have been shot while sitting in the chair. His reasoning? Hansford couldn't have been shot while sitting *in* the chair because he wouldn't have been able to *get out of* the chair.

That is some fancy footwork, even for a defense expert. It was also absurd. Assuming the theory had been based on fact in the first place, Danny Hansford had to remain seated, without moving, and let Williams shoot him. Was it not feasible that a man about to be shot might try to get out of the way?

If Hansford had been a quarter of the way out of the chair, or a third or halfway out of the chair, wouldn't he fall down, with or without control of his lower body? The chair was an armchair. Might a man grab the arms of the chair when shot, and take the chair to the floor with him? The only scenario that Petty considered was the single most unlikely shooting scenario possible, that Danny Hansford had made no effort whatsoever to avoid being killed.

But stop. We have taken the bait and followed Petty into fantasy land. This is a fairly universal rule: You don't get to make up your own evidence. There was *no* evidence that Hansford's spinal cord was damaged, "unquestionably" or otherwise, and Dr. Petty didn't cite any. Here is what he said: "Now what [the bullet's] velocity was when it went *near* the spinal cord, I don't know. It slowed up some. But the bullet was still traveling with *considerable* speed, and it *undoubtedly* in my opinion damaged the spinal cord."

There was no spinal cord damage in Danny Hansford's autopsy report. What actually was in the autopsy report? That the bullet passed *by* the spinal cord just before stopping. What mischief did the bullet perform as it passed? It nicked the dura. Here's what the autopsy said: "This bullet traveled through the sixth vertebra, causing injury to the *dura* of the spinal cord, but *not* entering the spinal cord itself."[99]

From that evidence, Dr. Petty created the conclusions that: (1) the bullet was moving with *considerable* speed and (2) it *undoubtedly* damaged the spinal cord. In truth, the bullet was less than an inch and a half from stopping in subcutaneous (soft) tissue when it passed the spinal cord and the autopsy report cited *no* injury to the spinal cord. The bullet nicked the dura, and the report didn't even describe that injury in detail.

A dura tear is not uncommon in surgery. We don't know how uncommon because it's widely presumed to be underreported. Estimates range from 2% for back surgeries[100] up to 17% in spinal surgical cases.[101] The primary symptom of a dura tear? A headache.

What did Dr. Petty do with his phantom spinal cord injury? Declare that if Danny Hansford hadn't been dead, he might have had a headache? No, Dr. Petty had a larger mission.

And yet he faced another hurdle. Even if he could claim to have kept Danny out of the radioactive chair, Danny still needed to be attempting to shoot

Williams from the far corner of the desk. Observe the inventive Dr. Petty. Having declared that Danny couldn't have been sitting in the chair when shot, he concluded that, therefore, Danny was standing at the *other end of the desk*. Seriously? Had Dr. Petty lost his mind, or did he think that everyone else had lost theirs? Recall Maxwell Smart. If Danny wasn't sitting down in Miami, he must have been standing up in Pittsburgh.

Dr. Petty was welcome to say that Danny wasn't sitting in the chair. A witness can say whatever he or she wants. Dr. Petty was also welcome to say that Danny was standing at the other end of the desk. But he linked them, without making any attempt to explain this remarkable theory. Dr. Petty checked off another item on his list—perhaps with a nod and smile to the defense table—and moved on.

Assuming that Dr. Petty moved Danny's feet to the other end of the desk along with the rest of Danny, what did he do about Danny's feet and head swapping places after Danny was shot? Nothing. He ignored it. Yes, it is reasonable to draw conclusions from a defense witness's failure to address an item of evidence that is damaging to the accused, particularly when that evidence falls directly within the witness's purported area of expertise.

Dr. Petty was the last expert witness on the defense witness list. The chair was still on top of the victim's body and pants leg. Somebody still needed to get Danny's feet to the wrong end of the desk, his legs crossed, and the chair over his backside. The prosecution team was probably cranking up the Rufus Thomas hit "Do the Funky Chicken" on their headphones, getting ready for what had to be coming next.

The defense had raised the headless-chicken theory with Dr. Draffin. But, remarkably, Dr. Petty didn't mention a chicken dance or any other form of barnyard gyration. He simply put the chair on the pants leg, adopting a brand new story for this new jury: Hansford had done it himself.

John Wright Jones might have been surprised by this theory, because it had been his belief that the dead man couldn't possibly have gotten the chair into that position himself. How about Dr. Joseph Burton? He had now testified twice without being able to explain the chair over Danny's body. But explaining the chair was child's play for Dr. Petty. He resolved an issue that had stumped everyone else, and did it in only a sentence and a half:

> In my opinion, this is a result of a *reflex* action. I believe that those legs
> were *thrust* under there in a *reflex* manner ...

With a "thrust" in a "reflex manner" Dr. Petty had explained the chair. But had he? Actually, Dr. Petty hadn't even explained his own sentence. He stated an opinion based on nothing. A bare assertion isn't evidence of anything if it isn't based on anything. Petty said the chair position was "a result of a reflex action." That was an *opinion*, not an explanation.

What reflex action? What kind of thrust? Taken apart and examined, Dr. Petty said that there had been a *result* of an *action* but didn't describe either. He spoke words—which can be confused with saying something meaningful—but his words were meaningless and weren't in any way connected to the evidence in the case.

Did he walk the jury through his thrust scenario? No. He simply said there was a thrust and that explained everything. Leaving the *how* untouched, he deftly moved on to explain *why* the scenario he hadn't described, explained, or demonstrated was supposedly possible. He said the chair was "less stable" from side to side than from back to front. This was because, he said, the back legs were closer together than the front legs.

It remains unclear why an MD is supposed to be an expert at crime scene reconstruction but this MD was testifying as a physics expert, and badly. His example is simply not a measure of relative stability. This doesn't mean the chair couldn't have been less stable from side to side, only that Dr. Petty didn't know much about physics. But the larger problem is that none of this meant anything. The stability of this chair from front to back *as compared with* side to side—even if correctly measured—had not been related to any issue in this case. If Dr. Petty wanted to explain a connection, he was welcome to do so, but he didn't.

Dr. Petty merely declared the radioactive chair "less stable" from side to side and used that new opinion to support one of the slicker moves one might ever see in a courtroom, a move straight from the professional version of the Lawyer Games Toolbox: He expressed his lack of surprise at a fact that hadn't been established. Here's how he did it. After declaring the chair less stable from side to side than from front to back, he testified that he was "not surprised" that the chair was "rocked and pushed." And with that flourish, he was finished.

Dr. Petty's testimony that he was "not surprised" that the chair *was* "rocked and pushed" only proved that he could be unsurprised by imaginary events. Was the chair "rocked and pushed?" There was no such evidence in the case, at least not yet. This was Dr. Petty's testimony so he could supply the factual basis himself. He merely needed to explain *when, how,* and *by what,* the chair was rocked and pushed and, most importantly, how these factors caused the chair to end up where it was found.

Did he do that? Of course he didn't. He simply presumed a fact not in evidence and used it as the basis of an opinion.

This isn't much different from Dr. Burton stating that the chair didn't "concern" him. What Dr. Petty is saying is that he's not surprised the chair ended up where it did. Neither of them, however, could explain how it happened. "I'm not surprised that happened" isn't an explanation for an event.

As an extreme illustration, suppose someone was killed and an acquaintance of the victim appeared to testify, arriving at the last minute from out of town. The acquaintance rushes in, takes the stand and testifies, "I'm not surprised Bobby did it, he hated the SOB." When informed that Bobby turned out to have been in Antigua and it's actually Tommy on trial, the witness then says, "I'm not surprised that Tommy did it; he didn't like the SOB either." That's hardly proof of who did what to whom.

As noted, Dr. Petty was welcome to establish the facts to support his hypothetical. All he had to do was explain and describe the thrust, reflex, rocking, and pushing that he claimed had occurred, and explain how those actions produced the position of the chair in the photographs.

With testimony this outrageous, I would like to have seen Dr. Petty asked to demonstrate his thrust-and-rock theory for the jury. He needed to come down from the perch of the witness stand and back up his testimony. This was a murder case. A witness should not get to stop by, say there was a "thrust," and go for cocktails. How did the Curiosity rover get to Mars? "On a rocket" is not an acceptable answer on an astronautical engineering exam.

Dr. Petty didn't demonstrate his theory and it's too late to call him down from the stand. But we can walk through his theory for him, with only one photograph (Figure 7). He could have done the same thing, but he didn't. This exercise might suggest why he didn't. According to Merriam-Webster, to thrust means "to push or drive with force."

As they say, "Do the physics." The rear leg nearest the desk is on Hansford's trousers. So that leg of the chair had to lift into the air to allow the trousers to slip underneath. This means the chair had to tip sideways, *away* from the desk, despite nothing striking it from that direction. The strike to the chair from Dr. Petty's thrust, if there had been one, would have come from the *front*, if the dead man was doing the thrusting.

Next, the chair, having tipped away from the desk onto two legs, had to stop and remain suspended in midair, balanced on its two legs, while the dead man crossed his legs (Figure 8) and slid himself back underneath the chair. When he was all set, the suspended chair then had to *reverse direction*, again for no reason, back toward the desk, and settle on the fabric of the trouser leg.

As if that wasn't enough magic, while the tilt, balance, and return were taking place, the chair also had to move a good two feet *toward* Dr. Petty's "thrust" (Figure 11). This move alone would require reversing the rules of physics regarding the transfer of kinetic energy. In Dr. Petty's imaginary universe, a car struck from behind would move *toward* the car that hit it. In sum, those were the components of Dr. Petty's opinion. Is there any question why he didn't try to explain it?

With the momentary nuisance of the chair out of the way, Dr. Petty moved on to the sequence of Williams's shots. Dr. Petty was unable to match the three shots with the recovered rounds, which he blamed on the police. He testified that if the bullets had been *properly preserved*, he could have told the jury which bullet went with each shot because there might have been *hair* or *shirt material* on the bullets—faulty evidence collection—right out of the handbook. Because the police had screwed up, Dr. Petty couldn't tell which bullet belonged to which wound.

The first bullet entered Hansford's chest and never left the body. Another bullet was embedded in the floor directly under the exit wound in Hansford's chest. Was Dr. Petty suggesting that this bullet might have come out of the left side of Hansford's head? If we assume that bullet came from the exit wound directly above it, that would leave the remaining bullet matched to the shot to the head. What did someone have to do to become director of the Dallas crime lab, look good in a suit?

Dr. Petty did demonstrate that the new defense team was aware that the ejected shell casings were a problem for Williams. From our diagrams, we know that they are tantamount to a map of Williams's movements around the room.

Dr. Petty had three explanations for where a shell casing might end up. First, using the Burton method, Petty testified that guns with side ejection ports eject shell casings sideways. There were no guns with side ejection ports in the *Williams* case. With top ports, the casings go up, he said. We knew that.

Next, Dr. Petty said that shell casings can bounce off hard surfaces and go literally *anywhere*. "Anywhere" is a broad term in any lexicon. We presume he meant anywhere in the study. The study contained a mixture of flooring, carpets, and carpet pads, the hardwood as covered as it was uncovered. Two of the casings were found at opposite ends of the room, with one between them. If Dr. Petty was suggesting that those three shots were all fired from the same spot and in the same direction, in sequence, he needed more than "shell casings bounce" to explain their positions. He was awfully close to "a thrust happened."

A witness in need can find a friend, indeed, in the Lawyer Games Toolbox. For Dr. Petty's third explanation for the shell casings, Dr. Petty testified that "somebody" could have kicked them. The mysterious "somebody" again, from the *Spector* case. If Dr. Petty was right, his unknown somebody had kicked each shell casing into a position that meshed perfectly with all other evidence in the case—if Williams was lying.

What might our friends Occam and Aristotle have said? What was the most reasonable explanation for the positions of the casings: that the shots were fired from the position and in the direction that the ejection pattern dictated, absent *evidence* to the contrary (Figure 13). If there was no need to take the evidence into account, many things become possible—including that "somebody" did "something" or a mouse developed a hoarding disorder.

Before he finished up, Dr. Petty addressed that irritating little skull fragment. So far, because the defense insisted on keeping the chair on its feet, the skull fragment was yelling "foul" at the top of its little voice. The fragment didn't fit with the chair upright. What if the chair had been on its side?

> If that chair had been, for example, overturned or lying on its side, that fragment of bone would not have been there because it couldn't have been situated on the chair seat at the time of the shot through the head.

The fragment would not have been there because—as his explanation meets its own tail—it couldn't have been there. I don't know if Dr. Petty was a parent but, if so, I expect his children heard a lot of "because I said so."

This is an astounding aspect of the *Williams* case. Defense experts simply don't deal with damaging evidence they can't explain, despite the requirement that "another reasonable hypothesis" conform to the evidence. Even Dr. Burton commented on the requirement in *Williams I*, that all the evidence must be considered and must support a conclusion. He might have ignored the rule, but he claimed to understand it.

Cross-examination of Dr. Petty was productive—for the prosecution. It's an advantage to know the evidence in the case. On cross, Dr. Petty exploded a persistent fraudulent defense claim about GSR: that time alone will affect GSR levels. According to Dr. Petty, time alone has *no effect at all* on residue.

He was talking about the shirt, so he probably thought he was helping Dr. Stone. But in the process he eliminated a claim that the defense constantly raised about the "twelve hours" between the shooting and the swabbing of Hansford's hands.

At the risk of over-complicating the Petty-Stone tag team effort on this topic, note that Dr. Petty's claim that the "residue" (on the shirt) wasn't going anywhere referred only to the passage of *time* and not to the *handling* of the shirt. If Petty's testimony isn't read carefully, it could easily be misinterpreted to mean that the shirt's history wasn't relevant. Did Petty explain the distinction? No. Who did? Dr. Stone himself (in Aldridge's previous cross-examination).

In conclusion, Dr. Petty—like Dr. Burton before him—couldn't eliminate Williams's guilt based on the evidence in the case.

> Q. [I]s there anything in the evidence or anything that you know of that would prevent the possibility that it was the victim who—that it was—that the victim was shot three times, as you have indicated, and it was the Defendant who then positioned himself about here (indicating the corner of the desk) and shot at the desk, and then placed the gun that he used to shoot the desk under the hand of the victim.

Is there anything in the evidence that you're aware of that precludes
that possibility?

A. No, that's a possibility, I suppose.

There are some benefits to being tried a second time for murder, such as the
opportunity to discover some "newly discovered" witnesses. In that spirit, newly
discovered Vanessa Blanton was called by the defense. She testified that she had
been living at 1 East Gordon Street in 1981, at the corner of Gordon and Bull,
across a corner of Monterey Square from Mercer House.

She had been working at a cafe that closed at 2:30 a.m. and, on one particular date in April, when she got home and got out of her car sometime
after 3:00 a.m., she saw a young man come out of the front door of Mercer
House and fire a gun up into the trees. She said that she had gone inside and
watched from a window. She hadn't called the police because she saw a police
car pull up. She hadn't thought it was important and never mentioned it to
anyone. She had heard about the killing later but never made any connection
between the two events.

Defense counsel went to lengths to emphasize that, had anyone come to
talk to Ms. Blanton, she would have talked to them. Of course, nobody had
known she existed, so her willingness to be found was not compelling. The
charges against Hansford in April of 1981 had been dismissed by Williams, so
there had been no search for witnesses. And the charges were Disorderly Conduct
and Criminal Damage to Property, for property damage *inside* the residence.

Fast-forward to 1983. Vanessa Blanton said she had been working at the 17
Hundred 90 restaurant when employees of Seiler's law firm heard Ms. Blanton
talking about the two cases—the cases she had never connected. They spoke to
her. She was interviewed by defense counsel, and here she was, on the stand, testifying at trial.

On cross, Lawton pointed out that the incident had occurred two years ago.
How had she remembered the exact date? She hadn't. Williams's lawyers had told
her the date.

As the reader knows, I don't have a problem with Williams's account of the
April incident being mostly true, in broad strokes. Because April doesn't bother
me, Ms. Blanton doesn't bother me. That doesn't mean her story didn't have
problems, though, and it didn't mean Williams was beyond arranging for a witness to help him out. There simply is no more information about Ms. Blanton or
any basis upon which to characterize her testimony. As unlikely as the story might
have sounded, there was nothing in the record to contradict it and the jury was
certainly entitled to believe it.

Besides, this was testimony about shooting a tree in April. Ms. Blanton had nothing to offer regarding Williams killing Danny Hansford in May.

The second miraculous coincidence—a new witness having been in just the right spot at just the right time to back up a story Williams needed to have backed up—should have been laughable, though I doubt that anyone was laughing at the prosecution table.

Claudina Delk Smith took the stand. It shouldn't require much imagination to figure out which random night back in 1981 she happened to remember vividly—May 2.

But how could she possibly help Williams? The shooting took place after two o'clock in the morning inside Mercer House. How likely was it that some random person would come along with some eyewitness testimony about a solitary date two years earlier covering the exact time in the early morning hours that Williams needed covered? Terrific question.

In May of 1981, Ms. Smith, originally from Savannah, had been living in Decatur (an Atlanta suburb). Smith testified that she was in Savannah with her son, visiting her cousin, whose apartment happened to be across Gordon Street, the street bordering Mercer House to the south.

Smith said that on May 1, 1981, she and her son had come back to her cousin's apartment from attending Night in Old Savannah, an event held in and around Johnson Square. Ms. Smith had gone out again, to visit an old friend, and returned around 1:30 a.m. After chatting with her cousin and talking with her husband by phone, she decided to go sit in Monterey Square, after two o'clock in the morning, by herself. Why? "'Cause I wanted to get out," she said.

She went to the opposite (north) end of the park from her cousin's apartment and sat on a bench. She was not alone. She said there were two teenagers on a bench near her. There was no description of the teenagers or what they were doing.

The timing was not only fortunate for Williams; it was miraculous. Danny Hansford was killed—according to the evidence—sometime between 2:00 and 2:22 in the morning. And along comes a witness who just happened to be sitting on a bench in Monterey Square on that exact night, during that small window of time. With that kind of luck, Williams should have moved to Las Vegas and slept on a casino floor between blackjack hands.

Then the lucky became luckier still. While sitting in the square, Ms. Smith heard gunshots—loud gunshots, she said. Not only did she hear them and immediately identify them as gunshots, she also recalled the exact *sequence* of the shots. The shots were all in a row. This would mean there was no gap—which we might think there would have been if Williams had shot Hansford and then grabbed a second Luger to fire his "fake" shot into the desk.

But there was a complication.

So far, Smith's testimony didn't cover all the possibilities. It wasn't clear how long Williams might have taken to plan out his setup of the scene. The "fake" shot could have come much later. To cover that possibility, Ms. Smith would have to have stayed in the park from the time the first shot was fired until the police were called by Williams, just before 3:00 a.m. So, what was Ms. Smith's testimony? That was exactly what happened.

But who would continue to sit on a park bench after 2:00 in the morning after hearing gunshots? Ms. Smith would, according to her testimony. She "kind of just sat there, rather frozen. It was quite frightening, and looked around, and remained in the square for some time ... twenty to thirty minutes. And then walked back across to the apartment." She didn't mention where the teenagers went, whether they were also frozen with fear or took off at the sound of gunfire.

But wasn't this great testimony for Williams? It appeared to be. In hindsight, however, she had just proved that Williams was lying. When making up facts, there is a risk of running into another fact coming the other way through the tunnel. Ms. Smith had *confirmed the missing minutes time gap*. She said she sat in the park for *twenty to thirty* minutes after the gunfire and then walked back to her cousin's apartment, right past Williams's house. Here is what she said she saw:

Q. Okay. Now as you walked back to the apartment, did you observe Mr. Williams' house?

A. Yes, I did. I had to walk in front of it.

Q. Okay, were there any police cars or other vehicles in front of the house at that time?

A. No, sir.

Continuing, she said the front door of Mercer House was open when she passed. In Williams's testimony, he said he opened the front door after he called the police. The police were at the house within ninety seconds of the phone call.

That means Ms. Smith was in front of Mercer House less than ninety seconds after Williams's call to the police. She had been in the park for twenty to thirty minutes after hearing gunshots. Smith had just confirmed the time gap between Williams killing Hansford and calling the police. We are assuming, for the missing minutes analysis, that Ms. Smith was telling the truth. That isn't likely, however.

Here's her story: After her fear from hearing gunshots thawed, it appears that she got up from her bench at the north end of the park, crossed Bull Street to the sidewalk in front of 423-425 Bull Street, crossed W. Wayne Street (bounding Mercer House on the north), and passed in front of Mercer House. "I walked in front of it," she had said. The front door was open. Williams had called the police, gone to open the front door, and disappeared into the house. The ninety seconds were ticking off rapidly. There was no sign of the police, no blue lights in the trees from police cars rounding the square. Smith then continued past Mercer House, crossing Gordon Street to her cousin's apartment. Still no sign of the police. She went inside. Still no sign of the police. She chatted with her cousin, and they went to bed.

Yes, the timing coincidence was incomprehensible but, in addition, consider her actions using basic human logic, which a jury is not only entitled to use but expected to use. Smith had just heard a volley of gunshots reverberate through the square. She was frozen with fright, unable to move, for up to a half hour. When she finally overcame her fear, she walked toward her cousin's apartment, directly past Williams's house. The front door was standing open. The key words here are gunshots, open door, mansion, rich man, and valuable antiques. Was someone in the house, robbing or killing the owner? Was there *a crime in progress*?

What was Claudina Smith's reaction in that situation? She strolled past a wide-open, lit-up Mercer House, apparently confident that nothing was going on inside. How was that possible? There is one obvious explanation: When constructing her story, she forgot what she wasn't supposed to know—that there was no continuing danger. Otherwise, her story doesn't account for *normal human behavior*.

It's impossible to believe that someone in that situation would not pick up a telephone once inside her cousin's apartment and call the police to Mercer House, or at least pick up her pace when passing it. Ms. Smith did neither. This is the place in the movie where we say, "Oh, please; nobody would do that." It's another example of why making things up is hard and smart people screw it up every day.

Much of this analysis is new. It's far easier to come up with these questions for Ms. Smith with time for calm, careful reflection. With a surprise witness on the stand, you do the best you can. Juries can sniff these things out pretty well when they trust their instincts. Some coincidences are just too coincidental.

What did Claudina Smith do later, when she knew about the killing and the time it had happened? Nothing. On cross-examination by District Attorney Lawton, Ms. Smith admitted that she knew what had happened as early as the next morning. She saw the news trucks outside and read the paper. But no, she didn't call anyone to tell them what she knew.

She claimed that she didn't say anything because she didn't know it was important. It was now October of 1983. She'd testified that she met Williams in November of 1982. She was now appearing as a witness in the trial of a murder case. It would be safe to assume that it dawned on her, at some point along the way, that what she knew might be important.

Q. And you—still you've made no attempt to contact any detectives, any police agency of any kind, the D.A.'s office, or [any] one. Kept to yourself what you knew, is that correct?

A. Yes.

Q. Waiting to tell it today?

A. (No audible response.)

The remainder of *Williams II* consisted of a two-pronged attack, to burnish Williams's application for sainthood and to relegate Danny Hansford's soul to hell.

The assault on the dead man was kicked off by previous victims, all of them miraculously still alive. Judge Oliver had allowed a rule change in this trial. In *Williams I,* witnesses had only been allowed to testify to Hansford's reputation for violence. In *Williams II,* they were allowed to say whatever they wanted about him. And there was no requirement that previous "acts" have been directed at Williams.

What was going on? The claim on the defense side would be that this evidence was relevant because it went to prove why Williams lived in fear of Danny, to make Williams's acting in self-defense more understandable. The claim was bogus. Danny was living in Williams's house and acting as his personal caretaker. At trial, Williams might have claimed to have been cringing with fear of Danny, but his actions said otherwise. In April, what had Williams said when the madman was firing off Lugers? "Now, let's put the guns away."

More to the point, Williams's general apprehension of fear related to Danny had nothing to do with this case. Williams was claiming that Danny shot at him. If Williams was telling the truth, Danny was trying to kill him. There is no requirement in the law to prove the reasonableness of your fear when someone is shooting at you.

What was the defense really up to? They weren't trying to prove Williams's fear of Danny Hansford. They were trying to prove, if they could pull it off, that Danny got into scuffles so he had obviously tried to kill Williams. In legal jargon, they were going to use "prior bad acts" to prove this bad act was also likely. Such evidence is considered so prejudicial that, absent very limited exceptions, it can't be introduced against a defendant. But Danny was the victim, not the defendant, so the prohibition against this evidence didn't apply. Judge Oliver placed no limitations at all on what the defense could dump on Danny Hansford's corpse.

To repeat, the reasonableness of an apprehension of fear in a case involving self-defense against an assailant shooting at the defendant isn't an issue. Williams didn't, for example, claim he'd shot Danny because Danny had gotten into a fistfight over somebody spraying his cat with insecticide. Nevertheless, we are about to hear about it. It was open season on Danny Hansford.

Barry William George Thomas was back for this trial. Barry testified that he had once been coming up from the basement when Danny came down the stairs and tried to kick him in the stomach for no reason. Barry testified that Danny's foot touched his stomach and that Williams held Danny back (Danny with the strength of a hundred men) while Barry escaped. That was Thomas's story—Danny "touched" his stomach with a foot.

Earl W. LeFevre was back to talk about the fight in his front yard. The story that George Hill had told Cook in *Williams I* was confirmed by Mr. LeFevre: George came back by himself, without Danny, chased LeFevre's son into the house, and in the process broke the door.

Douglas Seyle, now a former employee of Williams, followed what sounded suspiciously like a script.

Q. What was his (Danny's) reputation for use and abuse of drugs?

A. He used them a lot and he abused them a lot.

It's odd that such references used the generalized term "drugs" (or in this case "them") with no mention of a specific drug or any details. There was no foundation laid for how Seyle knew these things. And how had the case swerved so far off track that now a "reputation" for drug use was judged relevant in a murder case? What did Danny's reputation for drug use, profanity or jaywalking have to do with Williams's justification for killing him?

It's obvious why this kind of testimony is barred when used against a defendant. It's highly prejudicial (in this case, to the dead man) and irrelevant to the case being tried. If a priest had shot at Williams, he would have been justified in shooting back.

Had Williams said, "I had to shoot him because he smoked pot"? No. Had Williams said, "I had to shoot him because he touched Barry Thomas with his toe"? No again. How about "I had to shoot him because George Hill broke Earl LeFevre's door"? If Danny Hansford had stolen money from a Girl Scout and bought crack with it, did that mean Williams was telling the truth about the attack? Does that even require an answer?

Seyle had another task on his list of things to do for the defense. During earlier questioning of Cpl. Anderson about the April 1981 incident, Williams's lawyer had used a particular phrase, "playing possum," to describe Hansford's behavior. That phrase had never appeared in any prior statement or testimony until it was used—by Williams's lawyer—in Cpl. Anderson's cross-examination in this trial.

Now Douglas Seyle, who was no friend or fan of Danny Hansford, testified that Danny had *confided* to Seyle that he had been "playing possum" in April. First, who cared about April and what animal Danny had been impersonating and, second, Seyle had never reported this conversation to anyone until Williams's new defense team showed up, two years after the fact. Now, recalling it in 1983, he just happened to use the same phrase defense counsel had used.

A story was once told to me by a Savannah lawyer and wizened politician about old-time politics in Savannah. He told me of going down as a boy to a certain location where the political bosses would hand out names of dead people during elections. At a rate of so much per name, you would go vote the name, come back, get another one, and repeat the process.

This conjures up an image of a conference room in a law firm, the flaws in Williams's story being handed out to an assembled group of willing witnesses, along with a script for their testimony. It's only a fantasy, of course.

What about the cat? The next witness was another person fortunate not to have been killed by Hansford: Robert Charles Croyle. In June of 1980, Croyle had been a handyman at the apartments where Hansford lived. Croyle said he was spraying the apartments and didn't get an answer at Danny's door so he had used his master key and opened the door. The chain was on so, according to Croyle's version, he closed the door and went about his business.

Later, Danny showed up at Croyle's apartment and punched him in the face. This attack was totally unprovoked, according to Croyle. Croyle had done nothing at all, so he said—shades of Barry Thomas and the unprovoked toe attack. On cross-examination, Croyle categorically denied the possibility that he had stuck his spray wand through the gap in Danny's door and sprayed Danny's cat with rodent-killing chemicals. (Croyle will be back.)

This entire assault on Hansford was being constructed for one purpose only: to cast Williams as a man simply unfortunate enough to have been present when a killer had *predictably* snapped.

Contrary to my assurance that there was no voodoo in this narrative, the psychiatrists showed up next. It has always been fascinating to me that psychiatrists are so precise in their ability to predict behavior after the fact and so woeful at it in advance. They seem far better at "that was bound to happen" on a talk show than they are at "this is going to happen" when it might do some good.

Granted, Danny Hansford's childhood, with a hopeless and helpless young mother, was horrible. He was troubled, aggressive, an abuser of alcohol, a pothead, and likely not destined for greatness or a long life at his rate of self-abuse. Nobody would argue that Danny was a prize, other than in areas that Williams valued. But not every troubled kid who gets into fights or has a pot habit is a homicidal maniac. They can be a danger to themselves and a pain in the rear to others, but they are not all stone-cold killers.

This is not to excuse Danny Hansford's life, habits, or actions but is only to suggest that it was also not okay for someone to shoot him because he pissed them off. The attempt to prove that Danny was "just the type" to have shot Williams should be seen for what it was. The overwhelming physical evidence from the study on Monterey Square was far more relevant than Danny having trashed his room when he was fifteen (which had caused his mother to take him to Georgia Regional).

At the end of the day, it was possible that a jury might look at Danny Hansford and say, "Good riddance." The defense was banking on it. But the truth about Williams should not be lost in the process. This was the world Williams had chosen to inhabit. Danny Hansford was the wild child he wanted but, as the evidence showed, couldn't control or bend to his will. Most pointedly, if Danny Hansford "needed killing," that was not a decision James Williams was entitled to make.

Dr. Lester N. Haddad testified that, in December of 1975, he had been an emergency room physician at Memorial Medical Center when Danny Hansford, then fifteen, was brought in by his mother. After Danny was examined, the mother agreed to sign a committal slip to have Danny evaluated at Georgia Regional Hospital.

Dr. Simon Speriosu was employed at Georgia Regional Hospital in 1975. Originally from Yugoslavia, Dr. Speriosu was a psychiatrist. Danny was admitted on December 8, 1975, at 9:00 p.m. Dr. Speriosu didn't see Danny until two days later (December 10), the day Danny left, for an hour or less. Upon his release, Dr. Speriosu had a diagnosis that didn't sound good at all:

Q. Would you tell the jury whether or not there is a diagnosis called unsocialized aggressive behavior with emotional liability. Did I say that right?

A. Lability.

Q. All right, lability. All right, sir. What does that mean, sir?

A. This diagnosis is given to children and adolescents that show disobedience, quarrelsomeness, temper tantrums, verbal and physical aggressiveness. There is usually poor parent-child relationship in those cases. Destructiveness of property. That is generally the symptoms that one can find.

Sounds like Danny, all right. However, Dr. Speriosu went on to note that this assessment was very preliminary and that it would be necessary to evaluate Danny *over time* before making a real diagnosis. It didn't matter. The defense needed to build a killer from the ground up, so the jury was treated to this generalized testimony about unruly adolescents—from three and a half years before Williams met Danny Hansford and five and a half years before Williams killed him.

Fast-forward to 1979 and Danny's second contact with Georgia Regional, which was discussed by Nina Kelly in *Williams I*. Ms. Kelly was back but there was no dustup over her form-checking this time. Her testimony was restricted to what she had personally observed: Danny had been drinking; he said that some-one had hit him with a piece of wood; he had been sutured at Memorial Hospi-tal; his clothes were bloody; and he definitely did not want to be admitted. That was all she knew.

Stephen W. Richardson had been a social worker at Georgia Regional in 1979 and had seen Danny briefly. Richardson recalled the altercation and the stitches. He also recalled that Danny hadn't known why he had been brought to Georgia Regional. Richardson explained that Danny signed himself out two days later "AMA," or against medical advice. AMA meant that, though the hospital thought the patient would benefit from staying longer, they had no grounds to keep him.

Georgia Regional records, again admitted in bulk by the defense, included a signed copy of Form 1012 signed by the Chief Medical Officer approving Danny's 1979 release. There were two boxes on Form 1012. One box was labeled "Approved," and it was checked. The box below was labeled "Denied for the fol-lowing reason(s)." It was not checked. An additional form—Form 1010—was cosigned by Richardson and approved by the Chief Medical Officer. It carried the notation, "Patient not committable."[102] In lay terms, Danny Hansford was judged not to be a danger to himself or others. These forms are contained in and among Danny Hansford's Georgia Regional records; they were not mentioned or discussed at trial.

The defense continued with Dr. Aurel Teodorescu, the psychiatrist at Geor-gia Regional Hospital who saw Danny for a few minutes in 1979. The defense tried again, unsuccessfully, to get a diagnosis of psycho out of Dr. Teodorescu:

I put a *question mark* under diagnosis. Psychosis. Which to persist in this diagnosis you should follow the patient more time than *just once*, you know, just to see the patient the next day and the day after and some.

He told defense counsel that the hospital "can't keep him if he wants to sign out unless he's really bad." They could keep the patient "only in extreme situation and the patient is supposed to be *extremely violent, extremely dangerous,* and for himself and for the others."

On cross-examination by Spencer Lawton, Dr. Teodorescu explained further:

Q. There are patients at the hospital, are there not, who cannot sign themselves out voluntarily and are not allowed to leave whether they want to or not? Is that correct?

A. Yeah, these are extreme cases when that—real violent, real dangerous cases that are kept against their will and criminal offense pending against them, and—yeah.

Q. And in this case, no one took the steps which would be necessary to retain Danny Hansford at the hospital against his will?

A. No. They did as usual they do in these circumstances.

Q. These circumstances did not warrant that, did they?

A. Pardon?

Q. These circumstances did not warrant taking steps to keep Danny Hansford there against his will?

A. No, no.

Williams's lawyers were determined to do what Dr. Teodorescu said couldn't be done, no matter what he said. They only cared that Williams walk out of the courthouse when the trial was over. None of this testimony had anything to do with whether Williams was responsible for the death of Danny Hansford. It only went to the question of whether anybody should care.

This last two-day stay at Georgia Regional for Danny Hansford had taken place in July of 1979. Only four months later (November), according to Williams's testimony, he and this same Danny were playing backgammon and boy-toy games and having "occasional sex." The defense was now offering up this same Georgia Regional stay as evidence that Danny was a psychotic maniac. In April of 1981, Williams would ticket this same Danny Hansford to fly with him to Europe as a health-care guardian.

Judge Oliver would have been justified in tossing all of this evidence out as too remote and insufficiently connected to the events on trial—in other words, irrelevant to the matter before the court. But he didn't and the legal con game continued.

Speaking of just what the lawyer ordered, the defense witnesses progressed from a doctor who had seen Danny for an hour or less eight years earlier, to a doctor who had seen him for fifteen minutes four years earlier, to a doctor who had never laid eyes on Danny Hansford at all.

Dr. Henry A. Brandt, local neurologist and psychiatrist, was unique. He had come to court to assist the defense due only to what he called a sense of "civic duty." He was receiving a fee, but he explained that the money wasn't important; he was there to do what was right. As he soon made clear, that was to pronounce Danny Hansford a psychopath who must have attacked Williams because that is what psychopaths do. Dr. Brandt had never met or treated Danny Hansford. However, he had "pored over" Danny's records.

Dr. Brandt was a psychiatric counterpart to Dr. Burton. He spoke as if speaking to a civic club. This psychiatric evidence was so far from appropriate and relevant by this point that it's patently offensive. If Danny Hansford had been alive and on trial for having shot at James Williams, none of this evidence would have been admissible. And yet it was now admissible in Williams's trial, specifically to prove that Danny Hansford had fired the same shot. Danny Hansford was treated far worse as a crime victim than he would have been as a defendant.

Recall also that this evidence was supposed to be demonstrating why Williams was afraid of Danny Hansford—so afraid that Williams might reasonably believe Danny was shooting at him when Danny, well—shot at him. But what was this concerned citizen doctor doing? He wasn't testifying to anything Williams knew or believed. He was offering up an option that Danny Hansford was a psychopath. For what purpose? To suggest that Danny had done what Williams claimed Danny had done.

This trial had lost all connection to the question of Williams's state of mind. There is also a gaping hole in the base rationale for admitting this evidence. There would be no evidence whatsoever in any *Williams* trial that Williams had any knowledge of the contents of Hansford's official Georgia Regional records or the observations of any of these witnesses. Yet the assault continued unabated.

As we've noted, there's a reason why such testimony isn't admissible against a defendant accused of an act: It's grossly prejudicial and doesn't prove the facts alleged. For an example, if a man is wanted for a killing in Katmandu and it's undisputed that he has never set foot outside of the United States, proof that he was a raving lunatic wouldn't prove he committed the crime. This evidence in *Williams* was offered for one purpose: to prove that Danny Hansford had probably tried to kill Williams. It couldn't, and didn't, prove any such thing.

It would have been interesting to ask Dr. Brandt if Williams was capable of having killed Danny Hansford in a moment of rage. If he had said he couldn't answer the question without more information, the prosecution could have requested an hour-and-fifteen-minute recess—the total time spent with Danny Hansford by the doctors whose notes Dr. Brandt had pored over.

Some other questions I would have had for Dr. Brandt: Where were the bodies? How had Williams survived so long? To use the defense's favorite event—

April—why hadn't the psychopath killed Williams then, when holding a loaded Luger and facing a defenseless man?

What about the term "psychopath"? Brandt testified that the profession had stopped using the term because it was too general, too imprecise, then proceeded to use it (with obvious reference to Hansford), noting that "they" (psychopaths) don't care, that "they" (psychopaths again) have *no remorse*. This is where we might recall Joseph Goodman's testimony in *Williams I* about Danny's gushing remorse in a purported statement to Goodman about the damages to Williams's house in April.

Another question for Dr. Brandt begs asking. Dr. Brandt's "diagnosis" came from poring over Danny's Georgia Regional Hospital records. If Brandt was right, hadn't the doctors at Georgia Regional committed professional malpractice by allowing this man to leave—twice—even though he was clearly a killer?

And finally, while Brandt wasn't Williams's psychiatrist, he was a licensed psychiatrist testifying as a psychiatric expert. Could Brandt have shed some light on the psyche of a sophisticated man of means who is attracted to "rough trade" like Danny? Were the things that made Danny Hansford a wild, emotionally volatile young man the very things that attracted Williams, aroused Williams, and drove him crazy?

In other words, was it possible that Danny's demons caused the killing in the study, but that Danny was not the one who pulled the trigger?

Dr. Lester Haddad testified that he saw Danny a second time at Memorial Medical Center in August of 1980. Danny had been brought in suffering from an apparent overdose of Limbitrol. Williams had told the jury about this suicide attempt, saying:

> And he says, "I'm going to kill myself." I said, "Oh, yeah?" He said, "Yeah, you know those forty-nine tablets Dr. DeHaven gave you?" I said, "Yeah." He said, "I just took every one of them." ... I got on that phone that second and called Dr. Alton Williams. ... I said, "Dr. Williams, this guy has just taken these pills Dr. DeHaven gave me."

Did Williams ever tell the whole truth about anything? No physician *prescribes* exactly forty-nine pills. Did suicidal Hansford stop and count them? He was about to die, so what did he care? And Dr. DeHaven hadn't given Williams any Limbitrol. I will repeat this several times: Where did Williams get the Limbitrol and why was he taking it? Dr. Haddad told the jury what Limbitrol was:

> A. Mr. Hansford took approximately fifty Limbitrol, which is a tri-cyclic anti-depressant drug. It's a ... for someone who's depressed, and

also in combination with a drug called Librium. It's a combination drug, which is a benzodiazepine, is used for moderate anxiety, mild to moderate anxiety.

Q. Is that a prescription type medication?

A. Yes. Very definitely.

Q. All right, sir.

A. Usually prescribed only by a psychiatrist.

On cross-examination by Mr. Lawton, Dr. Haddad explained further:

A. No. No, this is a drug ... I don't ... I have never ever prescribed Limbitrol for anyone. Limbitrol is prescribed by psychiatrists for patients who have a psychiatric disorder.

Q. Do you know ... was this prescription ...

A. Or for *psychiatric problem*, pardon.

Who was treating Williams for a psychiatric problem? No one said. No one asked.

Dr. Haddad's testimony offered a great example of why they tell you in law school never to ask a question unless you know the answer (even though everyone does). On cross, Dr. Haddad said Danny hadn't been brought in for any kind of "mental problem." Seiler couldn't help himself, so he got up again and asked the following:

Q. I'm not trying to be facetious. You said that he wasn't brought in for any mental problem. Do normal people usually gobble up forty-two (sic) pills of any sort?

MR. LAWTON: I'll object to that, Your Honor. That's ... oh ...

A. I'd kinda like to answer that.

MR. LAWTON: May I take that to mean that I'm overruled?

THE COURT: I think so. Let's let him answer it.

MR. SEILER: I'll withdraw the question.

Picture a lawyer trying to backpedal in a courtroom. Dr. Haddad answered the question anyway, before Seiler could withdraw it:

A. Well, yes, normal people can take an overdose. It's very common, as a matter of fact.

Although Danny might not have had a "mental problem" because he took the pills, the person to whom the pills were prescribed apparently did. Where was Williams getting the Limbitrol, and why was he taking it?

Dr. Albert Patrick Brooks had been working in the Memorial Medical Center emergency room in August of 1980. Dr. Brooks testified, erroneously, that Danny had been treated "on several occasions" at Georgia Regional Hospital. (It was twice, Doctor.) After Danny got out of ICU, he had been transferred to Clark Pavilion for a psychiatric examination and had left the hospital on the tenth of August, three days after being admitted.

The final medical witness was the infamous Dr. DeHaven, who was infamous only for having been blamed so often for Williams's Limbitrol prescription. His testimony was straightforward and professional.

Dr. DeHaven specialized in endocrinology and first saw Williams on April 23, 1981. (He had said April 24 in *Williams I*, but the difference of a day was of no consequence in the case.) Williams had been referred to Dr. DeHaven, who had been told that Williams had passed out at a party. Dr. DeHaven discovered that Williams's diet was a mess and that Williams had been going without eating, substituting alcohol:

He was quite erratic in his eating. He stated that he never had an appetite, ate very erratically, would go long periods without eating, and would drink occas... some alcoholic beverages in lieu of meals, for example.

On cross-examination, the doctor tried to soften his comment about Williams drinking:

A. Yeah, Jim ate erratically. That may be a little misleading, as far as drinking his meals. He would often have some alcoholic beverages, maybe at the time of meals, and not eat.

Q. I think you said, "Taking alcohol in lieu of meals." That's what I have in my notes. Is that what you said?

A. That's what I said.

Dr. DeHaven confirmed, again: He had never advised Williams to have a constant companion, and he had not prescribed Limbitrol for Williams.

Williams had testified earlier to a phone call he claimed making on the night in question to a Bruce Muncher in Hinesville, Georgia. Williams said he made this call to ask his friend about vocational-technical school for Danny. This testimony was designed to show how kind and helpful Williams was, even just before Hansford's explosion into a murderous rage. Seiler asked the questions.

Q. And this was after you came home from the movie—was it before or after you began playing the Atari game?

A. I don't remember. I think it was after the Atari game and maybe before we started the board game. Maybe it was after the board game.

The truth was that this phone call had nothing to do with the board game or Atari game, only the "fool the jury" game. Regarding the time of the call, Seiler even took Williams through an explanation of Mr. Muncher's shift work to explain why Williams believed it was all right to be calling so late at night.

How much could this little story about the helpful mentor help Williams's defense? It was a trifle, at best. If he called Muncher, fine and thanks. But that wasn't good enough. Williams had to lie about it, led by his lawyer.

THE STATE'S REBUTTAL

Leading off its rebuttal phase, the prosecution called Paul J. Leslie, Jr. of Southern Bell, and Buddy Paul Houston of Coastal Utilities Telephone Company of Hinesville. According to their records, there had been a seven-minute phone call made on the night in question, from Williams's house to a Bruce G. Muncher in Hinesville. The time of the call? The call had been made at 9:41 p.m.

Williams had called Muncher before he and Danny ever left for the drive-in. At trial, Seiler made sure to establish that the call had been made after they got home, down to which game they were playing and why Muncher might be up at such a late hour.

It was obviously a lie, so why tell it? Seiler and Williams were working on the theme that there had been nothing but happy moonbeams at Mercer House before the "cocked rattlesnake" went off, that there had been no unpleasantness involving Williams in any way. In fact, Williams was even busy waking up his friend down in Hinesville to try to find Danny a spot in vocational school.

Williams could have gotten credit for calling Muncher. No one would begrudge him that. But the truth about it wouldn't have helped paint the picture the defense was trying to paint. So he lied about it.

Meanwhile, the prosecution had been forced to spend time and trouble tracking down a lie barely worth telling and bringing into court on subpoena two gentlemen who probably had better things to do: Lawyer Games.

In further rebuttal, Ofc. Robert E. (Gene) Roy of the SPD came on to authenticate the autopsy photographs that had been proffered into evidence during the trial. Officer Roy had taken the photographs. To this day, he swears he didn't take them and has no memory of the event. It is entirely possible that he blocked out the entire experience.

That comment is meant to be humorous. Less humorous is the fact that neither the photographs nor the original negatives from the Hansford autopsy can be found, despite the best efforts of the District Attorney's Office and the Savannah-Chatham Metropolitan Police Department. Stay tuned.

The final prosecution witness on rebuttal was Dr. Howard, who returned to address matters raised in the defense's direct case. Addressing a fundamental matter first, the diagram that the defense had been using throughout the trial to illustrate Williams's defense was grossly inaccurate. This was the diagram that Dr. Stone had admitted on cross-examination was merely a "pictorial representation." Dr. Howard explained:

> When anybody makes up a diagram, it's usually to depict facts or to depict a theory of how something happened, and in this case, it's the latter, it depicts a theory of how something happened. Unfortunately, it's not at all consistent with the facts.

Dr. Howard listed the following errors in the diagram.

> The shot to the back showed entry over near [Hansford's] arm and exit in the middle of the chest. According to the autopsy report and photos, the bullet went straight through the body.

Dr. Petty had "corrected" the autopsy report, but the defense hadn't bothered to correct its own diagram. Was this an oversight? Correcting the diagram trashed Williams's claim that he had shot Hansford in the back from behind his desk so, if an oversight, it was a convenient one.

The next mistake had to have been intentional: The defense diagram showed the shot that exited Hansford's chest striking the floor nowhere near where the bullet was dug from the floor:

> The rug very definitely—the hole in the rug very definitely shows that this missile [bullet] was found directly under this hole, under the body, so [the diagram] is completely at variance with what we see in the photographs and at variance to what we see with the description of the body and the photographs.

There were photographs of the points of impact of each shot, and copious testimony on the subject. The defense moved the bullet hole for their diagram. They don't get to do that. Does anyone still believe these lawyers were searching for the truth? Dr. Howard continued. The defense did the same thing with the head shot:

> Here we have the same thing. We have the bullet striking the floor about a body width away whereas, in actuality, it went into the floor, through the rug, about a half a body length—or width, excuse me body width away from the skull.

The photos are clear (Figures 15, 16), and the defense had them. In yet another distortion, the defense diagram showed Danny holding Luger 22A throughout:

We also see the gun remaining in a hand of the victim all the way to the floor. It's very clear that the first thing that happened after the victim was shot in the chest was that the hand clasped the wound, and that the gun is not stained with blood. Therefore, it's impossible that the gun remained in the hand … impossible that the gun—if any—remained in the hand.

So, the diagram was not merely a "pictorial representation" as Dr. Stone had claimed; it was a misleading diagram that was in direct conflict with the evidence.

Then, for the first time in the *Williams* case, someone talked about the hole burned into Williams's desk. Dr. Howard didn't have to address that evidence, and we know the danger. But Dr. Howard was correct: The hole in the leather and the ground-out joint were keys to the events that led to Hansford's death: "[W]e have on the table evidence of anger, where a cigarette is extinguished on the table. So that pretty much fixes the starting position of the victim."

It isn't clear why the next segment of Dr. Howard's testimony was left until rebuttal, but he then discussed the positions of the ejected shell casings, explaining how the casing ejection pattern indicated the firing positions. We know by now why I believe this is enormously important evidence. In hindsight, I believe it could have been front and center in the prosecution case, including in the first trial, to separate out the firearms evidence according to the weapon with which each item was matched (Figure 13).

What about thrusting legs and headless chickens? Dr. Howard pointed out that involuntary reflex movements of a dead man could not explain the evidence:

Purposeful movement is like moving a hand from under the chest, like rotating it and putting it on top of a weapon. I find … that … I think that's *impossible*. I also think that putting a leg under a chair and purposely moving a chair or kicking a chair up in the air, I think that's also *impossible*. Cadaveric movements may consist of a movement … where one muscle group pulls on the arm, or one muscle group pulls on a leg and/or vibratory movements with the muscles. I do not think that—especially under the condition of these wounds—that purposeful movement, like the lifting of a leg, or the rotation movement and lifting of the hand, are possible.

On re-cross of Dr. Howard, Seiler took a pass at addressing the ground-out joint and the hole burned in the desktop. The defense had tried ignoring them, but once Dr. Howard pointed them out, the defense had no choice but to try to deal with this evidence.

Seiler asked Dr. Howard if he was certain that Williams had been able to see the ground-out joint from his desk chair. Howard said he believed Williams could have seen it. (More importantly, the point was for Williams to see it. That was why Danny did it. It probably got him killed.)

Seiler suggested that Hansford was drunk and missed the ashtray. First, Hansford wasn't "drunk." Williams himself had testified that Hansford wasn't drunk, and his blood-alcohol content had been under the legal limit to drive at the time (dead people still weren't metabolizing alcohol in 1983). Dr. Howard pointed this out to Seiler when Seiler tried to testify again:

Q. All right, it's not unlike a drunk to miss an ashtray.

A. Whoa! Whoa! Let's not call point oh nine drunk.

Q. All right, then, I'll use intoxication.

A. In fact, we couldn't really talk about convicting him of driving under the influence at that level. Right.

Besides, there were other joints in the ashtray; it wasn't that hard to hit. And the burn mark was nowhere near the ashtray (Figures 21, 22). That wasn't exactly a near miss. Most importantly, the joint had been ground down into the desktop until it burned a hole in the leather—hardly the act of someone accidentally missing an ashtray.

With that brief glimpse of a likely scenario that led to Danny Hansford's death, the evidence in *Williams II* was complete and the case was once again handed over to a jury.

This second jury had heard much the same case as the first with respect to the physical evidence. The defense's new experts had used deceptive diagrams, irrelevant tests, and fantastical opinions based on fractured science in an attempt to find anything that might jar the case loose from its moorings. In the end, the funky chicken, bloody rag, boat anchor, photo juggling, rigged demonstrations, and trigger-pull charades had hopefully been exposed.

And yet, it's equally possible that this second jury saw only the show presented on the courtroom stage for their entertainment and not the sleight of hand or the secret pockets in the magician's cloak. Lawyer Games might only be visible when we know what to look for and when we have the time—to look under the rug, pull up the flooring, and check beneath the stage.

Figure 1

Figure 2

Figure 3

Figure 4

Figure 5

Figure 6

Figure 7

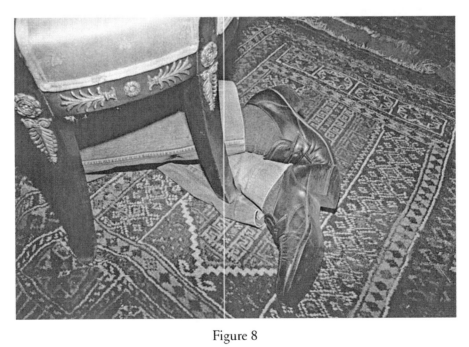

Figure 8

Figure 9

Figure 10

Figure 11

Figure 12

Evidence Matched to Luger 23A (Williams Weapon)
[Note: Shell Casings and Live Round are ENLARGED for viewing only.]

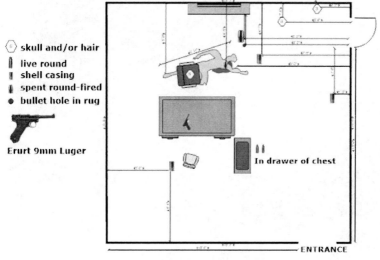

skull and/or hair
live round
shell casing
spent round-fired
bullet hole in rug

Erurt 9mm Luger

In drawer of chest

ENTRANCE

Figure 13

Figure 14

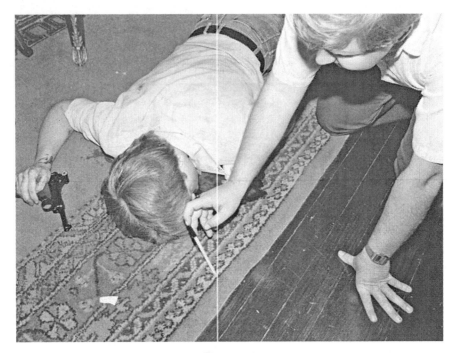

Figure 15

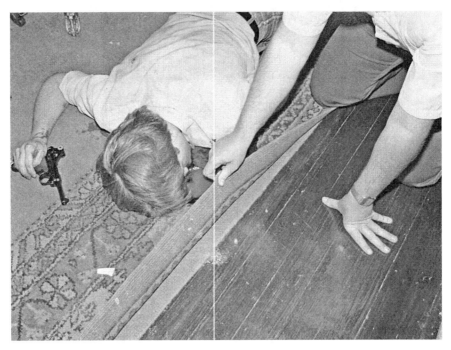

Figure 16

**HEAD ROTATION REQUIRED
WHEN HEAD IS RAISED**

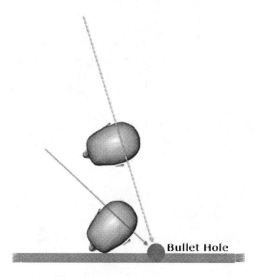

Figure 17

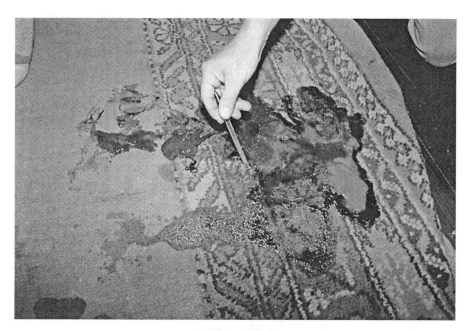

Figure 18

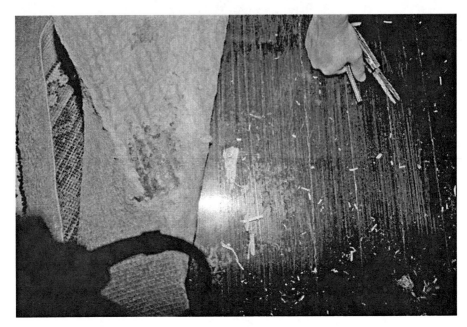

Figure 19

Evidence Matched to Luger 22A (The "Attack" Weapon)
[Note: Shell Casing, Live Round and Fragment ENLARGED for viewing only.]

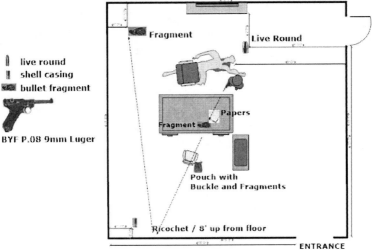

Figure 20

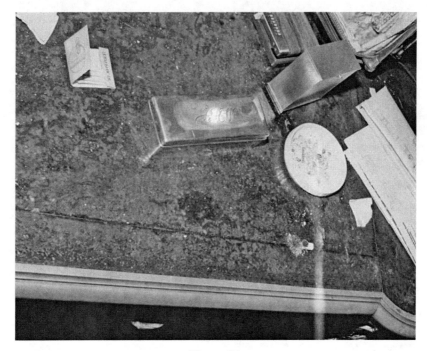

Figure 21

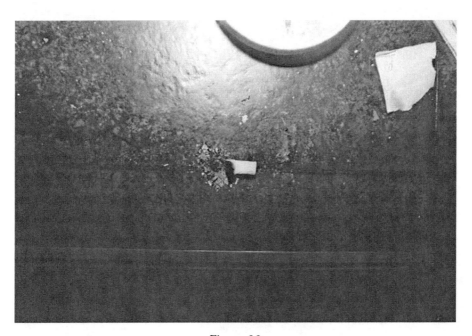

Figure 22

Figure 23

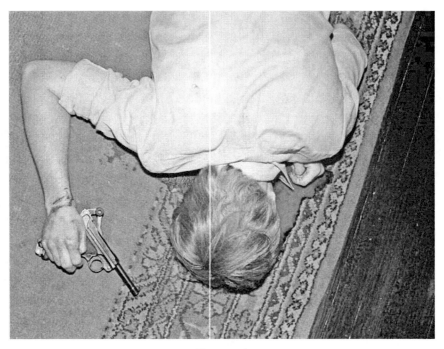

Figure 24

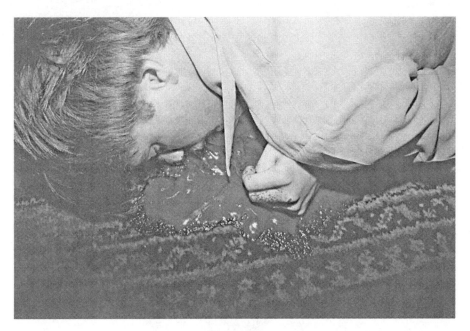

Figure 25

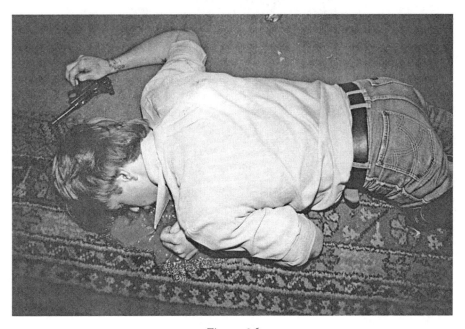

Figure 26

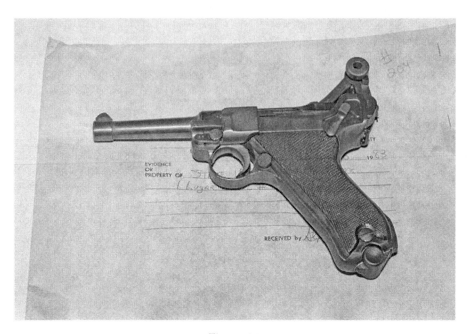

Figure 27

Figure 28

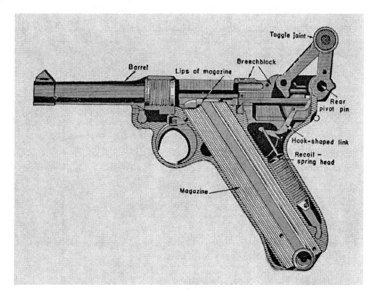

Figure 29

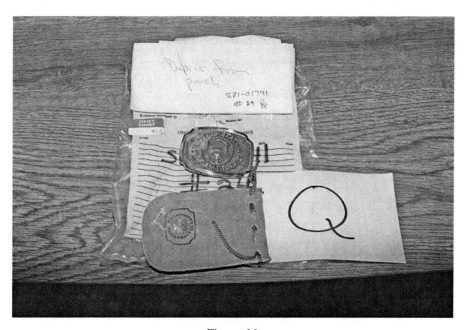

Figure 30

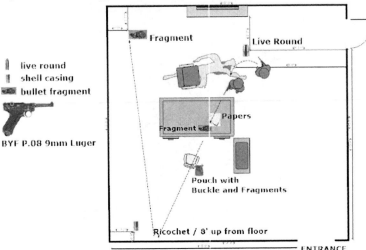

Evidence Matched to Luger 22A (The "Attack" Weapon)
[Note: Shell Casing, Live Round and Fragment ENLARGED for viewing only.]

live round
shell casing
bullet fragment

BYF P.08 9mm Luger

Fragment
Live Round
Papers
Fragment
Pouch with
Buckle and Fragments
Ricochet / 8' up from floor
ENTRANCE

Figure 31

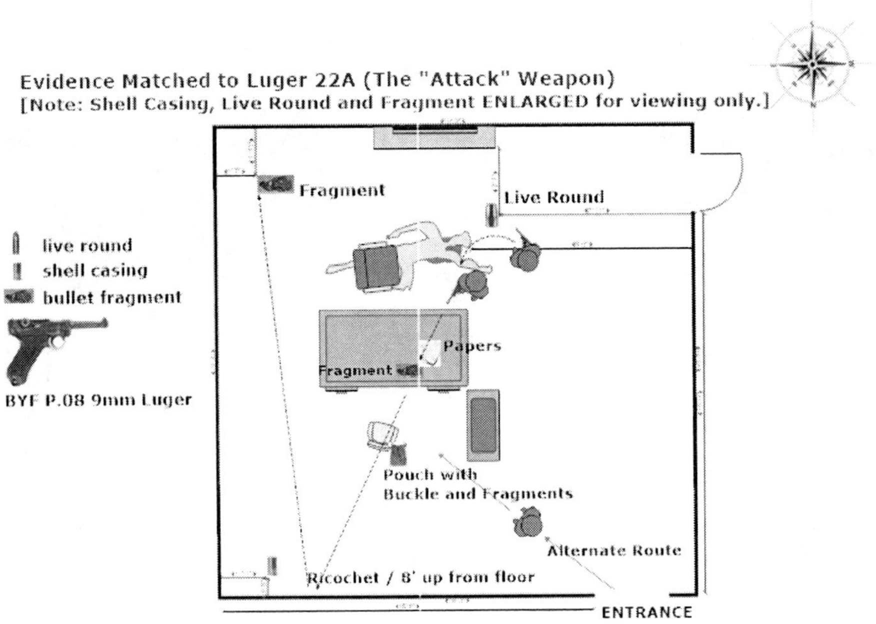

Evidence Matched to Luger 22A (The "Attack" Weapon)
[Note: Shell Casing, Live Round and Fragment ENLARGED for viewing only.]

live round
shell casing
bullet fragment

BYF P.08 9mm Luger

Fragment
Live Round
Papers
Fragment
Pouch with
Buckle and Fragments
Alternate Route
Ricochet / 8' up from floor
ENTRANCE

Figure 32

ALTERNATIVE FIRING ANGLES
SHOT No. 1

Solid = Trajectory required to match autopsy
Dashed = Normal expected trajectory

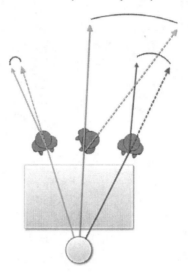

Figure 33

Figure 34

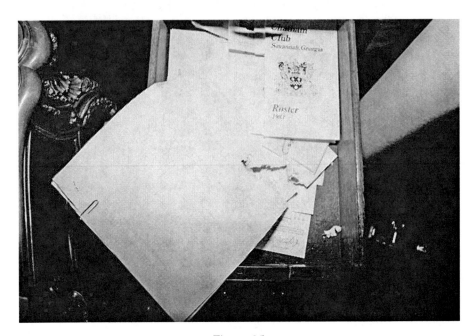

Figure 35

Figure 36

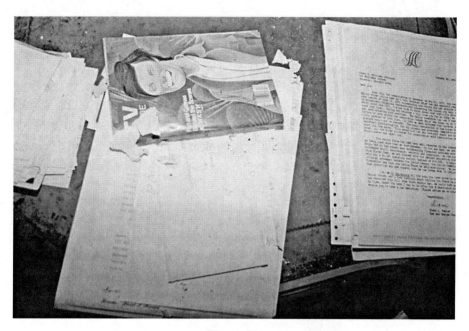

Figure 37

Figure 38

Figure 39

Figure 40

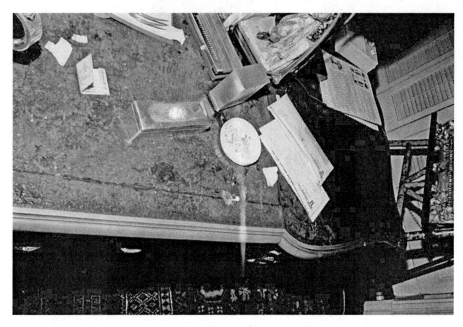

Figure 41

Figure 42

Figure 43

Figure 44

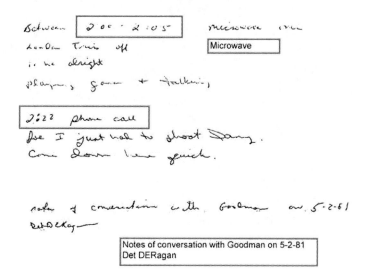

Figure 45

Figure 46

Figure 47

Figure 48

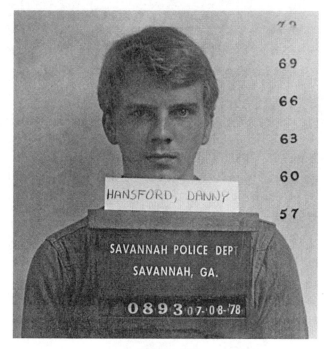

Figure 49

Figure 50

CHAPTER 21

THE VERDICT

F ollowing closing arguments and instructions on the law, another jury began its deliberations in the case of *State of Georgia vs. James A. Williams*.

On October 8, 1983, Williams was again convicted of the murder of Danny Hansford. The law in Georgia had changed since *Williams I* and an appeal bond was not permitted in murder cases. Williams was taken directly to the county jail.

CHAPTER 22

MOTION FOR NEW TRIAL—PANTS ON FIRE

The first step in an appeal is to file a Motion for New Trial. This was not a major event in *Williams I*. That would change by a factor approaching infinity in *Williams II*. The motion was filed on October 31, 1983.[103] It would not be ruled upon until the following August, approaching a year after the verdict—while Williams sat in jail.

How often is a Motion for New Trial granted? Not often, as we've noted, because a defendant's complaints typically focus on alleged errors by the same judge hearing the motion. There is, however, an alternative to telling the judge that he or she screwed up: discover yourself some brand-new evidence.

Williams's defense team had already demonstrated an aptitude in that area and soon, a blizzard of sworn affidavits began to appear, all filed by Williams's lawyers and all claiming to contain "newly discovered" evidence. The stream of affidavits continued until Judge Oliver finally issued an order setting a cutoff date after which no further "new evidence" would be accepted. This fountain of new evidence was a gross aberration. Legitimate newly discovered evidence is extremely rare. To have it sprouting like clover in a spring lawn was unheard of.

There are reasons that legitimate newly discovered evidence is rare. The evidence must (1) have been discovered only *after* the end of the trial; (2) have been impossible to discover earlier with the exercise of "reasonable due diligence" (meaning the reasonable efforts of a person honestly looking for it); (3) be "material" and not merely cumulative (more of the same thing) or impeaching evidence; and (4) be likely to have caused *a different result* in the case if it had been known and introduced at trial.

This combined hurdle is extremely high, as it should be. You don't want to waste the court's time, and you don't want lawyers playing games. With that said, let the games begin.

Because this evidence couldn't be cumulative, Danny attacking another stomach with his toe was no good. Something big was needed. Something that hadn't been known, that couldn't have been discovered, that didn't duplicate any other evidence, and that was big enough that it would likely have led to an acquittal of Williams.

Facing those insurmountable odds, what fell into the lap of the luckiest man on earth? A cavalcade of new witnesses to swear that Danny Hansford had been actively plotting to kill Williams right before he—coincidentally—tried to kill

Williams. A second plot involved only putting Williams in the hospital so Hansford could steal some jewelry.

The "newly discovered" murder plot was remarkable. It involved Hansford openly telling people he barely knew that he was going to kill Williams and take his money. The plot was notably short on details, such as how Danny was going to get Williams's money after killing him. But it would do in a pinch.

The stink coming from the affidavits should have gagged the court clerk who had to file them. But aside from the odor, there was another obvious flaw. According to the affidavits, they contained evidence of an actual plan—but none of the "plans" called for Hansford to go into an unprovoked rage and kill Williams for no rational reason.

What about the reasonable due-diligence requirement? Had this new evidence been *impossible* to discover? The calendar was approaching 1984. How had these murder plots remained undiscovered, despite the claims in the affidavits that Hansford had yapped about them all over town? By the end of 1983, two well-publicized trials had been conducted. Yet only after the verdict in the second trial did this gaggle of witnesses recall Danny telling them, two and a half years earlier, that he was plotting to kill Williams.

Despite these challenges to common sense, "new evidence" was pouring forth from defense counsel's word processors at the precise moment Williams was in need of some new evidence. Despite factors spelling F-A-B-R-I-C-A-T-I-O-N in large red letters, if someone was willing to swear an affidavit and a lawyer was willing to file it, the court was obliged to consider it.

So, the defense filed its Motion for New Trial, listing errors they alleged from the trial and the allegation that they had some brand new evidence. As required, the defense filed affidavits from their new witnesses, signed under oath, setting out what each witness would say should Judge Oliver give the defendant another "do-over."

What did the district attorney do when new witness affidavits began appearing on his doorstep like junk mail (a not-inapt analogy)? Spencer Lawton sent investigators to talk to the people who had sworn the affidavits. When allegations of buying testimony arose, Lawton called in the Georgia Bureau of Investigation, and GBI Special Agent R. Stone was assigned to assist District Attorney's Office Chief Investigator J. D. Smith.

Being visited by investigators can quickly impress upon a "new witness" the seriousness of the business into which they have inserted themselves. In *Williams*, the process exploded. Witnesses gave statements to investigators recanting their affidavits. When defense counsel was notified of the flip, new affidavits would appear claiming that the witness had never said what investigators claimed they had said (even when the statements to investigators had been recorded). These affidavits reasserting the original affidavits would then be followed by affidavits from investigators saying yes, the person interviewed had said exactly what had been reported (and often recorded). It was an affidavit avalanche unparalleled in criminal practice.

Up first is an affidavit sequence that had "Savannah" written all over it. James Franklin Kicklighter signed an affidavit saying that Danny Hansford had told him personally that he was going to kill Williams. The affidavit was filed on May 25, 1984. On May 26, Mr. Kicklighter was visited by Investigator Smith and SA Stone.

Mr. Kicklighter said the statement he had given Seiler had been a favor to Seiler because he had known Seiler since the attorney was a kid, that Seiler's mother had taught him in school, that he had gotten Seiler a job at the beach as a lifeguard and that, once, after he had been drinking and having trouble in the waves, Seiler had dragged him out of the ocean and probably saved his life. Seiler had told Kicklighter that this was the most important case he'd ever handled. So Kicklighter had done Seiler a favor with his affidavit.

Smith and Stone asked if Hansford had told Kicklighter he wanted to kill Williams. Kicklighter told them no. Danny had only said that he was mad at Williams and hated Williams for having him arrested and put out of the house (in April). Smith and Stone read Kicklighter's original affidavit to him twice, but he repeated that Hansford had never said he was going to kill Williams. In other words, the statement in the affidavit wasn't true.

They asked Kicklighter if he had read the affidavit that bore his signature and he stated that he had but that he was nearly blind in his left eye from cataracts and that he didn't really understand "legal stuff." When asked why he hadn't said anything for three years and two trials, Kicklighter claimed that he had been out of town for the first trial and hadn't wanted to get involved. He had only given the affidavit now because Seiler had called him and asked him to do it.

Smith's memo to the district attorney's office outlining this interview was dated May 29. A copy of the memo was provided to the defense. On June 2, the defense filed another affidavit from Kicklighter swearing that none of what Smith and Stone had said was true, that his first affidavit was all true, and that, contrary to what they said, he had excellent vision with his glasses. Apparently, Smith and Stone had made up the whole thing. Kicklighter did not explain how they knew about his cataracts. Kicklighter had either lied now in two affidavits or had lied to Smith and Stone in his interview.

On June 6, the district attorney filed an affidavit from a James Thomas, who knew Kicklighter from Thomas's work in maintenance at Kicklighter's apartment building. Thomas's affidavit said Kicklighter had a terrible reputation and that Thomas wouldn't believe a word Kicklighter said. Also on June 6, Investigator Smith filed an affidavit confirming the substance of the Kicklighter interview. Yes, Kicklighter had said exactly what Smith had reported. On June 8, GBI SA Stone filed an affidavit also affirming the interview content.

The story then became uniquely Savannah. On July 20, the defense filed two additional affidavits, but not about Investigator Smith or SA Stone. These affidavits were about James Thomas.

Myrtle Rowe, manager of the apartment building where Kicklighter had lived and Thomas had worked, swore that Kicklighter was a good fellow, that she wouldn't believe a word that James Thomas said (paraphrased), that Thomas was a terrible worker and would have been fired. Thomas wasn't fired. He left voluntarily in January of 1984.

Angela Stafford, assistant manager of the same apartment building, filed an affidavit confirming that Thomas was no good and not truthful. She claimed that she had smelled the odor of "marijuana and/or similar drugs" on his clothing. I don't know what "and/or similar drugs" she would have smelled or what they might have smelled like. Who uses such grammatical conventions as "and/or similar drugs"? Lawyers do. Stafford's affidavit, like that of Ms. Rowe, had been drafted by defense counsel.

Ms. Stafford also said that Kicklighter was a fine fellow and the only complaints they'd had about him had been for being drunk on the premises. Ms. Stafford started work at the apartments in January of 1983. Kicklighter moved out on February 12. Ms. Stafford had apparently gotten to know Kicklighter's reputation for being drunk on the premises very quickly.

That is a classic Savannah tale: cross-affidavits about who's a liar and a drunk.

But there was more funny business about Kicklighter's affidavit. Kicklighter barely knew Hansford but claimed that Danny had showed up at his door one night, having known where he lived because Danny had "followed him home from a party" one night in the past. Danny said he was hungry. Kicklighter let Danny in, gave him dinner, and let him sleep in Kicklighter's bed. Kicklighter slept on the sofa. Likely? I leave that to the reader.

Then, according to Kicklighter's affidavit, his brand-new friend told Kicklighter that he was going to kill Williams. Kicklighter never mentioned the plot to Williams. No, not even after Danny reportedly *did* try to kill Williams or after Williams had been tried and *convicted twice* for killing Hansford. Kicklighter hadn't uttered a peep until his dear friend Seiler, who had saved Kicklighter from drowning drunk in the waves at Tybee Island—gave him a call in 1984.

Danny also supposedly shared his murder plot with one Timothy Wayne DeLoach, an acquaintance Williams made in the Chatham County Jail. DeLoach swore his first affidavit on Thursday, May 3, 1984. Coincidentally—or not coincidentally—DeLoach also happened to know Sam Weatherly, Seiler's private investigator. Considering the connection, one might question how this "evidence" had been impossible for Seiler to discover until after Williams's second conviction.

According to DeLoach's affidavit, he had run into Hansford at a party shortly before Danny was killed. DeLoach said Danny had cocaine and told DeLoach that he got the money for it from a guy DeLoach figured was Williams. Danny told DeLoach that they should kill Williams and take his money. There was no mention of how this plot was supposed to work. DeLoach said he "knew" Danny to carry a .38 on the street and knew that Danny was "crazy" and "capable of violence." How many street punks use the phrase "capable of violence"? I would submit that none do—but this one did, in his affidavit prepared by Williams's lawyer.

DeLoach barely knew Hansford, if he knew him at all. No one had ever mentioned Danny and cocaine, not even Williams (it's not a street hustler habit; it's too expensive), or mentioned Danny in the same sentence with a .38 revolver. One would think it might have come up.

The weekend after DeLoach's affidavit was filed, the Savannah paper published a story, naming no sources, about exciting "new evidence" in the *Williams* case, along with DeLoach's name. Tuesday morning, May 8, Investigator Smith visited DeLoach at the county jail. DeLoach was furious. The following is lengthy, but the DeLoach affidavit will turn out to be one of the more powerful exhibits in the Lawyer Games prosecution of Williams's defense team:

> Mr. DeLoach replied, "I've been expecting you to come see me and I just want to say for the record, that this whole thing is a crock of shit. Those sons of bitches fucked me." I asked Mr. DeLoach if he was implying that the statement he had given to Mr. Williams' attorneys was false and DeLoach replied "That's right." I asked Mr. DeLoach who he was referring to when he said "They fucked me," and DeLoach replied, "That damn Sammy Weatherly and Sonny Seiler."
>
> DeLoach said that he had met Williams in jail and had agreed to help him. "Weatherly told me he was working for Sonny Seiler and a guy named Catts who are the lawyers for Williams. It was at this point that we agreed to a deal and I made a statement saying that I was at a party at a guy named Wainwright's apartment and that

Danny Hansford was there with drugs and money and that he got it from a "fag" named Jim. I was going to say Jim Williams but Weatherly said just say Jim. I also was originally going to say that I had sold Hansford a hot .38 caliber revolver, but Weatherly told me just to say I knew him to carry a .38. Weatherly told me that the District Attorney would tear me up because of my record but not to worry because they just wanted the court to believe Hansford was dangerous."

I asked Mr. DeLoach what he meant when he said he and Weatherly made a deal and DeLoach replied by holding up five fingers and saying, "Five of those will make you do a lot of things." I asked Mr. DeLoach was he implying that he had received five hundred dollars for his statement? Mr. DeLoach laughed and said, "Shit, Jim Williams spends that much for supper." I then asked Mr. DeLoach did he mean he was to receive five thousand dollars and he said "Yes." I asked Mr. DeLoach how and when the money was to be paid. Mr. DeLoach replied, "The deal is that after I made an official statement I was to get $2,500.00 and if they got a new trial I would get another $2,500.00." He went on to say that he had not received any of the money yet.

This information was provided to defense counsel. On June 6, Williams's lawyers filed the grandmother of all affidavits, a full nine legal pages of typed, polished lawyerspeak prepared by Seiler, supposedly containing DeLoach's words. The affidavit claimed that Smith had made up everything (again) and that the money suggestion had come from *Smith*, not DeLoach.

The affidavit also said that after Smith's visit, Investigator Smith and GBI SA Stone had involved DeLoach's family and that, feeling pressure, DeLoach had met with SA Stone on May 10 and had given him a recorded statement. The problem for DeLoach—and for Seiler—was that the recorded statement DeLoach gave to SA Stone confirmed *everything* Smith had reported, including the promise to pay for his affidavit—$2,500 up front and another $2,500 upon success. And it was all on tape.

Seiler was in a bind. Were we close to a confession in the Lawyer Games prosecution? How does a witness claim that somebody recorded him saying something he never said? DeLoach simply said, in his new Seiler affidavit, that the *recording itself* was a lie because he and GBI SA Stone had agreed in advance that the statement would be *made up*. Right. And I'm the real Batman.

If you believed before this precise moment that there were limits to what a witness would say or a lawyer would do, reconsideration might be in order. If necessary, just flip back and read this section again. I will wait here for you.

The supposedly "made-up" GBI interview with DeLoach also produced information about other new witnesses Seiler and Weatherly had rounded up.

RS: All right, was there any mention of another witness in this case who had also provided them with a statement?

TD: If I'm not mistaken, I believe his name is Gary Williams.

RS: All right.

TD: Or Wayne Williams or something, I'm not particularly sure.

RS: Who told you this?

TD: Sam Weatherly told me what all he had as far as evidence or some of what they had going for the motion for new trial.

RS: Did he indicate to you that they had paid that witness anything?

TD: There was an indication there, more than that, they indicated that it was a crock of bull to begin with. Every indication in my opinion points to that they knew that it was a crock of bull.

RS: You mean that Sam said he didn't believe the other witness statement?

TD: He said that there was room for improvement in the guy's statement at one time.

RS: Alright did they ever mention ever having paid any other witness in the case?

TD: There was one incident whether it is true or not or whether I've read it wrong, there was a witness who testified that they heard three or four shots on the night of the incident, murder or whatever it was. They indicated that she was taken care of.

That would be Claudina Delk Smith. Gary or Wayne Williams was most likely Joseph Williamson, who filed an affidavit claiming that Danny had been plotting to put Williams in the hospital so he could steal some jewelry.

DeLoach's nine-page typed affidavit denying this—and everything else he'd said on tape—was prepared by Seiler. Here is a sample of its content: "I realized the interest that obviously existed in the District Attorney's Office with regards to the Williams case and decided, at this point, to use my position in the matter for personal gain."[104] How likely is it that Timothy DeLoach either uttered or wrote those words?

At the same time, it would be appropriate to ask if the attorney who filed this affidavit believed it to be true. Was there any incentive for Seiler to falsify

DeLoach's second affidavit (setting aside the first affidavit for the moment)? Seiler had been accused, in separate statements given to a district attorney's office investigator and a GBI Special Agent, of agreeing to pay a witness for false evidence—evidence that Seiler filed in the record of a criminal case. A sworn affidavit is subject to rules related to perjury, and procuring and filing false affidavits is an ethics violation for a lawyer.

What were Seiler's choices? He could have filed his own affidavit, swearing that DeLoach made up the story to Smith and Stone about the payoff. If DeLoach had made it up, wasn't this the most logical step to take to get the truth out there—call DeLoach a liar, if that's what he was?

But Seiler didn't do that. Instead, he filed the second affidavit from DeLoach claiming that the Chief Investigator for the District Attorney's Office and a Special Agent of the GBI were both, separately, lying—even in the face of the recording of DeLoach's GBI statement. Why make that choice instead?

There are two possibilities. Maybe Seiler wanted to try to preserve DeLoach's original affidavit for Williams's benefit. However, that affidavit couldn't have retained any credibility at that point. DeLoach was useless to Williams.

What is the second possibility? That what DeLoach told Smith and Stone was all true, meaning that, if Seiler called DeLoach out and claimed that DeLoach had lied, it was virtually certain that DeLoach would launch into an accusation aria against Seiler, reaffirm what he had told Stone and Smith, and blow up Seiler's world and his legal career.

Given the choice, Seiler doubled down on DeLoach's original fairy tale about the murder plot, the cocaine, and a .38 revolver, despite a taped recanting of the tale by DeLoach himself. Even if he had filed two fabricated affidavits, Seiler would at least stay on the good side of a man who could threaten his law license. Faced with two bad choices, Seiler chose one.

Seiler filed DeLoach's second affidavit on June 6. On June 7, Smith and Stone both filed sworn affidavits confirming and reasserting everything in their reports.

As for DeLoach's family getting involved, DeLoach had said that Stone and Smith were the instigators of that intervention. As it turned out, DeLoach's brother, Terry, had gone to the jail to confront Timothy—on Monday, May 7, 1984, the day *before* J. D. Smith spoke with DeLoach for the first time. DeLoach might have felt pressure from his family to tell the truth, but it hadn't come from the district attorney's office.

What about the plot to put Williams in the hospital? Joseph Williamson's affidavit explained that Danny had wanted to put Williams in the hospital so he could steal some jewelry. Williamson also claimed to have seen Hansford firing shots in front of the house in April. He was almost positive that the shooter had been Danny, and he was certain that the shooting had taken place in the daytime. As we know, it happened after 3:00 in the morning.

When interviewed, Williamson said he hadn't mentioned anything about any of his "information" until an unidentified "lady" talked to him. The "lady" turned out to be his friend's mother, who happened to know Williams and Seiler.

There were other affidavits. Most talked about plots to kill Williams. But there was an affidavit from a Danny Ray Parker which claimed something quite different. Parker claimed Williams was offering money around the jail for witnesses, including one Timothy DeLoach. Parker's affidavit was filed by the prosecution.

The affidavit from Parker triggered a telling reaction from Seiler. Parker was lying scum—according to a fresh new affidavit of Kenneth Dilas, a fellow inmate of Parker, Williams, and Deloach. According to Dilas, Williams and DeLoach had had no contact at all at the jail, at least until November of 1983:

Williams and DeLoach, to the best of my knowledge, had no contact and did not correspond prior to my being transferred to the state prison system in November, 1983.

It wasn't clear why Kenneth Dilas would be privy to all contact and correspondence between the inmates at the county jail. Dilas also swore that conversations Parker claimed had taken place in the medical holding area of the jail couldn't have taken place because none of the three (Williams, DeLoach, and Parker) had ever been there.

Seiler also filed an affidavit from the sheriff, Walter Mitchell Jr.:

The medical holding area of the jail is designated as Pod 3-C. None of the three inmates (Williams, DeLoach, and Parker) have been assigned to Pod 3-C at any time during the period in question.[105]

All fixed? Not so fast. Examining Dilas's affidavit in detail, Dilas said he became acquainted with Parker when both were being *treated* in the *medical holding area*, Dilas for knee surgery and Parker for what Dilas claimed was herpes. There's more: Dilas also said he became pals with Williams in this same medical holding area:

He (Williams) was assigned to a single cell which had no shower, and he was brought to the medical holding area to shower and shave. He was often left *in our area* between 10:00 a.m. and 5:00 p.m. to shave, shower, and watch television[.]

By "our" area, Dilas is referring to himself and Parker. Sheriff Mitchell's affidavit was true, but only technically. Neither Williams nor Parker had been *assigned* to Pod 3-C, but that had nothing to do with whether they had been in the area for *other reasons*. Pod assignments were not the only indication of inmate interaction. The false impression intended to be created by one defense affidavit—Mitchell's—was exposed by another defense affidavit—Dilas's. Ironic.

To complete the connections, DeLoach and Parker *were* assigned to the same cell area during 1983. This was confirmed by both the Dilas and Mitchell affidavits. As to the contention that Williams and DeLoach had nothing to do with each other, Williams himself exposed that lie. On August 11, 1984, Williams wrote Timothy DeLoach this note:

Sam Weatherly will be by soon and I will ask him to get a copy of the David Hayes affidavit. We now have seventeen affidavits of all kinds.

... Keep things going. The DA has played all his cards and has about cornered himself. Thing are about to change for both of us.[106]

It's signed, "All the best, Jim." Any further question about whether DeLoach knew Williams and Weatherly, or how Williams was keeping himself busy at the county jail?

There's more to the affidavit blizzard than whether or not the affiants themselves were lying. Lawyers aren't allowed to file affidavits without taking responsibility for them. Lawyers are "officers of the court" and not mere bystanders. With respect to "newly discovered evidence" affidavits, not only must the affidavits meet the required criteria, but the attorneys filing them must also file affidavits of their own. The relevant affidavit in this instance was signed by Seiler, Catts, and Weatherly and was sworn on May 2, 1984. It stated:

In the opinion of the undersigned counsel, the facts set forth in the Affidavits of said witnesses are not cumulative only, are so material that had they been available they would probably have produced a different verdict, would have been offered by the defense if available, would not only have had the effect of impeaching the credit of any other witness, and were admissible at trial.

What this affidavit does not say is presumed: that the affidavits these attorneys are filing are not false. Reference to Williams's note to DeLoach might be in order.

To put it mildly, the affidavits were not persuasive to the court. Nor was the remainder of the Motion for New Trial. It was denied by Judge Oliver on August 26, 1984. Finally, the appeal could proceed.

But first, a brief jump in time is in order, to cover a fascinating series of discoveries. This information has not been previously discussed publically, because the information covers several years and wasn't raised in any formal proceeding.

In December of 1985, Investigator Smith interviewed a Billy Richardson at the Rutledge Correctional Institution. Richardson claimed he had been present when a Wayne Sexton had discussed with Sexton's wife whether Sexton should take money he'd been offered by Williams, while Sexton was in the Chatham County Jail, to "lie on the victim."[107] Richardson said Sexton's wife Carol had tried to talk Wayne out of it. Richardson didn't know if Wayne had taken Williams up on the offer. Smith later learned that Wayne Sexton had left the state and was separated from Carol.

In May of 1987, an inmate at the county jail, one Thomas James Padgett, was interviewed by Smith and Investigator Roger Orr. Padgett was off on the details but was adamant that when he was in jail after the second Williams trial, he and others had been approached by Williams to appear as witnesses for him to say that the victim had been a really bad and violent person, for which Williams was willing to pay $1,000.

Later that month (May 1987), Investigator Smith was contacted by a state probation officer who asked if Smith was looking for a Carol Sexton. Smith replied that he had been looking for Carol's husband Wayne. Using information supplied by the probation office, Smith contacted Carol Sexton. When Smith told her why he had been trying to find Wayne, Carol said she remembered the money offer episode herself. Wayne had come home from the jail on bond and told her that Williams "had offered to pay him to testify against the guy he had killed." She had begged Wayne not to get involved and didn't know if he had done it or not, though she knew he was easily swayed by money.

Thus, a year and two years after the affidavit blizzard was over, corroboration surfaced from two independent sources that Williams had been trying to buy witnesses at the county jail.

The question remains: Who was responsible for the false affidavit blizzard? The affidavits appear to have been produced either by Seiler or Seiler's investigator. Austin Catts was part of The Garland Firm in Atlanta, and, unless proved otherwise, my presumption is that he wasn't in Savannah drafting affidavits but it's possible.

The preparer of a document can often be recognized by format (some affidavits spell out page numbers, which is rare) and by the name of the notary (generally a staff member in the lawyer's office). There also can be clues within the syntax. For example, several affidavits contain the phrase "with regards to." The correct term is "regard," while "regards" are what we give to Broadway (thanks to George M. Cohan's song). This grammatical "tic" is a clue that the affidavits were probably prepared by the same lawyer.

Seiler wouldn't likely dispute that his office prepared affidavits. The question isn't who typed them but, rather, who composed their contents. Affidavits are routinely prepared by a lawyer to say things the way the lawyer wants them said. It's a standard (though not exemplary) practice. The witness then reads the affidavit, and if the witness agrees the affidavit says more or less what he or she would have said, the witness signs it before a notary. Reading the new witness affidavits makes this obvious. None of the statements was likely authored by the person signing it. That alone doesn't make the affidavit false; the facts can still be true.

The facts can also be demonstrably untrue. It's clear that facts in these affidavits were fabricated or the affiants lied to investigators when interviewed, and it's not credible that Seiler didn't know it. Is that conclusion shocking? Is it difficult to believe that a former state bar president, breeder of cute bulldogs, and prominent booster of the state university's athletic teams would do such a thing? If necessary, reserve judgment until this tale is complete, and then ask the question again.

In the meantime, another Savannah case might shed some light on the matter. In 1995, in the federal District Court case of *Knox v. Hayes*, Chief Judge Edenfield threw Seiler and his entire firm off the case for *knowingly* and *willfully* procuring a false affidavit of a key witness in the case. Seiler's violations in *Knox* included "incorporating both false and misleading statements in the affidavit" and "allowing [the witness] to sign it when both Seiler and [the witness] knew it was false."[108] In another portion of the opinion, Judge Edenfield made an observation that invites a comparison to *Williams*:

> In further support of his position, Mr. Seiler presents a second affidavit. ... The Court does not accord much weight to it. Aside from the fact that the affidavit was taken expressly to assist Mr. Seiler's defense

against Mr. [Steven E.] Scheer's charges, there is obvious irony in asking the Court to rely on an affidavit as proof of Mr. Seiler's good faith
conduct regarding another affidavit.[109]

Does the fact that Seiler was found to have knowingly produced a false affidavit in an unrelated federal case mean that he knowingly produced false affidavits in the *Williams* case? No. It doesn't prove that he did. It only proves that
he would.

CHAPTER 23

THE APPEAL

"**M**y role is to interpret the evidence, the physical evidence that's present." So said Dr. Charles S. Petty, defense witness in *Williams II*.

After the decision of the Georgia Supreme Court in the appeal of the conviction, this might have put Dr. Petty in violation of Georgia law, because the court was going to adopt a rule in favor of giving a jury in Georgia as little help as possible in figuring out a crime scene.

In a 4-3 decision written by Justice George T. Smith, the court reversed Williams's second conviction on the ground that allowing an expert witness in homicide investigations to testify to conclusions regarding the scene of a suspected homicide was a violation so serious that the case had to be reversed, even though the defense hadn't complained of the error and even though the error was deemed "harmless" by the court, hence striking a mighty blow in the name of jury ignorance.

The court said the *Williams* evidence was so easily understood by a layperson that allowing an expert in crime scene investigation—Detective Ragan—to draw conclusions from a crime scene invalidated the conviction. This was despite finding—for the second time—that the evidence fully supported the verdict. There was nothing wrong with the evidence. It simply wasn't complicated enough for the court's liking.

The decision also ignored the fact that the defense called its own experts. The supreme court believed the jurors could figure everything out on their own even though the experts couldn't agree on much of anything.

It was bad law. Requiring that juries be given as little help as possible in the interpretation of evidence hardly serves the cause of justice. The decision was also impossible to implement because it required those involved to guess what an appeals court might think of a given crime scene.

Justice Charles L. Weltner wrote a strong dissent. Justice Weltner noted the internal inconsistency in Justice Smith's opinion. If the evidence was so obvious that a lay juror could understand it, how could it be error to allow a detective to testify to the same thing? Justice Weltner noted, "Obviously, a dead man cannot place a chair leg upon the fabric of his trousers."[110]

Unfortunately, even Justice Weltner missed the point. If he believed a dead man couldn't place a chair leg upon the fabric of his trousers, he should have attended the *Williams II* trial to hear Dr. Petty claim that the dead man had done just that. These seven robbed justices sitting in Atlanta had no idea what a lay juror could or could not understand about the limitations of a cadaveric spasm or the implications of a 0.02 barium nitrate reading from a GSR swab. Even the dissent's analysis in the case was wrong.

As for the majority, perhaps most stunning was the fact that the court reversed the conviction based on an error that the defendant didn't allege. The defense did complain that Ragan shouldn't have been qualified as an expert, but the court disagreed. He was an expert—but, they said, specifically *because* he was an expert, he couldn't testify to opinions about the crime scene.

What was going on with this case? In the previous appeal, the court had allowed a defense attorney to add new facts and to testify in an appellate argument. Now they were finding errors that the defense hadn't even alleged.

How was the *Williams II* decision supposed to be followed in other cases? Would an appellate court have to rule on the complexity of every criminal trial in which an expert testified, and reverse convictions in cases that the court found weren't complicated enough to justify expert testimony? Would they need a scoring system? Under an eight in complexity, and the case would be reversed? Score an eight or higher on complexity and the experts could opine away all day? That's how much sense the court's decision made.

Then again, maybe the decision wasn't supposed to make sense. To take cynicism to its extreme, was the complexity argument merely a peg upon which to hang a hat in search of a peg? A reversal looking for a reason? As we say from time to time, stay tuned.

Even the dissenting opinion accepted the premise that you generally can't use an expert, even in a complex physical evidence case like *Williams*. I disagree. Justice Weltner took one item of evidence in isolation—the chair. *Williams* was not a case about a chair on a pants leg. It was a case about an entire study full of evidence that had to be pieced together like a puzzle.

I thought the decision was ludicrous at the time, and I still do. I'm sure the defense thought it was splendid. Both are only opinions. The supreme court wins, even if by one vote.

I do wonder if appellate justices occasionally forget their own past as well as the hundreds of hours of work and the pressure endured by so many people on both sides of a major criminal case, all of which they toss aside as if a trifle. Detective Ragan interpreting the crime scene evidence hadn't convicted Williams. The evidence that Ragan interpreted convicted Williams.

It didn't matter. Conviction reversed. Try him again.

But not just yet.

The following has never before been discussed publically. If some of it is hard to believe, that would be understandable. I make no representation as to the conclusions to be drawn; only as to the accuracy of the telling.

PART FIVE

TAMPERING WITH THE SUPREME COURT

CHAPTER 24

COCKTAIL TALK BITES BACK

While Williams's second appeal was pending in early 1985, I received a call in Atlanta from an attorney, Guerry R. Thornton Jr., who had practiced in Savannah for a time before moving back to Atlanta. Mr. Thornton wanted my advice regarding a conversation that he said had taken place in December between himself and another attorney following a holiday cocktail reception.

Mr. Thornton told me his conversation had been with a lawyer by the name of Don Samuel, who'd said he was involved with the defense of the *Williams* case. Donald F. Samuel had been a third member of the trial team in *Williams II*. Samuel was a member of The Garland Firm in Atlanta along with Austin Catts. The location of the alleged conversation was a hotel near The Garland Firm.

The substance of the conversation was astonishing. Mr. Thornton wanted to know what I thought. I advised him that he would need to communicate with the district attorney and that he would need to put his information in writing. That step usually has a filtering effect. Saying something is one thing; writing it down is another thing entirely.

The substance of what Mr. Thornton relayed to me was as follows: Mr. Samuel had told Thornton that he (Samuel) was involved in the *Williams* case in Savannah and that the defense was going to retain the Atlanta firm of Troutman Sanders to assist in the appeal. Troutman Sanders may have been the most politically powerful firm in Georgia at the time. The second name on the firm masthead belonged to Carl E. Sanders, a former governor.

The more startling claim was that Troutman Sanders wasn't going to do any actual work on the appeal but that former governor Sanders, should he run into members of the supreme court, would speak with them about the case. For those who are not in the legal business, were anything of the sort to take place, it would be a gross violation of canons of ethics governing both lawyers and judges. Having ex parte (without notice to the other side) communications with members of the supreme court would be as wrong as wrong can get.

Holiday parties can be dangerous things, particularly if one is partial to punch, eggnog, or open bars, but still, this was shocking. Or it never happened and Mr. Thornton made up the whole thing. I wasn't there. However, it's difficult to conceive of a motive for an attorney with no connection whatsoever to the *Williams* case to concoct such an incredible story. How would Mr. Thornton know that Don Samuel hadn't been in Casablanca or on tour with The Garland Firm bowling team on the date this conversation was supposed to have taken place? How would Mr. Thornton know that a lawyer named Don Samuel had anything to do with *Williams*?

To be clear, over time Mr. Samuel would deny every syllable of the allegation, including the punctuation. He did not admit to having met Thornton, much less having had the conversation. Again, I was not present for the alleged conversation, but some interesting facts are available.

In a later affidavit filed in another *Williams* battle (in 1987), Samuel mentioned that the defense had discussed bringing the Sanders firm on to handle the appeal and that he had not been happy about it because he had felt like "this prestigious law firm was going to replace me after all the work I had performed simply because the senior partners of that firm were so prominent."[111] So, there is evidence that associating the Sanders firm on the *Williams II* appeal was, in fact, discussed.

I have no personal knowledge of the factuality of the information relayed to me by Mr. Thornton. I only know what I was told, what I advised Mr. Thornton to do, and what he did. I suggested that he call Mr. Lawton, and that was the last and only action I took. Mr. Thornton did contact Mr. Lawton and relay to him the alleged Samuel conversation.

The timing of these events can get a bit jumbled because, though they related to the appeal in *Williams II*, no mention of them surfaced until much later. Information about the events might never have surfaced if not for a free-for-all that erupted after *Williams III,* described in a later chapter. So when the dates appear to jump, they are not typographical errors. The matter is taken up here only because it concerns the appeal in the second trial. Later, it was merely one salvo in a larger war.

This later, larger war prompted Mr. Thornton to confirm in writing his earlier report of the Samuel conversation. In August of 1987, Mr. Lawton sent a letter to Mr. Thornton setting out the substance of the information Mr. Thornton had reported orally, asking Thornton to confirm the information by affixing his signature. Mr. Thornton made a couple of minor corrections to the letter (for example, that the conversation took place in the hotel bar after the reception rather than at the reception) and signed it.

As a courtesy, Mr. Thornton also called Mr. Samuel and told him what he was doing. Mr. Thornton would also later include the substance of the alleged conversation in an affidavit filed as part of the later war—a brutal 1987 battle involving defense and prosecution dueling motions to disqualify each other. When the Thornton affidavit was filed in that case, all heck broke loose. Former governor Sanders would comment to the *Atlanta Constitution* at the time, calling the whole thing "an unmitigated lie."[112] Probably with emphasis.

Former governor Carl E. Sanders passed away in late 2014 but we will presume, for this narrative, that his position on this subject would not have changed appreciably.

Though the lid wouldn't blow off of this episode until the disqualification battle of 1987, the subject at the center of that explosion was the 1985 appeal of the *Williams II* verdict and the possibility that the defense had attempted to tamper with the Supreme Court of Georgia.

CHAPTER 25

THE POLITICAL SOLUTION

In everyday life, we assign credibility to statements or claims based on the information available at the time. We can only evaluate what we know. Occasionally, at some later time, a fact can come along that causes us to revisit the subject or even experience an a-ha! moment.

When I received the phone call from Mr. Thornton in early 1985, I had no idea that the district attorney had been contacted previously by Mr. Hal S. Hoerner with some starkly similar information. If the name seems familiar, it's because Mr. Hoerner was a character witness for Williams in both of his trials. Mr. Hoerner had been Williams's banker.

Mr. Hoerner had told Mr. Lawton, in this prior conversation, that Williams had called him from the county jail, relating that things were "looking up" and that *former governor Sanders* had become involved in his case. Hoerner said that Williams told him "these things are as much political as legal" and asked Hoerner to use his connection to Sanders (formed through Mr. Hoerner's involvement in Sanders's past political campaigns) to encourage Sanders's help with Williams's case. Mr. Hoerner had declined Williams's request.

With that background, imagine the effect on the district attorney when Mr. Thornton later related the story of a cocktail conversation about a "political" solution being pursued by the defense—through the Sanders firm. There was no indication that Hal Hoerner and Guerry Thornton had ever heard of each other, much less colluded together to make up two separate conversations on the same subject.

To continue the coincidence eruption, the supreme court reversed the *Williams II* conviction in June of 1985 and a new trial was scheduled. In June of 1986, the defense would file a motion to suppress evidence in the upcoming trial, and with the filing, a new attorney joined the defense team: R. David Botts, son-in-law of former governor Carl Sanders.

Mr. Lawton inquired about the purpose of Mr. Botts's addition to the trial team. Technically, it was none of his business, but he likely found the question irresistible. Remarkably, instead of telling Lawton it was none of his business, defense counsel answered the question: Mr. Botts was on the case for his expertise with the *parole board*. Williams couldn't be paroled until he was convicted, but maybe the defense was thinking ahead.

Again, none of this information was in the record of the case until 1987, and it arose then only because the defense had the brilliant idea of trying to have the entire district attorney's office removed from the case, which led to the district attorney asking for the removal of defense counsel—all of which led to removal of the lid on this material.

But returning to the main question—even if lawyers were willing to ex parte the supreme court, how was such a thing possible? One couldn't exactly call the court and make an appointment to exert some improper influence.

CHAPTER 26

THE CURIOUS CASE OF JUSTICE SMITH

They say it takes two to tango. The tango looks like it would take at least two, and a fire extinguisher. For a court to be influenced, it takes not only a willing culprit but also a willing court, or at least one willing member of the court.

The author of the 4-3 decision in *Williams II* was Justice George T. Smith. If, for the sake of argument, Sanders had been inclined to help Williams, he would have had no trouble getting in touch with Justice Smith. Smith had been a law school classmate of Governor Sanders (one class year apart), was a State Representative while future governor Sanders was in the State Senate and served as Speaker of the House during the final three years of Sanders's term as Governor. Smith was elected Lt. Governor as Sanders was leaving office (because of term limits) and was later elected to the supreme court.

So the gentlemen might have had each other on speed dial. That wasn't unethical. The real question was, would a justice of the state supreme court allow external, ex parte, communication regarding a case? Once again, we find evidence in a parallel case.

During the summer of 1985, when the *Williams II* decision was issued—a case pending before the supreme court (and in federal court) involved an important question of insurance law. The case was known as the *Nails* case (*Southeastern Fidelity Ins. Co. v. Nails*, 254 Ga. 555 (1985)). The federal court was waiting for the Georgia court to resolve a question of Georgia law in the case before proceeding. An attorney involved in the federal action was a Georgia legislator, a member of the House Insurance Committee, and a friend of Justice Smith. This attorney wrote a memorandum on the issue pending before the supreme court.

When the court's decision was announced, Justice Smith's opinion was almost a verbatim knock-off of the memorandum. The stark similarity was noticed by an Atlanta attorney who was a former member of the court of appeals. Despite rules of judicial ethics strictly prohibiting consideration of such outside information without disclosure, Justice Smith's friend appeared to have virtually written the Georgia Supreme Court opinion.

The supreme court vacated the opinion and issued another, with Justice Smith not participating, but that was not the end of it. At the request of Governor Joe Frank Harris, Attorney General Michael J. Bowers opened an investigation into potential charges of bribery and violation of Justice Smith's oath of office. That investigation was subsequently closed without a finding.

In the fall of 1987, another bit of information would appear from filings in the *Williams* mutual-disqualification mud fight. According to affidavits filed in October 1987, by District Attorney Lawton and Chief Assistant Lock, the AG investigation into Justice Smith and the *Nails* case had come up during a meeting in the district attorney's office with Don Samuel. According to Lawton's and Lock's affidavits, Samuel had told them that The Garland Firm had *also* given Justice Smith memos on cases before the court, at Justice Smith's request.

Thus, it appears that, had there been an interest in influencing the supreme court in *Williams*, one justice had been open to receiving extracurricular communication on cases—the justice who wrote the *Williams* opinion.

So what was the truth behind the allegations of improper influence regarding the *Williams II* appeal? Did someone sell the tale of an innocent, persecuted Savannah antiques dealer to Justice Smith? Did he hijack the opinion and find a peg upon which to hang a hat in need of a peg? I have no personal knowledge beyond what is related here. To mangle a paradigm, "Where there's smoke, there's smoke." I leave it at that and leave you, the reader, to exercise your own good judgment.

PART SIX

WILLIAMS III

CHAPTER 27

MOTION TO AVOID THE EVIDENCE

The third trial couldn't begin immediately because Williams's lawyers filed one of the more curious motions in the history of criminal practice—a motion to suppress the evidence in the case. But aren't such motions common? Yes. If you're sitting on a sofa carved out of cocaine when the cops knock, you're in trouble. But if your lawyer gets the sofa tossed because somebody screwed up the search, you can party on.

So what was the big deal about this motion in *Williams?* It was filed five years and two jury trials *after* the search. Challenges to a search are required to be filed before trial; otherwise, objections are waived as a matter of law. You don't try the case and complain about the evidence later.

A lawyer taking over a case might claim that the first lawyer committed malpractice by not filing a motion before the prior trial, but in this case, that would mean Seiler would have to allege malpractice against both Bobby Lee Cook (hardly an inviting undertaking) and himself. Seiler had handled the second trial and hadn't filed a motion to suppress either. What was he supposed to do now, claim he had committed malpractice and confess? The absurdity of the situation didn't faze him. Seiler and Don Samuel (who moved up a chair for *Williams III,* replacing Austin Catts) filed a motion claiming that the evidence in the trial they had just conducted had been illegally seized. What was their defense to their previous failure to notice or complain—that they forgot? Had it slipped their minds in the rush to pick out a tie for court?

How could they claim the original search was flawed without also admitting that they had been obligated to challenge it—three years before? As we'll see shortly, the defense motion was garbage and the witness who would prove the motion was garbage was none other than the defendant himself.

So why did Seiler and Samuel file the motion? Why not? Williams was out of jail thanks to the Supremes's new rendition of "Baby Love" and Williams was paying the bills, so why not file something, buy some time with Williams's money, and hope the district attorney would be hit by a bus. Whatever their reasoning, the motion was filed and a hearing was held on August 12, 1986, before Judge Oliver.

Detective Ragan testified. He advised that Williams's attorneys, Duffy and Shearouse, arrived at the scene within five to ten minutes of his and Det. Jordan's arrival, and that Duffy, like Williams himself, had offered Williams's complete cooperation.[113]

I did not testify at this hearing (or any other, obviously). If I had, I would have confirmed that I spoke with Mr. Duffy at the scene and that he had completely understood what was going on and raised no objection whatsoever. While I didn't testify, Duffy did. He confirmed that he was an experienced criminal defense attorney with *thirty-five years* of legal experience.[114] He also confirmed that there was no misunderstanding:

A. Well, that was obvious, he was a detective and there was a body laying there, and somebody was shot, so I had the right to assume that he was investigating the circumstances.

Q. To the extent of it, including conducting a search, is that correct?

A. No, sir, I don't know about that. Maybe—I assume he was, yes.[115]

Even though the motion was baseless, a side benefit was the State's opportunity to nail down the time of Williams's phone call to his lawyer. Mr. Duffy said it had taken him twenty-five to thirty minutes to get to the scene. He arrived five to ten minutes after Ragan and Jordan, which would mean 3:35 or 3:40. Add time to wake up, receive and complete Williams's call, dress and get in his car, and it was apparent that Duffy had been called by Williams right around 3:00, roughly the same time that Williams had called the police.

Duffy testified that, in fact, he told Williams to call the police and that it was his understanding that Williams had not previously called them.[116] More evidence that Williams called his lawyer just before he called the police, that is, *after* the missing minutes.

Surprisingly, Williams also testified. Although this was unusual, the defense had no choice if the motion was to have a chance. Williams had testified in his first trial that the police had been totally free to do whatever they needed to do, to go anywhere, and to look at anything. He had to explain that if the pointless motion was to have any point at all.

Williams confirmed that he had invited the police in and given them free rein. Yet now, five years later, he made the bizarre claim that this invitation had included a secret, unspoken limitation, one he had never mentioned. See, he had only called the police to "help" Danny: "I'm explaining that that meant to help Hansford and to see the damaged furniture and to determine that I called them to be of assistance to him."[117]

Williams shot a man, called a friend while the man lay dead on the floor, and then, more than a half hour later, called the police "to be of assistance" to the man he'd shot. The motion was denied by Judge Oliver.

The trial *still* couldn't begin, however. What did Williams's attorneys do after the denial of their frivolous motion? They appealed its denial, of course.

Normally, denial of pretrial motions can't be appealed. Appeals courts don't have the time to hear complaints about every ruling in a trial, but there are limited exceptions. The trial court can "certify" a ruling for immediate appeal, especially if disposition of the motion will effectively decide the case—such as in drug cases when the disposition of the drug evidence might effectively dispose of the case. The appellate court can agree or not agree to hear what's referred to as an interlocutory appeal. Judge Oliver certified his ruling, allowing the defense to ask the Georgia Supreme Court to hear it.

The defense petition was denied without comment. In Brooklyn, this would be the equivalent of being told "Fuhgeddaboudit." (For those unfamiliar with the term, the Urban Dictionary defines it, in polite terms, as "definitely no.")

Because of time spent wrestling with the Motion for New Trial and the Motion to Suppress, the third trial of Williams would not begin until May 19, 1987, three and a half years after Williams's previous conviction and more than six years after Danny Hansford's death.

Williams's third trial would take only sixteen trial days and the transcript would come to less than 1000 tidy pages. But the trial itself was no longer an accurate indicator of the size of the *Williams* case now that the Giant Panda had begun to grow and feast upon Williams's bank account.

CHAPTER 28

THE LEGAL ETHICS OXYMORON

Do not be fooled when a defense lawyer pontificates about the sacred "search for truth." If the truth helps their case, great. If the truth doesn't help, they will commit every ounce of their being to making sure the jury never hears it. They will attack a fact, the means by which the fact was discovered, the equipment that verified the fact, the inventor of the equipment, and the inventor's grandmother, if she has a record.

To be clear: Criminal defense lawyers are free to do whatever they want—within the bounds of the law—whether or not anyone else approves. Hopefully, they stop at the line marking the outer boundary of vigorous advocacy. Unfortunately, some only see that line in their rearview mirror. Equally unfortunately, the incentives built into the system don't help.

Yes, there are "Rules of Professional Conduct." However, the legal practice is, in effect, a large club that disciplines itself. The only surefire way to get in trouble is to steal money. Siphoning off a settlement check or dipping into an escrow account will get a lawyer every time. For trial behavior, however, discipline is as rare as a Michigan fan at an Ohio State pep rally. In most cases, the only real risk of being caught is being caught—and being made to cut it out. It's like the old *Truth or Consequences* game show, without the consequences part.

Inside the courtroom, a trial can resemble the Wild West without Judge Roy Bean to rein in the combatants. The rule is to fire away and keep firing until you're the last lawyer standing. That's inside the courtroom. Outside the courtroom, anything goes.

Before we part the swinging doors of the Longbranch Saloon for a third time, let's look at another unusual event in this unusual case that illustrates why legal ethics can be considered an oxymoron. The May 5, 1986, edition of *US Magazine* carried another interview with James Williams. This time he was singing a duet, joined by his defense lawyer.

CHAPTER 29

THE INTERVIEW

*U*S *Magazine* wasn't quite the *ABA Journal,* but for Williams's purposes, it was perfect. The banner at the top of the May 5, 1986, edition, for example, touted a story titled "Raquel Welch on Elvis, Prince, Bruce & Mick." The title of the article with the Williams–Seiler interview was "The Scandal That Shook Savannah."

The article was written by Rosemary Daniell. Aside from airing Williams's complaint that the district attorney was a big meanie for continuing to try him, the article showed that the defense team still had no idea how to attack the case against Williams.

After five years and the unsuccessful efforts of defense experts to explain the chair over Hansford's body, it was revealed that Seiler had known the explanation all along but hadn't bothered to share it with anyone. Not only that, but the explanation was so simple, it was incredible that everyone hadn't seen it immediately: "Perhaps they bumped the chair," which, Seiler explained, "was on castors and rolled easily."[118] He didn't say who "they" were, but he obviously meant anybody but Williams.

Williams had wasted a lot of money on experts while it was a simple matter of the chair rolling across two rugs and a carpet pad, stopping over Hansford's body, rising up while the dead man crossed his legs, and setting itself down on his pants leg. There was a good reason this explanation had not been heard in a courtroom: It was impossible and was based on invented facts.

What do the phrases "on castors" and "rolled easily" mean in common usage? Check the chair again. There are two small wheels on the two front legs (Figure 10). There are no wheels at all on the rear legs (Figure 8). If a car has two wheels in front but none in the rear, so that the rear end is sitting on the ground, is that a car "on wheels" that would "roll easily"?

The chair was halfway up Hansford's body. The chair didn't "roll easily" to that position after being "bumped." The chair didn't roll at all. How does one roll a chair with the design of this chair? By grabbing the back support of the chair, lifting the back legs off the ground, and rolling it on the front wheels, assuming they're in any condition to roll. The chair is impossible to roll accidentally and is designed that way.

Besides, even had the chair been able to roll around the room and up over Hansford's body, all this rolling around had to happen before Williams led the police into the study. Otherwise, there would have been no chair over the body when the police arrived and when Ofc. Stevens memorialized the chair's position on film. This has been covered extensively.

"They" couldn't bump and roll a chair before "they" showed up, so the only "they" who could have done anything with that chair was Williams. And Williams would barely admit knowing the word for chair, much less moving this one. Facts again. They can be bothersome in a criminal trial, though not so much in a magazine interview.

Besides, hadn't Seiler presented expert testimony that a dead Hansford had gotten the chair on top of himself with Dr. Petty's "thrust"? The bumped rolling chair contradicted evidence that Seiler had presented at trial. So which was the fib and which was the truth? Actually, neither was possible. But the question remains: Why hadn't Seiler mentioned the "easily rolling" chair at trial when Williams was facing a murder conviction?

Seiler also had the paper fragments on top of the Luger figured out: Williams was "scattering" papers. Except that there were no papers scattered at the scene. And if Williams had scattered papers, he should have thought to scatter some fragments *underneath* the gun.

If Seiler had had these simple answers, it should have been a walk in the park to spring Williams. He only had to use them during trial instead of saving them for *US Magazine*—except that it wouldn't have mattered. As the interview also explained, it was impossible to win the *Williams* case because Savannah was so homophobic that homosexuals had to arm themselves or risk being gunned down in the streets:

> "No one is going to acquit Jim in a jury trial in this county, because
> of one, homophobia, and two, ignorance," says Wade Bragg, who is a
> member of the Georgia Task Force on AIDS. "I wear what I want, go
> where I want. But I carry a gun—you have to."[119]

Maybe that's why Williams had a "carry-out" gun in his foyer. Who knew that homosexuals were being openly hunted in Savannah?

I am reminded of Bette Midler and Shelley Long riding through Harlem in a taxi in *Outrageous Fortune* when a worried Shelley points out that they haven't seen any white people for a while. Bette points and says, "There's one. … Oops, they got him." I'm visualizing Savannah's hunters of homosexuals and their shock upon learning that they missed one.

What evidence of Savannah homophobia was offered in the article? A criminal case in which US Army Rangers from nearby Hunter Army Airfield were accused of killing a visiting beauty pageant judge for what they thought was a come-on in an adult bookstore. Those men were in the US Army, *stationed* in Savannah.

Perhaps more fascinating than the article was information Ms. Daniell shared with the district attorney that did not appear in her article. According to Ms. Daniell, Williams told her that he had lied to the police and that his lawyers had told him to stick to the lie. She said Williams had later warned her not to publish the article and, when she refused to quash it, told her he would "get even" with her. She said that Williams also pulled out a Luger during the interview and that he told her he was hoping to plead guilty to voluntary manslaughter.[120]

Williams didn't plead guilty to voluntary manslaughter—despite discussions—and Judge Oliver's gavel finally struck again on May 19, 1987, announcing the commencement of a third *Williams* murder trial. No doubt, the prosecution was on the lookout for rolling chairs and paper scattering.

CHAPTER 30

THE TRIAL

For *Williams III* the cast once again changed. Kathryn Aldridge had moved to the US Attorney's Office and David Lock had taken over as Chief Assistant. The defense team consisted of Seiler, Samuel, and former governor Sanders's son-in-law, David Botts.

Even with two practice trials, the defense had a problem. What they had been practicing hadn't been working. The prosecution also had a problem. It was almost impossible to predict what the defense might do next, because the defense had demonstrated a willingness to do almost anything. No previous testimony was a lock, because if the defense didn't like it they would swap it for something better. After the affidavit fiasco, it wasn't out of the question that a new witness might appear to claim that she had been knitting sweaters for orphans in Williams's study and saw the whole thing.

The prosecutors could contact defense witnesses and attempt to talk to them. The catch is that no witness is obligated to talk to anyone. Other than talking to the witnesses, the only way the State could find out what the defense was planning was to read *US Magazine* and show up for trial while keeping a nervous eye on the door to the witness room.

THE STATE'S CASE

Leading off a *Williams* trial with Joseph Goodman was a tradition by this time. In *Williams II*, it had looked like Joe might have missed witness rehearsal, going back to his original 2:22 time for the "I shot Danny" phone call. He would more than make amends in *Williams III* by developing a severe case of mud brain.

It might have been reasonable to assume that Williams's lawyers would be limited—if by nothing else—by the testimony they themselves had elicited from Goodman at the prior trial. Under the rules of Lawyer Games, however, no prior statement was safe if it didn't help Williams. This was Goodman's testimony in *Williams II* on cross-examination by Seiler himself:

Q. So you got a call about two-oh-five, you talked to Hansford then.

A. Right.

Q. During that conversation; and then ten minutes later you got a second call.

A. Right.

Was it unreasonable for the prosecution to believe that those times were nailed down? After all, they had been nailed down by the defendant's lawyer. In hindsight, any such optimism would have been misplaced.

Mr. Lawton conducted the examination of Goodman. The first call? No problem: "shortly after two o'clock in the morning." What about the second call, the bright digital numbers on the microwave? Goodman's memory didn't go fuzzy. In fact, Goodman's memory had become *sharper* six years later. He was now certain that he hadn't looked at the clock *at all*:

> [B]ut I'm saying between the first call and the second call, I'd say between twenty, twenty-five minutes elapsed. But I *did not look at a clock* the second time.

The number 2:22 in Det. Ragan's handwritten note from the scene was not an estimate. It was a specific recollection with a specific source—a digital microwave clock. When asked what time something happened, does a person normally say, "I don't know exactly, somewhere around 2:22?" No, and neither did Goodman. Anybody who believed Goodman's story at this point should have been transported to the gullible farm for emergency treatment.

Spencer Lawton, with some practice at this by now, fought through another objection that he couldn't "impeach" his own witness. He then asked Goodman about his testimony from the most recent trial:

> Q. To which you replied, "two-twenty, two twenty-one, or two twenty-two, somewhere around there." Do you recall giving that answer to that question? (Pause) I know it's been a long time ago.
> A. If I said it, I must have said it, but I don't remember it.
> Q. Would it seem to you not to be true now?
> A. No.

It's not crystal clear what the second question and answer mean. Presumably Goodman is saying the prior statement does "not seem" to be "not true" so that might be akin to a confirmation. Trying to deal with Joe Goodman on the stand might have been somewhat like trying to walk a St. Bernard who spots a tasty poodle across the street. Who knew when he might bolt, or in what direction.

Now, strap in and grab a calculator. What followed on the part of Seiler was masterful, somewhat like watching a master of illusion at a Vegas dinner show doing math tricks. Beginning Goodman's faux cross-examination, Seiler first had to untie Goodman's call-time numbers from the pier before they could be towed somewhere else.

These are statements of Seiler from his cross-examination of Goodman (they are called statements because, as we know by now, Seiler typically testifies rather than actually asking questions):

- You said—correct me if I'm wrong—that you *estimated* the first call to come in around two-o-five.
- *Roughly*, and that's exactly what you said, *roughly*.
- So, that's an *estimate*, is it not?
- Right, and still, you were *estimating*.
- [Y]ou did not look squarely at the clock to get an accurate reading and therefore, your time increments are *estimates*.
- Now, taking in consideration that these were really only *estimates* …
- And you *estimated* that it would take three minutes.
- Now, you told me fairly that you had *estimated* the time of the first call …
- And what time did you *estimate* that you arrived at …
- And that's still an *estimate*.

Is there any doubt that Seiler preferred estimates to three glowing numbers on a digital clock?

It's time to add another charge to the Lawyer Games indictment. Goodman wasn't Seiler's witness, so Seiler had every right to cross-examine him and to use prior sworn statements of Goodman's to do it. But Seiler had a problem. Goodman's testimony in the previous trial, elicited by Seiler himself, didn't help.

Faced with this dilemma, what did Seiler do? He cross-examined Goodman using Goodman's prior testimony—from the *first* trial, not the most recent trial, in which Seiler had gotten answers he didn't like. Seiler didn't tell the jury he skipped a trial and the prosecution didn't bring it up. It's possible the prosecution didn't notice which transcript Seiler was using.

What Seiler did wasn't a crime. Prior testimony was prior testimony. He didn't have to say where it came from. If asked, he would have been required to show it to the other side and the prosecution could then have pulled Seiler's own cross from *Williams II* and gone back over it with Goodman.

From that point, Seiler testified and Goodman said sure, whatever. As we know by now, a telling sign that an orchestration is in progress and that no real communication is going on is when a witness answers a different question than the question that was asked.

Q. Okay, in fact you didn't even turn out the lights, you told us, in the bedroom before the second call came in.

A. After I finished smoking the cigarette, I turned the light out, yeah.

Seiler had the St. Bernard on a leash, doing his best to lead him, but it wasn't easy. What was Seiler up to? He was trying to fuzzy up the time, then take a page from John Wright Jones's playbook and use upside-down math on the arrival time.

Just as in the case of Jones's demonstration of advanced subtraction, however, there was no way the time gap could be eliminated, no matter how many tasty dog treats Seiler fed the St. Bernard. The time it would *reasonably* take for Goodman and Rushing to fully wake up, get up, change clothes, brush their teeth, get down to the car, get in, and drive to Mercer House was plenty of time for Williams to doctor the scene—period. The only question was the size of the time gap.

If Williams had called Goodman and said, "I'm going to shoot Danny in a few minutes because he's really pissing me off, so head down here," that would have been different. Goodman and Rushing could have gotten a head start and rolled up right after the shots were fired. But they didn't have a head start. It took time to get up, ready, out, and on their way. No math known to man could fix that. It should be no shock by this time that Seiler tried anyway:

> Q. So the next call came in ten minutes and you told us that; as soon as you got that call—and correct me if I'm wrong on this—that you told Nancy what the call was about and that the two of you got up and just put on what did you say, jeans and a T-shirt and docksiders? Not even socks.
> A. We had short sleeve shirts on and blue jeans and docksiders or topsiders. Both of us brushed our teeth.
> Q. Yes, sir. And you estimated that would take three minutes.
> A. I guess, yeah.

Who is testifying in this exchange? And three minutes? Were Goodman and Rushing members of Delta Force? In mere seconds, they're in a helicopter in full combat gear? Goodman might have been willing to agree with Seiler's time estimates but the jury could tally up the actions of Goodman and Rushing on their own and come to their own conclusion.

Here's some meaningless trivia: People in Savannah didn't wear socks with Top-Siders in the '80s. They probably still don't. It wasn't a sign of hurrying; it was a Savannah fashion statement.

Seiler then totaled up his time segments: three minutes to get up, dress, brush their teeth, get in the car, and head to Mercer House; eight minutes to drive (which is almost certainly understated); one minute for the duration of the "I shot Danny" phone call. A total of twelve blazing Delta Force minutes.

Seiler then subtracted his twelve minutes from the arrival time, just as Jones had done and—presto—he's moved the second phone call to 2:48. If we recall Goodman's testimony about the cigarette, it has now taken him something like forty-five minutes to smoke part of one cigarette.

Finally, note that Seiler's time calculations are no longer estimates. Goodman's times that Seiler insisted were "rough" and "estimated" had suddenly become razor-sharp, quartz-calculated time units. Goodman's memory was crap—until it was useful—and then it was caviar. More Lawyer Games.

The exercise was also pointless. This was often overlooked, but the defense had to move the *first* time—and it was practically carved in granite: 2:58 minus 2:00 (or 2:05) still equals almost an hour of missing minutes. The second call didn't prove when Williams shot Hansford. It only proved when Williams *told Goodman* he'd shot Hansford. It's easy to miss the distinction.

If the defense wanted Williams's second call to Goodman to be later, fine. Williams could start staging the scene before calling Goodman. Or, if Seiler wanted to insist that Williams had done it in twelve minutes, as unlikely as that might be, then he had done it in twelve minutes. If the park angel, Claudina Delk was coming back, they were going to need to fix her testimony with its twenty to thirty minute time gap, if it had been noticed, so stay tuned.

Besides, the time that Williams took to do what he did was not nearly as important as what he did during the time he had. Less time would only mean he was in a bigger hurry and thus more likely to make the mistakes that he obviously made.

Realistically, how much time could it take to: pick up the chair, grab another Luger, shoot his desk, pull Danny's arm out from under his body, and put the Luger under his hand—five minutes? Add a minute for Williams to ponder the tragedy that had befallen him and Goodman might have been less than halfway to Mercer House.

Call times aside, Goodman was far from finished. Phone call times were a minor problem compared to the radioactive chair.

Consider a rhetorical question: Do friends lie for friends in court? Is water wet? Would Goodman lie for his friend of twenty years, the man who had seduced him as a teenager, the best man at his wedding, the only person other than Goodman's future wife who called him JoJo? First, let's review some of Goodman's direct testimony under examination by Spencer Lawton in *Williams II*:

Q. Okay. But that—you wouldn't have touched anything inside the room? No movable objects or anything?

A. No, they would not—the police officer said, "You can't go in there."

On the same question—whether Goodman went into the study—the following is from Seiler's own cross-examination of Goodman in *Williams II*:

Q. You say you *did not go in that room* at that time?

A. No, I didn't.

With this background, what would Seiler and Goodman try to pull off in *Williams III* in the sacred search for truth?

> Q. All right, what we're talking about is, you *did go in there* and you got a good look at the body.
>
> A. Yeah, I looked straight down at it.

Seiler continued testifying for Goodman. Note which are longer, the questions or the answers.

> Q. Straight down at it. Such a look that you said in one statement that you'd never forget it; isn't that correct?
>
> A. That's right. I won't.

I have been unable to find any Goodman statement containing Seiler's representation but it's certainly possible that the sight might have been unforgettable.

> Q. You didn't see a chair straddling that body, did you, sir?
>
> A. No, I did not see a chair.
>
> Q. And if there had been a chair there straddling the body, you would, of course, remember that because you told the police in the statement you gave them that you'd never forget it. Isn't that a fair statement, sir?

So that there is no confusion about this answer, Goodman never gave a statement to any police officer or investigator that related in any way to the radioactive chair. Whatever it was that Goodman would never forget, if he made that statement at all, it was not related to the chair.

> A. Well, I'd never seen a dead body before, so that's something that sticks in your mind for a long time.
>
> Q. Right. And if you had seen a chair straddling that body, you would have certainly remembered it.
>
> A. I probably would have, but there wasn't no chair.
>
> Q. There was no chair. And you went in there the same time Anderson did.

Seiler's conflating time with position and distance. Note Goodman's prior testimony, that an officer stopped him, telling him "You can't go in there." The time when Goodman tried to walk into the study didn't matter. Where he was allowed to go did. Seiler was trying to finesse the issue by treating them as the same things. Goodman tried to help:

> A. He was just in front of me.

Anderson might have been "just in front" of Goodman, but only until Goodman was stopped at the door to the study.

> Q. All right, let me show you, just to make sure that we don't leave this point unnoticed, let me show you what's been identified as Defendant's Exhibit 69. Do you recall seeing a chair over the body like that?

A. No.

Q. You're sure of that?

A. I'm sure.

Q. If it had been there, you would have seen it.

A. Yes, I would have.

JoJo Goodman should have been taken directly from the stand to perjury jail and left there for a very long time, and Seiler should have gone with him. Seiler needed a witness, and he got one. It's no shock who that turned out to be: Williams's friend and bag man.

It would be hard to imagine a more blatantly orchestrated piece of deception. The prosecution had to be thinking, *What will these people come up with next? Hansford was never shot at all and is living with Elvis in Memphis?* Seiler was eliciting testimony that contradicted testimony that Seiler himself had elicited in the previous trial of the same case. There is no possibility that he didn't know what he was doing.

A man who had barely peeked into the room according to six years of statements and sworn testimony was now standing over the body, making a chair magically disappear, despite photos and copious testimony that made either of those suggestions impossible. Nowhere in Goodman's prior statements or testimony had there been mention of going more than barely past the study threshold—as if police officers at a homicide would ever, in a defense lawyer's wildest dream, allow a stranger to stroll into the scene and walk over to check out the dead man.

What about the statements Seiler referenced? In his formal recorded statement, Goodman had said he got "about that far" inside the door, without any indication of how far that was. His descriptions elsewhere in the statement were that he "looked in the room" or "looked in his office."

But what about looking "straight down" at the body? In his formal statement, did Goodman really say he'd looked straight down at the body? Not exactly. He did say he looked down. The rest was Seiler's invention. Here's what Goodman did say:

> "[I] got about that far inside the door and as soon as I looked ... I didn't look *up in the air* I just looked *straight down*. I never seen a dead body like that in my life."[121]

Goodman looked *down* instead of *up*. On the stand at trial, that statement was massaged to suggest that Goodman was standing over the body. He wasn't and it wasn't what Goodman had said. It didn't matter; it helped the defense so Seiler restated it to his liking and used it.

What about the prior trials? The defense knew the chair was slightly important. Had it slipped their minds to ask Goodman if he had gone right up to the body and whether he had seen a chair over the body? No. The problem for the defense wasn't that Goodman hadn't been asked. The problem was that Goodman hadn't provided the answer they needed: "Q. You say you did not go in that room at the time? A. No, I didn't." The solution? Change Goodman's answer. Poof—the chair disappears!

The only thing that had disappeared was any shred of credibility that Goodman—or Seiler—might have had left. But the *Williams III* trial jury didn't know any better. As far as this jury knew, the trial had barely started and the first witness—a prosecution witness—had just said there was no chair over the body.

Bobby Lee Cook is known for a story from the '50s about the trial of a moonshiner and Cook's cross-examination of the crooked sheriff. Cook claimed he pulled the sheriff down from the witness stand and whipped him on the floor of the courtroom after the sheriff threw a coke bottle at him and that the judge let it go because everybody hated the sheriff and believed he deserved a whipping. Somebody needed to pull JoJo Goodman off the stand and whip him, right there in the courtroom. And then they could have taken a few minutes to deal with Seiler.

But pause the film. Did this make sense, even for the goofy Goodman we've come to know? The lie was so blatant that there was no chance of it going undetected. There are fibs, white lies, and whoppers. This was a double whopper with cheese.

We'll return to this, but before finishing, Seiler and Goodman again raised the possibility that police officers had made coffee without giving Goodman any. There is no clue why Seiler thought this was compelling evidence:

Q. Making coffee?

A. I didn't see them make coffee, but it sounded like they were making something with spoons and glasses. I don't know if they were drinking water, making a milkshake, drinking coffee, I don't know, but they were doing something in the kitchen.

He also didn't know if they were baking a Bundt cake, but what was the point of this testimony and what relevance did it have to Williams's shooting of Danny Hansford?

Goodman was handed over to the prosecution for what was, technically, redirect examination. It was unfortunate that the man Williams immediately called for help after killing Hansford was allowed to masquerade as a prosecution witness. Goodman needed to be questioned to within an inch of his life and sent to bed without his supper. Spencer Lawton showed Goodman a photo (Figure 5).

Q. Is that what presented itself to you when you looked in that morning?

A. That's the only angle that I saw the body, yes.

Q. That's the only angle at which you saw the body?

A. Because I was only about that far inside the door.

Check the photo. What had happened to standing *over* the body, the testimony Seiler had given while pretending to cross-examine Goodman? Goodman
had a habit that had to have been maddening to the defense team. As soon as they
had his testimony where they wanted it, he would do something unpredictable.
And he was doing it again. This sequence must have caused pencils to snap at the
defense table. Lawton referred Goodman again to the photograph.

Q. I'll hold this up, so I hope that the members of the jury can see,
and I'll ask you if you will to point to the two chairs that you just
pointed out to me.

A. This one over here on the right and this one way back here in the
back. It's real dark, you can't hardly see it, but it's way back here in the
back.

Q. All right, is it where that shiny reflective light is?

A. Yeah, right where the little light is.

Q. The vertical round area?

A. Right.

Q. We want to be sure everybody gets a chance to see it. If you will,
just put your finger—I'll give you this and ask you if you will, point
with that to the chair that you are now talking about.

A. You see a shiny light here?

Q. Okay, where would that be positioned in relation to the victim's
body, as best you can tell, looking at that?

A. Way behind it.

Q. Like over the feet?

A. I can't say that. I can't see the feet.

Q. In the lower portion of the back?

A. I can't see anything but this right here. I can just see where the chair
is, the back part of the chair.

Q. Okay, but you—but I believe you testified that you took no special note of that at the time, is that right?

A. The only thing I saw was the body and the gun under his right
hand.

Q. Okay.

A. That's the only thing I saw.

What was the object with the "shiny reflective light" on it in the photograph? The same chair, in the same location, over Hansford's body, exactly where
it had been found. It was that darned thing called photographic perspective again.

As difficult as it might be to grasp, in Goodman World, he had been telling at least part of the truth. He thought the chair was "way back here in the back" because the photograph was two-dimensional and he had either convinced himself, or allowed Seiler to convince him, that the shiny spot on the chair was "here in the back" rather than where it actually was.

Referring again to the photograph, Lawton confirmed with Goodman that this was the image of the study as he had seen it. In other words, Goodman had barely been inside the study door, the position from which that photo was taken. Lawton asked him again, to be sure. Goodman replied:

A. [A]s soon as I got *inside the door*, this other policeman said, come on, let's get out of here, let's go somewhere else, and they took us back to the back.

Q. All right, and he told you, you couldn't go in there then.

A. He told me I couldn't go. I was going right on in there.

Q. But you followed his order and left.

A. Yeah.

Q. All right.

A. But I was in the door, you know, a couple of feet. I was inside the door a couple of feet.

Goodman was barely inside the study door. He had never looked "straight down" at the body. Seiler's latest photo flimflam had collapsed. What did he do about it? That question probably isn't necessary to ask at this point. He got up again and tried to fix it—but he only got into more trouble with Goodman's reply:

A. I saw the body and the gun. That's what I saw.

Q. And you didn't see any chair straddling the body, as you've told us.

A. I didn't see a chair. I *didn't look* for a chair.

Not to be deterred, Seiler tried again:

Q. And you got right up and you saw the body, you said you remembered it, never forget (sic) it, and you didn't see a chair over it.

A. Not then.

Notice Seiler did it again, testifying to what he wanted to hear. Goodman had shown the jury where he had been and what he had seen. They could look at the photograph and see for themselves. A jury is specifically instructed that a lawyer's questions *are not evidence*. Seiler hadn't been at Williams's house that night, unless he knew something he wasn't sharing. He was not a witness, no matter how badly he might have wanted to be.

What was the defense suggesting? That Cpl. Anderson—the only possible culprit, given the time frames involved—had grabbed a chair from somewhere in the room and put it over the body at a crime scene? For what possible brainless purpose was Anderson supposed to have done this? Did the SPD protocol for homicide investigations say, "Immediately cover the victim with furniture"?

Assuming Anderson didn't do it, did anyone else have access to the chair and a reason to move it? Right. James Williams.

ID Ofc. Donna K. Stevens was back to authenticate the photographs. Once again, she agreed that items moved during evidence collection did, indeed, look moved in her photographs. The scene had been secure while being processed. No, she couldn't see through walls.

The same problem surfaced again with respect to the timing of Stevens's photographs. Nothing that a ghostly spirit might have done after Stevens took her establishing photos could ever change the original condition of the scene. If Stevens's photos had been placed in order, a lot of unnecessary garbage would have been prevented and tactics exposed. Spencer Lawton made the points that needed to be made, in a reasonable world, in both *Williams II* and *Williams III*, in his examination of Ofc. Stevens.

From *Williams II*:

A. Once Ragan arrived, I stopped what I was doing at that point and went to talk with him, and showed him what I had *already photographed* and asked him what he wanted from that point on. It was in his control, you know, as far as if he wanted *more* photographs or *different angles* or whatever.

And from *Williams III*:

Q. [A]nd while you were in the room, will you state whether or not you moved anything without first taking a picture of it in its original position and then in its altered position?

A. Prior to the detectives arrival, I didn't even touch anything, much less move it, but after their arrival, if we did move anything, it was photographed long *prior to that* and then *again afterwards*.

Clear enough. However, it wasn't enough to keep the subject from coming up again and again. Maybe going beyond the extra mile might have helped in this case. Ask Ofc. Stevens to order the photographs or even print out oversized proof sheets showing the negative numbers and place them into evidence. Then, if the defense continued to suggest that an unknown "somebody" had kicked the evidence around the room, or continued to ask who was left guarding the study door hours after it mattered, the irrelevance of these efforts would be apparent. The value of hindsight is once again demonstrated.

We won't review the shuffle game in *Williams III*, because it was essentially the same as it was in *Williams II*.

Corporal Anderson once again took the stand. By 1987, Anderson had left the SPD because of a deteriorating medical condition. Anderson might have wished that he had been secondary on this call. As primary, he had become Suspect No. 1 in the great chair caper because of his five minutes of authority over the scene preceding Stevens's arrival.

A quick word about Mike Anderson and a silent salute—for a job well done and for never losing his sense of humor in the process. Mike Anderson had been named Policeman of the Year in 1984, but the illness that forced him from the police force would take him only twelve years later, at the ripe young age of 42. We will return to *Williams*, but I leave this admonition to all concerned: Anyone who suggests that Mike Anderson did anything other than his job, at the highest level of professionalism, should be ashamed of themselves.

Anderson repeated that he had been either in the study or at the study door from the time of his arrival until ID's arrival five minutes later. Some people went in, but always with him and always behind him. No one touched anything or disturbed anything. Williams was calm.

The only new defense tactic was to ask Anderson why the chair wasn't listed in his report. He explained, once more, that he had not been the ID officer or a detective on the case and had only made a quick, preliminary scan of the scene, secured the room, and called it in.

As for the chair leg pinning Hansford's trousers to the floor, there was good reason why Anderson might not have catalogued that particular aspect of the scene: you couldn't see it from the front of the chair (Figure 14). Cpl. Anderson apparently hadn't noticed it for the same reason Williams hadn't noticed it.

EMS Tech George W. Segall (spelled Siegel in the *Williams II* transcript) was back. He testified that he had checked Hansford's vitals, confirming that Hansford was dead. He hadn't touched the wrist, arm, or hand. He was the only tech who went into the study. He was in the study for no more than two minutes. Nobody touched anything while he was there. On the way out, he and his partner went to the back of the house and inquired if anybody needed any kind of assistance. All said no and they left.

The defense again tried to make the case for Williams's distress. Segall said Williams had been in the back of the house, had been calm, and had required no assistance. The inquiry only confirmed Williams's composure during the initial stages of the investigation.

There were no surprises with Det. Ragan. No, he said, the coroner hadn't touched the body. EMS had determined there was no sign of life, so after conferring with Segall, Dr. Metts had left. Ragan again explained that he asked Jordan to bag the hands. He again confirmed that Ofc. Stevens had not climbed up on Williams's desk.

Then a clue appeared: Det. Ragan was asked if the paper fragments on top of the Williams Luger (Luger 23A) had been small and light:

Q. Extremely light, were they not?

A. They were small paper fragments.

Q. And would it be fair to say that the slightest movement of any article on the desk that may create *a wind or a breeze* could easily disturb those small particles?

An educated guess would be that a gust of wind was coming. Wind disturbing the paper particles was an odd approach, however, considering that the particles were found *on* the weapon; this mysterious "wind or breeze" that might "disturb" the particles would have blown particles *off* the weapon. Was the defense suggesting that there had been even more fragments of paper on the Luger than had been found there?

On redirect, Lawton went directly to the paper fragments. For Williams to be telling the truth, as we know, there had to be paper debris *underneath* his Luger, no matter what was on top of it. Either item of evidence—on its own—made Williams's story impossible. Though they both confirmed the same fact, they were separate items of evidence. The defense had to account for both.

Mr. Lawton proved that the prosecution, as well as the defense, can benefit from a practice trial. Prosecutors apparently recalled Seiler's paper fragment photo scam from the previous trial.

Q. Detective Ragan, who removed the weapon from the desk?

A. I did.

Q. Did you notice any paper fragments under the gun when you did?

A. No, sir, I did not.

Detective Ragan's cross-examination had been relatively light combat, about as brutal as ballroom dancing. But going quietly was not in the defense team's DNA. Rather than having become suddenly docile, the more likely possibility was that they had something up their sleeve.

With the testimony of Detective Jordan, a giant flashing hint appeared.

Detective Jordan was now a seventeen-year veteran of the department and had been promoted to the rank of sergeant. He went through the arrival with no changes. Later on, just before Hansford's body had been picked up for transport, he had bagged Hansford's hands: "I went in, the funeral home was waiting outside, and I bagged the hands of the body." What did he use? He used paper evidence bags.

With Det. Jordan's cross-examination, the approaching rumble of artillery could be heard. The defense showed where they were going, though not how they planned to get there. Why had Jordan bagged the hands?

A. To keep [prevent] contamination, yes, sir.

Q. And that's because if you hadn't done it then, then whatever gun-shot residue, if any might have been on the hands, could have (sic) knocked off; am I right about that?

A. Theoretically, yes, some of it could have been brushed off.

The difference between the question—suggesting that *all* ("whatever") GSR could have been "knocked" off—and the answer—that *some* could be "brushed" off, might seem meaningless, but it wasn't. Jordan was correct.

Seiler's question was a hypothetical based on nothing—a tactic we've seen before. There had been no testimony that anything had been knocked anywhere. Boiling this question down, Seiler had simply asked if something could happen (residue being knocked off) without bags on the hands. That's like asking if a car left outside could have become covered with snow. There still had to be evidence that it had snowed for the question to matter.

If Hansford's body had been run through a car wash, that might have gotten rid of some residue. But strapped to a gurney in the back of a hearse? Not likely. In other words, un-bagged hands provides an *opportunity* for mischief but not the mischief itself.

Still, something was coming. Too many questions were asked about bagging the hands. Seiler asked Jordan where he had gotten the bags. "Sergeant Ragan handed them to me." The kind of bag? They were paper. Jordan did not remember what color the bags were (they were brown in *Williams II*). He used evidence tape to secure them.

He was asked if he could have swabbed the hands at the scene. Yes, Jordan said, he could have, technically, but the procedure he used had been standard SPD procedure during the entirety of Jordan's seventeen years on the force. He also said it wouldn't have made any difference.

Q. Doesn't it seem to you that it would have been a better and clearer and more protected test if you had done it that way?

A. Not particularly, no, sir.

Q. Why not?

A. If the hands are bagged, they're the same as they would have been inside the house.

Q. Suppose they are knocked around in the bags during all the han-dling and taking him to the funeral home and the x-rays and all the other things? You don't think that would have made any difference?

A. I don't think it would make that much, no, sir.

The defense was going after the GSR. There was no longer any doubt about that. The questions followed Jordan to the autopsy.

Q. Do you recall whether or not the hand wrappings were still on the body when you got there?
A. That's the first thing I did, was take the hands off the—the bags off the hands to swab the hands.
Q. And you did that by yourself, did you, sir?
A. Yes, sir.
Q. Were they the same bags that you had put on?
A. Yes, sir.
Q. You're sure of that?
A. I had no reason to think that they wouldn't be.

What was the suggestion? That a "somebody" had come along and swapped the evidence bags for other, identical evidence bags?

Note that Seiler asked, "And you did that by yourself, did you, sir?" There are two meanings to "by yourself." One means without assistance. The other means you were alone when you did it, which seems to be the inference of this question. To be clear, Det. Jordan said he un-bagged the hands himself, not that he un-bagged them with no one else present. Present at the autopsy, in addition to Dr. Draffin and the morgue staff, were Dr. Metts and Ofc. Roy of the SPD ID Unit.

The autopsy report includes Dr. Draffin's personal observation of the hands, "which have been previously bagged."[122] Detective Jordan had not been off in a dark corner, alone with the body.

Seiler asked Jordan about blood remaining after he swabbed the hand, suggesting that the swabbing hadn't been thorough. Yes, Jordan explained, there had been blood on the wrist, but you don't swab the wrist in a GSR swab. He swabbed the "pocket," or webbing, of the hand, and the top of the back of the hand.

I would like to insert an inaudible scream before the next question. The defense couldn't let go of the bogus time-lag issue. The defense's own expert, Dr. Petty, had testified in the previous trial that GSR does not deteriorate over time. Nevertheless, the defense clung to the fallacy:

Q. Now, would you agree with me if what you're telling us is so, you people let twelve hours pass between when Danny Hansford shot the gun and when you finally got around to doing the hand swabbings.
A. That's correct.
Q. And there's no reason why it couldn't have been done right at the scene.
A. It isn't necessary.

Q. Could have been any of the time you were there.

A. It isn't necessary to do it that fast.

Dr. Howard had also confirmed that time was not an issue. As a matter of fact, GSR has been detected on immobilized suicide victims as long as five days after the event.[123] We should also not miss the statement in the question above. There was no evidence, aside from Williams's own statement, that "Danny Hansford shot the gun." That was why there was a murder trial in progress.

The defense was spending too much time on this issue for this to be a fishing expedition. Whatever the defense was up to was going to be about GSR: the bagging, the time, and everything in between. They were going to try to explain how virtually all of the GSR that should have been on Hansford's hand had disappeared.

It's easy to forget during this exercise that nothing the defense did could ever put GSR *on* Hansford's hand. They could only try to explain away the GSR that *should* have been there. Even if they were successful, this wouldn't—and couldn't—prove that Hansford had fired Luger 22A. But they had to explain the lack of GSR. If Danny didn't fire the Luger, there was no self-defense in this case.

Another clue that something was up with GSR showed up in Seiler's cross of Det. Jordan, but it was bizarre:

Q. Are you absolutely sure those hands were bagged before they left the house?

A. I bagged them.

The hands had been bagged at the scene by the same detective who removed them at the autopsy. Others had been present both when the hands were bagged and when the bags were removed. Yet now, in the third trial, was the defense going to question whether they had been bagged at all? If the prosecution had had a defense-prediction machine, by now they had turned it off, put it away, and applied for a refund. Because it didn't work.

The defense had a long hill to climb. A "knock" or two wouldn't explain the extremely negative GSR levels on Hansford's hands: zero antimony and essentially zero barium. There were also too many questions about the autopsy and the un-bagging of the hands, which occurred well after transport of the body. Something else was undoubtedly coming.

Roger W. Parian now had seventeen years' experience with the State Crime Lab. He covered the paper, firearms—everything he had covered in the previous two trials. Chief Assistant David Lock asked Parian about cartridge ejection from a Luger. Parian confirmed that shells eject up and slightly forward. He also said the direction depends on the angle of the Luger: "[I]f you think somebody is shooting downward, it would tend to go that way (forward). If they were shooting upward, you might expect to find it back of the shooter."

On the trigger-pull issue raised by Dr. Stone in the prior trial to explain how Hansford had missed the barn while standing in front of the barn door, Lock elicited compelling evidence from Roger Parian without Parian uttering a word. While handling Luger 22A during his testimony, Roger Parian had pulled the trigger twice without even realizing he had done it and, when Lock pointed it out, a surprised Parian explained that although the trigger pull might be stiff, "it still works." In other words, a shooter's purpose is to shoot something; they don't drop the barrel and fire into the floor because the trigger is stiff.

On cross-examination, the defense returned to GSR, this time with questions about the materials used. Yes, Parian said, he had used a "commercial" kit for the GSR testing of Luger 23A; Sirchie was the brand name. The questions suggested that a commercial kit was less reliable than one the lab might have made on its own.

This is another tactic straight from the Lawyer Games Toolbox, to question anything related to the collection of the evidence. If the lab had used kits made in the lab, the defense would have asked why they hadn't used commercial, professionally prepared kits from a reputable manufacturer—like Sirchie.

Sirchie is one of the world's leading providers of forensic tools to law enforcement. The company, founded in 1927 by Francis Sirchie, provides forensic tools, including GSR kits, to law enforcement agencies in more than a hundred countries. This is not a plug for the Sirchie company. I note it only to point out the corrosive effect that a pattern of suggestive questions can have if they go unanswered.

This Lawyer Game tool—*if you did A, why not B or, if you did B, why not A instead*—goes hand in hand with questioning every imaginable thing an investigative agency didn't do in a given case. The GSR kit questions were a variation on the same theme: *Who are these Sirchie people? Where is this company located?* Yes, the defense asked Parian where the company was located. At the time of the *Williams III* trial, I could not have told you where the company was located—nor, most likely, could the defense without looking it up. I checked. The Sirchie headquarters is in North Carolina.

Don Samuel asked Parian, once again, about Danny's BAC and the rate at which alcohol is metabolized. Again, Parian didn't catch what was going on, or he didn't know the correct answer. It wasn't like Samuel didn't know better. Seiler had gotten into this area with Dr. Howard, suggesting that Hansford had been drunk at the time of his killing. Unfortunately, Roger Parian again told the jury the rate at which alcohol is metabolized by *live* subjects.

Presuming a corpse to be a live person is not an innocent oversight if it's fair to assume that a lawyer preparing a question understands the question. Presumably, Roger Parian, a chemist, answered the question as a chemist, not a pathologist, and didn't know any better. This wasn't explored further. It was a minor issue—Hansford could have been a drunken blob and, if he didn't shoot at Williams, Williams doesn't get to kill him—but it would have been nice to correct the misconception, if for no other reason than to shine a light on the defense's tactics.

Returning to GSR and the gathering storm clouds, Samuel asked Parian how GSR gets on hands, and this time, Parian answered the "real" question.

Q. Where does the gunshot—how does the gunshot residue get on
your hand with a revolver?
A. Well, *either type of weapon*, it gets on your hand because of the
cloud, or the smoke, soot, that's produced in the firing. There's a lot
of gasses produced that try to expand rapidly around the gun and they
meet air resistance and they fall back onto the shooter and they get on
the hand.

The "attack" bullet from the Luger would have left the barrel slightly above the speed of sound, along with gasses trying to "expand rapidly." In other words, there is blowback from air resistance, in addition to GSR released from the breech at the top. Parian concluded, "So there's two mechanisms there in this particular weapon, how you would get or why you would get gasses on your hand."

The next issue, the effect of time on GSR, raises a question about the ethical obligations of lawyers. How far can a lawyer go in service of a client? One boundary is clear: A lawyer cannot "suborn" perjury, meaning consciously offer testimony that the lawyer knows to be a lie (at least that's the rule). Does the rule apply to a position taken on a matter of evidence that is clearly specious—for example, the notion that GSR will disappear if you simply wait twelve hours? If you can get a jury to buy it, even if you know it's BS, is that okay with everybody? This is only a theoretical question, but it might be an interesting topic for a Lawyer Games panel at a law school.

Williams's defense still couldn't let go of the fallacious time issue even when Roger Parian pointed out the irrelevance of time so long as the hands are protected:

Q. And it makes no difference where you swab hands?
A. No. They usually—a lot of times, they bag the hands before they
move a body and it doesn't make a difference on a body, cadaver, you
don't get absorption of these elements, and so you can do the swabbing
at a later time in another location.

Detective Jordan had testified that departmental policy was to bag the hands and swab as part of the autopsy. The Crime Lab was not a part of the police department. Parian wasn't the person to ask about the protocol. Predictably, the defense asked him anyway.

Roger Parian was a chemist. He agreed with Samuel that it would be better to do the swabbing at the crime scene, then corrected himself to clarify that he, *personally*, would rather swab at the scene. Of course he would. Any chemist would, personally.

It would have been helpful if Det. Jordan had been asked to explain the protocol. In the prologue, I noted that a victim's body is evidence. The reason for bagging hands is simple: to provide for collection of *all* evidence related to the body at the same time—at the autopsy. For example, if there were fingernail scrapings to be taken for tissue or blood, a blood-splatter pattern to be analyzed, or wounds to the hands and arms, manipulating the hands and applying chemical wipes at the scene could disturb such other evidence. The protocol has a purpose. This point wasn't made.

Speaking of Lawyer Games, the next move by Don Samuel was creative—though there are other terms that might describe it more accurately. Who would have guessed that Roger Parian was involved in a secret conspiracy to convict Williams all the way back in 1981? Conspiracies are a popular item in criminal cases, whether real or not.

Don Samuel confronted Parian with an interdepartmental memorandum that Roger had sent to Randy Riddell in 1981 asking how Mr. Riddell wanted to handle the test results from the Luger test firings. It was now 1987, in the midst of the third trial. Yet Samuel was puffed up with outrage over a conspiracy to hide evidence (the hand swabs from the Luger 22A test firing), the analysis of which had, in fact, been provided to the defense *six years before*.

The following is Samuel exposing the conspiracy through Roger Parian. It is not clear if he was waving the memo in the air, but it would fit.

Q. Mr. Parian, were you all going to hide the results of the gunshot residue test?

A. I had no intention of hiding anything, just wanted to make it easier to—for Randy, not having to report the results on the computer if they didn't need to be.

Even reviewing this cross-examination today, I can't tell what conspiracy Samuel was talking about. He had not apparently listened to any of the GSR testimony. In order for any conclusions to be drawn about GSR from swab results on Hansford, there had to be evidence that the weapon deposited GSR. Recall the original GSR discussion, the scenarios that would help or hurt Williams—both required a positive GSR weapon test. If the swabs Parian sent to Riddell were negative, they had no evidentiary value, one way or the other. But, to Don Samuel, waiting to enter the swabs in the computer record and give them evidence numbers until their relevance was determined was a conspiracy.

As we know, the test results had proved to be significant, had been entered into the system, and had been provided to the defense—six years earlier. Samuel was concocting a conspiracy from his imagination. Parian's memo also hadn't been written on parchment with invisible ink. It was an interdepartmental memo, transmitted through official channels. The key word is "memo." The conspirator had supposedly put his conspiracy down in a memo?

How ironic that this outraged lawyer conjuring conspiracies to convict his client expected everyone to simply take his word for the fact that he'd never heard of a lawyer named Thornton, hotels, bars, holidays, or cocktails.

Returning to the original Luger 22A test firings, the next tactic involved trying to scramble up the ammunition again. Roger Parian had already answered the same questions in *Williams II*. Assuming that Samuel had reviewed the prior testimony of the witnesses he was to examine, what would he do with the knowledge that the ammunition had not been scrambled? He would pretend that he didn't know the truth, to see if he could get a better answer.

Parian had explained in *Williams II* that he used original ammunition for the one-shot and two-shot tests. It didn't matter. Samuel tried, once again, to get Roger Parian to say that he might have used the newer ammunition first. Parian didn't remember the sequence, so to some extent, Samuel was successful with the ruse.

On redirect, Mr. Lock tried to straighten this out. He asked Parian if he remembered the sequence. Parian answered, "I think the first shot and the second two shots were actual evidence ammunition, but I didn't write that down and I remembered that—seemed like I remembered that *at the second trial*. I can't swear that they weren't the last three, but I don't think they were." He was right. He had "remembered that at the second trial."

Here is Roger Parian's testimony from *Williams II*:

Q. Okay, which shots were fired using rounds that were in the clip?

A. Those were the first three. The one shot, and the two shot sequence used the ammunition *that came with the weapon*, and the three shot sequence was ammunition—similar brand, Remington Peters nine millimeter Luger, that I had at the laboratory.

Roger Parian was not shown his prior testimony to refresh his recollection. No doubt Samuel knew what Parian had said at the previous trial. If so, he knew the truth but, in service of his client, preferred some non-truth, if he could swing it.

Mr. Parian lost his concentration in one other area. He was asked about factors that could influence where shell casings end up. Samuel likened an ejected casing to a rubber ball. Roger Parian agreed. A shell casing is nothing like a rubber ball except that both are objects and both can bounce. It's a false analogy. A grizzly bear and a rabbit both have fur, but feeding a carrot to a grizzly bear is a bad idea. They are not the same thing.

As we know, the casing giving the defense the worst case of indigestion was the casing near the west wall (Figure 7), between the chair and table. No bounce known to man could get that casing into that position from a shot fired into Hansford's back from behind Williams's desk, so Samuel tried to swap it for a rubber ball that might make the impossibility seem more feasible.

These smaller issues might seem inconsequential. They are not. The cumulative effect can be to cast a cloud of uncertainty over a case, which in turn can influence how all of the evidence is viewed by a jury. That is exactly the reason the defense does it.

The looming question now was where the defense was going with all of these GSR questions. There was ample other evidence to convict Williams of murder and stupidity without any mention of GSR, but the defense was focused on it to an inordinate degree. This was a major clue that Seiler had another new evidence angel or a magic rabbit loosening up backstage.

Dr. Draffin acknowledged Dr. Petty's correction of the written autopsy report with respect to the location of the bullet entrance wound in the back. It had been a transcription error. The correct number was 11 cm, not 19 cm. This also conformed to the hole in front of the shirt (11 cm right of center) and the exit wound in the chest (9 cm right of center). As noted earlier, this was not a disputed correction, though the correction hadn't managed to find its way into Dr. Stone's inaccurate diagram in *Williams II*.

On cross, Samuel returned to the bagging of the hands. Yes, Dr. Draffin testified again, he was positive the hands had been bagged. What was so difficult to understand? Why would Dr. Draffin have written in his autopsy report that the hands were bagged if they had not been bagged? But a shark doesn't circle in the water with a knife and fork and a napkin tied around its neck for no reason.

Stop the tape. Something critically significant just passed unnoticed in this trial.

There were two questions Dr. Draffin should have been asked—by the *defense*—but only one was asked. The fact that *both* questions were not asked shines a spotlight on what, if true, might have been the largest fabrication in the history of the *Williams* case. These are the two questions Dr. Draffin should have been asked by the defense:

Were the hands bagged?

With what kind of bags?

The first question was asked. The second question was not. There is only one reasonable conclusion from that omission. This is new information (more accurately, a new insight). It relates to Seiler's magic rabbit, who has not yet made an appearance. The prosecution had no reason to ask either of these two questions, knowing what they knew at the time. The defense had extremely compelling reasons to ask both, but didn't—which told an even larger truth. More to come, shortly.

Randall Riddell returned and addressed the increasingly popular topic of GSR. By this time, Riddell had performed 3,000 GSR tests and testified approximately 150 times regarding the subject.

Riddell explained again, hopefully for the last time, that there is no urgency to swab for GSR: "If the residue was deposited on the hands, unless there were certain unusual things that may have happened, the residue will still be there; it's not going to go anywhere." He added that, if hands were bagged, "I don't know that it would make any or much difference *how long* the hands had been in the bag."

He reiterated that the swab samples from the Luger tests had revealed "significant" levels of "elements characteristic of gunshot residue." Then he reviewed the exceptionally low residue levels on Hansford's hands. Antimony was *absolute 0.00* across the board. The barium levels were also extremely low. He explained that by testing the subject and the weapon he had been able to draw conclusions that could not be drawn with only one of the tests. As before, Riddell testified, "It's very unlikely that Hansford fired the weapon." He added that the 1983 re-tests had not altered his opinion.

On cross-examination by Don Samuel, there were no surprises with respect to the tests, particularly regarding the 1981 tests. So, if the prosecution was looking for warning flags related to GSR, there were none, not from this cross-examination.

Riddell's cross-examination did contain another trick from the bottomless trick bag, however. This one backfired and, depending on the jury's sense of humor, may have provided some comic relief.

The technique is legitimate. Lawyers will bring in a book or scientific journal that the expert recognizes and agrees is "authoritative" and then ask questions about an article appearing in the journal. A variation of the approach was attempted by Seiler with his subpoena for a police officer's personal book to use in questioning Cpl. Anderson. The article or item chosen will, naturally, have something in it favorable to the lawyer's position. Here's how that worked out for Samuel in his attempt to use the gambit to finesse Randall Riddell:

> Q. Are you familiar with studies that almost universally [say] if you swab a person's hand a second time you'll still get antimony? Are you familiar with those studies?
>
> A. Yes, sir, I remember reading a study like that.
>
> Q. All right. It's in one of the two journals you read. So if someone swabbed Danny Hansford's hand and got zero, if they swabbed it again, according to that study, he might get antimony or barium? The second swabbing will pick up antimony and barium, even if the first—regardless of the first, the second could still pick it up?
>
> A. I believe that *the article you're referring to* did not show any situations where none was detected the first time and metals were detected the second time.
>
> Q. You're absolutely correct.
>
> A. What counsel is referring to is when metals were detected the first time in significant amounts, and then [the analyst had] gone back and done it again, and then they found some more.
>
> Q. That's right. But the point is that the first swab doesn't pick up all the antimony and barium.
>
> A. Correct.

It isn't obvious because Samuel covered it well, but a defense lawyer just got schooled by a witness. Initially, Riddell had said he remembered reading a study "like that." Very general. Samuel then moved in, asking Riddell about a *specific* study in a *specific* article, and misstating the conclusion. Riddell then quoted the *specific* study back to Samuel, correcting him in the process. Interestingly, when Riddell corrected him, Samuel readily agreed. Samuel knew what the study said—and didn't say—before he asked the question, but he was prepared to misstate and misuse the result to influence the jury, if he could get away with it.

But there is more to this exchange than a humorous look at a lawyer and witness in a high-level fencing match. What about the study Samuel brought up; what did it actually show? As Riddell explained, the study had found that, when GSR was detected "in significant amounts," a second swabbing can pick up even more residue. In other words, the swabs from the Luger 22A test firing probably *didn't pick up all the GSR* given off by the gun.

Samuel had obviously been referring to the swabbing of Hansford's hand for residue (suggesting that GSR might have been there even though the swab didn't pick it up—the suggestion Riddell had shot down). However, the same would apply to the swabs of Roger Parian's hand from the *Luger* test firing. In other words, according to this study Samuel cited, if Jordan had gone over Parian's hand again, the GSR levels would have been *even higher*—which made it even *less likely* that Hansford's hands could have been so extremely clear of GSR (if he had fired the Luger). This exchange actually bolstered the State's case though this wasn't noted at the time.

On redirect, David Lock asked Riddell about trigger pull, making the point again that Lock had already made with Roger Parian:

Q. Did the gun—you testified you all fired the gun several times, is that correct?

A. Yes, sir.

Q. Did you ever have any trouble firing it, that you recall?

A. Not that I recall.

Dr. Howard, the final witness for the prosecution, began with the topic that had moved to the front of the *Williams* case train: GSR. On direct by Spencer Lawton, Dr. Howard told the jury that he had never had any trouble with tests on hands that were bagged and tested later. He confirmed, again, that the time interval alone was *irrelevant*.

Then Dr. Howard went directly to the bottom line: Luger 22A produced significant GSR, and there had been virtually no residue on Hansford's hands. The only possible conclusion was that Danny Hansford *did not fire* that weapon. If the defense didn't have some magic in the wings, the GSR wasn't going away, but Williams was.

Leaving GSR for a moment, Lawton moved to the event and he and Dr. Howard committed to telling the jury Dr. Howard's theory of the killing. Hansford was sitting in the chair, was shot and went to the floor, along with the chair. The body was on the floor for the second and third shots, probably fired from behind the desk, by Williams leaning over the desk, though he could have rounded the desk. They were similar to coup de grâce shots that he saw frequently, one to the head, one to the chest (or through the chest in this case).

This decision to put forth a prosecution scenario in a self-defense case is a judgment call, as I've said, and impossible to second-guess. To use a variation on an example used earlier, if you tell me you didn't turn in your homework because your cousin's dog ate it and I prove that you don't have a cousin, I don't need to prove what you were doing last night instead of your homework. Taking that on would only muddle the issue for no good reason.

If the State could easily prove that Williams's self-defense claim was a pack of lies wrapped in untruths, why assume the additional burden of proving a particular scenario? It's a rhetorical question. It was a strategic decision impossible to evaluate without interviewing the *Williams III* jurors.

But we saw Dr. Howard, in discussing his theory of the case in *Williams II*, pronounce that the chair had gone over backward and that this was the *only way* it could have fallen over. We won't cover the entire direct and cross of Dr. Howard—his reconstruction wouldn't come as a surprise to anyone at this point, though we can differ on Williams's firing position—but on cross-examination, the defense predictably and rightfully confronted Dr. Howard with his prior testimony.

His prior testimony was obviously wrong. He had said the chair had to have gone over backward. Quite obviously, it hadn't. A lot of fur flew between Dr. Howard and Don Samuel before Dr. Howard finally dismissed the conflict. No matter what he had said before about the direction in which the chair had fallen, the important point was that the chair had to have been toppled over in order to find the skull fragment stuck to the seat. Dr. Howard admitted that his prior testimony had to have been a mistake because it didn't jibe with the evidence. That's what a witness should do. Regrettably, all of them don't.

Considering how linked Williams's defense was to the chair not falling over at all, it's curious that Williams's lawyer would engage in a debate over the direction it fell. But this was about proving Dr. Howard wrong about something, no matter what it was. This is not unlike Dr. Petty ceremoniously "correcting" the autopsy report, thereby only confirming that the shot through Hansford's back was almost perfectly vertical. Similarly here, if the defense wanted to insist that the chair had toppled over sideways instead of backward, that was their privilege, though the theory contradicted their client's self-defense claim.

Desperation can lead to some seemingly strange moves. The *Williams* defense needed something—anything—to talk about, whether it was cops making coffee, a moving pouch, the direction a chair had toppled over—anything other than a hand, a thumb, blood, paper fragments, GSR, and a chair leg on a dead man's pants.

The remainder of Dr. Howard's cross didn't produce anything startling, other than another attempt by Seiler to claim that the Crime Laboratory was nothing but a shill for the prosecution while the defendant's hired guns bathed in holy water. This absurdity has been addressed before. The idea that defense experts (experts who are well paid for testimony that is routinely rejected) are unbiased is laughable. Dr. Howard put the role of the scientists at the State Crime Laboratory into perspective, for those who cared to listen: The Crime Lab also processed evidence for the defense if the lab received a reasonable request, and did not testify exclusively for the prosecution in criminal cases.

The defense had uncovered another conspiracy, however, revealed dramatically by Don Samuel, on cross-examination of Dr. Howard. Samuel had another incriminating piece of paper to wave, even if only figuratively. Dr. Howard couldn't deny he knew about the paper, because the paper bore his signature. Before trial, the defense had subpoenaed the Crime Lab's raw data on the GSR tests and Dr. Howard had sent the data to the district attorney for delivery to the defense. Dr. Howard's cover letter said "good luck" at the bottom.

Don Samuel confronted Dr. Howard with this smoking gun. Again, the defense had this supposedly damning evidence because the prosecution had given it to them, along with the data. With the rate at which the Crime Lab and SPD were getting caught documenting their own conspiracies, they were making the Keystone Cops look like Scotland Yard's finest.

I don't know what the "good luck" salutation proved, other than how deeply the defense had to scrape the barrel for anything to divert the jury's attention. The prologue of this book contains Dr. Howard's pointed comment following his review of photographs of the crime scene: "The son of a bitch is lying." There doesn't seem to be anything overly sinister in his wishing good luck to the district attorney who was engaged in proving it. The defense saw conspiracy in the words "good luck," but the defense probably saw conspiracy written in their morning cereal.

With that, the prosecution rested its case in the third trial of Williams. It was time to find out the identity of the magic rabbit everyone knew was coming.

THE *WILLIAMS* DEFENSE

No doubt there was some silent speculation taking place at the prosecution table about who would lead off for the defense in this third trial. Williams again? Burton again?

Neither. Instead, an obscure name from down the witness list rang out in the courtroom. The defense called Marilyn Biggs Case, RN to the stand. Nurse Case might not have looked like a magic rabbit or actually hopped to the witness stand, but Seiler the magician could have been forgiven a quick bow to the audience nonetheless. Marilyn Case was not merely a rabbit pulled from a hat. She would prove to be a twelve-foot rabbit on steroids.

Marilyn Case testified that she had been employed for the previous fifteen years in the emergency room at Candler Hospital. She further testified that she had previously been a "deputy coroner" for Dr. Metts. I had never known that Chatham County had a deputy coroner but Nurse Case claimed that Dr. Metts had deputized her and she had been his deputy for a while. She didn't mention any cases she had worked, and she wasn't asked.

It would normally be presumed that she had been interviewed by the prosecution, but it isn't clear from the record how much anyone knew about her. More to the point, what was she doing there, and why was she leading off the defense case? Marilyn Case was there for one purpose: to help the defense try to explain away the lack of GSR on Danny Hansford's hands.

Suddenly, the curious questions to Ragan, Jordan, and Draffin about the hands and bags made sense. The strategy was preposterous, but this group of lawyers had long since proved that preposterous was child's play for the truly gifted. According to Ms. Marilyn Case, Detective Jordan hadn't bagged Danny Hansford's hands at all—she had.

Case testified that she had been on duty in the Candler emergency room on May 2, 1981, when the body of Danny Hansford arrived. According to Case, Dr. Metts had called her and alerted her to "bag the hands," meaning—as dramatic music rises on the movie soundtrack—the hands had *not* been bagged at the scene. This would mean that Det. Ragan had lied and everyone else had apparently been too blind to notice or were in on the conspiracy. Case had also come armed with her own evidence. She had a copy of the admission form from the hospital for Danny Hansford's body.

This is only the beginning, but first, stop and rewind. Case had barely hit the stand and there was already a major problem with her story: It couldn't have been true.

Dr. Metts had gone to the scene, pronounced Hansford still dead at 3:45, and left the scene. He was there for maybe ten minutes, according to Det. Ragan's testimony. Hansford's body was received at Candler more than four hours later, at 7:52 a.m.[124] It was only 3.5 miles from Mercer House to Candler Hospital, on a Saturday morning on lightly traveled streets. This meant the body likely left Mercer House somewhere in the vicinity of 7:30–7:40.

Jordan had returned from Williams's bond hearing and bagged the hands immediately prior to Fox & Weeks removing the body, meaning that Jordan's bagging of the hands—which no one had questioned for more than six years— took place almost *four hours* after Metts had left the scene. In other words, Marilyn Case was claiming that Dr. Metts gave her instructions based on information that he didn't have—and couldn't have had. Dr. Metts couldn't have known whether Hansford's hands had been bagged or not. There are other reasons this story made no sense, but for now, suffice it to say that it should have fizzled on launch. It didn't.

Nurse Case continued her testimony by offering up her own documentation. On the admission form for Hansford's body were three blank areas for recording information. They were captioned "Nurse Assessment," "History and Physical," and "Orders and Treatment." Each box contained various entries consistent with the title of that box, with one notable exception. In the "Nurse Assessment" box, there was a handwritten entry with an oversize asterisk next to it. It read: "Hands bagged bilaterally in ED per mscasern."

The note was not under "Orders and Treatment," where it normally would be if bagging the hands had been ordered by a physician. Rather, it was under "Nurse Assessment," which in common English usage means "evaluation or observation of *existing* facts." The written note also reads "hands bagged" rather than "bagged hands." This suggests an observation rather than an action taken. Was it mere syntax, or something else?

Stopping for a moment, let's ask, what was the potential impact of this claim, with nothing more? Aside from the clear allegation that Det. Jordan had simply made up the entire hand-bagging scenario, *if* the hands had not been bagged at the scene, in practical terms, how much might this help Williams? Was it enough to explain the absurdly negative levels of GSR on Danny's hands? What if Danny had, in fact, ridden to the hospital without bags on his hands? Considering that GSR didn't evaporate on its own, it was absurd to suggest that almost every molecule of residue had vanished on the quiet ride to Candler Hospital. The defense needed something else.

It should shock no one that Nurse Case answered the call. "Ask and ye shall have it said under oath" had become the theme song for the defense. Unlike "hands bagged," Case's second claim was not supported by anything. It did not appear on her form or anywhere else. Nurse Case testified that not only had she bagged the hands at the hospital but she also claimed that she had bagged them using *plastic garbage bags*. She said they were the only bags she could find.

Assuming, against all odds, that this testimony could be true—that Nurse Case had bagged the hands at Candler Hospital and that she had done it using plastic garbage bags—we ask again, what was the potential effect on the GSR results? Minimal. The body had traveled only 3.5 miles to the hospital, strapped down and tidy. Randall Riddell had testified in *Williams I* that the hands could be bagged with "paper or plastic bags," though paper was preferable. As outlandish as Case's story might have been, how could Nurse Case's story disappear virtually every trace of GSR?

In the hands of any aggressive defense lawyer worth their salt, what might only be "preferable" to Randall Riddell (paper over plastic) is a mole hill begging to be made into a mountain, complete with chair lifts and ski lodge. Nurse Case was not there, however, to build the lodge. She was not a GSR expert. Case was only the setup witness. Her testimony only removed Det. Jordan's paper bags from Hansford's hands and replaced them with plastic bags. Her testimony didn't suggest what effect the switch might have. That would be left to a cleanup hitter—another witness—to come later. The reader is allowed one guess who Case's tag-team partner might turn out to be. By now, the reader can probably write that part of the story.

As for Nurse Case and the second element of her claim, the plastic garbage bags, there are a number of questions that come to mind. To begin with, what was she thinking? Despite years of ER experience and her stint as a deputy coroner for Dr. Metts, she didn't know what kind of bags to use? And if she hadn't known, why hadn't she asked Dr. Metts, who—she claimed—had asked her to perform the task?

According to Case, she had advance notice to be prepared, but she took no steps to see that she knew how to correctly perform the task she'd been assigned. Who else might she have asked, if she had forgotten to ask Metts?

Dr. Metts had ordered x-rays, which was also noted on the form—in the correct box. Case testified that Metts had asked her to call Det. Jordan when the x-rays were completed. She did call him, as also noted on the form. In other words, she had Jordan's *phone number*. When Danny Hansford's body came in at 7:52 a.m., Jordan and Ragan were still *at the crime scene*. If Case didn't want to ask Dr. Metts how to bag hands, she could have called the detectives on the case. Of course, if she had done that, it's likely they would have asked her what the hell she was talking about. But we're assuming—for discussion only—that she was telling the truth.

Nurse Case didn't do any of these things. She didn't call Jordan to ask how to bag the hands, to ask him to bring her some bags, or to send someone to the store. This was also the emergency room, where victims of gunshots, stabbings, and other violence were taken. It was Friday night into Saturday morning. It was highly likely that there was a uniformed SPD officer either on site or nearby, along with hospital security.

Case also could have called SPD dispatch and asked them to have someone bring her a couple of evidence bags or to send an ID tech by the hospital. Officer Gordon had previously testified that there were seven ID officers in the ID division. One of them, Ofc. Stevens, was still on duty. Case could have had a fully equipped evidence van come to the hospital. She did none of these things, despite having claimed experience as a deputy coroner who went to crime scenes and regularly dealt with law enforcement officers.

Returning to Dr. Metts himself, the irrationality of Case's story is even further exposed. If Metts had experienced a sudden panic attack about bags on the hands after he left the scene, wouldn't he call the detectives who were still at the scene with the body?

What about Case's written note on her form? Was it legitimate? Was it written by her, and when she said it was? We'll assume that it was, until proved otherwise (stay tuned). If she wasn't telling the truth, what could explain the notation?

This was the question that was examined in detail by Spencer Lawton on cross-examination. The form was ambivalent—because of the placement of the notation and its syntax—and that was where the prosecution focused its efforts.

The theory goes something like this: Metts had to call the hospital to order x-rays for projectiles, which accounted for making the phone call that he indisputably made. If Metts had to call anyway, might he have mentioned to Case to *confirm* that the hands were bagged?

If so, might Nurse Case have made a note of her *observation* on her form? She might well have written "hands bagged" on the form under "Nurse Assessment." That was far more reasonable than the story she had brought to court. This is where the prosecution directed the attention of the jury, to the ambivalence of the form.

One question screaming for an answer is this: Which one person could have cleared this up immediately? As we will see shortly, there were quite a few people who could have settled all of these questions but the most obvious would have been Dr. Metts. But Dr. Metts was never called as a witness in this trial. He was on the witness list but was not called by either side. It's curious. But one conclusion is inescapable: If Dr. Metts could have corroborated Case's testimony, the defense would have brought him to the stand on a golden throne.

Why the prosecution didn't call him isn't clear. It's possible Metts didn't remember and told the prosecution that he didn't remember. But he could have been called anyway. He could have been asked how he could have told Case to bag hands he hadn't seen in hours, or why he didn't call the detectives who still had the body at the house. His history with GSR testing could have been explored. He could have been asked if he had ever had a case in which hands were ordered bagged—it's quite common in suspected suicide cases—and the detectives had forgotten.

Had he trained his former deputy about gunshot cases? Had he discussed with her the type of bags to put on the hands? If she'd been out on other gunshot calls, had she not spoken to him on those cases? Had bagging hands ever been discussed? Might she have used plastic bags because she'd been taught that it was the bagging that mattered and that plastic would work just fine in the short term? What was the practical difference, in his view, between paper and plastic? What does "preferred" mean? Had he ever seen plastic bags destroy all traces of GSR? There are probably other questions left off of this list.

Case's direct testimony continued. When the x-rays were complete, she called Det. Jordan as requested. She hadn't thought to mention the hands. Defense counsel suggested that this was Jordan's fault. Even in answering Seiler's question, note how carefully Case chose her words:

Q. Okay, now, did you have the occasion to notify any detective pursuant to Dr. Metts' instructions?

A. At nine forty-five a.m., I notified Detective Jordan that the x-rays were complete and that I had done everything Dr. Metts had instructed me.

She testified in spy code. "I had done everything Dr. Metts had instructed me." Why the careful phrasing? Jordan was a detective on the case. Wouldn't she want to assure him that everything was all square with the body? Might she have said, "Dr. Metts called it in and we did the x-rays, which are ready, and I bagged the hands like he said, so that's all taken care of," or some version of the same thing?

Marilyn Case had claimed experience with crime scenes. If so, she would have dealt with police officers all the time. But now she was speaking in code to avoid saying the secret word, "bagged"?

Seiler was ready with the "nobody asked me" defense:

Q. Did he at that time ask you whether or not the body had arrived in bags, the hands were bagged, or anything like that?

A. No. He did not *ask me* that.

This was asinine. Why in the world would Jordan ask Case those questions? He had bagged the hands himself. Of course, though, Seiler kept at it:

Q. Did the detectives ever come back and *check with you* to see if the body had arrived with hands in bags?

A. No.

It was the fault of the detectives that they didn't call to make sure Fox & Weeks hadn't stopped on the way and taken the bags off of Danny Hansford's hands? Just as Dr. Petty had tried to use Williams's scene tampering—pulling the hand out from under the body—as evidence of Williams's innocence in the previous trial, Seiler was trying to use Case's story to corroborate itself.

If Jordan knew he had bagged the hands at the scene, asking Case if they were bagged would have been patently ridiculous. If Jordan knew he hadn't bagged the hands at the scene, he would have had even less cause to ask if the body had arrived with bags on the hands. Was Seiler suggesting that if detectives didn't assume, in 1981, that a nurse might make up testimony six years later, it was their own fault?

There were more defects in the logic of Nurse Case's story. Her phone call to Det. Jordan about the x-rays was noted on her form, but only the time, not the content of any conversation that took place. Case testified on direct that she hadn't had *any* memory of the receipt of Hansford's body at the hospital and hadn't even recalled the *occasion* until the form had been shown to her by defense counsel. Those thinking ahead get a trophy. There was nothing on the form about her conversation with Det. Jordan.

If her vacant memory had been refreshed only by the form, how could the form have refreshed her memory as to things not on the form? Despite this apparent problem, once on the witness stand, Nurse Case's memory had become laser-clear about all manner of collateral minutiae related to this past event.

Now we can return to Dr. Draffin and the *two* questions he should have been asked by the defense:

Were the hands bagged?

With what kind of bags?

Question one was asked and answered, but the critical question is the second question. If the bags on Hansford's hands at the autopsy were plastic, Det. Jordan had been lying for six years and had committed perjury in three murder trials. Slam dunk. If the bags on the hands at the autopsy were paper, Nurse Case was lying and should have been prosecuted for perjury.

The fact that Don Samuel didn't ask Dr. Draffin the second question speaks volumes about the defense and their magic rabbit's testimony. There were any number of other people who could also have been asked this second question: anyone who had been at the autopsy, in the admitting area, in the radiology department, on the morgue staff, or even Ofc. Gene Roy, who had taken the autopsy photos. But the most obvious two were Dr. Metts and Dr. Draffin.

Dr. Metts was never called as a witness, but Dr. Draffin had been explicitly cross-examined about the bags. Samuel never asked Dr. Draffin the second question. If Case was telling the truth, as soon as Draffin had said, "plastic garbage bags," it would have confirmed Nurse Case's statements and ended Det. Jordan's career as a law enforcement officer.

There are only two possible reasons why Samuel wouldn't have asked the second question: He didn't know the answer, meaning he wasn't sure if Case was telling the truth, or he did know the answer and knew she wasn't. No defense attorney in history has passed up an opportunity to corroborate his or her own witness's testimony through a witness for the prosecution. Why the defense would pass up the opportunity in this case does not require superhuman powers of deduction. The only reason not to ask the question was to avoid having it answered.

What about the prosecution? Even though they didn't appear to know what Nurse Case was going to say in advance, could they have re-called Dr. Draffin to the stand and asked him the second question? Yes. If he said paper, Nurse Case was finished and defense counsel could have surrendered their law licenses at the close of the trial.

It's possible that Dr. Draffin didn't remember. I spoke with him and he did not recall ever having been asked the question at any point during the history of the case. After a couple of decades, he had no recollection of what the bags on

Hansford's hands had looked like, though he did believe he would have noticed something as unusual as plastic garbage bags on the hands. To be clear, I do not claim today that Dr. Draffin has any current recollection of the type of bags that were on Hansford's hands. He does not.

Could the prosecution have called any of the other witnesses listed above? Certainly. And, most to the point, the autopsy photographs themselves could have been examined to see if there was a photo of the hands prior to the un-bagging. This can't be done today, because neither the photos or negatives can be found.

This is second-guessing of the highest order. The initial reaction to a witness like Marilyn Case, a medical professional, is to focus on how her testimony and Det. Jordan's testimony could both be true. This led to examining the obvious ambivalence of the admitting form.

But with Case's plastic-bag claim, there was *no* possibility that her testimony and Det. Jordan's testimony could both be true. The option was "paper or plastic." If Case had only been asked to check the hands rather than bag them—assuming for now that she'd been told anything at all—the paper bags that Jordan had put on the hands would have still been there at the hospital and later at the autopsy. If she had put plastic garbage bags on the hands when the body arrived, the bags would have been on the hands later in the day and at the autopsy. One of them—Case or Jordan—was lying and the way to unmask the liar was to prove which type of bags were on Danny Hansford's hands.

For an extreme example, if Case had claimed that she had removed Hansford's clothes and dressed him in a clown suit when he arrived at Candler, it would obviously have occurred to someone to ask Dr. Draffin—and everyone else who had seen Hansford's body after its arrival—whether the body had been dressed in a clown suit.

Case's claim that she had put plastic garbage bags on the hands didn't suggest a similar response. The cross-examination of Nurse Case focused on the admission form. Because the bagging had been noted under "Nurse Assessment" rather than "Orders and Treatment," wasn't it possible that the note reflected an observation rather than an action?

Nurse Case wouldn't budge. Maybe Dr. Metts had asked her to make sure the hands were bagged rather than telling her to bag them. No way, she said. Not possible. It's always suspicious when somebody claims a foggy memory but is adamant about facts that favor whichever party put him or her on the stand. Nurse Case wouldn't tolerate any suggestion that she could have been mistaken.

Sometimes, witnesses slip up. While Nurse Case was denying that she could be mistaken, she told Lawton, "No, sir. If the hands had been bagged, I would have documented that in the nurse's assessment portion." Exactly where she had put it.

When the slip was pointed out, she only dug in her heels harder. It didn't matter what she had just said; she refused to entertain the slightest possibility that she could be mistaken six years after the fact. And thus ended the remarkable testimony of Williams's magic rabbit, the latest defense version of the "newly discovered" witness.

We have to jump forward in time for a moment to cover some facts not known at the time of this trial, in the interest of getting to the bottom of this. Dr. Metts wasn't called at trial, but in August of 1987, he would file an affidavit in connection with a peripheral matter. Just as Nurse Case had, Dr. Metts chose his words carefully. Seiler drafted the affidavit. The affidavit was obviously intended to suggest that Metts was corroborating Case's testimony. It did nothing of the kind. This is what Dr. Metts said, in part: "It is not possible for me to have personal recollection of all of the orders on patients and autopsies that I have been involved with over the years."[125]

His affidavit could have ended there. But what he couldn't say as a matter of fact, he then tried to say through a vague inference. Dr. Metts said the entries on Case's form were "consistent with my discussions with the detectives and the desired purpose of the Hansford autopsy."[126]

What does that mean, if anything? Essentially nothing. Detective Jordan's testimony was also consistent with both factors. The affidavit was meaningless to distinguish between Case's and Jordan's testimonies.

What "discussions with detectives" was Metts talking about? According to testimony at trial, Dr. Metts and detectives decided at the scene to bag the hands and run GSR tests. That "discussion" had nothing to do with Case's claim. In fact, Dr. Metts's discussion with detectives contradicted Case's story. That discussion called for the hands to be bagged at the scene, not with garbage bags at the hospital.

As for Dr. Metts's second phrase, the "desired purpose of the autopsy," the desired purpose of the autopsy as it related to GSR was to swab the hands, nothing more and nothing less.

What about the initial statement, that Dr. Metts couldn't remember every case he had handled? Note that Metts didn't actually say he had no memory of this case. With the opportunity to say just that, he chose to hedge. Wouldn't it have been simpler to say, "I have no recollection of this case"? Is it not also curious that he recalled the specifics of his "conversations with detectives" and the "purpose of the autopsy" in this particular case but couldn't recall his conversation with Case? Were they not equally memorable?

This is one of the more cleverly crafted affidavits one might ever see, crafted by Williams's attorney. It denied nothing, admitted nothing, and meant nothing.

So, are we splitting semantic hairs? After all, would a doctor ever say something that was not true?

Merely in the spirit of uncovering every conspiracy in sight, is it conceivable that Dr. Metts feigned a lack of recollection to avoid destroying the testimony of one friend—Marilyn Case—and the most important case ever handled by another friend—Frank W. Seiler? Dr. Metts had longstanding relationships with both.

Perhaps tellingly, Dr. Metts would be quoted some years later in a certain well-known book as follows: "Hell, I'd have shot Hansford, too." Metts did not indicate whether he would have required Hansford to shoot at him first. Metts's statement—if true—is a shocking and, frankly, offensive admission by a medical professional.

What about Metts's relationship with Seiler? In 2013, Metts became embroiled in a GBI investigation into possible expense irregularities within the coroner's office, leading to his resignation. The local attorney quoted in news reports regarding the upstanding character of "Jimmy" Metts? None other than Frank W. Seiler.[127] As we will see later, when James Williams himself suffered a future tragedy, the first action Seiler would take was to personally drive to Dr. Metts's house, before calling the police.

The point here is not to suggest whether Seiler's friend Jimmy Metts knew or didn't know the truth of the Case testimony. It is only to caution that one not assume that someone couldn't be favorably disposed toward the defense because the county wrote them an occasional check. Metts was certainly not favorably disposed toward Williams's victim, according to his quote.

Back to Nurse Case and the garbage bag garbage. No matter what bags were put on Hansford's hands by whom, they were still on his hands at the autopsy later that day. Such a sight should have stood out in flashing neon. It is stretching the incredible beyond its limits to believe that none of the seasoned professionals present would have noticed. Could Marilyn Case have lied? Do people lie in court, even people who seem really nice? Is that question still necessary to ask?

A police detective can also lie. Some people believe that's all the police ever do. In this case, however, it made no rational sense. For six years, through multiple trials, Det. Jordan had testified that he was asked by Det. Ragan to bag the hands, that he bagged them using paper evidence bags, that he couldn't find any string and sealed the bags with evidence tape, tape with EVIDENCE written on it in red letters, and that he un-bagged the hands at the autopsy—specific, detailed testimony. Det. Jordan's written report on the autopsy said this:

> On 5-2-81, at approximately 1400 hrs., I attended an autopsy at Candler General Hospital. Present was Officer Roy, Identification Section, Dr. Draffin, Pathologist; Candler General Hospital Staff; and

Dr. James C. Metts, Jr., Coroner. Prior to the start of the autopsy, the hands of the victim were unbagged and this writer conducted a swabbing of the victim's hands with a solution of five percent nitric acid in an attempt to find any gunpowder residue. This was forwarded to the Crime lab.[128]

If Jordan had not bagged the hands at all, would he calmly walk into an autopsy with at least four others present (the report doesn't indicate how many "Hospital Staff" were present), see two plastic garbage bags on Hansford's hands and, having no idea where those bags came from, think nothing of it?

If Det. Jordan was lying, he had been lying at the time of the first *Williams* trial, when memories were very fresh and autopsy negatives were far more likely to be where they were supposed to be. Was it credible that Jordan would have seen plastic garbage bags on the hands at the autopsy but testify that they were paper bags, knowing that Metts, Draffin, Roy, Fox & Weeks personnel, officers at the scene, x-ray technicians, or any number of other hospital personnel—not to mention the autopsy photographs—could blow up his career?

Further, are we supposed to believe that Det. Jordan didn't bag the hands, didn't do a thing about it, but showed up at the autopsy with a GSR kit? Then, when testifying at trial, knowing he had never bagged the hands, he simply made up an entire scenario involving when he returned to Mercer House, who was there, who handed him the bags, why he hadn't used string but substituted evidence tape, down to the color of the text on the tape?

Jurors are called upon all the time to resolve conflicting testimony. In doing so, they are entitled to use their grown-up brains, their common sense and their built-in manure detectors. They are perfectly entitled to disbelieve a witness if the testimony doesn't pass the sniff test or doesn't comport with the other evidence in the case.

There is no item of evidence in the entire *Williams* case record—other than Case's claim—that contradicts Det. Jordan's account of his actions. At the same time, there is no evidence whatsoever in the case—other than Case's own testimony—that conclusively corroborates her claim, including her admission form.

What about an item of evidence that could have settled the matter without question? In the prologue I noted, "Something not being where it should be is often as important as what is there." As we know, Robert E. (Gene) Roy was the ID officer at the autopsy. In researching this book, I asked him if it would have been his practice to photograph the body before the autopsy started, and he told me that not only had it been his practice but it also was standard SPD practice at the time. He agreed that there was a good chance that there were photographs showing Hansford's body before the autopsy began.

Terrific. All we had to do was check the autopsy photos. If there was a photograph showing the hands, that would solve the "paper or plastic" mystery once and for all. This led to my harassment of a number of innocent victims within the judicial and law enforcement communities, all to uncover a startling truth.

The negatives from the Hansford autopsy are missing. In fact, there are no Hansford autopsy photo negatives in the police department files, the superior court clerk's files, or in the files of the district attorney, the superior court, the GBI, or the State Crime Laboratory. To quote Gene Roy, who took the photos originally and who lead the search, along with Ofc. Michele Schiro, "They are not where they are supposed to be."

Weren't autopsy photos used at trial and, therefore, marked as exhibits? At trial, autopsy photos are used to demonstrate the means and manner of death. There wasn't any testimony in *Williams* that required—as far as anyone knew at the time—showing the body before the autopsy began. So, even if there were photos showing the body—and the bagged hands—before the autopsy began, they would not have been printed for trial.

Seiler had asked Det. Jordan on cross-examination—or, more correctly, stated to Det. Jordan:

Q. You don't usually photograph that procedure, do you?

A. It's not necessary.

That wasn't the right question. Whether or not photos were taken of the un-bagging of the hands, photos had very likely been taken of the *body* prior to the autopsy. At least that was the protocol. Today is too late to find out what those photos might have shown; the negatives are "not where they are supposed to be."

Obviously, we have to ask the screaming question. Is it possible that, at some point in time, the defense or someone acting on their behalf managed to remove the autopsy negatives from police department files? I do not have the answer to that question or any basis upon which to hazard an answer. Perhaps one day they will show up behind a file cabinet, merely misplaced.

Before we leave Nurse Case, we detour for two additional items of evidence that were not available to the prosecution at the time of trial.

(I) Case was interviewed, on October 5, 1987, by District Attorney's Office Investigator Jean Anderson. Ms. Case was adamant that she *always* completed the admission form before signing it and that, once it was signed, she *never* went back and entered anything on the form. Ms. Anderson repeated the question *five times* during the course of the interview, each time receiving the same unequivocal answer.[129]

(II) The admitting form was analyzed by State Crime Laboratory handwriting specialists. It was determined that the "hands bagged" entry was placed on the form *after* Nurse Case's signature.[130]

Despite all the sound and fury, all Marilyn Case could accomplish—if the jury believed her at all—was to keep Hansford's hands unprotected on the hearse ride to the hospital. According to Case, her garbage bags went on as soon as Danny Hansford was rolled into the emergency room. Someone still had to remove the abundant GSR that should have been on his hands.

Curiously, the defense didn't follow Ms. Case with her tag-team partner. Williams himself was called next. It was Williams's third shot at the case. He should have had it down. He also should have had his own story down, but he didn't. He was still making revisions.

He continued to maintain that Danny had never lived with him. He coupled that with his fainting fear and claimed—for the *third* time—that Dr. DeHaven had told him to have someone with him "at all times." Williams continued to make this claim despite knowing that Dr. DeHaven had testified that he had never said any such thing and was likely to testify to the same in this trial.

Williams said Danny Hansford hadn't been working anywhere else. Joseph Williamson had put it like this in his statement to GBI SA Stone in connection with the previous affidavit blizzard:

RS: Based on what, made you think he was a hustler?

JW: Through being in the parks and getting hooked up with a wealthy man.

RS: How did you know he was hooked up with a wealthy man?

JW: Because he was living with James.

RS: How did you know that?

JW: Because he had told me, his house was right there in one of the parks and he said "I stay there, man." You know he'd talk about, "You know, yeah, I used to hustle and, you know, I kind of made it big now," and things like that you know. Just general conversation.[131]

It seemed that everybody but Williams knew Hansford was living with him. But this jury only knew what Williams told them. Notably, neither George Hill nor Gregory Kerr was on the prosecution's witness list.

Danny's 1980 suicide attempt was back with its inconsistencies intact: Danny took exactly forty-nine pills of Limbitrol prescribed by Dr. DeHaven, who hadn't prescribed them, as everyone knew by now. Williams clearly liked the story and was going to continue telling it, regardless. I would like to have asked

Williams about this Limbitrol story. Did he have a shrink? Was he being treated for a psychiatric disorder? Why did he continue to lie about where the Limbitrol came from and about Dr. DeHaven's advice?

Williams's testimony then turned to Danny's violent nature and gave Williams another chance to showcase his ability to exaggerate everything he said. He recounted the fight involving Earl LeFevre. Recall that Mr. LeFevre had confirmed Hill's account at the previous trial. Here's how Williams—who had not been present at the fight—described the same event:

> A. There was a Mr. LeFevre that lived across the street and Danny and
> a friend of his got in a big argument there and they sort of beat up the
> mother and father, kicked their front door down, and went in the
> house and did it.
> Q. Where did that occur?
> A. I could reasonably say it was in 1980.

Yes, Seiler asked *where* and Williams answered *when*—because he wasn't really listening. But wasn't Williams's made-up version of the event certain to be exposed? Earl LeFevre was on the witness list. Nobody had beaten up Mr. LeFevre, and nobody had touched Mr. LeFevre's wife. Danny hadn't broken down any door or gone in the house. The defense had to know this. They had tried the last case.

Williams didn't give a damn what anybody said. He continued to say whatever he wanted, even in the face of certain contradiction. This is not normal behavior. It's usually reserved for megalomaniacs and politicians. Why his lawyers let him continue to do it is impossible to answer. Maybe he was uncontrollable, but there is nothing to be gained from having your client constantly contradicted by his own witnesses.

A note about the trial process: Even when witnesses are sequestered—kept out of the courtroom—the defendant is not. The defendant, who has a legal right to "confront" his or her accusers, is present during the entire trial. So Williams was aware of the testimony of every witness. He had heard them contradict him. Yet he showed up the next time and told the same whopper, if not some other version. There is no rational explanation for this behavior.

Next was Danny's fight with Bob Croyle, the handyman. Recall that Croyle had testified in *Williams II*, swearing that he hadn't sprayed Danny's cat. Williams told the story again, contradicting his own witness:

> He went up to spray the apartment and couldn't get in, but he used
> his pass key and the door opened just a few inches, so he took this
> wand—I guess that's what you'd call it—it's an extension for a sprayer,
> he stuck it in the door, sprayed. He couldn't see where he was spray-
> ing. He sprayed Hansford's little cat. Hansford later got up, smelled
> the spray, the cat had been sprayed, got furious.

Williams had just impeached his own witness, in advance. The defense could try their case however they chose, but having seen this happen time and time again, defense counsel might have wanted to spend less time creating new witnesses and more time coordinating the witnesses they had, including their client. Next, Williams impeached himself:

> He went down and found Croyle at his employer's place and beat him
> up, threw him against the concrete wall and against the concrete,
> stomped him, hit him, and told me about it.

Croyle was on the defense witness list. According to Croyle's prior testimony, Danny had come to his apartment to confront him and the entire confrontation had taken place in the hallway, with Croyle subduing Danny by himself. These lies were small. Why did they matter to Williams? Why couldn't he just tell the truth? Maybe Williams's lawyers would say Croyle was lying instead of Williams. They could tell us which testimony they put up was perjured and which wasn't.

Back to the April incident. Could it possibly change after all the statements, reports, interviews, and testimony? Of course it could.

In this telling, Williams said Danny dropped by at 2:00 a.m. to borrow money for his date. This time, though, Danny actually got $20 from Williams and left. Six years after Williams first told this story, somebody must have realized that, if Williams was going to claim Danny was going on a date, Danny needed to actually leave for this date.

But, as before, patching one hole can leave another. Imagine a sheet that's slightly too small for a bed. You can tug it here and there all night, but covering one corner will leave another corner uncovered. In the next breath, Danny was back—with no mention of a date, the $20, or having left at all. He was upstairs, shooting the floor and getting arrested.

What about the aftermath, later that day? That should have been a simple matter—but not for Williams. He testified that Danny got out of jail a week later. He didn't. Danny got out of jail later *the same day*. And he didn't just get out; Williams and Goodman went to get him. All of this was documented by Goodman's statements, police reports, and jail records.

These nuggets of mendacity could have been exposed and dragged back and forth across the courtroom, but hindsight is not only clear-eyed; it also has a lot of time to ponder such matters. In addition, it might have taken a full-time staff merely to track the changes in Williams's stories. Nonetheless, Williams's compulsion to fabricate and elaborate does provide a window into the mystery of the man himself when given the time to track the footprints of his changing stories through the case.

Several times during the 1980 presidential debate (yes, there was only one), Ronald Reagan coined a response to a number of allegations of the incumbent,

Jimmy Carter, with the famous line "There you go again." Over time, it became a part of the lore of politics. The district attorney probably didn't have lawyers to spare, but if he had, it would have been fun to have an ADA stand up every time Williams told another whopper and say, "There you go again," until Judge Oliver threw them in jail.

Williams's lawyers could have helped Williams by giving him a calendar. Williams again claimed that he had to take Hansford on his Europe trip per doctor's orders. And, of all the doctors he could have chosen, he chose Dr. DeHaven again. "Dr. DeHaven says somebody has to go with me because I'll be carrying a certain amount of cash." There he goes again! Now Dr. DeHaven was a security consultant.

Williams finished up with window dressing—the part-time employee story, the suicide attempt, the violent drug abuser, and Williams's own abhorrence of all drugs and alcohol—and finally got to his third try at describing the shooting for a jury.

The beginning changed, again. In *Williams I*, Williams and Danny were playing backgammon after the Atari game when Hansford exploded for no reason. In *Williams II*, they had moved on from backgammon to some "little board games" when the spontaneous combustion occurred. This time, they were still playing backgammon, Danny was winning, and Williams said, "Well, looks like you're just too good for me tonight, Danny." (Goodness, that's painful dialog.) This time, rather than exploding for no reason at all, Danny exploded over a compliment. According to Williams, immediately after the compliment, "that other personality took over like that."

Danny's raging raged on, as it had before. Then Williams and Danny were in the study with the phone call to Goodman. The moment the phone was back in its cradle, Danny was raging again but Williams asserted himself: "And I stood up and I said, Danny, you have done as much damage in my house tonight as you're going to do."

After this ultimatum, according to Williams, Danny said, "Savannah's a rotgut place." Was he serious? Danny Hansford of the seventh-grade education was supposed to have uttered those words? It's shocking he didn't break into "It's the Hard Knock Life" from the musical *Annie*. This was also a new line, never uttered before in statements or testimony.

Danny then left the study to go damage the house he'd just been warned not to damage, returning moments later to kill Williams for no reason. And then the story changed in a far more important way. After six years, it appeared that someone on the defense team had noticed the live 9mm round on the rug between Danny and the fireplace.

Up until this moment in Williams's third trial, Danny had never even slowed down before uttering his "You're leaving tonight" B-movie line and firing at Williams. In the prior trial, Hansford had been "moving like lightning," rounded the corner of the desk, raised his Luger "right up," and "started firing." This is what Williams had told Seiler about the sequence on direct examination in *Williams II*:

And I had the phone in my hand when he came from my right, right around to the end of the desk with his right hand right down by his leg. He had a pistol in it that I didn't see until he turned, right at the end of that desk. He said "I'm leaving this town tomorrow, but you're leaving tonight." And he took that gun right up, and he started firing.

Now fast-forward to 1987, Williams testifying in *Williams III* about the same event:

His right arm was down by his side and he said, "I'm leaving tomorrow, but goddamn it, you're leaving tonight," and he took a pistol and pointed it dead at me.

And—stop—Danny didn't fire. The story screeched to a halt. Danny had the Luger pointed "dead at" Williams. But Williams hit the pause button and took a detour, to patch a hole:

He fumbled with the pistol. I was seated at my desk like this. He came across this way. When I saw that gun pointed at me, I got up just like this, I had a chest of drawers there, I pulled the top drawer out. It had a pistol in it, too.

Then, as if in a sci-fi movie, Williams finally unfroze the frozen Danny and allowed him to fire his Luger: "He *fired at me* from over there."

But Williams must have gotten confused. Or he got lost with his new story, so he repeated the fumble line, even though Danny had already fired:

He fumbled with the gun. *I think he jacked it back*, I don't know, maybe he did. It was a delay of about a half second or a second. I took my pistol. I was so scared, all I knew is that I had to keep that man from killing me and I had to do it right then, I couldn't sit around and think about it.

(A rather obvious question asks itself: Shouldn't Williams be dead by now?) And from *where I was standing*, I shot him one time, just shot, and as he was going down, I kept shooting *from that position* and I fired several times.

After six years, Williams suddenly remembered, "I think he jacked it back." Williams had never uttered anything of the sort, whether in a statement or testimony, prior to this moment on the stand in his third trial. He had either rejected the possibility that Hansford had "jacked" the weapon or had left no time for it.

While he was at it, Williams had shoehorned "from where I was standing" and "from that position" into his description, to keep himself behind the desk. It's not normal syntax. The way to tell is to say it. See if the phrases fit naturally. Then see how it sounds with the phrases left out.

With his brand new story, Williams had two challenges: (1) Hansford had to stop and "jack" a round into an already occupied chamber while not getting shot by Williams in the process, and (2) Williams had to get the round to eject where it was found, only two feet and seven inches from the south wall, past the hole in the rug made by the shot through Hansford's head (Figure 13). That was a long way from the corner of the desk.

If Danny Hansford had been at the corner of the desk with the pistol pointed "dead at" Williams, any live round Hansford ejected by "jacking" the Luger would have ended up where he was standing,. Getting the live round behind him to where it was found was nearly impossible.

This impossibility was already resting on a stack of improbabilities. For Williams to be telling the truth, Danny Hansford had to have taken the longest, most circuitous route ever taken by a killer to his intended victim—stopped in the middle of the room, racked a round into his weapon, then turned, approached Williams, gave his little speech, raised his weapon, and fired (Figure 32). And he had to accomplish all of this without being gunned down.

Regardless of the implausibility of the story, Williams now recalled for the first time that Danny had "fumbled" with a weapon he hadn't fumbled with for six years. Improving memory over time is not common, but it tended to show up whenever needed throughout the *Williams* case. No one would choose to be tried multiple times for murder, but there is one advantage to practice trials: the chance to work out the kinks in your testimony.

But witnesses who ramble can also make mistakes, such as not noticing conflicts with other areas of evidence. This time, Williams took an eraser to Seiler's lawyer math. It hadn't been known exactly when Hansford was shot. The second call only established when Williams *told Goodman* that he'd shot Danny. But Williams now testified that Danny started "raging" again the very instant the receiver was hung up from the first call. He threatened a painting and raged out of the room. Before Williams could grab the phone and call the police, Danny was racing back in and the killing sequence began.

Williams had just set the time of the killing very close to the first phone call. The first call had never moved from its 2:00–2:05 time frame. This meant Danny was almost certainly dead by 2:10 or 2:15. The police weren't called until 2:58.

Williams had just established at least as large a time gap as that established by Goodman's 2:22 on his microwave clock.

This testimony from Williams came on direct examination by Seiler. It wasn't raised again. Did Seiler blink at this revelation? No. If he noticed Williams's slip, it wasn't apparent. At the same time, Seiler demonstrated his skill at slipping his own testimony into a question:

Q. [D]uring that *brief period of time*, did you ever touch Mr. Hansford after the shooting?

A. I never went near the body.

In whose universe is over a half hour a brief period of time? This is a textbook example of using a question to cover a false statement, a technique mentioned early on in our discussion of the Lawyer Game Toolbox. Moving down the defense checklist, what about the chair? Had Williams picked up the chair, moved the chair, or touched the chair? He didn't say. Seiler didn't ask him those questions. Instead, he asked:

Q. Would there have been any reason for you to move that chair at all?

A. None that I can think of.

This is an incredibly roundabout way to ask Williams about evidence that could send him away for life. Where were the following questions?

- Did you touch that chair after Hansford was shot?
- Where was that chair before the attack began?
- Was Hansford sitting in that chair at any point that evening?
- Did Hansford kick the chair when he fell to the floor?
- Did you see the chair lift into the air after Hansford hit the floor?
- When you took the officers into the study, was that chair over Hansford's body?
- If not, where was it?

Williams was on trial for murder. He was the only eyewitness. He was in a position to know the answers to all of these questions. Seiler had asked Joe Goodman questions about the chair that he never asked his own client. As to the question Seiler did manage to ask Williams, if Williams couldn't think of "any reason" for him "to move that chair at all," how about to cover up evidence that Hansford was at the other end of the desk, unarmed, sitting in the chair and smoking a joint, when Williams exploded and shot him to death? That might qualify.

Seiler and Williams, the duo from *US Magazine*, then reached the paper-debris evidence, evidence that destroyed Williams's defense all on its own. This relates only to the paper debris on *top* of the weapon. In the first trial, Williams hadn't touched a thing. In the magazine interview, Seiler had him shaking papers. In the second trial, Williams had been "throwing things away" until Seiler fed him the answer Seiler wanted: looking "underneath the papers" for "Joe Good-man's phone number."

The six flaws in that last claim have been covered. Williams's lawyers were not dumb. I came up with six in a matter of minutes. No doubt they could do the same.

So what happened in the third trial on the same evidence? Under oath once again—which apparently had little effect upon him—Williams said he hadn't been looking for Joe Goodman's number "under the papers" or anywhere else: "I just sat on the edge of the desk and I called Joe Goodman and I said, Joe, could you get on down here right now?" Recall that Williams now had to claim he sat on the edge of the desk because sitting in his office chair, which he had done in his first trial testimony, inconveniently conflicted with the evidence of paper and lead debris on the chair seat.

Where were the shaking papers? Gone. The search for Goodman's number? Gone. It had never made sense to be looking for Goodman's number, so Williams and his attorneys grabbed an eraser and a fresh pencil. Williams sat on the edge of the desk and called Goodman, without looking up anything. He and Seiler continued:

Q. What did you do after that conversation?

A. Ran around the desk and found the phone number for *Bob Duffy*, the only lawyer I knew at the time.

As difficult as it might be to believe such blatant changes in a witness's testimony, Williams was now looking up Duffy's number, not Goodman's. We also know, from the Motion to Suppress hearing, that Duffy wasn't called until very close to 3:00. It was impossible for Williams to have called Goodman, Duffy and the police at the same time. We made this note in *Williams I*: The police were on site in ninety seconds; Goodman and Rushing lived on the southside of Savannah.

But something was still missing. Williams needed to get paper fragments on top of his Luger. Running around to look up Duffy's number wouldn't do it. Did he shake anything or look under anything? No. He looked in his phone register. Williams said the number was in a "little punch pad that you have to keep phone numbers in." Where was his punch pad? On his desk (Figure 9).

Could Williams get paper fragments on top of the Luger with the "little punch pad?" A button releases the cover, which flips up, away from the Luger. If there had been any paper fragments on top (assuming this only for argument), they would have been flipped away from the gun. Even more telling, neither Williams nor his lawyer suggested that his "little punch pad" had anything to do with the paper debris on his Luger.

In fact, Seiler and Williams offered *no* explanation whatsoever for the debris on top of Luger 23A. This is frankly astounding. Did they *forget*? This single item of evidence proved that Williams hadn't shot Danny Hansford in self-defense, and yet it *wasn't addressed.* There is no rational explanation other than confusion and oversight on the part of the defense.

In *Williams II*, Seiler had provided the scenario involving Goodman's number by testifying for Williams. He had also been the source for the paper shaking story in the *US Magazine* article. Yet, at trial, both of those stories were missing— as was any other explanation for the paper debris on Williams's Luger.

This is almost inconceivable but perhaps keeping track of changing testimony from trial to trial can become confusing. There is an old saying to the effect that lying is hard, because you have to remember what you said. Whatever the reason, the defense left out *any action* by Williams that could have even arguably explained the paper fragments from the supposed "attack" shot having ended up on top of Williams's Luger.

What about Williams's changing stories? A disturbing aspect of Lawyer Games, quite aside from the *Williams* case, is that some lawyers might believe changing their client's story to better fit the facts is brilliant. If a previous answer is going to get you in trouble, changing the answer is really quick thinking. But what if the witness is lying? Shouldn't that bother somebody? Perhaps law schools could increase their legal ethics requirements and eliminate instruction on how to tie a perfect four-in-hand knot in a silk tie. That would be a start.

Seiler and Williams, the dynamic duo of truth slayers, finished up their work with the irksome chair by leaving out a few more questions. Williams testified that he went into the study right behind Cpl. Anderson and was no more than five feet from the body. And that was it. After Seiler had again made the point that Williams was in perfect position to see anything and everything, he wasn't asked anything about what he had seen.

The final entry in Williams's third campaign against the evidence was a claim telegraphed in the *US* interview, that the chair had wheels. According to Williams, there were wheels on the *rear* legs of the chair. If the witness oath was still taken by placing one hand on a Bible, in Williams's case the Bible might well have burst into flames.

> A. The chair was sort of horseshoe shaped, the front being the flat part
> of the horseshoe and rounded in the back. That (sic) legs were closer
> together than the front legs were *and there were rollers on them.*
> Q. Coasters?
> A. Coasters, little short rollers.

They're called "casters" or "castors." The problem is that there were no castors—or coasters—on the rear legs of the chair (Figure 8). The castors were on the front legs. Were Seiler and Williams going to suggest that the chair "rolled easily" on those wheels, which Seiler had claimed in the magazine article? If so, wouldn't

Williams, the owner of the chair, be the witness to cover the topic? But Williams wasn't asked anything about his experience with that chair, including its penchant for rolling around the room when "bumped" by unknown forces.

Having finished sanding, patching, and touching up his story, Williams was faced with his favorite pastime, being cross-examined by District Attorney Spencer Lawton. Lawton asked what had become of the Europe trip in Williams's attack story. In the latest version, Williams had only mentioned the people Danny was ranting about before deciding to kill Williams. Williams's answer to this question contained a slip of the tongue: "The night Danny and I argued on May the 2nd, he screamed out, amongst a lot of other things, he said, 'You gave my trip to London away.'"

The significant phrase was "Danny and I argued." Arguing is different than sitting quietly while a madman goes berserk over a compliment about his backgammon skill. This was a small slip but a clue to what actually happened.

I would have had another nagging question for Williams, if only out of curiosity. Danny was originally going on the trip to Europe in case Williams fainted. It was now 1987. The first and only report of Williams fainting was in early 1981. It would have been interesting to know who had been acting as Williams's constant companion, for medical reasons, since he had killed the last one.

Lawton pushed Williams hard on the contradictions in his portrayal of his relationship with Hansford. Williams agreed that he had known Hansford to be violent, that Hansford had shot off a gun in the house and torn up the house, that he had a dual personality, and was "burned out" on drugs, incompetent, and undependable. But yes, Williams said, he had planned to take Hansford to Europe to watch over him.

As was his habit, Williams continued to speak like a bad crime novel when describing events. Returning to the April incident, the police were now pursuing Danny "hot on his heels." Who speaks like that in daily life? We have touched on this, but this tendency seems to betray a need in Williams to be the star of his own adventure, filled with decadence and dangerous characters. He created his exaggerated phantasms without any appreciation at all for the risk that people would see he was lying. All that seemed to matter was the current rewrite of his personal drama.

In keeping with this theory, he claimed that Danny had "bodily attacked the three policemen" in April. Not according to Anderson or the police report. Not according to the charges filed. And not according to Williams's previous telling of the event. But Williams didn't flinch. I refrain—unlike Dr. Brandt—from psychoanalysis. I don't feel qualified. But these stories are, at best, odd. At worst, they reveal a pathology that is difficult to ignore.

Williams did not like the district attorney, Spencer Lawton. If that wasn't apparent to this jury yet, his personal dislike at being questioned by Lawton would finally reveal itself and allow the jury a hint of the volatility that might lead the dapper man to grab a Luger in anger. When Lawton pushed Williams on the incongruities about his April story, Williams blew.

Q. Do you remember Corporal Anderson mentioning that he met
you at the door and that you showed him the gun and pointed that
the gun had been broken up and pointed to upstairs, indicating that
Hansford was up there—

A. Uh-huh.

Q. ... in a violent rage and would not be taken alive?

A. I never said will not be taken alive. *That's a cold-blooded lie.* You see,
the man ...

Williams tried to back up, but he was too late. He had given the jury a glimpse, even if a small glimpse, at his temper. Sometimes a glimpse is all it takes.

Williams next unveiled a creative new approach to Hansford's upside-down body position. Welcome to Danny Hansford and roller disco. Since 1981, Danny had been at the corner of the desk, firing his Luger. Even though it was unlikely that Hansford had fired the shot, there was no disagreement about the position from which it had been fired. But that was no good. Williams and his lawyers knew it. The body was upside down. Here are samples from Williams's new version of the same event:

A. [Y]ou see, *he was moving.* He had a certain *momentum going.*

A. I would assume he was *moving* this way.

A. He was *moving* and he was still walking and talking, but *he shot
along there,* but I think he went on that way some. He fired first and
he was still *going that way* and when I fired at him, he was *along* in that
position.

A. You see, *he was in motion.*

A. He was coming this way, around the desk, in a fast *motion.*

A. He shot it at an angle there, but he *kept going that way* and when I
shot him, he was directly across from me. I would say, to be as accurate as possible, when he fired *he was in motion,* going this way.

The defense knew the body didn't make sense where it was, so Williams put Hansford on roller skates. He was all over the place—and for no reason, if his intention was to actually hit Williams with a bullet. It would have been a mira-cle, under Williams's new scenario, if Hansford had even managed to hit the desk. So where was Danny again?

A. And when he got about where my finger is now, right here, if you
were standing right here. If you were standing right here, that would

be about the right placement that way.

Q. Exactly directly across from you and your chair.

A. Uh-uh, no. You've got to understand, the chair is over here. I left the chair to get that drawer like this and I came up.

Q. All right, then he would be exactly across from—

A. Along here.

Q. Well, that's going to put me exactly across from your chair—

A. Well, it depends on which way you want to look at it. You're also exactly across from me.

It sounds like the famous Abbott & Costello "Who's on first?" routine. More importantly, none of this fit the evidence in the case. The shooter had to be at the desk corner. The physical evidence (papers, ricochets, mark on the wall, bullet fragments) and consistent expert testimony—from both sides—put him there. That didn't matter to Williams. If Williams needed Danny to be moving, Danny had to get moving. But Williams's new version had a problem. He couldn't have Hansford in two places at once. You can't pay physical evidence to lie—only people.

Run some of Williams's roller-skating Danny scenarios and see how it works out. All of Williams's versions—in order to create the upside down body—require Danny's upper body to move toward the large caliber round that just slammed into his chest, while his legs fly in the other direction. Putting Danny on roller skates doesn't allow Williams to flip the laws of kinetic energy transfer any more than Dr. Petty's MD degree did for him.

Return for a moment to the diagram of varying bullet paths examined in connection with Dr. Howard's testimony from *Williams II* (Figure 33). We saw what happens to the bullet path as Hansford is moved to Williams's left. If Danny had "kept going that way" from the corner of the desk, as Williams now claimed, observe what happens to the bullet path: it becomes even more extreme. In fact, it becomes impossible to match to the autopsy results. This was not examined in this trial but we are aware of this evidence so we consider it in our inquiry.

As Williams continued his testimony describing the attack, he collided head-on with the shell casing evidence: "I shot three times without stopping. Three shots without a fraction of a second between them." The three ejected shell casings from these shots were recovered from three very different locations, however, two of them on opposite sides of the room (Figure 13). It might have been helpful if Williams had held up a flag when he told the truth so the jury would have known when to pay attention.

Thus came to a close the testimony of James Williams in his third murder trial. It isn't possible to objectively analyze Williams as a witness before a fresh jury. His constantly morphing tales can generate out-loud laughter. This was his own murder case, yet he continued to spew inconsistencies and contradictions like an old jalopy belching smoke and oil. He was an outrageous raconteur and probably entertaining at parties. Though it might seem impossible to imagine anyone taking him seriously when his stories are viewed over time, it would be a mistake to apply that impression to one trial before a single jury. The jurors might have found him charming.

Vanessa Blanton Alexander, the first park angel, returned to tell her tale of the April incident involving Hansford shooting a tree at 3:00 a.m. Ms. Alexander was now the beverage manager at the 17 Hundred 90 Restaurant where she had been working at the time of the prior trial. She repeated the same testimony.

Ms. Alexander's story was fortuitous for the defense, but fortuitous things happen. There is one question about her reasoning. She testified that she was scheduled to enter Emory Law School in the Fall, so she apparently had an interest in the law. Yet she had now testified twice that she hadn't felt any need to tell the police what she knew because she saw the police drive up. The fact that the police drove up after the fact meant that they didn't know what she knew. She was an eyewitness. She had information and chose to keep it to herself.

Ms. Alexander may well have been telling the truth, no matter how coincidental. That was not bloody likely in the case of Claudina Delk Smith.

Claudina Delk Smith was now living in Thunderbolt, a small nautical municipality abutting Savannah to the east. By 1987, her story had changed along with her address.

Ms. Smith had been to Night in Old Savannah with her son and cousin. In *Williams II*, she said that she then went to visit a friend, Ms. Thad G. Johnson, and knew what time she had left her friend and returned to her cousin's apartment, so she knew what time she went to sit in the park.

This time, there was no sign of Ms. Johnson in Ms. Smith's testimony. Ms. Smith was back from Night in Old Savannah and then she was in the park. More remarkably, Seiler actually didn't ask her *what time it was*. Ms. Smith never testified in *Williams III* as to what time she went to sit in Monterey Square. Seiler must have forgotten to ask, considering the importance of the question. The omission is inexplicable.

Why had Ms. Smith gone to sit in the park in the middle of the night? She'd changed her mind for this trial.

Here's what Ms. Smith had said in 1983:

My husband and my cousin had gotten into something of an argument (on the phone), and I simply wanted to get out of the house and enjoy the evening.

Here's what Smith said in 1987:
I'd had a nice evening and my cousin doesn't smoke, I respect that,
and I went outside to get some fresh air and smoke a cigarette.

The argument on the phone was gone. Getting out of the house to enjoy the evening was gone. In its place was an urge to smoke a cigarette. There had been two teenagers sitting on the next bench in 1983. They, too, had disappeared from her story.

Asked what happened while she was in the park, Smith said she heard "several loud gunshots fired all at once, very rapidly." Just what the lawyer ordered, and it only took one question. Loud gunshots, all at once, very rapidly. Just like Williams had said. Perfect, everyone could go home. But hold on a second. There were a few questions for Ms. Smith to answer.

How did she know that she'd heard gunshots without a second of hesitation? Not everybody knows what gunshots sound like, particularly gunshots fired without warning inside a brick mansion almost a block away, echoing through an empty square at night. Most people go through a process of elimination, normally starting with fireworks. Any account of a shooting in an open space is almost always accompanied by "and then we realized they might be gunshots." Ms. Smith, however, had it instantly: loud gunshots, all at once, very rapidly. Ms. Smith did not mention having previously seen combat.

In the previous trial, Ms. Smith had destroyed Williams's story about the timing of the killing and had confirmed the huge time gap between the killing and his call to the police. That had to be fixed. The defense had to believe that the prosecution had gone over Ms. Smith's testimony and spotted this poison pill lurking in her tale.

It should be no mystery by now what would happen to this little problem for *Williams III*. Ms. Smith changed her testimony. Had she reviewed her prior testimony with Williams's lawyers? She was their witness. They put her on the stand. Would a competent lawyer review what his or her witness had said at the previous trial?

What did she say this time? This time, she said she had sat out in the park for "at least ten minutes, probably about fifteen minutes." She cut the time exactly in half. The obvious question is the one always asked in such a situation: Was her memory better in 1987 than four years earlier? But that question hardly has to be asked in this instance. This was not a fender bender. Smith was a defense witness in a murder case with a crippling time gap. Anyone who thinks she had not met with Williams's lawyers since 1983 or reviewed her testimony from the prior trial should just stop reading.

Is this an accusation? If there is an accusation here, the facts and circumstances are making it. This is merely a reasonable interpretation of the evidence—

and it might be completely wrong. Perhaps Claudina Smith came up with the change all by herself, with no clue that her change worked in favor of the man who had put her on the stand.

How did cutting the time in half work in Williams's favor? It drastically reduced the conflict between Ms. Smith's and Williams's stories. The defense was stuck with the fact that Goodman and Rushing lived a certain distance away and had to get up, get dressed, get in the car and drive to Mercer House, but no cops after fifteen minutes was far better than no cops after thirty.

Last time, Smith didn't say where the shots had come from. This time, with her improving memory, she decided that the shots had come from behind her. Was the defense trying to emphasize that the shots came from Mercer House? Where else would they have come from? How many killings were taking place on the same square in 1981?

What did Smith do after hearing gunshots? She was frozen with fear, just like before. This time, though, she knew the gunshots had come from behind her, in the direction of Mercer House. With this new information, when her fear thawed enough for her to move, what did she do? She got up and walked *toward* the gunshots. Generally, only soldiers and law enforcement officers voluntarily move *toward* gunfire.

This flaw in her tale had been there in 1983, but now the flaw was even more egregious. The time between the gunshots and her movement was cut in half and she knew the direction from which the gunshots had originated. Only knowing Williams's story could account for her lack of concern. She heard gunshots, walked toward them, passed in front of a mansion full of valuables with the door wide open, and didn't even hurry her stroll, much less call the police.

Her timing problem with this sequence had not disappeared. Williams didn't open the door until after he called the police (at 2:58). The call response time was ninety seconds. Williams consumed some of those ninety seconds hanging up the phone, walking to the front door, opening it, and going wherever he went to wait for the police to arrive. The door was open when Smith passed, yet Smith never saw Williams, a blue light, or a police car. The whole tale was patently absurd. The ridiculous timing coincidence had now been narrowed down to a coincident few seconds between 2:58 a.m. and 3:00 a.m. on May 2, 1981.

Some people might consider slotting a spacecraft for orbit entry around Mars, a planet anywhere from 35 million to 250 million miles from Earth (depending on relative orbits), to be a matter of some precision. But it appears that Claudina Delk Smith could claim her own timing trophy. She had managed to match her passing of Mercer House back in 1981—over 52,000 minutes prior to her testimony in 1987—to a single slot of less than ninety seconds—on the exact night and time that Williams and his lawyers needed a witness.

Before she was finished, Ms. Smith tidied up one more string she had left hanging from her prior testimony. She had said there was a car sitting across from Williams's house. This time she took care of it without even requiring Seiler to waste a question. She simply added, "but it had been there, I believe, when I walked out in the first place. It did not arrive while I was there."

To revisit some earlier speculation, why was the defense concerned with accounting for the mystery car? Was there some concern that a jury might wonder if that car was Goodman's car, if perhaps he and Rushing had arrived more than once at Mercer House? There was no other testimony relating to a car in front of Mercer House or what the presence of a car might mean. What is interesting is that the defense felt the need to account for it in Smith's story.

It's also remarkable that Smith was not only monitoring the time, along with the number and spacing of sudden gunshots on the night in question, but was also monitoring traffic in front of Williams's house, from the other end of the park, facing in the opposite direction. Note that she had testified to the shots having come from behind her, meaning Mercer House was behind her—she was at the other end of the park, facing the other way, but she was positive that this car could not have arrived while she was in Monterey Square. Did she monitor every car that rounded the square and make sure it didn't stop in front of Mercer House?

On cross-examination, Ms. Smith again admitted that she hadn't mentioned any of this for years. She also refused to even consider that she might be mistaken about the number of shots or their sequence.

Consider: If we were to put ten people in Monterey Square, fire off shots inside of a brick mansion almost a block away in the middle of the night and not let them write anything down, what would we likely get if, two and a half years later, we asked our ten people what had happened (the 1983 trial)? We would get ten different answers. If we asked them six years later (the 1987 trial), they might have forgotten what they'd been asked to remember. Yet Smith would not even consider the possibility that she didn't remember everything with exactitude. This is where jurors have to use their own human experience to weigh the credibility of a witness.

As to her failure to say a word for years, Ms. Smith fell back on the "nobody asked" response. She "didn't have any reason to think the police would be interested." That statement wasn't credible. She admitted that she saw the news vans and police cars the next day. She knew someone had been killed in the house. How could any thinking person believe that the police wouldn't be interested? But Smith chose to play hide-and-seek with the police instead of walking out the front door, crossing the street, and telling somebody what she knew.

Ms. Smith also had a new explanation for having kept her secret: She had read a crime book written by a coroner and thought there would have been a house-to-house investigation. The coroner who wrote the book would probably agree that it would also be helpful if citizens who were witnesses to a killing would let somebody know, rather than waiting for a house-to-house investigation.

Why look at these fault lines within Claudina Smith's tale? Because constructed stories often don't get little things right. A juror is allowed to bring their common sense to the trial, and if something triggers an "oh, come on!" moment, that's a perfectly valid and legitimate basis for dismissing a witness's testimony. That's the law, not an opinion. Jurors are the final arbiters of the credibility of witnesses. Because people lie under oath, and they're not always good at it.

The violence witnesses were back, no more violent than in the previous trial. Barry W. G. Thomas was no longer employed by Williams by 1987. He told of the attack on his stomach on the basement stairs.

Next came the man with the deadly spray wand, Robert Croyle. His story was the same: Everything took place at the apartments, and Croyle subdued Danny by himself in the hallway. There was no sign of Danny going to Croyle's job, throwing him up against a concrete wall, or "stomping" him.

Earl LeFevre repeated what he'd said before about the fight in his front yard: It was George Hill's beef with Earl's son. Danny left and George came back later. There was no sign of anybody doing anything to Earl's wife or of Danny breaking a door. Mr. LeFevre never saw Danny again.

These three "violent" events were supposed to be the tracks of a natural-born killer. Based on this evidence, if Danny Hansford had lived in one of the legitimately rough neighborhoods in America, he wouldn't have measured very high on the scary scale. This doesn't mean Danny Hansford was not a troubled young man. However, with the defense having been granted free rein to prove that Hansford was a "cocked rattlesnake," it would be reasonable to expect more than Danny touching somebody's stomach with his foot or getting pulled into a fight over George Hill's hat. This is not an excuse for Danny Hansford's nature or behavior, but an argument with a janitor over spraying a cat does not conjure up the image of a homicidal maniac.

If an attack with a toe couldn't do the job on Danny's image, maybe a shrink parade could. The defense had shuffled the order of their witnesses, like a baseball manager juggling the lineup when their team isn't hitting. In the prior trial, the initial defense witnesses had been Williams, Stone, Burton, and Petty, and the shrinks had come later. This time, after Nurse Case and Williams, the defense put up the park angels, the violence witnesses, and the doctors, holding the case evidence experts for last.

Only speculation suggests why the defense switched up the witness order. Considering that Stone, Petty, and Burton hadn't swayed the jury last time, the defense might have decided to soften up the victim first before getting to the case evidence. Another way of putting it is that the defense would prove that the victim was "a bad man who needed killing" up front to improve the jury's view of their expert testimony coming later. In the spirit of trying something else if what you're doing isn't working, it made sense.

Dr. Aurel Teodorescu didn't testify in person. Apparently, the doctor was not available. His prior testimony was read into the record. This procedure is entirely proper in appropriate circumstances, when a witness is legitimately unavailable. The previous trial testimony is read aloud with lawyers reading the questions and answers. Obviously, his testimony didn't change.

Maybe there was a shrink golf tournament somewhere, because Dr. Speriosu's *Williams II* testimony was also read into the record.

Dr. Albert Patrick Brooks appeared in person. He testified that he had been working in the Memorial Medical Center Emergency room in August of 1980. Danny had reportedly swallowed a bottle of Limbitrol, a prescription for anxiety and depression. Danny's stomach was pumped. He was given charcoal, some medication, and a bowel stimulator, and put in ICU. When he woke up he didn't know where he was, freaked out, and had to be restrained.

Dr. Lester M. Haddad returned, also in person. There was only one notable difference in *Williams III*. On cross-examination of Dr. Haddad, Lawton tried to get some more information on Limbitrol.

Q. That was for an overdose of something called Limbitrol?
A. Yes, uh-huh.
Q. All right, is it correct to say that that's a drug that's prescribed for a psychiatric disorder?
A. Yes.
Q. Would you prescribe it for a condition of hypoglycemia?
A. No. Definitely not.

This produced a lesson for lawyers, not to get too casual. Probably to fix the suggestion that Williams was being treated for a psychiatric disorder, Seiler waded in on redirect.

Q. What about, Dr. Haddad, for stress? Would it be appropriate medication for someone who's under a good bit of anxiety or stress?

A. Limbitrol? That's quite a strong agent. I don't think one would or should prescribe Limbitrol for just stress, unless perhaps a psychiatrist felt it was important to prescribe it.

Q. Suppose it's stress—

A. I would not prescribe—I was in private family practice for three years, as well as work in the emergency department, and for situational or daily type stress type situations in normal patients, we—I would not prescribe Limbitrol. I think that that's—I think that's a *major drug*. I think that that should be prescribed by *psychiatrists*.

It might have been a good idea to get out of there, but no. Remember, these guys couldn't manage to shut up, even when it was for their own good.

Q. What about in cases of anxiety, where it might lead to hyperventilation? Would it be appropriate in that instance?

A. I am not familiar with that usage. Now, perhaps you should *ask a psychiatrist*. But I can only say I'm board certified in family practice and emergency medicine and in those areas we would not use Limbitrol.

This Limbitrol was crying out for an explanation. Some doctor had prescribed it—not Dr. DeHaven—and Williams obviously didn't want to reveal who the doctor was or the reason it had been prescribed for him. If there was a doctor out there who was treating Williams, why didn't someone call them as a witness and get to the bottom of this Limbitrol mystery rather than asking peripheral witnesses for theoretical diagnoses and indications for the medication?

This is the USDA-approved indication for Limbitrol: "Limbitrol is indicated for the treatment of patients with moderate to severe depression associated with moderate to severe anxiety." These are things to watch for: "mood or behavior changes, anxiety, panic attacks, or if you feel *impulsive, irritable, agitated, hostile, aggressive*, restless, hyperactive (mentally or physically), more depressed, or have thoughts about suicide or hurting yourself."

Did any of those symptoms apply to Williams? How about on the night he shot Danny Hansford?

Dr. Henry Brandt returned, to continue his public service (for a fee). He went over the "antisocial personality," explained that the profession didn't use the term "sociopath" any longer, then used it anyway.

Dr. Brandt listed the criteria for the diagnosis of someone as a "sociopath" and testified that a person only need fit three. When he listed the criteria, the entire courtroom might have cringed, considering how common they were. A group bus ride to Georgia Regional Hospital might have been in order.

Dr. Brandt's testimony wasn't any more enlightening in 1987 than it had been in 1983. For those fond of voodoo, Dr. Brandt might have done as well with some owl's teeth on a string and some possum eyeballs in a jar. On cross, he admitted that no, he had never attempted to speak to Danny's mother or any other member of Danny's family. Presumably he didn't need to, since he had pored over Danny's records from visits to Georgia Regional eight and twelve years earlier.

With his service to the community complete, Dr. Brandt was excused.

All that was left of the third Williams trial was for the defense's hired guns to take another crack at the circumstantial evidence that was still screaming "pants on fire" at James Williams. Very little new has been learned about the case, though a great deal has been learned about the second theme of this narrative— the extent to which some combatants in a legal war will go to win. The bottom of that pit is not yet in sight.

Dr. Irving C. Stone was back from Dallas, without his boss, Dr. Petty (who was not listed as a witness for the defense and did not appear). The defense couldn't resist, once again, trying to drape Dr. Stone in a cloak of impartiality before he testified to a fresh jury. Stone testified that he had first come to Savannah without knowing "what value he would be to the defense."

Good for him. Hopefully, no witness would guarantee the defense a result ahead of time. And if they did, they presumably wouldn't be stupid enough to say it.

We've seen this impartiality charade. It's not technically objectionable on relevance grounds. But it would be far more honest—and far less irritating—if hired guns would just testify and drop the halo act. These witnesses might as well testify that their one true wish—like Sandra Bullock in *Miss Congeniality*—is "world peace."

The better question, rather than asking if these witnesses are saints in suits, would be to ask how the dime-store testimony such as that seen so far in *Williams* ever works with a jury: half-baked, untested theories offered up as science, tests that don't have anything to do with the evidence in the case, diagrams that are only "representations" so they can misrepresent the evidence, all such sorts of nonsense.

These types of witnesses are the trial practice equivalent of hecklers at a political rally. What they're yelling isn't as important as making sure that nobody can hear whatever the speaker is saying. The distractions and misdirection can also work, because real life is not *CSI Savannah*. Crimes are not antiseptic events. A murder scene is more like a splattered Pollack painting than an engineer's AutoCAD® design. And with scientific evidence, there is always a way to fuss around the edges, take facts in isolation, and muck around in the details to create some chaff to confuse the fact-finding radar of a jury.

For example, you could argue that DNA tests can't say *absolutely* that blood A came from defendant B, because DNA evidence deals in probabilities. In the *Simpson* case, DNA tests of blood recovered from the back gate at Nicole Brown Simpson's condo did not say that the blood came from Orenthal James Simpson. Rather, it said that only 1 in 57 *billion* people would have the exact markers Simpson shared with that blood. One could argue that this was only "circumstantial" evidence that the blood was his. But considering there are only about 7 billion people on planet Earth even today, that argument wouldn't (or shouldn't) fly very far.[132]

Relevant testimony should be admitted. Then the combatants can argue about it and the fact finder can decide how much weight it's to be given. But the suggestion that a defense lawyer's hired gun is pure while scientists testifying for the prosecution are inherently crooked is pure manure and is offensive. Defense lawyers should stop doing it. Not surprisingly, none of this reasoning made a bit of difference in the *Williams* case. With Dr. Stone's inspiring testament to his own impartiality complete, he got to his actual testimony, led by Don Samuel.

They began with the shirt. How far away did Williams have to be when he fired the shot into Hansford's back? Much like before, ignoring the handling of the shirt, Stone opined that the weapon had to be three feet or more away.

Another quick note about Stone's absolute cut off at three feet: If three feet was the outer limit and there was absolutely no gunpowder particulate beyond three feet, the particles that would be present at that outer limit would be the last sturdy little particles that out flew the rest. In other words, the amount of particulate at the outer limit would be relatively small. Losing the few particles at the outer limit would require much less disturbance of the shirt than greater quantities deposited at closer distances.

Dr. Stone couldn't have been unaware that the shirt's history was important. He'd admitted, on cross-examination in *Williams II*, that the handling of the shirt could have affected his results. Regardless, he ignored the shirt's history to deliver an opinion favorable to Williams. Stone told the jury that Williams's Luger had to be three feet or more from the shirt and he was finished. The defense had been rabid about the protection of Hansford's hands. But, because it suited their purposes, the lack of protection of the shirt was ignored.

But hold on a second. Is that really what Stone said?

Believe it or not, there is another layer to this—one so subtle that it is impossible to detect without a magnifying glass. Dr. Stone didn't technically say Williams's Luger had to have been three feet or more away. That was the *impression* he and Samuel created. The clever lawyer and well-trained witness had struck again. This was Dr. Stone's actual testimony, with some additional words inserted:

> Based [solely] on my [unadjusted] tests in 1983, I would—it's my opinion that the gun was no closer than about three feet to the—the gun was no closer than three feet to Danny Hansford's shirt.

The words I have added clarify what Stone was saying. Here's the logic trail: Stone's "tests in 1983" didn't detect residue on the shirt, but the failure to detect residue was only *one factor* to be considered. The shirt's history was another. That history *wasn't considered* in his "tests in 1983."

According to rules of construction, Stone's statement "based on my tests" means "based on my tests as constituted and conducted." This can be mind-bending, but that's why these things are so difficult to detect as a trial is flying by. If the explanation sounds more confusing than Stone's answer, think of it like this: "Based on my tests [using a car in a garage], it did not snow last night." The statement without the bracketed words doesn't account for last night's snow storm. If you didn't know better and heard the statement alone, you would certainly get the *impression* that it hadn't snowed.

Dr. Stone's "tests" did not account whatsoever for the lack of protection of the shirt or its handling history. So the tests were limited by their parameters to a factual situation not present in the case being tried. Regardless of the limitations of Dr. Stone's tests, Samuel and Stone then doubled down. They used Stone's unadjusted three feet for another rigged demonstration:

> Q. Could Jim Williams have stood over Danny Hansford and shot *like this*?
>
> A. No, not in my opinion.

Samuel didn't need an expert for this demonstration. He could have put a third-grader on the stand and given the kid a measuring tape. Samuel was, in effect, asking Stone if the distance between two points was less than 36 inches while holding his arm stretched out. Dr. Burton had done the same thing by going the wrong way around the desk to find a demonstration that wouldn't work.

A legitimate seeker of truth might have asked, "Is there any reasonable scenario that would allow Williams to fire the shot through Hansford's back after coming around his desk?" That question wasn't asked. Yes, it is fair to ask why not.

Dr. Stone had brought some even newer "newly created" evidence to *Williams III*: the results of a "tilt test" he had performed out in Dallas. The prosecution hadn't been informed of the test, hadn't been invited to observe it, and hadn't been provided with any report of it being held or a copy of the data it produced.

Stone testified that he had used a Luger he had at the lab—*not* the weapon in the case being tried—to conduct a "test" of the effect on GSR deposits of tilting a Luger down to fire it, because the "attack" shot had been fired at an angle into the desk. A lab assistant got up on a table and fired Dr. Stone's Luger toward the floor. Dr. Stone then checked his assistant's hand for residue and concluded that detectable GSR would definitely be reduced by *70% to 90%* (for antimony and barium, respectively) in *any shot* fired from *any Luger ever made.*

Dr. Stone might not like this description, and it wasn't the one he used, but that was the meaning of this exercise he called an experiment. He applied the result from *one shot* from a random Luger to a different Luger (Luger 22A) without any attempt to compare the two weapons. This meant Stone was applying his result generally, to any Luger ever made. The only required components of his test were that the weapon be a Luger and that it be tilted. If this sounds suspicious, it should.

The larger problems were (1) the weapon Stone used, and (2) the test itself. The weapon that Dr. Stone used had deposited *no residue at all* in 20% of his previous tests with it. So was his test result due to the weapon he chose or the effect of tilting the weapon? There was no way to know: he only fired one shot. That was his test. His results were so extreme—a 70% reduction in antimony and 90% reduction in barium—that the results alone cried out for verification and re-checking. Did Stone fire the weapon again to check his results? No. These were great results for his client; why mess with a good thing—one shot and he quit.

There was also no indication of who had swabbed the lab assistant's hand or how the swabbing had been performed. If Stone did the swabbing himself: Beware a scientist conducting his own test while hoping for a particular result. This is a distant cousin of Burton failing to raise the end of his string another inch in Williams's study because of the potential affect on his fee.

But we're not finished. Stone prefaced his testimony about his tilt experiment by claiming that primer residues "basically go up, straight up." No, they don't. The statement is patently false. To the contrary, the evidence in the case was that primer residues: (1) are discharged in a *cloud* from the open breech of the weapon, and (2) come out of the barrel, meet air resistance, and form a *cloud* around the weapon. The second cloud in particular, created by air resistance, would be created no matter what direction you aimed the weapon. But Dr. Stone was presuming all the GSR came out of the breech at the top. With that assumption in hand, he tried to turn that discharge cloud into an arrow.

What was Dr. Stone doing? He was pretending GSR was emitted from the Luger in the form of a contained shaft so he could "aim" it—and then aim it away from Hansford's hand, to explain where the Luger 22A GSR might have gone. You can't aim a cloud, so Stone turned a cloud into an arrow, or a column of residue, going "straight up." And he had a visual aid. He used a rubber stopper tossed into the air to demonstrate his "straight up" notion.

What had Dr. Stone done, vigilant reader? Right. He had used a deceptive substitution to mislead a jury, much like a rubber ball and a shell casing. If Dr. Stone merely wanted to demonstrate the direction of up, he could have tossed anything into the air, even Mr. Samuel, but it would have had no relevance at all to the way in which GSR is discharged from a Luger.

Stone also told the new jury about his bloody-rag test even though it had been discredited in the previous trial. No, he didn't tell the jury that his test wasn't based on the case evidence, at least not on direct examination.

Stone then helped Samuel roll out the nutty assumption that Samuel had tried to establish with Roger Parian: that the original and replacement ammunition had gotten switched, which might have thrown off the first (most important) Luger 22A firing test, the one-shot test. The ammo-scrambling scenario was so scrambled that it probably didn't make any more sense to the jury than the testimony does on review. It was unfortunate that Parian hadn't been reminded of his prior testimony, where he had recalled the sequence. The bullets had never been scrambled, and the defense knew it. It's pointless at this point to point out that they didn't care.

What was Dr. Stone's primary mission in this trial? To deal with the lack of GSR on Danny Hansford's hands. The "tilt test" was one example. His bloody-rag test was another. Or switching up the ammo. Each area dealt with GSR residue. So Dr. Stone, the defense GSR expert, would naturally be Marilyn Case's tag-team member, to take her plastic bag story and disappear the GSR from Hansford's hands, right? Wrong.

The defense didn't ask Dr. Stone anything about hand bagging or the paper vs. plastic question. It is reasonable to ask why the defense didn't question their GSR expert about the 800 lb. GSR gorilla that Marilyn Case had left sitting in the middle of the courtroom. It's reasonable to conclude that Dr. Stone wasn't asked because he couldn't be counted on to provide the answer the defense wanted.

David Lock conducted Dr. Stone's cross-examination and deserves thumbs-up for a job well done. First, the trigger pull was not all it was cracked up to be.

Q. Okay, so in fact, it's relatively easy to pull that trigger, is it not?
A. If you know that you're going to—yeah, you can do it.
Q. I mean, I did it with my thumb and my index finger without even supporting the—
A. Right.

Mr. Lock also displayed a wry sense of humor that only a student of the *Williams* trials might have appreciated, while making another point about trigger pull:

Q. Let me ask you this: If somebody had a—if somebody was fairly strong, let's say they could pull a door off its hinges, would they have any problems firing that gun?

A. No, sir.

When Danny was admitted to Georgia Regional at age fifteen, he had been accused by his mother of having pulled the door to his room off its hinges. No, trigger pull didn't explain how Danny Hansford could miss the side of a barn and hit a cow in the pasture instead.

Lock took Dr. Stone through a number of cleanup questions about the GSR tests run by the State Crime Lab (in 1981 and 1983) and the Dallas lab (in 1983). Stone agreed that his test scores would have been more accurate if the same person who'd swabbed Hansford's hands had swabbed Stone's hands. He agreed that the machine the Dallas lab had in 1983 was not as "good" or specific as the machine Randy Riddell had used. He agreed that the test would be more reliable if the same ammunition was used. He also agreed that the Hansford antimony and barium levels were remarkably low.

How about Stone's Luger tilt test and his use of a rubber stopper tossed into the air to illustrate his theory that residue from Lugers went "basically up."

Q. [T]his little thing you did using the little stopper and throwing it up in the air, that's not really an accurate showing of how that occurs from the gun, is it?

A. No. It's just for *demonstrative* purposes. It's *illustrative* of what might happen.

Q. Okay, now, the residue that comes from a gun would diffuse a little more than that, would it not?

A. Yes.

Q. And so it might cover a wider area; it wouldn't just go straight up in the air and come straight back down.

A. No, sir.

The stopper was for "demonstrative" purposes but was not "an accurate showing." Meaning Stone used his stopper to demonstrate an *inaccurate showing* for the jury, just as he had used an inaccurate diagram for "presentation" purposes in *Williams II* without disclosing that it was inaccurate until he was found out on cross-examination.

What about the weapon in Stone's tilt test? Yes, he revealed, 20% of his firings with that weapon in previous tests had produced no residue at all.

Q. There is no way you would ever publish an article with this, is there?

A. No, sir.

Q. How many times would you have fired it before you published an article?

A. Probably thirty, thirty-five times.

For an *article*, Dr. Stone would have done a lot of testing. This was only a murder case. Dr. Stone had an explanation: He only fired one bullet because of *time limitations*. Lock wasn't buying it. He pointed out that all tubes containing swabs from all the test firings go into the machine at the same time. Stone agreed. So, Lock surmised, the time required for the analysis was only the time required for the test firing itself—the time it took to wash the hand, fire the gun, and swab the hand. Stone agreed again.

Stone was preparing testimony for a murder case, but he found the time required to fire the weapon even one more time to check his extreme results too burdensome. Stone also confirmed that he had not made a report of this test or provided his results to the prosecution.

Lock challenged Dr. Stone on another one-shot test he had debuted on direct but that we haven't covered yet. Stone fired his pet Luger one time, again, and went to his office, where he "did paperwork" for two hours. Afterward, he checked his hands for residue. He didn't find any. On cross, Dr. Stone agreed this had no relevance to the facts of the *Williams* case. It hadn't stopped him from sharing it with the jury.

In all of these examples, Dr. Stone had presented misleading or completely irrelevant evidence and allowed a criminal trial jury to believe it mattered. Mark this as Exhibit A in case Dr. Stone is denied witness sainthood should his name come up on the list. And who was orchestrating this series of rigged up chaff? Williams's lawyers, playing Lawyer Games.

Although the defense didn't ask Dr. Stone any questions about hand-bagging with respect to GSR, the prosecution did. What about hands not being bagged until the body got to the hospital?

Q. Even if they were not bagged for several hours and moved to a certain extent from one location to another, would that significantly effect (sic) it?
A. Sure could.
Q. It could.
A. Yes, sir.
Q. It's all according to whether somebody rubbed their hands real good or something of that nature, is it not?
A. True.

With respect to the exit wound in Hansford's chest and the "shored" wound debate that received more attention than it merited, the defense firearms expert then proceeded to knock down the entire house of cards. The lack of a "shored wound" in the chest (which the defense claimed would have been there if the chest had been flat on the floor when the bullet exited the chest) was supposed to prove that the body had not been on the floor for the shot through the back.

Lock asked Stone about the shored wound issue. Dr. Stone agreed with Lock: Even with a body facedown on the floor, an exit wound could be in an area of the chest that would not be flush to the floor because of muscle structure in that particular area. Dr. Stone then caused the theory to collapse altogether. He testified that he couldn't tell from the exit wound in the chest alone if Danny Hansford's body had been on the ground when the shot in the back had struck or not. This completed David Lock's cross-examination.

Redirect examination signaled the return of the testifying lawyer. Don Samuel combined Stone's invalid tilt test, the debunked theory that GSR disappears through time alone, and the irrelevant bloody-rag test into one monster question in an attempt to resuscitate them all at the same time. Leading your own witness is a no-no. Samuel did it anyway, testifying for Dr. Stone while pretending to ask a question, something that he and Seiler did continuously:

Q. And with respect to the Danny Hansford analysis, the evidence
shows that the gun was shot down, that the hand hit the shirt, and
that the swabs were taken some twelve hours later.
A. Correct. Those all would reduce the residue.

Not only incorrect, but categorically false. Samuel's testimony masquerading as a question was based on evidence that either did not exist or had been discredited. Also note that the question in the transcript is not followed by a question mark.

First, what about the allegation that "the evidence shows" that "the hand hit the shirt"? "The evidence shows" is an improper form of question, if that mattered by this point. Samuel's statement would be more appropriate (whether or not true) in a closing argument. For example, Dr. Petty testified in *Williams II* that a thrust put the chair on Hansford's pant leg. Did that mean "the evidence showed" that that's how the chair ended up where it did?

It might be a small difference but, "There is testimony to the effect that" is far different than "The evidence shows." But during the course of a trial you can lose track of every minor violation and these things pass. Besides, the thinking goes: If you're seen jumping up constantly to object, the jury might not like you. It's a fine line. Lawyers will often push the boundaries, to see what they can get away with. They can wear down the opposition. The technique was on full display in *Williams*.

What about the "hand hit the shirt" point? Was Samuel adopting the dead man with the springing hand and perfectly bouncing Luger? What the evidence "showed" was that Hansford went to the floor clutching both hands to his chest

THE TRIAL | 321

and died on the way down. The evidence then "showed" that Williams came along later and pulled his hand out. That's a compelling reading of the evidence, entitled to at least as great a stake to the "evidence shows" label.

Samuel was welcome to ask Dr. Stone a hypothetical based on some facts Samuel might want to suggest had been established. The jury could then decide whether his foundation was valid or not. But his statement that "the evidence shows" was nothing more than a self-serving claim and—again—a lawyer's statements and questions are not evidence. Finally, of course, the "hit" was not described in any detail, in keeping with other examples we've seen: reflex action, thrust, twist, knock, tilt, bounce, kicked, and other non-specific terms tossed around the courtroom, none of which stand up to even the most basic scrutiny.

Second, how many times by this point had witnesses testified—for the prosecution and defense—that time alone had *no effect* on GSR trace elements? The passage of twelve hours was *meaningless* in relation to GSR, as a matter of settled science. You might as well ask if a chunk of metal would disappear if you left it on your kitchen counter while you went to work. Both Stone and Samuel knew the contention to be false. Maybe that's why Dr. Petty wasn't back for this trial. He knew better and had said so. Dr. Stone was contradicting every other witness to ever testify on the question, including his own boss.

Third, the statement that the weapon was shot down(ward) was correct, though the only evidence demonstrating the effect of pointing the weapon down was based on an invalid test.

Finally, even though Samuel's predicate statement was one-third false and two-thirds misleading, it was then used to support an unsupportable conclusion. Unfortunately, Dr. Stone flubbed a great closing line.

Q. Is it remarkable, then, that there is so little *antimony* on his hand?
A. No. It would have been remarkable if *they* were left, if *they'd* been there.

Samuel said "antimony" but Stone answered "they." That is what happens when an actor blurts out their line without listening to the other actor. I expect Samuel was supposed to say antimony and barium, and Stone just said his line without paying attention. If this had been a play, they could have worked it out in rehearsal, but this was the performance, so it only sounded awkward.

It also wasn't true. Note the word "then" emphasized in Samuel's question above. Here's a translation [Q. and A. are both mine, not from the trial record]:

Q. Given these things you've agreed with me are true, even though they might not be, don't you agree with me that we are absolutely right?
A. Yes, absolutely.

As Don Samuel's final act of obfuscation, he went even further. He had Dr. Stone agree with *him* that Dr. Howard agreed with *both of them*. To pull this off, Samuel used one premise *rejected* by Dr. Howard and another *never presented* to him. Samuel could have asked Dr. Howard the question he asked Stone, but he hadn't. Samuel clearly couldn't handle Dr. Howard, so he waited and had his own witness testify for Dr. Howard.

> Q. And will you agree with me that, I think it was Dr. Howard who testified that, without the proper bagging, all the gunshot residue tests are absolutely meaningless?
>
> A. That is correct.
>
> Q. Thank you.

First, what did "without the proper bagging" mean? Filling the bags with ice cream? Here is what Samuel had actually asked Dr. Howard with regard to the passage of time:

> Q. All right, is it not true that not once, not once, did anybody ever do a test to see what happens twelve hours later, with or without bagging, six hours without, six hours with?
>
> A. No, we've done that *many times* and the results have been good.
>
> Q. You've done tests where the body was dead for six hours with fifteen people walking around the room and then you bag his hands and drive him half way across town, put him into a hospital, give him x-rays, bring him down to the morgue, then have the autopsy performed, then take the bags off and then do—you've done tests like that?
>
> A. Have I done tests like - - -
>
> Q. Anything close to - - -
>
> A. Wait a minute. Wait a minute.
>
> Q. Anything close to it?
>
> A. Oh, yes, *many times* we have checked hands that have been bagged *under those circumstances*, particularly in suicides, and the results are very often good.

Dr. Howard hadn't agreed with Samuel. He had *rejected* Samuel's premise. What about the use of plastic bags? Samuel *never mentioned* plastic bags to Dr. Howard:

> Q. And of course, in all your answering with respect to the gunshot residue test, you're assuming that absolutely there was proper bagging, proper procedures in protecting the hands; correct?
>
> A. That's correct.
>
> Q. And needless to say, if that's not true, if it changes that hypothetical, your opinions—all these tests and everything, would

mean nothing at that point, if you change that hypothetical, part of the hypothetical.

A. That's correct.

Why didn't Samuel ask Dr. Howard a specific question? Why didn't he ask Dr. Howard about the effect of plastic bags, if that was what he meant? Why play games, hiding behind the phrase "proper bagging"? Dr. Howard might have agreed that filling the bags with ice cream wouldn't be considered "proper bagging." But no one was entitled to answer for him. If Samuel wanted to know what Dr. Howard considered "proper bagging," why didn't he ask him? That's the point of examining a witness.

For example: "Dr. Howard, assume plastic rather than paper bags were used to protect the hands in this case. How would that affect your conclusions?" On the other hand, "Assume somebody did something wrong; wouldn't that be bad?" doesn't cut it.

Let's cover a few points about the question Samuel did ask Dr. Howard. Here it is again:

Q. You've done tests where the body was dead for six hours with fifteen people walking around the room and then you bag his hands and drive him half way across town, put him into a hospital, give him x-rays, bring him down to the morgue, then have the autopsy performed, then take the bags off and then do—you've done tests like that?

Taking Samuel's premises one at a time: (1) There were never fifteen people in the entire house, much less in the study; (2) the 3.5 miles to Candler Hospital might have been "half way across town" if Savannah was 7.0 miles wide, but the body was in a Fox & Weeks hearse, so the ride was probably smooth and the residue wasn't going anywhere; (3) it is not clear where Samuel was suggesting the body be taken, if not to the hospital; (4) x-rays don't make GSR disappear; (5) the un-bagging and swabbing were done *before* the autopsy, not after. That's five flaws in logic or intentional misstatements of fact by one lawyer in only one portion of his exchange with one witness.

This is Lawyer Games on full display. Samuel knew there weren't fifteen people in the study but said it anyway, knowing it wasn't true. What do you call that where you come from? But it goes with the territory in trial practice. As an acquaintance of mine, an extensively educated medical professional, said, "Don't all lawyers lie? You kind of expect that, right?"

I'm not sure which page of this book we're on but if the reader is getting tired of seeing the same charade play out over and over, feeling a little fed up and possibly a shade disgusted, then I'd say we're on track. This is what it looks like behind the curtain.

But back to the question Samuel did not ask Dr. Howard: the effect of paper vs. plastic bags on GSR collection. It wasn't asked for two likely reasons. First, Dr. Howard testified *before* Marilyn Case, and asking the question would have tipped off the prosecution. Second, Dr. Howard was a national authority in the world of forensic criminalistics. Williams's lawyers couldn't risk having Dr. Howard shoot down a theory before it was even launched.

More remarkably, the defense also didn't ask Dr. Stone about plastic bags and their effect on GSR, despite the fact that he was the defense GSR witness. We might feign surprise but we all know who was destined to tag into the ring to finish what Case started, a man whose talents were especially suited to the task.

By 1987, Dr. Joseph Burton appeared to be trying to surround his nemesis, Dr. Howard. Dr. Burton had managed to have himself named medical examiner for three Metro Atlanta counties: DeKalb, Cobb, and Paulding.[133] His fee for his testimony was up to $1,500 a day plus expenses.

Seiler had Dr. Burton testify, again, to his own impartiality. Despite the fact that it's silly, which we've covered, there's also a hidden flaw buried within this practice. Doesn't the jury have to believe a witness is impartial in order to believe the claim of impartiality?

What would the defense take up first with Dr. Burton? Surprise: the GSR evidence. The witness who didn't believe in GSR would testify about GSR while Dr. Stone, the defense's GSR expert, was on the way to the airport. The *Williams* case could have retired the "unusual" trophy by this time.

Burton delivered the same civic club lecture as before. He informed everyone that a negative gunshot test meant nothing. The bailiff's nephew knew that by now. A negative GSR test, standing alone, meant nothing. This was akin to George Carlin's comedy newscaster giving sports results: "Here's a partial score: 3." It doesn't mean a lot without the second part: the *weapon test* to go with it.

To suggest how out of style GSR testing was, Burton then declared that they didn't do GSR tests anymore in Cobb County. Well, they did, he said, but they had to have a sign-off from the DA's office. Which meant what? The defense had just presented its own GSR expert, who not only believed in GSR testing but had performed GSR testing *in this case.*

How about the FBI? Had they checked with Dr. Burton for guidance? According to the May 2011 *FBI Law Enforcement Bulletin*: "GSR findings continue to add value simply because numerous population studies have shown that GSR is not normally found on the average person."[134] Burton's testimony that GSR testing was useless was, itself, useless.

It was clear by the time of *Williams III* that Dr. Burton didn't perform tests or do much science himself. He waited until his team was at the goal line then trotted onto the field, took the handoff, ran behind the marching band into the end zone, and spiked the ball. He was here to do the same with the pesky GSR evidence.

Burton agreed completely with Stone's tilt test, though he had never performed such a test himself, simply based on what he cited as common knowledge. To become "knowledge" at all, scientific theories are subjected to rigorous peer review, published, and confirmed by further studies that successfully duplicate the tests and results. The distance between one shot fired from a faulty Luger to "common knowledge" in science approaches infinity, yet no leap was too large for Burton.

Undeterred by modesty or lack of scientific foundation, Dr. Burton then took the garbage-bag handoff from Case and headed for the end zone. The only expert in the case who was not qualified to render an opinion on GSR was going to wipe the GSR from Hansford's hands with a proclamation. Burton announced that plastic bags, with the body "in a refrigeration unit for five or six hours," would destroy *any trace* of GSR through *condensation.* Cue the orchestra: This was obviously intended to be the big finish for the defense. It would have been more compelling if it had been related to the evidence in the *Williams* case. It wasn't.

The defense was rightfully proud of themselves for digging up the hospital admission form for Danny Hansford's body. They should have read it. The body was not released to the morgue until 12:15 p.m. The autopsy commenced at 2:00 p.m., one hour and forty-five minutes later. By the time somebody got Hansford's body to the morgue, checked it in, and got it into a refrigeration unit (assuming it ever made it into a refrigeration unit—which was not asked), it was likely to have been less than an hour and a half before it was taken out again for the autopsy. There was no evidence whatsoever in the *Williams* case that Danny Hansford's body had even been *in the morgue* for "five or six hours," much less "in a refrigeration unit." Burton's testimony was invalid on its face. (This is new information. It was not pointed out at trial.)

Aside from the flawed basis of his proclamation, Burton made no attempt to either explain it or support it. Dr. Joseph Burton seemed to be the only expert witness alive who could offer conclusions on scientific subjects without reference to any actual research that he or anyone else had ever done on the subject. He cited no studies, data, tests, prior cases, authoritative journals, or treatises—nothing whatsoever in support of his conclusion.

The term "refrigeration unit" even requires description. Morgue units aren't freezers. Generally, they're kept at a range of 2 °C (35.6 °F) to 4 °C (39.2 °F). The normal temperature of a refrigerator is 35–38 °F.

Undeterred, Burton proclaimed, "Plastic bags allows (sic) condensation or moisture from the hands to condense inside the bag." The key word is "allows." All this means is that, with plastic bags, condensation might be possible under certain circumstances—circumstances *not present in this case*. This is similar to the notion in *Williams I* that wind could have interfered with GSR distribution inside the study. There was no evidence of any condensation in the bags on Hansford's hands.

It probably isn't necessary to point out that this entire area is irrelevant if Det. Jordan did exactly what he said he did. This is why the paper-vs.-plastic debate was a larger issue than simply who was lying—Case or Jordan—and why the defense stayed away from the subject with Riddell, Howard, Stone, and Draffin. Why wasn't the effect of plastic bags brought up with these witnesses? Because the defense knew what Dr. Burton was going to say. If he was going to scrub the hands squeaky clean without requiring the silly business of relevant facts, actual studies, research, or other cases to back him up, why risk giving real GSR experts or Dr. Draffin a chance to screw that up?

What about this condensation claim, unfounded as it might have been. Where was the morgue staff to testify to times, temperatures, and protocol? What about Ofc. Roy, Dr. Metts, and Dr. Draffin, all of whom were present at the autopsy? Even if they had been subject to mass hypnosis and had not noticed plastic garbage bags on Hansford's hands, had they noticed water flowing out of the bags when the bags were removed? Wouldn't that have been slightly unusual?

In particular, wouldn't the man performing the autopsy have noticed? From Dr. Draffin's autopsy report: "Examination of the hands, which have been previously bagged, shows blood clots on both surfaces of both hands."[135] Why didn't the defense ask him if the hands he examined were wet? The blood was still there, undisturbed. Had the GSR been washed off—every last sign of it—while the blood was left undisturbed?

But Dr. Draffin wasn't asked. None of these witnesses was asked about the paper-vs.-plastic question that was now threatening to take over the case. It was the defense's big surprise, but they wouldn't allow anybody but Burton to touch the subject. The implication is clear.

There is a terrific lawyer joke that we might apply to Dr. Burton. First, by way of disclaimer, most lawyer jokes are actually told by lawyers. The question is: Why were lab rats at Johns Hopkins replaced by lawyers? Because lawyers are more plentiful, the students don't become as attached to them, and there are some things you just can't get a rat to do. In this case, I have beat the lawyers up enough, but I can apply the joke to Dr. Burton without a bit of remorse.

Burton moved on, to keep Danny's body in the air for the head shot. We don't put much emphasis on the question, for reasons already explained, but this testimony says more about Burton than about the issue. He used an actual analogy—a watermelon in place of Danny Hansford's head. His conclusion? If a watermelon was on the floor and you shot through it, you would expect to find watermelon juice and pulp on the rug. This passed for science in Burton's world.

He then concluded that because there was no blood and brain tissue (watermelon juice and pulp) on the rug near the hole in the rug, Hansford's head had been—presto—*eight to ten inches* in the air when he was shot. Burton didn't explain why he picked eight to ten instead of seven to eleven or any other pair of numbers. Regardless, the watermelon analogy is bogus. Most people would say, "If I shot a watermelon with a 9mm Luger, I think I'd see some watermelon and juice on the floor even if you raise it eight inches." They would be right.

What's the problem? A watermelon isn't a human head; its internal composition is nothing like a human head, and it doesn't have a blood pressure. A heart can stop pumping. Blood pressure can drop to zero from a 9mm bullet that severs an aorta (as in this case). This isn't worth belaboring. Whether or not Danny's head was off the floor when struck, the analogy is as full of holes as Burton's watermelon.

But he's not alone in that respect. Almost every example used by these defense experts throughout the history of *Williams* was misleading: a watermelon for a human head, a rubber stopper for a cloud, a rubber ball for a brass shell casing, an anchor to represent the squeezing of a trigger. A steeple could represent an umbrella; after all, they both point up.

What could have been done instead? Perform tests dropping actual shell casings on a rug with a pad underneath and see what happens. Safety-check Luger 22A and allow the jurors to squeeze the trigger. Show GSR discharge clouds in a high-speed photo. These are simple examples. Avoiding them suggests that these simple examples didn't help the story the defense was spinning. That would likely be Detective Aristotle's conclusion.

Dr. Burton had a second, not-simple explanation for why the body had to be off the floor when the head was struck. He claimed the head had to be in the air for the skull fragment to bounce onto the seat of the chair (with the chair remaining upright, which Williams's story required). But, not surprisingly, he left something out. He can't simply raise the body off of the floor. If he raises the body, he has to *rotate* the head, to keep the exit wound and impact point in the floor aligned. Rotating the head causes the bullet path to become more and more vertical. We can illustrate the effect (Figure 17). The exit wound in the head has to remain aligned with the bullet hole in the rug. There is no choice. If the body is raised, the head has to rotate.

This spells serious trouble, for Williams: As the head rotates and the bullet trajectory becomes more vertical, Williams also has to rise, in order to strike the same entry point in the head (refer again to Figure 17). He would eventually have to get some stilts or jump up on his desk.

In other words, Burton didn't consider the effect of his example on the *other* evidence in the case. When the other evidence is included, Burton's example *hurts Williams's case* rather than helping it. But this is what can happen when a witness deals with one item of evidence in isolation, trying to justify a conclusion in reverse. This is a new analysis and a new illustration.

There is another flaw in Burton's example which is becoming far too familiar. He presumed the chair had always been where it was found, upright. But it wasn't. The chair was placed there after Hansford's death. Using the defendant's scene manipulation to justify a scenario that supports the manipulation isn't kosher. Nevertheless, witnesses have done it repeatedly.

What else could Dr. Burton take care of with his magic wand? He could take a moment to dismiss all GSR evidence in the case. This was Dr. Burton's grand finish:

Q. And based on your expert opinion and the evidence you've reviewed and the tests you've seen conducted, can you draw any conclusion whatsoever as to the absence of gunshot residue ... absence of significant gunshot residue on Danny Hansford's hand?

A. There is no scientific basis to draw any conclusion or opinion from that.

This should be recognized by now as vintage Burton. It's a proclamation without any foundation. We have to translate Samuel's question once again: "Based on your expert opinion, what is your expert opinion?"

At least other defense witnesses did battle, but Joe Burton didn't even bother to suit up for the game, aside from selecting a suit for court. He merely showed up and declared "no scientific basis" for anyone else to be entitled to an opinion that differed with his. There are a number of new possible nicknames for Burton, should he ever require a replacement.

The privilege of cross-examining Dr. Burton fell to Spencer Lawton. Back to GSR, one last time. What followed is what happens when a witness doesn't review any testimony or evidence in the case and is asked questions for which they hadn't been prepped in advance.

Dr. Burton admitted that he was not aware that the same person who had swabbed Danny Hansford's hands had also done the swabbing for the test firings done by Roger Parian. He agreed this would make those tests more valid than the tests done in 1983 in either Atlanta or Dallas.

How about that pesky skull fragment? The following moment should be laminated. Dr. Burton was going to agree with Dr. Howard. He was also going to contradict Dr. Petty from the prior trial, but this jury wouldn't know that.

Mr. Lawton asked Dr. Burton a hypothetical:

Q. Suppose that he had been seated in that chair and, realizing that he was about to be shot, had begun to rise from it and then was shot in the chest and then, as he fell forward, knocked the chair over. And suppose further that when he did, by whatever the attitude of the chair, whatever it did, where it wound up, it had the seat of the chair facing generally in that direction. Is it possible, in your opinion, that a small fragment of bloody skull fragment could be thrown up against the seat of that chair then and stick there?

A. Somehow it could, yes.

Thus the cross-examination of Dr. Burton ended with his agreement to the feasibility of Dr. Howard's theory of the killing. This was also the only rational explanation ever offered for the presence of that skull fragment on the seat of the chair.

On redirect, Samuel tried working on Hansford's upside-down body position, but it didn't make much sense. Burton explained that the head could end up where the feet were because "their legs essentially drop out from under them." That statement cannot be analyzed, much less refuted, because it's impossible to visualize.

Surprisingly, Lawton decided to re-cross Dr. Burton about the chair. He asked Burton if Hansford could have been sitting in the chair, legs crossed, seen that he was going to be shot and, when shot, fallen to the position where he was found. Burton replied, "He could have if the chair was not in the position we see it in the photographs at the scene." Exactly right, Doctor. That's why Williams had to pick up the chair. It was not in the position we see "in the photographs at the scene."

As its last witness, curiously, the defense re-called Ofc. Stevens to the stand. In Seiler's never-ending search for elephants roaming the study, he had discovered another clue. He took Stevens through several photographs in which a portion of a shoe might appear. Stevens went through the photos, noting the owner of each shoe. Seiler still made no effort to place the photos in context. Nor did he suggest any conclusion from the footwear survey.

Most of the shoes belonged to Stevens, from photos she took while pointing the camera down. Corporal Anderson's shoes made a brief appearance, as well as the distinctive footwear styling of Detectives Ragan and Jordan. That was it. Still no sign of Don Samuel's fifteen people in the study.

There was only one pair of shoes that Stevens was unable to identify. She speculated that they might have belonged to Dr. Metts. They didn't. They were mine. I confess to wearing a pair of Hush Puppy moccasins, but my defense for the fashion choice is that it was a long time ago and I dressed in a hurry. No, I was not standing on the body or the desk.

In *Williams III*, the defense's character witnesses had been sprinkled throughout, probably to accommodate the witnesses' schedules. We didn't cover them as they appeared to avoid breaking the flow of the substantive evidence. Notably, Williams's mother and sister testified on his behalf for the first time. Williams's mother, Blanche Williams, testified that James hadn't gotten into fights growing up other than with his sister, which Mrs. Williams said didn't amount to anything.

On a related note, Williams's mother attended this trial, whereas Danny Hansford's mother was not allowed to be present in the courtroom. Williams's lawyers placed Danny's mother under subpoena for the sole purpose of keeping her out of the courtroom, where she might present a sympathetic image. Witnesses are routinely sequestered to prevent one witness from hearing the testimony of the others. In this case, Williams's lawyers invoked the rule against Danny's mother, for another transparent reason: They didn't want to remind the jury that the pit bull had a mother. They never called her as a witness. It's a common ploy and a clear abuse of the sequestration rule.

If I had been presiding, I would have asked counsel for a commitment on the record as to their intention to call Hansford's mother, the basis for her testimony, and an anticipated time frame for her testimony. Absent satisfactory answers to those questions, I would have told her to come in and have a seat. She had a right to hear the trial of the man accused of killing her son.

The other character witnesses whose testimony was sprinkled throughout the third *Williams* trial were: Dorothy Kingery (Williams's sister), George E. Patterson, Cora Bett Thomas, Deborah Friedman, Jan Corbett, Lucille Wright, and Theron Spencer. Hal Hoerner did not appear. He had probably been removed from Williams's holiday party list as well for telling the district attorney about Williams's call from the jail and his request to intercede on Williams's behalf with former governor Sanders.

Following closing arguments and Judge Oliver's instructions to the jury, another group of twelve retired to a jury room to deliberate in the case of *State of Georgia vs. James A. Williams*. With one exception, those involved in the third *Williams* trial have always believed that they knew what happened next. They have been wrong.

CHAPTER 31

THE NON-VERDICT

On Tuesday morning, June 9, 1987, before the jury was sent off to continue its deliberations, counsel met with Judge Oliver in chambers, where Spencer Lawton reported a phone call he had received from one James Harty. Mr. Harty worked for the Medstar Ambulance Service. Mr. Harty reported that he had received a phone call at 2:30 a.m. that morning from a woman he understood was a member of the *Williams* jury. This woman had asked a number of questions specific to the evidence in the *Williams* case. Coincidentally, the jury had already reported to Judge Oliver that they were deadlocked and could continue deliberating "until hell froze over" but would not likely be able to reach a verdict.

Judge Oliver decided to put Mr. Harty on the record. Mr. Harty joined the group, was sworn, and related his story: A woman had called the ambulance service, asked if she was speaking to a paramedic, and said she had some questions. It came out that she was on the *Williams* jury. She said she was the only one who thought the man was innocent. According to the caller, the rest of the jury wanted to convict Williams because "he was nothing but a 'faggot,' they don't care if he lived or died and go (sic) to hell or whatever, you know."[136]

A disturbing aspect of the questions this juror had asked was how confused she was about the evidence. If her questions were reflective of the jury's understanding, it had to have been shocking to the lawyers. At the time, however, the task was to find out who she was.

Meanwhile, the defense had heard, loud and clear, that this woman was the lone holdout for Williams. They were one vote from a third guilty verdict. At least four times during the session in chambers, defense counsel asked Judge Oliver to declare a mistrial. Judge Oliver declined.

Judge Oliver decided to convene court normally and ask the jurors the standard questions asked after an overnight recess. Included among those standard questions is whether the jurors have discussed the case with anyone. There were no positive responses. The mystery juror wasn't talking.

Because that didn't work, everyone returned to chambers and each juror was brought in and questioned by Judge Oliver individually. Mr. Harty was present, observing. The jurors were asked whether they had called or spoken to a paramedic about the case. There were twelve jurors and one alternate. If the culprit was discovered among the twelve, the alternate would take that juror's place. Mr. Harty did not have the juror's name, only a voice.

The twelfth juror called in was Cecilia Russell Tyo. When she was asked the questions, she had a slightly different answer than the others had. Rather than simply say no, she said, "Not about the case."

THE COURT: Did you specifically telephone a paramedic about this case?

JUROR: No.

THE COURT: You haven't talked to anyone about it?

JUROR: Not about the case, no, sir.

There was something about the way she answered the questions that appeared odd. Unfortunately, Judge Oliver was doing the questioning and he was decidedly unaggressive. These were jurors. He was being polite. After a cursory examination, Judge Oliver sent Ms. Tyo back to the jury room. Mr. Harty then spoke up, telling Judge Oliver that her voice sounded familiar. She was not called back, and there was no follow-up.

What should Judge Oliver have done? That calls for hindsight and speculation. What he was certainly authorized to do, based on the fact that her answers were unlike the others and the fact that Mr. Harty said he thought he recognized her voice, was to bring her back and question her more closely. But he didn't. Judge Oliver merely said that because all jurors had answered no, as far as he was concerned, he had a clean jury.

He didn't have a clean jury. He had credible evidence, from a disinterested party, that one of his jurors was lying to him. He had a jury that had told him they were deadlocked and that hell could freeze over before the situation changed. The juror who had contacted Mr. Harty had told him exactly the same thing as well as the exact vote breakdown. The caller had to be a member of this jury, had to be the lone holdout blocking a verdict, and was clearly in violation of the rules governing juror conduct.

You simply cannot let that go, announce you have a clean jury, and pretend nothing is wrong. The last opportunity to salvage this trial ended when Judge Oliver halted the examination of Cecilia Tyo. He had effectively granted the defense a mistrial. It was only a matter of time.

The jury continued its pointless deliberation and, predictably, Judge Oliver was forced to declare a mistrial. The jury ended deadlocked 11-1 in favor of a guilty verdict. Celia Tyo was the lone holdout. Afterward, she was interviewed in the press. I don't know if she shared the following during jury selection, but I doubt it.

Cecilia Tyo says her own experience with domestic violence taught her that "If you have never experienced fear in your life, you never know what you will do. Can you imagine a wild dog coming at you?" She once had an argument with a drunken "gentleman friend," she said, during which he "grabbed me by the throat." As she was slipping into unconsciousness, Mrs. Tyo said, "I took a fillet knife and stuck him in the ribs."[137]

Tyo didn't say if she had killed the man. As to Tyo's allegations to the paramedic and the press that the jurors were against Williams because of his sexual preference, the foreperson of the jury, Barbara S. Hubbard, responded publicly. From her open letter to the *Savannah Morning News*:

> "The jurors for the James A. Williams trial handled themselves with dignity and the utmost respect for the law," Mrs. Barbara S. Hubbard told the Morning News. "Not once was the word 'faggot' used during the deliberations. We were very much aware of the consequences of our decision. We were entrusted with a man's life. Each person (juror) examined the evidence and reviewed his or her notes (on testimony). Our decisions were based on these two things only. Mr. Williams' sexual practices were not presented as evidence in trial, nor used in the jury room," she added.[138]

Mrs. Hubbard conveyed the same sentiments in a letter to Seiler.

But that is not the end of the story of Celia Tyo, holdout juror. Was she a principled woman, alone in her belief in Williams's innocence, standing her ground? Until now, the assumption has been yes. That assumption has been wrong.

Cecilia Tyo was not merely a concerned citizen—or, rather, she wasn't concerned about what people thought. Tyo was the live-in companion of a notorious suspected safe burglar familiar to local and state law enforcement authorities. Detective Ragan had personally executed a search warrant at Ms. Tyo's house, along with GBI SA Stone (whose name should be familiar from the affidavit blizzard). This is new information, related directly to me by Everette Ragan during my research for this book.

What was Cecilia Tyo doing on the *Williams* jury? The prosecution didn't know who she was. Detective Ragan did, but he wasn't present for jury selection. As the lead detective, normal practice called for Ragan to attend the entire trial, including jury selection. In *Williams III*, however, Ragan's immediate supervisor would not allow him to take time from his regular duties to attend the trial and allowed him to go to court only to testify. Detective Ragan didn't know Tyo was on the jury until he took the stand and saw her sitting in the jury box. He recognized her immediately. According to Ragan, if he had been present during jury selection in *Williams III*, "She would never have been on that jury."

That jury could have stayed in the jury room until hell froze over and hosted the Winter Olympics—Cecilia Tyo was not going to vote to convict James Williams, who retained his title as the luckiest man alive.

After the inevitable mistrial, it was decision time. Would the State try Williams a *fourth* time for the same crime? No sooner had the courtroom door closed behind him than District Attorney Spencer Lawton announced that he intended to do just that.

PART SEVEN

EVIDENCE NEVER HEARD

CHAPTER 32

THE ADVICE NOT TAKEN

On September 30, 1987, Barry W. G. Thomas was interviewed by Investigator J. D. Smith. Thomas had left the employ of Williams in August of 1985. He had run the business while Williams was in jail, but according to Thomas, Williams had never so much as thanked him and their relationship had gone from personal, to strictly business, to nonexistent. He had decided to "get on with his life."[139]

The interview contained two highlights. The district attorney's office had been in touch with an individual from London, a Mr. Kamal. Thomas related that Williams had been introduced to the mystic (Thomas's term) in London, that Williams was fascinated by the man and had brought Kamal to Savannah to counsel Williams.

Mr. Thomas did not know about the upcoming trial (then set for October) and had not been subpoenaed, but the most notable thing Mr. Thomas related was an opinion. He said that the death of Danny Hansford could have been prevented if Williams had "listened to he and other workers and had ended his relationship with Hansford."[140]

This was the aspect of the Williams–Hansford relationship that mattered, not the *existence* of the relationship but the *nature* of the relationship—in particular Williams's attachment to Hansford and his unwillingness to let Hansford go. According to Barry Thomas's comment, he and others had seen the same thing and had warned Williams to break the tie. Which Williams did, eventually, but probably not in the manner they had envisioned.

CHAPTER 33

THE DISAPPEARING MYSTIC

There were twenty-three months between the end of *Williams III* and the opening day of the fourth trial, for reasons that will be explained shortly. A lot can happen while a case is in pause mode. New witnesses can appear. Old witnesses can disappear. As *Williams* would prove, even *new* witnesses could disappear.

A. James Kamal of London, England, did not refer to himself as a mystic; that was Barry Thomas's term. Mr. Kamal called himself a paraphycologist (not misspelled). In late June of 1987, after the *Williams III* mistrial, Mr. Kamal wrote to Savannah's chief of police, relating that he understood James Williams was awaiting retrial on the charge of having killed his homosexual lover and that Kamal had received a number of threatening phone calls from Williams. Williams had told Mr. Kamal that he was coming to London, and Mr. Kamal was concerned for his safety. He wanted to know if Williams was entitled to travel as a condition of his bail.

The letter was brought to the attention of the district attorney's office. On September 17, 1987, Chief Investigator Smith communicated with FBI Special Agent G. Sears to request assistance in contacting Mr. Kamal, with the idea of possibly obtaining his testimony regarding Williams's violent nature. The following day, Smith spoke with SA Huggins with INTERPOL. As Huggins instructed, Smith sent a teletype requesting assistance.

On September 23, 1987, Smith received a phone call from Det. Sgt. Peter Smith in London who informed Smith that he had located and interviewed Mr. Kamal, that Kamal had some "very important information about Mr. Williams and the crime scene," and that this information would be detailed in a formal statement to follow.[141] Mr. Kamal had indicated that he was willing to testify at Williams's fourth trial. Detective Sgt. Smith also indicated a willingness to testify if necessary.

All of this activity was directed only toward using Mr. Kamal as a witness to Williams's violent nature, in rebuttal of Williams's professions of gentility. Mr. Kamal's statement was forwarded to Smith through the INTERPOL office in Washington, DC. According to Kamal's statement, he had first met Williams in 1979 in London, introduced through a friend. He had later counseled Williams about a "relationship with another male." Kamal had told Williams he should "get rid of this man by ending the relationship amicably."

Kamal said that Williams had counseled with him again some six months later and told him he had shot this other male and had put the gun in the dead man's hand.[142] Williams was in London for this conversation which, according to the time sequence he outlined, must have been during the trip that Williams and Goodman took to London and Geneva in May of 1981.

Mr. Kamal hadn't contacted the district attorney. He had only contacted the chief of police to find out about Williams's bail conditions because he was afraid of Williams. The district attorney's office tracked him down, still thinking he was a potential witness regarding Williams's violent nature. Kamal had not been trying to hurt Williams. He had been trying to avoid being hurt *by* Williams.

Mr. Kamal reported in his statement that Williams had left a painting with him in London. When Kamal had taken it to Christie's Auction House in London to have it valued, they had told him it was a fake and Kamal had relayed this to Williams. Kamal said that Williams became upset and accused him of stealing the painting. Twice a week for weeks after, Kamal had received phone calls from Williams of "a very abusive and irrational nature."[143] Williams had sent a letter "saying that he was coming to England to sort me out. I understood this to mean that he was to offer me personal violence."

Kamal also recalled the following: "I remember on one occasion whilst in Savannah with Williams we went out to a dinner party. Prior to going out he put a gun in his pocket and said that the negroes in the square sometimes cause trouble."[144] This must have been Williams's "carry-out" gun. Apparently, it was not only to protect him from hunters of gay men.

But that was not all Mr. Kamal knew. In a follow-up interview, he related what Williams had told him about the details of the killing. Williams said he had been sitting at his desk and his "boyfriend" was reading a poem in a "mocking" fashion. The poem was one that Williams had written and he blew up over the boyfriend reading his poem "in a mocking fashion." Williams told Kamal that he took a gun out of the desk drawer and shot the boyfriend.

Mr. Kamal was a purely professional associate of Williams. When he had come to Savannah in 1979, Kamal had met Williams's sister and mother and had later counseled with the sister on two or three occasions in London. Kamal's trip to Savannah had been paid for by Williams and Kamal had stayed at Mercer House. He had seen Williams only twice in America: once on the Savannah visit and on another occasion in New York.

Testimony from Mr. Kamal would be difficult if not impossible to impeach for bias, and the confession that Williams had made to him was supported by the evidence, a clear advantage over Williams's self-defense claim. Kamal's testimony would be devastating.

Arrangements were made to fly Kamal to Savannah for the fourth trial. As required, Kamal was added to the witness list provided to the defense. As it would turn out, the fourth trial would not begin in October because a lawyer "mud fight" had broken out, requiring postponement of the trial. But the defense didn't miss Kamal's name on the revised witness list.

On October 15, 1987, Mr. Kamal reported to Lawton that on the previous day, a private detective had "gained entry" to his office and spoken to his secretary. Kamal thought the private detective was from a firm in New York, but he was not certain. The investigator had wished to interview Det. Sgt. Smith and Kamal. The secretary told the man that Kamal did not wish to see him.

Kamal further related that he was "finding the whole thing a very big strain." He also mentioned an F. W. Seiler but there is no indication of the context in which Kamal used the name. Whoever visited or contacted Mr. Kamal, it clearly rattled him. On July 8, 1988, Seiler requested court permission for Williams to make a business trip to London for a week to ten days. I do not know if this trip was made or, if so, whether Williams paid a visit to Mr. Kamal while in London.

The fourth trial of Williams would not commence until May of 1989. Mr. Kamal was on call as a witness, to come when needed. When time for trial arrived, however, Spencer Lawton received a letter from Kamal's London physician, a Dr. Nicola Burbidge, explaining Mr. Kamal's inability to travel because of stress. Dr. Burbidge reported, "I do not think his stress levels are likely to settle in the near future and have prescribed some benzodiazepines." Too bad she didn't prescribe Limbitrol. The irony would have been priceless.

Aleph James Kamal's testimony was never heard.

CHAPTER 34

THE DISAPPEARING PINK MINK

On March 28, 1989, Mr. Allen Brock was interviewed by Chief Investigator Smith and District Attorney Lawton. His transcribed interview consumes forty-two typewritten pages.[145] Allen Brock was a friend of John Berendt (author of the "Midnight" bestseller that we will get to in the Epilogue). Originally from North Carolina, Brock had been living in New York. Berendt had told him to drop by Savannah if convenient when Brock headed to Florida for a long-delayed vacation and Brock had stopped over in Savannah on his way to Key West. As Brock had a facility with antiques, Berendt had introduced Brock to Williams.

Thereafter, while in Key West, Berendt had called Brock and told him that Williams wanted to hire Brock if he was interested. Brock said he was and Williams then called and offered him a position. After some negotiation, Brock moved to Savannah and went to work with Williams. As partial compensation, he was given the use of Williams's place at Indian Bluff in Richmond Hill and was also promised use of the parlor floor of Williams's house at 10 East Taylor Street (nicknamed "Yellow Bird") on the opposite corner of Monterey Square from Mercer House.

Mr. Brock worked with Williams for less than two months before Williams became angry with him for not being willing to work with Douglas Seyle and, according to Brock, for correcting Williams regarding some issues regarding antiques on which Williams did not enjoy being corrected. Brock said he refused to work with Seyle "because he's illiterate. He does not know his left from his right and when we're carrying a $40,000 piece of furniture, I don't want to be there when the piece of furniture hits the floor."[146]

So the working relationship didn't work out. As to the *Williams* prosecution, Brock made several significant revelations. According to Mr. Brock, he had overheard a phone conversation that he interpreted to mean that Williams was paying off the witness who said she was in the park and heard the gunshots. This was the second time this allegation had surfaced. Timothy DeLoach had said the same thing in his interview related to the Motion for New Trial affidavit blizzard in *Williams II*.

Brock also reported that he had asked Williams about the controversy over the sequence of shots out of curiosity and that Williams had simply told him, without prompting, that he (Williams) had gotten mad and shot Hansford.[147]

Brock also related that Williams and Berendt had discussed the killing and that Williams had told Berendt that his first instinct was to wrap the body up in a rug and put it in the trunk of his car, then drive it out to the airport and leave it there. Brock stated that John Berendt did not know that Brock was divulging this information and he asked that Berendt not be told that he had said anything. He also said that in his opinion, John Berendt "knew everything."

When asked if he knew why Williams hadn't put the body in the trunk and left it at the airport, this was Brock's explanation:

A. Ah, he just figured he could just call and say that it was an accident, self-defense, and you know. And let me try to get this straight. Whenever he talks about the trial and about what happened, it's like he's in a trance. It's like he's hypnotized himself to believe these things. And he speaks in a very monotone. If I could describe to you in better graphic detail the mannerisms in which he relates these things (inaudible). I don't doubt the man did it, I really don't. I think he got drunk, I think they got mad. He's drunk every night, every night. And every room of course has a bar. And, ah, I think he got drunk, got mad and shot the guy. I don't think there were any, I think he's just that cold hearted.[148]

When asked if he had any information as to the relationship between Williams and Hansford, Mr. Brock related the following:

Q. In your opinion is Jim Williams gay?
A. He's as gay as a pink mink. I'm gay. Well the whole show is gay. Well it was a homosexual relationship, there's no two ways about [it].
Q. Is that with Hansford?
A. Yeah. Yeah, he said he had a huge dick, just fucked the hell out of you, great. He's as gay as a pink mink. I'm gay, John Berendt's gay.
Q. I mean was that why Williams was keeping Hansford around?
A. Oh yeah, sure. He didn't have any home skills at 18 years old.
Q. Do you have any reason to think that it was Williams' purpose to rehabilitate, save Hansford from himself?
A. No, because Jim Williams' interest as he has showed to me is solely with Jim Williams. And, you see, Danny Hansford in my opinion was but a play thing. Just as he had intended I would be and that Douglas Seyle is.
Q. Has there been a trend that his, that he tends to want younger guys?
A. Right, that's the general.[149]

Allen Brock's name was added to the witness list provided to the defense for the fourth trial of Williams, now set to begin on May 1, 1989. On April 19,

1989, the district attorney received a letter from Brock, posted from Raleigh, North Carolina. Mr. Brock advised that he had been angry with Williams when he gave his (forty-two-page) statement and that part of what he had said was exaggerated and much of it was false. Brock advised that if called as a witness, he would have to repudiate most of what he had said in his interview and that he would not be testifying at the trial.

Allen Brock's testimony was never heard.

PART EIGHT

LAWYER MUD FIGHT

CHAPTER 35

THROW OUT THE LAWYERS

As the courtroom doors closed after the *Williams III* mistrial, Spencer Lawton told the scrambling media outside the courtroom:

I'm disappointed, as I'm sure you can imagine. But on the other hand, two juries have heard it before now and they decided. This one was unable to decide, and I'm quite confident that another jury will be able to decide. So far as I see it, the score is thirty-five-to-one for conviction and I'm confident that, if we bring it back and get a jury that is willing and able to decide, then we'll get the right result.[150]

The defense not only didn't like the fact that Lawton intended to try Williams again—they didn't even like the way he said it. So they did what lawyers do when they get mad: They filed something. On August 13, 1987, the defense filed a Motion to Disqualify the District Attorney and His Assistants, asking the superior court to remove the District Attorney—and his entire office—from the *Williams* case. The following day, they filed a Motion and Plea to Bar Further Prosecution, claiming a double-jeopardy violation.

Was this a minor bump in the road? Hardly. The *Williams III* trial ended in June of 1987. The fourth trial would not begin until May of 1989. The disqualification fight was not a formality; it was a bloodletting. And it took the case an untold distance from the central issue of the case, the killing of Danny Hansford.

What did the defense want? They didn't want Williams tried again, and if he was tried again, they didn't want Lawton doing it. It's difficult to imagine what they hoped to gain. The double-jeopardy claim was baseless. As for trying to decide who could prosecute their client, the defense team seemed to have forgotten that voters elect the district attorney to represent the interests of the public, not the interests of defendants—who don't, as a rule, like being prosecuted.

Personally, I'm thankful for the defense motions, because they led the Georgia Supreme Court to correct the finding of prosecutorial naughtiness from *Williams I*. How was that possible? It was possible because Williams's lawyers got too clever for their own good and opened the door.

On the motion to disqualify, the defense made two claims. One was related to Mr. Lawton's thirty-five-to-one comment. The second was an allegation that Lawton's office had committed misconduct by not giving the defense Hansford's hospital admitting form as part of the autopsy report. That might have been fine, even if the claim had no merit, but the defense couldn't resist adding the word "again" to their motion and citing the Anderson report controversy from *Williams I*. Then they piled on, attaching an affidavit from Bobby Lee Cook wherein he said that, on second thought, he hadn't been given the hospital admitting form, either.

It's likely that there were some self-congratulatory backslaps shared in some law office conference room or local tavern over this piece of cleverness. It wouldn't last long.

Spencer Lawton, reacting to Seiler's motions with something less than unbridled joy, subpoenaed Cook as well as David Botts to testify at the hearing on the motions. Picture lawyers with their hair on fire. The defense moved to quash the subpoenas, but Judge James W. Head—who had taken over the case—refused, leading to one of the more unusual sights you will ever see in a criminal case: a district attorney questioning a defense lawyer under oath on the witness stand.

As it turned out, Cook couldn't recall, in the several hundred murder cases he had tried, ever seeing a hospital admitting form for a victim included in an autopsy report. For good reason. A hospital admitting form isn't part of an autopsy report. An admitting form from the hospital that receives a dead body has no relevance to the autopsy. This should be obvious from the fact that autopsies are not always conducted at hospitals.

But there was far more to Mr. Cook's brief appearance. Unable to resist adding "again" to their motion, the defense left the door wide open to review the Anderson "fresh" bullet-hole debacle. So Lawton questioned Cook about the *Williams I* appeal and the allegedly "withheld" Anderson report. Shockingly, Cook, who had known all about the report in his oral argument before the supreme court, didn't know anything about it in 1987. Judge Head halted Lawton's examination without explanation and let Cook go.

Judge Head then prevented Lawton from even putting David Botts on the stand. Judge Head hadn't quashed the subpoenas for the two lawyers but prevented Lawton from completing his examination of Cook and from examining Botts at all. Regardless, the earlier appeal had been reopened by the defense. We will return to this later as the mud fight escalates.

After two hearings on the defense motions, Spencer Lawton, apparently having had his fill of playing Hit Me Elmo for defense lawyers, filed his own motion. On October 20, 1987, the district attorney filed a Motion to Disqualify and Discharge Counsel for Defendant, asking the court to remove Seiler and his firm from the case.

The grounds listed were two: (I) Negligence and Incompetence and (II) Unethical and Unprofessional Conduct. Picture lawyers with their hair already on fire and add a bee colony to their underwear. On November 2, 1987, Judge Head issued orders denying all motions filed by the defense and the district attorney.

The State can't appeal much of anything, so it was up to the defense. Why the defense thought the supreme court was going to remove a prosecutor's entire office from a case isn't clear, but Lawton had been right as far as his math was concerned. It was 35-1 in favor of guilty, so another appeal might have appeared attractive in lieu of beginning the fourth trial. The defense filed an appeal of Judge Head's denial of their motions and asked the supreme court to hear it on an expedited basis.

In a surrealistic flashback to the previous *Williams* appeals, a confidential news source called Lawton on Friday, December 4, 1987, to tell him that, according to Carl Sanders, the supreme court had denied the defense motion for expedited appeal. On the following *Tuesday*, the clerk of the supreme court called to inform Lawton that the court had issued an order *that day* denying the motion. What did former governor Carl Sanders have to do with the *Williams* case in the Supreme Court of Georgia in 1987? And how did he know the court's decision four days before it was issued? Apparently, no one asked him.

The defense then filed a straight, normal-time appeal from Judge Head's order. On May 26, 1988, the supreme court issued an eighteen-page decision affirming Judge Head's denial of both of the defendant's motions. In the supreme court's order, because the defense had included its "again" allegation related to the previous (*Williams I*) allegation of wrongdoing that had caused the reversal in that case, the court revisited the *Williams I* appeal decision.

Using the same language that the court had used in 1982 to reverse Williams's first conviction, the supreme court stated, "[I]t is clear that *no intentional 'corruption of the truth-seeking function of the trial process' by the prosecutor has been established here.*"[151] This didn't change the prior outcome—it was too late for that—but I found the correction welcome, nonetheless, because I felt responsible for having missed the snake's rattle on a long-ago morning in Judge Oliver's chambers.

The mud fight wasn't over, however. The fourth trial still couldn't proceed. Incredibly, the defense filed a Petition for a Writ of Certiorari in the United States Supreme Court, asking the high court to review the denial of their double-jeopardy claim. The trial had ended in a mistrial; there was no double-jeopardy claim. In August of 1988, the Supreme Court denied the defense petition—without comment.

What had been achieved, if anything? The district attorney's office had gotten a welcome "correction" to the *Williams I* decision while the defense had lost every legal point but had gained a huge time-out to regroup. A rule of thumb for a defendant: If you keep being convicted when you go to trial, don't go to trial. However, there is a limit and there are only so many motions that can be filed by a creative legal team. Eventually, if the State doesn't forget about you—which wasn't likely—the gavel raps again.

PART NINE

FOURTH TIME'S THE CHARM

CHAPTER 36

CRIME SCENE? WHAT CRIME SCENE?

By the spring of 1989, the case against James Williams had rested for more than eight years on a solid foundation of forensic evidence. It had withstood three trials, theories that would challenge the imagination of a science-fiction writer, and testimony that changed to fit Williams's needs seemingly on command. Yet, when the fourth trial of Williams was moved 135 miles up the Savannah River to Augusta, somewhere along the way, a strange thing happened: The case became about persecution rather than prosecution.

At least that was the new jury-new story theme of the defense for jury number four, as Seiler would exhort the jury to "Let my man go!" The theme found a receptive audience—twelve citizens of Richmond County, Georgia. On May 12, 1989, these twelve would return a verdict of not guilty in the case of *State of Georgia vs. James A. Williams.*

"Let my man go!" had always been the underlying theme of the defense of Williams. The question wasn't whether Williams had killed Danny Hansford in a blind rage—which should have been clear to anyone. The question—lurking under the surface of the defense attack on the dead man—was only whether Williams should be blamed for it. It took eight years for Williams to finally finagle from a jury, sitting in another time and another place, the answer that he wanted to that unspoken question.

But wait—what was the *Williams* case doing in Augusta, Georgia? And what happened to flip the result on its head? We'll get to that, but the transformation of the case itself, from prosecution of a killer to persecution of the accused, was as shocking as the ultimate outcome.

During research for this narrative, I dropped by Athens, Georgia, to visit with David Lock, the third and last chief assistant district attorney to try the *Williams* case—and the only one to try it twice. Leaving Athens, I headed on to Savannah to continue knocking dust from the case. As I drove, something Mr. Lock had told me continued to replay over and over in my head. No matter how many times I went over it, it did not make rational sense.

Mr. Lock had told me of his conversation with a juror immediately following the announcement of the verdict in the fourth trial. After accepting the juror's thanks for his work and professionalism, Mr. Lock had asked permission to pose one question, which the juror had readily granted.

His question: "What about the crime scene?"

Her answer: "What did that have to do with it?"

What did the crime scene have to do with a case based on physical evidence from the crime scene? If the *Williams* case had drifted that far from a chair, hand, blood, paper fragments, and an upside-down body, it had not only lost its way—it had lost its mind.

On the drive to Savannah from Athens, my helpful rental car GPS took me south to I-20, then east, before turning south again. While still trying to make sense of what this juror had said, I noticed one of those large green signs growing larger on the right shoulder as I approached. It simply said, "Carl Sanders Highway." Interstate 20 between US 441 and Augusta is named after the last Georgia governor from the city of Augusta and founder of the Troutman Sanders law firm.

No, I do not believe Carl Sanders had anything to do with the fourth *Williams* trial, held in Sanders's hometown. It only brought home to me what a long, strange trip the *Williams* case had been by the time a bailiff said, "All rise," on May 1, 1989, in the Law Enforcement Center in Augusta, Richmond County, Georgia.

But first, what was the *Williams* case doing there?

CHAPTER 37

ABUSE OF VENUE—
SEARCH FOR A CLUELESS JURY

On March 1, 1989, Judge James W. Head issued an order transferring the fourth *Williams* trial to Augusta, Georgia. The sole consideration cited was "the extensive pretrial publicity generated during the course of the three prior trials of this case."[152] This decision was wrong on the law and may well have contributed to the ultimate outcome of the case. "Pretrial publicity" is not, as a matter of fact or law, inherently evil. Nor is it just cause, on its own, for moving a trial.

Interestingly, when denying the defense's attempt to remove the district attorney's office from the case, Judge Head had found that the defense team had been far more active in the media than had the district attorney. Defense counsel and Williams were openly trying the case in the press. The prosecution was not. Judge Head's opinion in that earlier proceeding stated, "The court can but conclude that defendant has actively participated in pretrial and post-trial publicity to proclaim his innocence of all charges in the indictment."[153]

More importantly, publicity does not decide trials. Did Judge Head think people in Augusta didn't know about the *Williams* case? They certainly did by the time it arrived in town. Augusta knew the outcome of the previous three trials, just as Savannah did. What Judge Head did not do, and should have done, was answer the "so what" question. Given that there was publicity about the trial, so what? What did he believe the effect of that publicity was, specifically? The only legal "authority" cited in his opinion was *Uniform Superior Court Rule 19.2*. Here is what that rule actually says:

Rule 19.2. Criminal

When a criminal action is to be transferred to the superior court of a county different from that in which initially brought, the superior court judge granting the venue change, unless disqualified, shall continue as presiding judge in the action.

The rule has nothing to do with the legal standard for a change of venue and a blanket reference to pretrial publicity is inadequate justification for moving a trial. Simply because people have heard about a case does not mean that those called to jury service are rendered—as a matter of law—incapable of coming to a fair decision.

The notion that a trial, to be valid, must be held where nobody has ever heard of it is not based on any legal principle. The jury system itself represents a rejection of just such a notion. There is a presumed nexus between the jury pool and the person on trial. In fact, until the fourteenth century, the jurors were the witnesses in the trial.

If ever there was a defendant who had public perception problems, it was Jeffrey Skilling of Enron fame, whose trial was held in Houston, the home of Enron. In upholding the denial of Skilling's request to move the trial, the US Supreme Court observed:

> Our decisions have rightly set a high bar for allegations of juror prejudice due to pretrial publicity. ... News coverage of civil and criminal trials of public interest conveys to society at large how our justice system operates. And it is a *premise of that system* that jurors will set aside their preconceptions when they enter the courtroom and decide cases based on the evidence presented.[154]

Did anyone follow the trials of O. J. Simpson, Casey Anthony, Jodi Arias, or George Zimmerman? If pretrial publicity alone disqualified a city from hosting a trial for a crime committed within its jurisdiction, some trials would have to be moved to Tristan da Cunha, reputed to be the most remote place on earth.

Publicity is not the issue. The issue is *prejudice,* and a finding of *presumed prejudice* is extremely rare, reserved for only the most outrageous cases. A case reviewed in the *Skilling* decision in which a trial had been moved involved a videotaped confession by a suspect in a bank robbery, kidnapping, and murder. The confession was obtained without counsel present, taped without the defendant's knowledge, and shown repeatedly on local television.[155] This was an especially rare case. But, absent such egregious facts, cases are not moved simply because people have heard about them. The Supreme Court explained in *Skilling:*

> Prominence does not necessarily produce prejudice, and juror impartiality, we have reiterated, does not require ignorance. *Irvin v. Dowd,* 366 U. S. 717, 722 (1961) (Jurors are not required to be "totally ignorant of the facts and issues involved"; "scarcely any of those best qualified to serve as jurors will not have formed some impression or opinion as to the merits of the case."); *Reynolds v. United States,* 98 U. S. 145, 155–156 (1879) ("[E]very case of public interest is almost, as a matter of necessity, brought to the attention of all the intelligent people in the vicinity, and scarcely any one can be found among those best fitted for jurors who has not read or heard of it, and who has not some impression or some opinion in respect to its merits."). A presumption of prejudice, our decisions indicate, attends only the extreme case.[156]

If it's impossible to seat a jury that can fairly weigh the evidence in a case, a court may have no choice but to move the trial. However, the inability to seat a jury cannot be presumed simply from a case's public notoriety. And in today's world of ubiquitous communication, certain sensational cases are as well known in Topeka as they are in Tampa.

The issue is *prejudice*. Judge Head didn't consider the issue of prejudice, according to his order. He looked only at the fact that there had been publicity in the case. Jeffrey Skilling presented several hundred news reports along with sworn affidavits from actual experts who had done extensive work on attitudes about the case in the Houston area. Even then, his case was not moved and the Supreme Court agreed with the decision. Where was the evidence of *prejudice* in the Williams case? It was nonexistent. A high-volume rant from Williams or his lawyers is not evidence.

The only way to know you can't get an unbiased jury, absent extraordinary evidence of actual prejudice, is to try. Call in a larger than normal jury pool if you like and voir dire (question or examine) the pool. If you can't seat a jury, then deal with the issue. The court should be looking for bias, not ignorance. People who follow the news are not *presumptively biased* as a matter of law. It's a bogus concept. Juries also are not supposed to be pulled from remote places to sit in judgment about something that happened in another community in which they have no interest. The law, in fact, *dictates* that a criminal case be tried where the crime took place.

Williams claimed in the media, "I think we should have a change of venue." He said, "I think Savannah has been pretty much brainwashed by the news media."[157] There was no evidence to support Williams's claim—none. In all three *Williams* trials, prominent members of the community had testified to Williams's character. Williams nor his lawyers would ever cite a single example of prejudicial media coverage of the case. Williams had been convicted by the evidence, not the evening news. Yet the position of Williams and the defense was that publicity made it impossible to get a fair trial in Savannah. But that wasn't the whole story.

It was obvious from Williams's *US Magazine* interview and from statements by Don Samuel that the defense was suggesting that Savannah was homophobic and would not give a gay man a fair trial. The following statement of Samuel to the press was quoted in Judge Head's order denying the defense's earlier motion to disqualify the district attorney's office:

> "If the DA does (retry the case), we'll be here," said defense co-counsel Don Samuel of Atlanta. "I'm confident we can (acquit Williams) - if we can get a jury to pay attention to the evidence and not the prejudice."[158]

Aside from the fact that the evidence had been the last thing of interest to Samuel, the notion that going to Augusta from Savannah would be to escape a homophobic city for an oasis of tolerance displayed a willful ignorance of both cities.

There is nothing evil about Augusta. It's a normal, medium-size city along the Savannah River, 135 miles northwest of Savannah. Augusta is a consolidated city (with Richmond County) with a population slightly below that of Savannah (if consolidated with Chatham County). At last count, TheGeorgiaVoice.com, a statewide site for the LGBT community, listed 10 gay or LGBT organizations in Augusta and 12 in Savannah. What does this prove? Not much, only that the cities are roughly comparable in size and in the number of LGBT organizations. Anyone who thinks that Augusta was San Francisco in 1989 is deluded or not telling the truth.

Was Savannah biased? I am virtually certain Savannah was biased against someone pumping three 9mm rounds into someone else without justification. But whether the killer and the victim were lovers or Lutherans didn't make a bit of difference. If Williams's definition of fair was a city that wouldn't care if Williams had shot Danny Hansford, then Augusta or Albuquerque might have been a better choice than Savannah. But if headed to Augusta searching for tolerance, he was far more likely to find indifference. As one juror later divulged, "Not living there made it a lot easier to decide."[159] Perfect.

CHAPTER 38

THE MISSING TRIAL

The official record of the fourth trial of James Williams no longer exists, as I will explain shortly. But before proceeding to an examination of what is left of *Williams IV* in the public record, let's briefly review three unique trials that we have been conducting together in the pages of this book, only one of which has taken place entirely in a courtroom.

In a sense, we have been conducting three inquiries—or trials—involving the following: (1) the official criminal trials of Indictment No. 34,982, *State of Georgia vs. James A. Williams*; (2) the factual culpability of James A. Williams for the death of Danny Lewis Hansford, distinct and aside from the courtroom verdicts; and (3) the Lawyer Games trial of defense lawyers, expert witnesses, and prosecutors.

The prologue of this book included a commitment that the reader would come to know more about the second of these questions—the factual culpability of James Williams for Danny Hansford's death—than any jury that ever tried the criminal case. That trial is complete. Anyone with a shred of doubt that James Williams shot an unarmed Danny Hansford and doctored the scene after the fact should return to page one and start over.

The Lawyer Games trial will continue—our descent beneath the surface, to watch those who pull the levers to create the scene played out on the stage above. The term "aboveboard" originated with card games, the board being the playing surface and aboveboard referring to hands above the table, where they could be seen. In theater, the "boards" refers to the stage itself and the label might apply here. The scene played out on the stage—above the boards—should comport with this aboveboard definition: "in open sight; without tricks, concealment, or disguise."

In trial practice, whether or not the definition fits depends entirely on those beneath the boards, pulling the levers. We have seen them at work, without the magician's curtain or cloak. In the case of *Williams*, we might be better served by looking at antonyms of aboveboard, antonyms such as: deceitful, devious, or underhanded.

The Lawyer Games trial will continue, but the verdict should be clear, as much as it might leave unfulfilled our wish that the criminal justice system really did work to filter out duplicity in the search for truth, so as to honestly separate the guilty from the guiltless.

The official trial of *Williams* will continue as well, but without the trial record. There is no trial record: thus the title of this chapter. In this instance—unlike the missing autopsy negatives—there is no mystery. We know what happened to the record of the fourth trial. It was destroyed.

This news will undoubtedly disappoint those who were relishing another review of bullet holes, headless chickens, and our friends antimony sulfate and barium nitrate, but there are no transcripts of the fourth trial. There was no conviction and only the defense can appeal, so there was no appeal. Because there was no appeal, the record was not prepared, which would have included transcribing the testimony. For some reason, the only portion of the fourth trial of Williams that was transcribed was the closing arguments of counsel. Maybe the lawyers wanted to read their speeches.

But what about the court reporter's audio recording, stenographic tapes or stenomask recordings (depending on the method used). Transcripts could be prepared today from the original materials maintained by the official court reporting service. That would be true—if the materials existed.

The designated court reporting service in the jurisdiction was operated by William (Bill) DeLoach for almost sixty years. Following his passing in July of 2012, the appointment was awarded to Bill's daughter, Janet DeLoach. In early 2013, Janet destroyed all records from the 1980s—including *Williams*—to free up storage space.

CHAPTER 39

WHAT HAPPENED?

The fourth trial of Williams did take place, and something obviously happened to flip the verdict after three trials and thirty-five votes of fair-minded jurors in favor of conviction. Defense counsel would no doubt supply the answer: super-lawyer brilliance. If so, I would ask how super they were if it took them eight years to get it right.

As noted earlier, Samuel told the media after *Williams III*: "I'm confident we can (acquit Williams) - if we can get a jury to pay attention to the evidence and not the prejudice."[160] It was an odd comment at the time, calling for "attention to the evidence" when Williams's lawyers had spent three trials and six years trying to scramble the evidence into an unrecognizable goulash.

In any event, Samuel and Seiler did achieve a variation of the theme in *Williams IV.* They managed to get a jury to pay attention to the *claim of prejudice* and ignore the *evidence*. We will look at a number of factors—in addition to super-lawyer brilliance—that might have made that possible.

Seiler boldly promised the fourth jury, "Don't think for one second you are going to hear the same trial others have heard." What did he mean, that he'd finally figured it out or that he'd been saving his good stuff for last?

Was this trial different? Every trial is different. Was the evidence different? Not according to observers, with one caveat. There would be another surprise witness in *Williams IV* with a sudden recollection from eight years earlier, but it wasn't even clear that she was in the right courtroom.

The physical evidence against Williams didn't change—because it couldn't change. That evidence couldn't change after 3:00 a.m. on May 2, 1981, when Williams greeted Savannah police officers at his front door with the words "I shot him; he's in the other room." Within minutes, the crime scene was secured and shortly thereafter it was frozen in celluloid. Those original photographs, taken by Ofc. Doris K. Stevens, had caused Dr. Larry Howard to reach a conclusion as valid in 1989 as it had been in 1981: "The son of a bitch is lying." No evidence ever appeared to disprove that observation.

The most compelling indication of what happened in the fourth trial remains the juror comment to David Lock—the jury didn't believe the case was about the crime scene. As someone who was standing in the study less than two hours after three Luger slugs ripped into Danny Hansford, it's difficult to imagine that the case was about anything else. Nevertheless, we will take a look at how that astounding shift of focus from the evidence at the crime scene to the persecution of a defendant might have occurred.

Seiler told the Augusta jury that they could assume that things for Williams had "gone his way" in the case. Being tried a fourth time for murder is a very odd definition of things going your way, in my view. Thirty-five citizens voting to convict you isn't something to brag about. If things had gone Williams's way, he'd have been home sipping a refreshing vodka tonic and mentoring another young man from his refinishing shop.

But that was the pitch: a promise of a different trial and a claim that Williams was right where he wanted to be. That is merely lawyer strut, not evidence. It's the fighter before the fight, brimming with confidence, standing nose to nose with his opponent before anybody has thrown a punch. Inside the ring, though, several factors might have been at work, including:

- a disinterested jury,
- a harmless old man,
- a moved-trial stigma,
- a crippling legal ruling,
- a criminal-case shelf life,
- a flock of angels, or
- a case-weary prosecution.

A Disinterested Jury

The Augusta jury wasn't indifferent to duty. Disinterested in this context means only having no community interest in the outcome. Any jury under the circumstances would be susceptible to a case of "who cares." That might be overstated, but it refers to the disconnect between the community and the participants, exacerbated in this case by an eight-year gap.

This effect was touched upon in relation to Judge Head's decision to move the trial out of the community where the crime occurred. The same move was made in the O. J. Simpson case, with the consent of the district attorney, also to no good effect.

I don't believe that former district attorney Spencer Lawton agrees with me on this point about *Williams IV*. For some reason, the phrase "disinterested jury" carries an attraction that I am not convinced is justified. So, we can all respectfully disagree on the point. As noted, it was a decision within Judge Head's discretion.

A Harmless Old Man

James Williams was approaching sixty years of age and, according to more than one participant at this trial, was very different in demeanor and attitude. Williams, whether legitimately or as a strategic decision, seemed to have shed his arrogance. Rather than looking like a man about to give the order for his tanks to destroy a village, he simply looked like an amiable older man who smiled at jurors and joked around with court personnel.

The change could well have made a significant difference to a jury. Watch how often jurors glance at a defendant, gauging body language, demeanor, and attitude. It can matter. According to observers, Williams appeared to be a harmless older man—in other words, a man who wasn't likely to kill anybody else. And if he did, it wouldn't be in Augusta.

The Stigma of a Moved Trial

A change of venue can do more than find a "disinterested" community. A change of venue can also attach a stigma to a case. Why are trials moved, in the public perception? Because the defendant "couldn't get a fair trial." Cases are not moved to afford the State a fair trial. That can't happen.

When a trial comes to Augusta from Savannah, what does that tell a jury? That this case has a disease and it's up to the good citizens of Augusta to provide the cure. Under those circumstances, it would be easy for a jury to believe that, if they don't reach a different verdict than the other juries, what's the point?

A Case-Crippling Ruling

The factors above are subjective. A less subjective factor was a ruling by Judge Head prohibiting the prosecution's experts from explaining the evidence to the jury. We noted after the *Williams II* appeal decision that the impact of that decision would reappear. It reappeared with a vengeance in *Williams IV*.

At the time of *Williams IV*, according to the supreme court, an expert was permitted to state his or her opinion that, "based on his experience and training in the field of criminal investigation and crime scene reconstruction, the physical evidence was consistent with a hypothetical sequence of events surrounding the shooting."[161]

Using that language, someone like Det. Ragan or Dr. Howard could be presented with a particular "hypothetical sequence of events" and asked if, in their expert opinion, the facts of the case supported it. Experts couldn't lay out their opinions from scratch, but a lawyer could lay out a hypothetical and the expert could opine as to whether the evidence was consistent with the hypothetical. If the distinction sounds silly, that's because it is. Courts do make silly decisions now and then.

Previously, a lawyer could present a hypothetical based on the evidence, such as: "Assume, if you will, there is a chair leg on the pants leg, blood here, no blood there," et cetera. The expert could then be asked to share his or her opinion about what it all meant.

Another way to do it would be to ask if the expert had reviewed the evidence in the case and then ask if he or she had been able to form an opinion based on that review. If the expert said yes, the expert would then be asked to share that opinion. Basic crime-scene reconstruction.

However, at the time of the fourth trial, under a case known as *Coleman* (interpreting the *Williams II* decision), a lawyer was only permitted to lay out a "hypothetical sequence" and ask the witness if it was "consistent with the evidence" in the case. Form over substance. But that was the rule.

It got worse. Judge Head then applied an even more restrictive rule in *Williams IV* than the supreme court had set out, effectively crippling the State's ability to present its case. The *Coleman* decision had involved a veteran detective. The supreme court had said it was "*allowable* for him to assist the jury by stating his opinion that, based on his experience and training in the field of criminal investigation and crime scene reconstruction, the physical evidence *was consistent with a hypothetical sequence of events* surrounding the shooting."[162]

In *Williams IV*, despite that clear prescription from the supreme court, Judge Head refused to allow the prosecution to ask Det. Ragan if the physical evidence *was consistent with a hypothetical sequence of events* in the case. The same reasoning would apply to Dr. Howard. The effect was to handcuff the State and whack them in the knees for good measure.

But didn't the defense have expert witnesses? Wouldn't they also be handcuffed? The difference was, the defense *sought* confusion. Preventing the prosecution's experts from organizing the evidence was playing the defense's tune. They weren't going to complain that Dr. Howard wasn't allowed to tell the jury (in scientific terms) that the son of a bitch was lying.

Did the ruling have an impact? Interviewed later, District Attorney Lawton suggested that, because of Head's ruling, the testimony of Dr. Larry Howard had been "so severely restricted as to render it completely ineffective."[163] I generally respected Judge Head, but there is no question that two decisions he made in *Williams IV* negatively affected the case. The first decision was his choice to move the trial. I would have opposed the decision for all the reasons we've discussed, but it was discretionary and I would have lost the argument.

The second decision was to prevent the prosecution's experts from interpreting the evidence. He put the State's witnesses in straitjackets, and to what purpose? The effect was to deprive the jury of guidance. Jurors are free to give testimony such weight as they choose. To prevent them from hearing testimony at all is the most severe action a judge can take. Pardon my failure to see the benefit to the criminal justice system of keeping a jury adrift on the sea of evidence without a compass.

How, exactly, does guaranteeing that a jury receive as little help as possible serve the search for truth? There is no constitutional right of a defendant to a confused jury.

A Criminal-Case Shelf Life

The defense also had what might not seem like an advantage: the passage of time. When Seiler exhorted the jury to "Let my man go!" he was asking how long Williams should have a murder case hanging over him as a matter of basic fairness. I can answer the question, technically, but it's not always seen as a technical question. Defense attorneys hammer the point, as I would in their position. It's effective.

Though not officially, there might be an expiration date on a criminal case—not for a "cold case" in which the perpetrator isn't known until DNA evidence reveals that the town baker is wanted for a 1960s homicide in Kansas City. Time spent hiding doesn't count, but after the prosecutor has the case and suspect, the clock does begin to tick, even if silently.

In July of 2013, a justice of the Quebec Court of Appeals issued an order refusing to extradite an individual to New Hampshire for a fourth murder trial, despite a claim by authorities that new evidence, including DNA evidence, had been secured connecting the man to a murder committed in 1988. The justice ruled that there was no precedent for subjecting someone to the "stress and tribulations" of a fourth trial.[164] That decision is highly questionable—tantamount to arguing that it couldn't be done because it hadn't been done before—but I do not discount the expiration-date concept. It is possible that the *Williams IV* jury imposed its own quadruple-jeopardy rule.

There is a phenomenon in the criminal law known as a jury's power to pardon, which is a distant cousin of Cook's "Did he need killing?" theory. A jury can, in fact, do whatever it wants in acquitting a defendant, whether or not the acquittal comports with the evidence. The jury doesn't have to explain its reasons to anyone, and its decision is final.

There's no evidence that the *Williams IV* jury "pardoned" Williams. This is only to suggest that delay, which is ordinarily seen as an enemy of a defendant, can eventually turn to the defendant's benefit. Could it be that the judge in Quebec was expressing a personal rather than a legal opinion, that there is a point when enough is enough? Might the jury in *Williams IV* have simply said, "Enough is enough," and sent everyone home?

A Flock of Angels

Of course, *Williams IV* would not have been complete without surprise new witnesses to join the flock of angels protecting Williams. The first, Ms. Angela

Douglas, was a new witness but not a surprise witness. She was given to the defense by the district attorney's office. She might be called "the witness who probably maybe remembered something." Angela was so unsure of what she was sure of, it's not certain that she had the right body or right case.

Ms. Douglas, from Savannah, indicated that she had not really been following the case (so much for pretrial publicity having poisoned the population of Savannah) until she had seen Marilyn Case's name mentioned. Douglas knew Marilyn from Candler Hospital.

Ms. Douglas's testimony? She helped with intake on emergency room patients, and one of her duties was to place the hospital identification bracelet on a patient's arm. She testified that she "probably" would have had trouble getting the bracelet on Hansford's wrist if the hands had been bagged, because she wouldn't have been able to get the bracelet over the bags.

Pause a moment and think. Yes, exactly. Douglas admitted on cross-examination that the bracelets were *snap-on*. She could have put the bracelet on even if Danny's hand had been stuck to a bowling ball. She still claimed her memory was impeccable. She clearly remembered that Hansford had been shot in the forehead. Well no, he hadn't. But yes, the defense put this witness on the stand.

The truly surprising new witness was Debbie Blevins, Danny Hansford's former girlfriend. Eight years after the fact, she finally testified in the case—for the defense. Danny might have wanted to break up with her posthumously. Maybe Williams had comforted her in her time of grief. Maybe he had bought her a car. Debbie testified that Danny had a "hostile attitude" toward Williams and others. "He couldn't keep a job. He didn't want to work. He drank and did a lot of drugs."

There's that code word again—drugs. How are drug users normally referenced? They're cokeheads, meth heads, tweakers, sketchers, speed freaks, or pot heads. No one lumps all drugs together, except when testifying for the defense in a *Williams* trial. Apparently, Debbie had also forgotten her previous recorded statement in 1982 claiming that Danny didn't mind work at all and thought it was cool that he could go to work right downstairs.

It's just odd to see the victim's girlfriend testifying for the man who killed him. Not to mention, it brings up an obvious question for both Debbie and Williams: Why were you two both dating Danny Hansford if he was a piece of human garbage?

Debbie's testimony did backfire slightly on the defense. Asked about Danny's living arrangement, she simply said that he lived with Williams.

A Case-Weary Prosecution

In sports, it's very difficult to beat a team four times (counting the Tyo jury as a third conviction). There is no doubt that Spencer Lawton, David Lock, and their staff were totally committed to their task and duty. The effect of this phenomenon on a team is not conscious.

Personally, I don't know that I would have had the resolve to do it all over again—a fourth trial on the same evidence. But there wasn't much choice for the prosecution, unless a plea agreement could be worked out. There were plea negotiations before the fourth trial, as there had been at other times during the *Williams* prosecution. Recall that Williams told the author of the *US Magazine* story that he was hoping to plead guilty to voluntary manslaughter. A deal was never reached.

In any event, it wouldn't be unheard of for the prosecution to have had to fight a subconscious letdown while the other team, sick and tired of getting whipped, showed up breathing fire. It's an effect experienced frequently in sports. It might or might not apply in trial practice. We don't know, because cases simply aren't tried four times.

This still doesn't explain a jury not following the evidence, however. Gravity should trump lawyers, no matter how fired up they get in the locker room. But the possibility of an involuntary letdown can't be discounted. This is how upsets happen.

Might other factors have been at work, factors that had little impact when the case was fresher but came into play as the distance in time from the event increased? The following analysis is extraordinarily difficult and undoubtedly unfair, but is also necessary if we are to fairly complete the "what happened?" inquiry. With respect to the prosecution, three possible factors stand out:

(1) The foundation of the case was rock solid. Within reason, Williams could have been convicted before the lunch break on the first day of trial using three photographs. A natural tendency is to rely on that foundation and to resist being pulled into the magic forest with Williams or into Lawyer Games with his attorneys and, in the process, becoming diverted by the chaff and confusion they were cultivating at every opportunity.

(2) Confidence in this strength of the evidence could lead to being less aggressive with respect to the continual changes in the stories that Williams's defense rolled out for each new jury like an automobile company churning out new models for the new model year, or with respect to the continuous violations of evidentiary procedure such as repeatedly leading witnesses. Nobody wants to irritate a jury with constant objections and some lawyers take advantage of this as we've mentioned.

Did the gloves need to come off in *Williams IV* because the advantage had shrunk with the passage of time and a new, disconnected jury? Was it even more important to show the jury that the defense was trying to manipulate them? Did it actually become important to unmask the messenger in addition to exposing the flaws in the message?

(3) As a corollary of the first two factors, was it possible that, when Judge Head cut the legs out from under the prosecution's witnesses, the prosecution wasn't prepared to compensate? To stretch a sports analogy, if your star passing quarterback goes down, can your team flip a switch on the fly and become a grind-it-out running team? Put another way, having been through three trials relying on Dr. Howard to bat cleanup, was the prosecution prepared to play the game without him?

That is the ultimate question from the analysis: Was the prosecution prepared to deal with Judge Head's muzzling of their experts? One answer is that no prosecutor could have handled it, and that is a compelling argument. It's difficult to punch to much effect with pillows on your fists. And you can't deal aces when the house has removed the aces from the deck. So, quite unfairly, we raise the question but don't answer it.

It's simply impossible to pronounce that any certain thing *should* have been done, that one or another thing would have saved *Williams IV*, or even whether saving *Williams IV* was possible under the circumstances. But we always ask more questions after a loss than after a victory, whether in sports or in law, so we do it here. To be fair, adopting a bare-knuckles approach alone might not have mattered in the end and might only have resulted in a two-month trial with the same result and some hefty contempt of court fines to pay.

This is one instance when hindsight is not 20-20.

Gunshot Residue

This final note is not about the GSR evidence itself but about the fact that the prosecution led off the fourth trial with it. As a strategic matter, I would want the clearest, most easily understood evidence of Williams's culpability in evidence before delving into antimony and barium. It might have been a scheduling issue, which David Lock agreed was a possibility. Dr. Howard was retired from the State Crime Laboratory by 1989 (after thirty-two years).

Other than this possibility, I don't know why the GSR evidence led off the trial. I have an opinion, however—admittedly in hindsight: Scheduling issues can't be allowed to decide the presentation of a case this important. I am aware that's easy to say when you're not there, but that's my view of the question. This was a new jury, and GSR is science, replete with unfamiliar jargon, concepts, and decimals. It would be akin to starting a criminal trial with a professional DNA witness. The jurors' eyes could glaze over before their seats were warm. Of course, the issue might not have been with the GSR evidence itself but, rather, with Dr. Howard not being permitted to interpret it.

I've heard it suggested that the State should have left the GSR evidence out altogether, that it was too murky and confusing. I disagree. If Dr. Howard and Randall Riddell were not allowed to interpret the results, this opinion could change, but the GSR evidence in the case was overwhelming and conclusive. I simply don't know that I would have led off the case with it. Whether or not this had an effect on the case can't be known.

In the end, there is no magic bullet that explains the verdict in the fourth *Williams* trial. In the end, all that matters is the official record—who got the W on the official score card. That was the defense team. The coveted W went to Seiler and Samuel, perhaps the only team in history to win a game by a score of 13-35.

CHAPTER 40

THE VERDICT

In the end, members of an Augusta jury joined each other in a silent *Amen!* to Seiler's exhortation to "Let my man go!" Righteous indignation is a penny a pound in criminal trials. I'm surprised lightning doesn't strike more courtrooms.

For reasons unknown and indecipherable, the fourth trial of James Williams appears to have turned into a debate over what Williams was doing in a courtroom in 1989 rather than what he had done in his study in 1981. That debate was won by Williams and his attorneys.

The jury returned a verdict of not guilty and gathered around to congratulate Williams on his victory. Eight months and two days later, he was dead.

CHAPTER 41

NOT INNOCENT

News sources, web sites, and casual commentary routinely repeat the misstatement that Williams was "cleared of all charges" or found to be "innocent" by his Augusta jury. Nothing could be further from the truth. If James Williams had been cleared of all charges, he would never have been tried.

Juries don't clear people of charges. People are cleared of charges when, for example, it turns out they were in Casablanca when the crime was committed. "Cleared" indicates a judgment that a person did not, as a matter of irrefutable fact, commit the acts alleged, yet it has continued to be erroneously suggested that a jury found Williams "innocent" of the murder of Danny Hansford. That contention confuses *legal* responsibility with *factual* responsibility. It is no small thing that a jury verdict acquitting a defendant is termed "not guilty" rather than "innocent." There is a significant difference. It can help to insert the word "proved" into the phrase: not proved guilty. "Innocent" is not a choice on a jury verdict form.

What about the juries themselves? Is it possible that the first three were "flawed" and the fourth finally "got it right?" After his acquittal, Williams certainly preferred the fourth jury. "This jury was wonderful," he opined to the *Atlanta Journal-Constitution*, obviously pleased as punch with the Augusta twelve.[165] I do not know if they received invitations to his holiday party that year, but I would not be surprised. He seemed quite taken with them.

But no, there was nothing wrong with the first three juries (other than the presence of Cecilia Tyo on the third), and the fourth jury was no better than the other three. Williams's lawyers never complained of the juries impaneled in the first three trials. The prejudice screed from the defense came only *after* the verdicts. The defense had no problem with a jury until the jury didn't buy Williams's story.

It simply isn't possible to evaluate *Williams IV* in isolation. We know too much to ever put those blinders back on. In the end, I come back to the simplicity of this case.

For an example, I will share a recollection of Barbara Wright, the court reporter for the first, third, and fourth *Williams* trials. Court reporters see everything, and someone with Barbara's experience has, quite literally, seen it all. I asked Barbara if she could explain the verdict in the fourth trial. Nothing remarkable about the trial had struck her, no shocking change in the evidence. Here is what she did say:

The one thing that sticks in my mind so vividly from the first trial onward was that beautiful color photograph that was blown up and showed the chair leg sitting on Hansford's pants leg. Right. When he fell over, the chair just jumped up and got on his pants leg. That is such simple evidence of the fact he rearranged the scene that I would have convicted him on that alone.[166]

I agree. Perhaps we should have blown that photo up to 8 x 12 feet, hung it from the ceiling of the courtroom, and said, "The State rests." The case was that simple. Anyone suggesting that James Williams was factually innocent of the unjustified killing of Danny Hansford is delusional, unaware of the facts, or a member of the defense team.

Nevertheless, in May of 1989, a jury spoke, and this time, there would be no appeal. The prosecution doesn't get do-overs.

I must confess to having been wrong about the *Williams* case. For many years, I had said when asked that, knowing what I knew about the evidence, Williams would be convicted a hundred times if tried a hundred times. I did not fathom any twelve people on earth cutting him loose. It wasn't possible. I was wrong.

Somehow, after eight years of bloodless yet ferocious battle, Williams's defense managed to turn off the lights in the study and take the jury out onto the veranda for cocktails. As the juror said, "Not being from there made it a lot easier to decide."

What the jury found was that Williams had been "not proved guilty" in a courtroom. What they did not find was innocence. There was none to be found.

CHAPTER 42

REGIS EST MORTUUS: THE KING IS DEAD

An argument can be made that the guilty did not ultimately slip away through the fog in *State of Georgia vs. James A. Williams.* Convicted twice, coming within one juror's tainted vote of being convicted a third time, ultimately cut loose by a jury some eight years after the fact, Williams was found dead in his mansion on Monterey Square on January 14, 1990.

Despite rumors to the contrary, Williams did not die behind his desk, in the hallway, or in the kitchen. He died lying across the threshold of his study, wearing nothing but a white tee shirt. His arms were bent up to his chest, his hands in loose fists. Had Danny Hansford's right hand been placed back underneath him, their positions in the end would have been strikingly similar (Figure 50. This photo is cropped as a courtesy).

Williams's causes of death, based on an autopsy performed at Memorial Medical Center by Dr. Manuel L. Alvarez on the morning of January 16, 1990, were (1) congestive heart failure, (2) cardiac arrest, and (3) unknown.

Williams's body was discovered by Douglas Seyle at 8:00 p.m. on Sunday, January 14, but it appeared that Williams had probably died the previous night. The Sunday paper was still outside when Seyle arrived. There was evidence that Williams had been entertaining and Seyle indicated that Williams had had guests on Saturday night, though Seyle didn't know who they had been.

In news reports, Seiler cleaned the story up. He claimed that Williams had probably died earlier on the day he was found because, although the Sunday paper was still outside, Williams had risen and "fixed himself a cup of tea." Aside from the fact that it was impossible to know any such thing without witnesses, the story was also highly unlikely, unless Williams was in the habit of walking around downstairs in nothing but a tee shirt in broad daylight.

After Seyle discovered the body, he first went to the home of Walter Hartridge, an attorney in Seiler's firm who lived nearby. Hartridge then called Seiler, who drove in and accompanied the other two back to 429 Bull Street. After viewing the situation, they went to the home of Dr. Metts, leaving Williams on the floor.

I do not know why they didn't call the police or EMS, unless this is a common reaction to a death in the Mercer House study. Dr. Metts was out of town, so the trio returned to 429 Bull Street and called Williams's personal physician, Dr. Joseph Heffernan Jr.

Dr. Heffernan drove in from Tybee Island, determined that Williams was still dead, and called the police. Officer M. Galipeau received the call from dispatch at 9:25 p.m. and arrived at Mercer House at 9:27 p.m., roughly an hour and a half after Seyle had discovered the body.

Dr. Heffernan told Ofc. Galipeau that he had been treating Williams since 1985 and that Williams had no history of heart problems. Dr. Heffernan advised that he had prescribed medications for Williams but that Williams did not appear to have been taking them. This is not entirely accurate, though not critical. Williams did have a history of irregular heartbeat. Toxicology from his autopsy also revealed the presence of acetaminophen and either quinine or quinidine. Quinidine is commonly prescribed for treatment of arrhythmia (irregular heartbeat).

Williams also produced a positive HIV scan. Lastly, his lungs were congested with areas of pulmonary edema, essentially a collection of fluid in the air spaces in the lungs, which can lead to respiratory distress and cardiac arrest.

As for the circumstances surrounding his death, there is a final irony: If Williams died on Saturday night while entertaining guests, his guests did not see fit to stay after Williams hit the floor. Or to call for help.

PART TEN

THE TRUTH

CHAPTER 43

A SILENT STUDY SPEAKS

In the segment from my *Williams I* closing argument included in the prologue, I said Danny Hansford might be screaming still, for someone to listen to him. I also owe an obligation to the reader to repay the patience and care it has required to take this journey deep into the belly of the beast.

The following is the puzzle from the study on Monterey Square, solved—without leaving out or altering any item of evidence. It relies on the physical evidence, the analysis of that evidence, and the testimony and statements of witnesses, whether or not they were ever heard at trial. It even includes two live 9mm rounds from the drawer of Williams's desk-side chest that were never mentioned in the trials of the case but were matched to Williams's Luger 23A, having been ejected from that weapon.

With that preamble, let the silent study—and Danny Hansford—speak.

Danny Hansford was a slim 5'11" twenty-one-year-old, well-endowed male hustler. James Williams was a self-made aristocrat, a 6'2" country boy who had done very well for himself, a fixture of Savannah society, and comfortably wealthy. James was as gay as a pink mink and had a taste for young men. He even liked a bit of "rough trade," as in Danny Hansford, street-corner hotshot.

When they met, Danny was working Bull Street and the parks, selling himself to anybody "who wanted to pay for it."[167] Danny wasn't gay. As he put it, "I suck dicks and get fucked by different people for money."[168]

Danny didn't drop by looking for a job in Signore Geppetto's woodworking shop. Williams took Danny off the street and took him home to Mercer House, a gift Williams bought for himself. With Williams's wave over from an idling Jaguar, Danny had leap-frogged the hustler pecking order, straight to the mansion on Monterey Square. As Danny told Joseph Williamson: "[Y]eah, I used to hustle and, you know, I kind of made it big now."[169]

Williams led two lives: society sophisticate and sexual predator. He had seduced Joseph Goodman, a youngster he had known since the age of twelve, when Goodman was sixteen or seventeen. He took Danny in when Danny was nineteen. He kept a number of young men in his refinishing shop, paid in cash.

Danny was not a shop worker other than occasionally helping move a piece of furniture. He was Williams's private dancer, kept by Williams with money, a car, gifts, pot, and alcohol—whatever Danny wanted in order to keep doing what Williams wanted him to keep doing.

Debbie Blevins, Danny's real-life girlfriend, thought Danny had the upper hand in the relationship with Williams, though she didn't know why. For whatever reason, Danny knew he could push Williams's buttons and get what he wanted. He would pick fights on purpose, knowing that Williams would feel guilty afterward and do something to make up.

Williams had a problem where Danny was concerned. The wild child in Danny attracted Williams and excited him. Williams craved drama and wrote his own as he lived it. But Williams also liked young men for another reason: He had to be in control. Possibly hiding a deep-seated insecurity, he sought boys from "the parks" to supplement his drawing-room friends.

There was never any doubt who was supposed to hold the cards and who was supposed to submit in the dalliances Williams chose—until he met Danny Hansford. Nobody could control Danny—not his disaster of a mother, not Debbie, and not James Williams.

The more Danny refused to behave or behaved badly, the more possessive and obsessive Williams became. Williams didn't mind Debbie as a person, but he wanted Danny to himself. He told Danny to give her up, but Danny wouldn't do it. Danny asked Debbie to marry him virtually every day until she finally made him stop. He was "super super" serious about her, and she wasn't ready for that. Danny might have been as obsessed with Debbie as Williams was with Danny.

On April 2, 1981, a Thursday night, Danny and Debbie were at Mercer House, playing gambling games with Williams and having "a few cocktails" as they always did. Danny was insanely jealous where Debbie was concerned. Williams laid claim to being bisexual and Danny thought Williams was flirting with Debbie. After he took her home, Danny came back and had it out with Williams, starting a monstrous argument.

Sometime around 3:00 a.m., Danny grabbed a Luger that Williams kept in his bedside table and fired it into the floor of Williams's bedroom. Then he went downstairs, made a mess in the living room, went out the front door, and fired a shot at a tree.

Williams called the police and a belligerent Danny was hauled off to jail. Later the same day, after Danny cooled down, Williams went to the jail with Joe Goodman and got him out. Later, Williams took Danny with him to see Judge Lionel Drew in municipal court and dismissed the charges.

Debbie was furious with Danny for what he'd done. She refused to see him for a week. He begged her to forgive him and told her he was going to get her a gold necklace.

Meanwhile, Williams needed to take a buying trip to Europe. On April 10, Williams made reservations for himself and Danny to travel to London and Geneva. The departure date was May 3, 1981. Danny told Debbie about the trip and wanted her to go, too.[170]

Danny asked Williams about taking Debbie with them to Europe. Instead of adding Debbie to the trip, Williams called Delta Airlines on April 24, took Danny off the trip altogether, and put Joseph Goodman on instead.

Williams claimed it was his stance on drug use that caused him to take Danny off the Europe trip. The only evidence of Williams's anti-pot stance was his claiming he had one. Joe Goodman said Danny was off the trip because Danny had court dates. Then he said it was because Danny had passport problems. There is no way to resolve these claims.

It's also possible that Williams took Danny off the trip because Danny brought up taking Debbie and Williams had told him he didn't even want Danny seeing her. Danny didn't pay much attention to anything Williams said, according to George Hill.

Meanwhile, Williams had bought a gold necklace Danny wanted. A condition of Danny getting the necklace was that he stop seeing Debbie. Instead, Danny gave the necklace to Debbie.

On April 29, Danny told George that he and Williams had gotten into a huge fight about the necklace and Debbie. Williams had asked Danny why he wasn't wearing the necklace. Danny had told Williams that he gave it to Debbie, and Williams had exploded. Williams had gotten mad before and told him to get out, but Danny told George he was seriously worried that Williams might really mean it this time. This was the last time George, who had to go out on a job with his tugboat crew, saw his friend alive.

Danny giving the necklace that Williams had given him to the same girl whom Williams had forbidden him to see was more than a slap in Williams's face; it was a fist to the gut. Williams didn't tolerate such behavior from the street trash he had bought for himself. Williams was supposed to be the boss.

Williams was furious with Danny but, predictably, didn't throw him out. Williams was incapable of fighting off his addiction to the boy he couldn't tame. Friday night, May 1, would be a chance to smooth things over before Williams and Goodman left on Sunday for Europe. Williams and Hansford went to a drive-in movie—a Friday-night date in a place where they wouldn't be seen as a couple and could sit in Williams's Jaguar in the dark. Danny smoked some weed and drank some whiskey. Williams probably inhaled at some point during the film, having little option as an air-breathing mammal. They got back to Mercer House after midnight.

When they got home, they played a video game and some backgammon, but it got ugly. They argued about Debbie and about the trip. Williams had a few of his usual cocktails, to relax, having eaten very little during the day, despite the warnings not to mix alcohol with the Limbitrol that had been prescribed for him by his psychiatrist and not to drink his meals. The argument escalated.

Danny was angry about Williams taking him off the Europe trip. Williams was furious with Danny for giving the necklace to Debbie. Danny knew how to push Williams's buttons, and he sat across the desk, smoking a joint and giving Williams hell.

Just after two o'clock, Williams had heard enough. Fine, he would call the damn trip off. He called Goodman, waking him up, telling him the trip was off. Danny got on the phone and told Goodman not to "put it on him" and that he hoped Goodman wasn't mad about Williams canceling the trip. Danny was slurring a little, but he always slurred a little. He sounded normal to Goodman. Danny told Joe that he and Williams were talking and playing a game.

But Williams and Hansford were also in the midst of an escalating fight. They were making 2:00 a.m. phone calls and arguing. Williams later told an associate in London that Williams had written a poem that Danny was reading. Was Williams trying to fix things with Danny before going away? Had he written a poem for Danny? If he had, how might Danny—particularly an angry, petulant Danny—have treated such a thing, knowing Danny's temperament?

Turning Williams's poem into a mockery was another shot to Williams's solar plexus. Williams was not a gentle man, though a gentleman in public. Debbie Blevins and George Hill had both been shocked at how fiercely Williams and Danny fought. Whether it was with a poem or something else, Danny was working Williams's buttons as only Danny could.

Williams was not rational where Danny was concerned. Williams's friends, including the manager of his shop, had told him to get out of the relationship, but he wouldn't do it. Or couldn't.

Williams pulled his Luger from the top drawer of the chest next to his desk. He told Danny to stop, but Danny didn't. Danny amped it up instead, repeating Williams's poem back to him with heightened sarcasm. Williams racked the Luger's slide, ejecting a round that was already chambered, and told Danny to stop again, with no effect. Danny laughed, and Williams racked another round, threatening Danny again.

Not only did Danny laugh at Williams and make fun of his poem, but he made fun of Williams's antics with the Luger. With Williams's Luger pointing dead at him, Danny took a long drag on his joint and leaned over, pressing the burning tip of the joint into the leather top of Williams's desk and turning it, grinding it into the tooled leather top of Williams's Louis XV desk while suggesting what Williams could do to himself. Williams could see the hole being burned into the leather. He snapped.

Erupting in anger, Williams raised the Luger. Danny realized what was happening and tried to rise from the chair, but his feet were tucked under the chair and his ankles were crossed. Danny grabbed the arms of the chair and started up out of the chair as Williams fired, striking him in the left center chest. The empty cartridge was ejected, bounced off the desk and ended up on the floor behind Williams's chair.

The shot to Danny's chest completely severed his aorta, dropping his blood pressure instantly to zero as blood gushed into his chest cavity and a lung pierced by the 9mm slug. Danny fell forward, taking the chair down to the floor with him, as Williams rose from his desk chair.

Danny's body hit the floor, his head turned to his right, both arms underneath him, his hands both clutched to his chest wound, aspirating blood from his lung, out through his mouth, and onto the rug to the right of his head. Following Danny's body to the floor with his weapon, Williams leaned out over his desk and fired again, striking the right rear of Danny's head. The round passed through the back of the head and exited the other side, piercing the rug and ending up underneath it. The spent shell casing ejected forward, toward Danny's body, ending up just past his head on the rug.

The force of the shot threw the back of Danny's head toward the fireplace, until his head reached the limit allowed by the neck muscles, causing his head to rebound in the other direction. His head ended up resting on his right cheek.

Meanwhile, Williams was rounding his desk (clockwise) in a blind rage. The chair Danny had been sitting in was toppled over on its side. Coming up on Danny from the rear and slightly right of center, Williams fired another round, into Danny's back, a final exclamation point. The bullet went straight through, on a slightly upward and leftward path, exited the chest, and embedded itself in the hardwood floor directly beneath the exit wound. The spent shell cartridge was ejected toward the west wall and ended up a foot from the wall, underneath a chair.

Danny was facedown on the rug, blood beginning to flow from the chest wound and from his mouth. Both arms were raised up to his chest, both fists clamped over his thumbs in a classic death grip. Danny's fists were clamped so tightly that he may have suffered from a mild cadaveric spasm, a form of instant *rigor mortis* to the extremities that can result from sudden violent death.

Williams saw what he had done as he tried to slow his racing heart, trying to sort through what had happened and what he should do. He paced the room, finally walked back behind his desk and slumped into his chair, putting his Luger down on the desk in front of him. He came to a decision, picked up the phone and called his friend, Joe Goodman.

Goodman had smoked most of a cigarette, put it out, and rolled over after the first phone call when the phone rang again. Goodman got back out of bed and answered it, looking at the clock on his microwave. It was 2:22 a.m.

Williams told Goodman he had shot Danny. Goodman asked the natural question: "Is he dead?" Yes, very dead, get down here and hurry. Williams hung up. While he was thinking about it, he grabbed the two ejected live rounds from his Luger and put them in his desk-side chest, which is where they were found during evidence collection in the study.

I am leaving a gap here intentionally. I have beaten Joe Goodman up enough. I will let him worry about the next thirty-six minutes. Goodman either got there early and helped Williams or he didn't. The difference has nothing to do with Williams's case.

Williams set back upright the chair in which Danny had been sitting, but he didn't notice four things: (1) how far the chair was over Danny's body, (2) how far the chair was off from its previous position, (3) that a rear chair leg had pinned Danny's pants leg, and (4) that a small, bloody skull fragment had stuck to the seat of the chair while the chair had been on its side.

Williams went upstairs and grabbed another Luger from the holster in his bedside table and went back to the study. He had to think of how to do this. He circled out into the room. He looked back toward the door of the study and saw his imaginary scenario take shape, the next scene in his personal melodrama.

Williams racked a round into the Luger, not thinking that there was a round already in the chamber, thus ejecting a round onto the rug between Danny's head and the fireplace. Then he went to the corner of the desk and, deciding he needed undeniable evidence that Danny had shot at him, aimed the Luger down and fired at the desk. He heard the bullet ricochet when it hit a metal buckle inside a leather pouch on the desk. The remains of the bullet glanced off the north wall.

Then he retracted the slide on the Luger, until he could get at another live round in the chamber. Misaligning the round, he released the slide, jamming the round in the slide.

Turning to Danny's body, he kneeled down, pulled Danny's right arm out from under his body, turned his hand palm down, partially opened the fingers, which were surprisingly stiff, placed the second Luger on the rug, and lowered the hand on top of the grip. He stood, checking his handiwork. He didn't think about the thumb tucked against the palm of Danny's hand.

He thought back to April. It was the same Luger, the same Danny. There was a police report about the April incident. It was perfect. In a truly inspired moment, Williams decided to create a "call back" to April. He went to the hall-way, turned a chair on its side, then went to the living room, where he smashed a video game console, turned a table over—being careful to put a pillow under the top to protect it from real damage—and turned over a silver tray with some glassware on it—the same silver tray turned over in April.

Then he decided he needed something that would seal it, something distinctive. He pulled the grandfather clock out from the wall, turned it, laid it down near the floor, and dropped it. If JoJo was there, he helped. If so, he and Rushing waited while Williams called his lawyer, Robert Duffy. Duffy told Williams to call the police. If there, Goodman and Rushing left, drove around the square, and parked.

Ninety seconds later, two squad cars came around the square. Goodman pulled up and parked—for either the first or second time—as Anderson, White, Chesler, and Gibbons were exiting their vehicles, and fell in between them, with Nancy Rushing, to mount the stone steps.

At the front door, Williams said, "I shot him; he's in the other room."

Could some peripheral assumptions above change? Sure. But, in the end, this puzzle picture is complete and matches the picture on the puzzle box. It also has a major advantage over Williams's tale: It conforms to all of the evidence and conflicts with none of it—which a story should—if it's the truth.

PART ELEVEN

SUMMATION

CHAPTER 44

THE DISTRICT ATTORNEY VENDETTA

Detective Ragan's report of May 5, 1981, to the head of the SPD Detective Division, Major J. E. (Jim) Weaver, concluded as follows: "At this time, I request this case [be] closed by Arrest and Formal Charges." That made two of us.

Despite rumors fanned by Williams that his prosecution was a vendetta or politics on the part of District Attorney, the notion is absurd. I was the one who recommended the arrest of Williams at the scene, and I didn't know James Williams from James Oglethorpe.

What did Spencer Lawton do? He prosecuted a case brought to him through normal channels. It's not as if the office was short of work. At the time, we were working to clear a backlog of well over a thousand felonies inherited from Mr. Lawton's predecessor. Most prosecutor's offices are inundated with criminal cases. There are people who don't understand that, if there's a law against doing something, you're not supposed to do it. These people are called criminals. There are a lot of them.

As for the fact that Mr. Lawton continued to try Williams rather than just letting him go with a gift bag, Williams continued to be retried because Williams had the bad form to keep getting convicted (twice, within one vote of thrice). The reversals of the first two convictions turned on side issues that had *nothing* to do with the evidence in the case and the 11-1 mistrial was the result of an infected jury.

The suggestion that Lawton was trying Williams for political reasons was nothing but self-serving tripe. Fanning the rumor was only one more component of the defense strategy of trying the cases of *Williams vs. the Prosecutor*, *Williams vs. the Police*, and *Williams vs. the Victim* rather than the case against Williams himself. One might be led to believe that James Williams was the most important criminal defendant in the history of Savannah, but I can assure you: one killer is the same as another.

By way of disclaimer, I had previously worked in the district attorney's office and returned to the office when Mr. Lawton won election. I was his Chief Assistant until such time as I left to accept a gubernatorial appointment. I still consider Spencer Lawton a friend. However, I am confident he will not agree with everything I say in this book. But that's nothing new; he never did.

CHAPTER 45

LAWYER GAMES: THE VERDICT

Played in the shadows and dark corners of the criminal justice system, Lawyer Games is a game within the game the public sees, when the public is paying attention at all. Most trials don't attract a passing glance from the public. Very few attract the attention that a Manson, Simpson, Buono, Anthony, or Arias attract, and even those cases, as rare as they were, were not tried four times.

But *State vs. James A. Williams* was—tried four times. And because it was, we've been offered the rarest of opportunities, to watch opposing legal forces do battle, retreat, adjust their battle plans, and attack again, across a legal landscape covering close to a decade. We've waded into the crossfire, armed with hindsight and a manic attention to detail that might have occasionally driven the reader to distraction.

Such a level of dissection is seldom possible. It also isn't likely to be worth the effort, because not all lawyers behave as Williams's lawyers did. I've called them legal juvenile delinquents, but such advocates do more than spread teenage mischief. They undermine the justice system.

That system relies on two sets of oaths: one spoken and one unspoken. The witness takes a spoken oath, or affirmation, to tell the truth, and can be prosecuted for the oath's violation if caught. The other oath is that presumed by an attorney appearing before a tribunal. When that second oath is violated—the oath that lawyers will procure the truth and speak the truth, whether as to a fact or a point of law—there is seldom any recourse.

No attorney reviews the rules governing legal ethics every day, but most don't have to—they follow those rules instinctively because the rules are grounded in commonly understood ethical values. Some, however, willingly bulldoze through ethical boundaries and leave the rules in the mud beneath the bulldozer's churning tracks.

Yet the process is too often seen as no more than a Lawyer Game. Even what passes for legal analysis on news programs can turn into a commentary on cleverness. Too many observers buy into the notion that it's all about which side just made the slickest strategic move.

In some circles, for example, barring an opposing witness from visiting the scene of a crime, challenging the witness at trial for not having visited the scene of the crime, and then creating a specious argument to keep the jury from knowing the truth, would be applauded as brilliant. It is, in the sense that a jewel heist might be considered brilliant. More accurately, it is a deliberate attempt to have a jury base its decision on a falsehood.

In the real world, a falsehood would be called a lie. Inside a courtroom, it can be inspired advocacy, depending on the audience. The public often believes the law is a game, too, while having a very negative view of those who play it. As noted earlier, an extremely bright medical professional commented to me, matter-of-factly, "Don't all lawyers lie? You sort of expect that, right?" The best response I could muster was, "Not all of them," which I do sincerely believe.

But the criminal legal field includes unique incentives that distort the system. A verdict of not guilty cannot be overturned. In such a system, when a lawyer is willing to exceed the outer limits of advocacy, it can become extremely difficult to keep the proceedings from degenerating. Let me be very clear—not all criminal defense lawyers cross that line, and not all prosecutors are pure. But there is a critical difference: A prosecutor's egregious misconduct can be appealed. Misconduct by a defense lawyer cannot ever be appealed by the State in a criminal case.

This explains why appellate decisions in the public record are relatively free of cases involving the conduct of criminal defense lawyers—their actions can't be appealed. Once a verdict of not guilty is returned, it's over—in the United States.

But this book is not a dissertation on all criminal cases, and the title is *Lawyer Games*, not *Defense Lawyer Games*. Considering the lashing dished out to defense lawyers in *Williams*, what about the prosecutors? Didn't they do anything wrong?

"Wrong" is a harsh word. Are there things that could have been handled differently? Anywhere in this narrative where a notation such as "this was not done" appears, the assumption can be made that the subject was considered worth my time to explore and the reader's time to read about it. However, whether something not done rises to the level of wrong would require us to be clairvoyant.

We've talked a lot about science, possibly more than some of the scientific witnesses did. To test two theories (or two possible strategic choices in this case), we would have to try the case again using each option and see how it went. Much like Dr. Howard couldn't start shooting people to test dead-man-falling theories, we can't retry a case several different ways to see what might happen.

Some things are mentioned here that were not noticed at the time they came up at trial. It's always preferable that nothing be missed, based on simple common sense. More information is always better. Cases are built on facts. Facts are good. But never missing anything in a trial isn't realistic. It's impossible to declare that something missed "should" have been noticed without standing in another lawyer's shoes at the time. I've lived with this case for many years and thought of it often, and yet I noticed things in this review that never occurred to me before.

But, of course the prosecution wasn't perfect—which applies to the first trial as well as the rest. I would not try the same case today. We were young but enthusiastic. For a personal example, I was not nearly as vigilant as I "should" have been about a toxic word lurking in a police report and a snake lurking inside a lawyer suit.

In the end, the *Williams* case was won three times (discounting Celia Tyo's hijacking of the third jury, which I don't consider legitimate). So prosecutors (leaving myself out for the moment) did a lot right. Equally significant is what they did not do. The distance between most lawyers and perfection is probably more accurately described by a symbol—∞—than by a distance. But I simply don't see in the *Williams* case record the behavior from the prosecution that was on abundant display from defense counsel, with the exception of John Wright Jones, who, in my opinion, comported himself as an aggressive, honorable advocate for his client.

The prosecution didn't waste months arguing spurious motions while their client sat in jail. Williams's first lawyer lied, whether through omission or directly—to the superior court or the supreme court, or both. The lawyers who followed almost certainly appear to have procured and filed false evidence, filed motions with no legal foundation, and were accused—though never convicted—of attempting to improperly influence the supreme court in the appeal of the case. This does not include the examples covered here of attempts to confuse, distract, and mislead multiple juries.

Those lawyers are not unique, however. Naughty-lawyer jails could be filled by the population of legal juvenile delinquents roaming the hallways and courtrooms of criminal justice centers. Does anyone think Simpson's lawyers hesitated for a second to put into evidence Dr. Henry Lee's "newly discovered" footprint from the murder scene, to suggest the presence of a second mysterious assailant, or that Simpson's lawyers didn't know it was a footprint in cement from the time the walkway was originally poured?

Following the infamous Dr. Lee to the *Spector* case—did Spector's lawyers give in when Dr. Lee was accused of having removed and hidden evidence from the crime scene? One did, which proves my point that all lawyers are individuals and should be judged as such. Dr. Lee's act was only exposed by a lone defense lawyer who refused to go along with protecting him and admitted that she had seen him do it.

From another California case, the Hillside Strangler trial of Angelo Buono, one attempted abduction was supposed to have involved an Excalibur kit automobile.[171] The police hadn't found such a vehicle, and the defense ridiculed the very notion of such a distinctive car being used in an abduction in broad daylight. The defense not only knew all about the car, but bragged about it later to prosecutors.

384 | LAWYER GAMES

In the same case, a detective who testified to Buono having a gap between his front teeth was brought down from the stand and forced to look into Buono's mouth and admit that there was no gap. The defense didn't tell anyone about the dental work that had closed the gap. Were these shades of Dr. Gantner being challenged for not visiting a scene that the defense had refused to let him visit?

What about Seiler's attempt to misrepresent Goodman's view of the body and chair from just inside the study doorway? When the Buono defense brought in a witness to testify that she could see the back of Buono's shop clearly from her apartment and had never seen anything like the prosecution was claiming, the defense had photographs to prove the excellent view of the shop from her apartment. What they didn't tell the jury was that the view from the apartment was blocked, so the defense team's investigator had gone out on the fire escape to take the pictures instead. When the jurors were taken to the apartment to see for themselves, a request vehemently fought by the defense, sure enough, they couldn't see a thing.

Did these other lawyers present intentionally misleading or false testimony or conceal and manipulate evidence in a murder case? Of course they did. The deeper question is, did they care? The same question could be asked of Williams's lawyers, though by now the answer should be obvious.

In sum, I simply don't see the condescension, derision, and outright deception on the part of the district attorney and his assistants that permeated the DNA of the defense teams. Even Bobby Lee Cook, until his waltz with lady perjury on appeal, displayed a certain sense of decorum while trying to beat the State's brains out—even if he did call me a son of a bitch. I can't even say he was wrong on that count. It's a subjective judgment.

If anything, my critique of the prosecution would be that they could have been a factor of ten more combative when the delinquents showed up. Where that might have led, I have no idea. Contempt citations and jail cells for all? Perhaps. But it might have been worth it. As some fellow once wrote, "Whether 'tis nobler in the mind to suffer the slings and arrows of outrageous fortune / or to take arms against a sea of troubles ..."[172]

Of course, Spencer Lawton, Aldridge, Lock, and Sparks might have merely been exerting more self-restraint than I might have under similar circumstances. That would not likely surprise anyone who knows me.

CHAPTER 46

THE LAST BRASS PLAQUE

After eight years and four trials, some things about the *Williams* murder case remained constant. Even after being visited by fact jugglers, magic rabbits, and snake-oil peddlers, the evidence never changed. Williams's killing of Danny Hansford remained as clear on the last day of the last trial as it had been when homicide detectives first saw the puzzle with unexplained pieces spread around Williams's study.

An "expert" claiming that a donkey could give birth to a penguin is not evidence (other than evidence that some people will say anything). It would not surprise me to read, one day, of a defense expert testifying that a frog could play the harmonica, given enough practice. To believe Williams's fractured tale, one would have to be willing to buy a ticket to a harmonica concert given by Kermit.

To quote Justice Weltner again, from his *Williams II* dissent, "Everyone knows a dead man can't put a chair leg on his trousers." Justice Weltner might have been surprised what a dead man can do once an "expert" gets their hands on him. The *Williams* witness parade—with fantastical tales of headless chickens, leapfrogging dead men, bullets bending in flight, bloody rags that weren't there scrubbing hands that weren't scrubbed, and boat anchors pulling triggers—was dazzling, as well as astounding for its analytical shallowness and scientific pomposity.

David Lock shared with me a gut impulse he had during trial to call a witness's bluff, particularly as to the chair, and challenge them to come down from the stand to demonstrate their theory. I believe his gut was right—I would like to have seen him follow it. Come down from the safety of the witness stand, Dr. Petty and Dr. Burton, drop a Luger, close your eyes, fall to the floor, jerk around like a flounder plugged into a wall socket, and re-create the chair and Danny Hansford's position.

It is difficult to imagine a defense spending so much time and money to produce such a collection of junk in the form of testimony. I would not have advised taking the jalopy they pieced together onto the highway. You could leave pieces strewn behind you and end up sitting on the side of the road with nothing but a seat and a steering wheel, like a character in an old silent movie.

But somehow James Williams managed to drive that coughing, smoke-spewing jalopy away from the Richmond County Courthouse—only to drop dead eight months later. Even as Williams's heart stopped on the floor of his study, in the distance, wafting over the marsh, through the moss-draped oaks and into the heart of Historic Savannah, the faint sound of tour buses could be heard, warming their engines.

I suggest one more brass plaque for Savannah's Historic Landmark District, to be erected in Monterey Square, directly in front of Mercer House.

It should simply read: "He Did It."

PART TWELVE

EPILOGUE

CHAPTER 47

A BOOK, A MOVIE, A TOURIST TSUNAMI

The Book

Midnight in the Garden of Good and Evil is known in Savannah as "The Book" or simply *Midnight*. John Berendt's book spent over 200 weeks on the *New York Times* Best Seller List, sold millions of copies, has been translated into twenty or more languages, became a major motion picture directed by Clint Eastwood, and sparked a tourism tsunami that swept Savannah up in its wake and caused the city to lose its collective mind in the process.

The Book purported to tell the story of James Williams's killing of Danny Hansford and the murder case that followed. The Book was not, however, about the crime, in my opinion. Nor is The Book on trial here—so long as it's understood for what it was: a literary work loosely wrapped around a murder case. At various points within its pages, The Book is a distant cousin of the truth, the absolute truth, and anything but the truth.

In my view, The Book was more a *product* of the *Williams* case than it was about the case. The killing and the trials of Williams for his murder attracted the author's interest, so he went to Savannah after the second trial, hung out with Williams and his defense lawyers, took up residence in Savannah for several years, and eventually wrote a book about the city, using the murder case as literary *entrée*—in other words, a reason to be at the party.

Contrary to what might be expected, I didn't dislike the book. It was, in my view, a well-written mix of fiction and nonfiction, like cotton candy spun around a central shaft of moderately sturdy cardboard. I like cotton candy. Who doesn't?

The Book should never be mistaken for nonfiction, however. It contained a variety of facts: true facts, garbled facts, facts ignored when inconvenient to the narrative, and other facts wholly made up, presumably having been judged more interesting than the real thing. The chief problem with Berendt's tale was that he placed himself in Savannah, involved in events that never took place or that took place long before he arrived.

If there is any question about the objectivity of The Book, one need only know that the author had a contract with Williams, drawn up by Williams's defense attorney. Would you imagine that the late, great Vincent Bugliosi, author of *Helter Skelter*, had a contract with Charles Manson?

Berendt took up with the defense team. As a result, Seiler was rewarded with a part in the film adaptation of the book, along with his dog UGA, the University of Georgia mascot. (To be clear, UGA is a damn good dog and is not responsible for his owner.)

While the foregoing is criticism of The Book, it is not criticism of the writing. There is a difference. The Book was a finalist for the Pulitzer Prize in nonfiction, until it was removed by the committee, reportedly because of the number of inaccuracies in it. It didn't get on the list in the first place without having literary merit.

In 1998, a special report was written for the *Fulton County Daily Report* (at the time, the official legal organ of Fulton County, county seat of Atlanta) by Marcel P. Dufresne, Associate Professor of Journalism, Investigative and Computer-Assisted Reporting, and Journalism Ethics at the University of Connecticut. The article was titled "'Midnight' in the Garden of Fact and Fiction." The article included the following quote from John Carrol, Editor of the *Baltimore Sun* and a Pulitzer board member: "While I'm not hung up by a liberal interpretation of events, as a journalist I'm not prepared to call it nonfiction."[173]

I do not contend that the work wasn't worthy of a Pulitzer. I'm not a Pulitzer judge. The Book was merely in the wrong category. It remains ubiquitously referenced even today as a work of nonfiction. It wasn't.

The Book and this narrative have nothing in common other than the same crime as a starting point. For example, this book contains references, and there are no fictitious characters.

I have always believed that the reality of *Williams* was far more interesting than the fiction: Four murder trials; a changing cast of notorious attorneys, including one of the most famous defense attorneys in America; claims of prosecutorial misconduct; claims of defense lawyer misconduct; claims of police misconduct; claims of witness payoffs; witnesses appearing and disappearing, swearing, recanting, and un-recanting; a British paraphychologist; involvement of the GBI, FBI, and INTERPOL; a female paramour of a criminal landing on a jury; allegations of scandal involving a former governor of the state and the state supreme court; and surprise witnesses coming out of the woodwork. For my nickel, all that is more interesting than a transvestite lounge act, invisible dogs on leashes, and flies on strings, none of which had the slightest thing to do with the *Williams* case.

There is a final irony related to The Book and its film adaptation, The Movie. Each of them contains what I believe to be a clue to the truth. Perhaps his contract with Williams wouldn't let John Berendt reveal what he knew, but there is evidence that he knew the truth, revealed in a fictional conversation between fictional Minerva and fictional Berendt appearing within the closing pages of The Book. If you like, grab a copy and see what you think.

I never spoke with John Berendt, and he never sought me out at the time. By the time he arrived in Savannah, I was in Atlanta, and by the time he wrote his book, I was gone again, from Atlanta to Washington, DC. I don't know if he thought his book told the real story of the Hansford killing, but it didn't appear to me that he assumed that task. The Book seemed far more interested in the figurines in the curio cabinet than in what happened in the study on the fateful night in question.

But before anyone gets too agitated, let me assure you again that I did enjoy The Book. It was well written, in my water-cooler opinion. I can separate the fact from fiction. After that, as they say, what's not to like?

A cautionary note: For readers of The Book who experience a sudden compulsion to visit Savannah, you will love it. But do not be disappointed not to find voodoo rituals, packs of invisible dogs, or roaming male hookers on Bull Street. As for finding ghosts in Bonaventure Cemetery, I have two grandparents, two parents, two sisters, two aunts, and an uncle residing there, and as far as we know, they all stay put.

The Movie

The film adaptation of *Midnight in the Garden of Good and Evil*, written by John Lee Hancock and directed by Clint Eastwood, staring Kevin Spacey, John Cusack, Jude Law, and UGA the bulldog, had an insurmountable task: to capture the essence of Savannah.

Optioning a bestselling book to adapt for the screen is done a lot in Hollywood. At the time, there was no bigger best-seller than *Midnight*. The movie was released on November 21, 1997, at the end of The Book's astounding run on the *New York Times* Best Seller list. It was a no-brainer. With a book people were gobbling up like candy, what could go wrong?

Films that can't go wrong are often the films that do go wrong. I believe the film suffered because the story was not compelling enough to drive a film. Was The Book about a murder case or was it about a glib transvestite and quirky characters? My belief is that The Book failed the film more than the film failed The Book. There was no spine running through it—not the stuff of which Mr. Eastwood's best work is made, in my opinion.

Eventually, I did walk up Third Avenue from my studio apartment in New York City and sit in the dark for two hours and thirty-five minutes, taking a nice trip of the sort I might take on a tour bus. It was a treat to see my hometown on the big screen.

The film's path reminded me of tourists one sees in Savannah, reading a brass historic marker downtown. When finished, they look around, trying to figure out what to do next, and eventually wander off, scanning their tour map for something else interesting. Every time the film didn't know where to go next, it grabbed Lady Chablis like an alcoholic with a taste for cheap wine. Clint Eastwood and Kevin Spacey are people I hold in high esteem. Again, I think the story failed them—no story, no film.

The Book, The Movie, and the *Midnight* frenzy all suffer from an attempt to hang ornaments on Savannah when, in truth, Savannah is remarkable in its own right. It's much like a small European city stuck on the coastal point of a Southern state.

As mentioned above, there is a "clue" in The Movie as well as The Book. At the 2:01:50 mark, fictional John Berendt (John Cusack) is visiting Williams (Kevin Spacey) in jail. Williams tells Berendt a story—a very different story than he told the police or the jury. As Williams relates the story, it appears on the screen, in flashback: Danny comes into the study with a Luger, gives a little speech, and tries to shoot Williams. But in this version, the Luger doesn't fire at all. While Danny is staring at his non-firing Luger, Williams decides to shoot him anyway. He shoots him once in the chest, walks around his desk, and fires two more shots, into the back of Danny's head and into his back. He then takes Danny's Luger, fires off a "fake" shot at his desk, and slides the Luger under Danny's hand.

There are differences between this version and some physical facts, but there is enough correlation that I believe Berendt, the screenwriter (John Lee Hancock), Clint, or all of them, knew Williams did not shoot Danny Hansford in self-defense.

In The Movie, as factional Berendt expresses his shock that Williams just admitted lying to the police and everyone else, the phone rings with news that Williams's conviction has been overturned. His "confession" is cut short and never heard again. I believe this scene is a dog whistle within the movie—a silent callout that says, "We know what really happened."

Or maybe I'm mistaken.

The Tourist Tsunami

The *Midnight* phenomenon is not the first example of the City of Savannah becoming caught up in popular-culture mania. Portions of *Forrest Gump* were also shot in and around the city. Forrest (also known as Tom Hanks) sat on a bench eating his box of chocolates at the southernmost entrance to Wright Square.

Savannah's pride at having been the site of this historic chocolate-munching moment grew to the point that some thought it would be a wonderful idea to build a statue of Forrest Gump eating his box of chocolates on the "historic" site where it took place. Once it was pointed out that Forrest was not a real person, the movement lost steam.

Perhaps, instead, the city should have commissioned a statue of Danny Hansford, who ended up sparking an influx of tourist dollars into Savannah unparalleled in the city's history. He did far more for Savannah's tourist trade by being shot dead by Williams than Forrest Gump ever did by eating a box of Whitman's.

Neither the City of Savannah nor the office of tourism has ever apologized for feeling good about the blessings of *Midnight:* tourists flowing into Savannah seeking voodoo, transvestites, decadent gentility, stashes of Madeira wine, invisible flies and pooches, and who knows what other nonsense. Nor has Williams's sister, who moved into Mercer House and started charging admission to the scene of the most famous killing in Savannah since General Lachlan McIntosh, Commander of the Continental Army in Georgia, shot Button Gwinnett, one of the signatories to the Declaration of Independence, in a duel in 1776.

In The Book, Berendt suggested that the most dominant common desire of Olde Savannah was that the city never change. In a delicious bit of irony, The Book itself began the end of that quaint fantasy. And the city welcomed the attention, without a thought that it was celebrating a killer in the process.

The *Midnight* obsession is inexplicable. How many coffee mugs has another famous killer sold? Yet, for more than twenty years, there stood "The Book" Gift Shop, where you could buy coffee mugs, ornaments, note cards, a photo of Williams in front of Mercer House, and a variety of "Bird Girl" memorabilia, from earrings, to lapel pins, to a candle molded in her shape.[174]

For those curious about what really happened one dark night in a mansion on a moss-draped square, hopefully this narrative has also been of interest.

Mercer House

Following Williams's death and the subsequent death of his mother Blanche, Williams's sister, Dorothy Williams Kingery, took over Mercer House. She later declared the name of the house to be Mercer-Williams House. When I checked the website where tour tickets were reserved, it was called the Mercer Williams House Museum. I suppose calling it a museum allows you to charge admission.

I am not sure what to say about selling tickets to see the place where your brother shot his young lover. Maybe it's best to say nothing. Several people have relayed to me that Ms. Kingery is a very nice woman, and I presume that is true.

I have also been told (Savannah does love its gossip) that her brother didn't like her, so maybe that's why tourists claim they have seen him haunting the upper floors. Maybe he's mad that she ended up with the house.

As for the name of the house, I refer to it by its original name: Mercer House. Ms. Kingery can, of course, call it anything she wishes. But adding the name of a killer to the name of a landmark identified with the Mercer family is a choice I have chosen to reject.

ENDNOTES

1. Supplemental Report of M.J. Anderson, 05-02-81, CRN-81-0500398.

2. Louis XV bureau plat with tooled leather top, ormolu acanthus mounts and sabots, serpentine edges, cabriole legs and large drawer hardware, either created by or in the style of J. Dubois. Source: Roderick A. Hardy, Hardy Halperin, Inc., Atlanta and Palm Springs.

3. Sotheby's Catalog, Lot 399, sold October 20, 2000.

4. Supplemental Report of M.J. Anderson, 05-02-81, CRN-81-0500398.

5. Written, signed statement of Joseph E. Goodman, 05-02-81, 10:30 a.m., Witnessed by D.E. Ragan.

6. Supplemental Report of Det. D.E. Ragan, 05-05-81.

7. Teel, Leonard Ray. "Strengthening Their Case." *The Atlanta Journal Constitution* 24 Nov. 1985: M12.

8. BYF, "P.08", Caliber 9MM., Semi-Automatic Pistol, Ser. No. 5378. Official Report, Georgia Bureau of Investigation, Division of Forensic Services, S81-01741, October 21, 1981 (Item 22A).

9. Photo Credit: Savannah Morning News Archive.

10. In 2011, Bethesda was renamed Bethesda Academy. It is no longer an orphanage.

11. Georgia Department of Human Resources, Georgia Regional Hospital at Savannah, Records, Social Summary, December 8, 1975.

12. Ibid.

13. Debra Lynn Blevins, Transcribed Statement, District Attorney's Office, January 5, 1982.

14. Ibid.

15. Scardino, Albert. "Williams' Exclusive Interview." *The Georgia Gazette* 6 May 1981: 1A.

16. Joseph E. Goodman, Transcribed Statement, District Attorney's Office, October 12, 1981.

17. George Alan Hill, Transcribed Statement to District Attorney's Office Chief Investigator J.D. Smith, January 4, 1982.

18. Ibid.

19. Ibid.

20. Joseph E. Goodman, Transcribed Statement to District Attorney's Office Chief Investigator J.D. Smith, October 12, 1981.

21. George Alan Hill, Transcribed Statement to District Attorney's Office Chief Investigator J.D. Smith, January 4, 1982.

22. Debra Lynn Blevins, Transcribed Statement to District Attorney's Office Chief Investigator J.D. Smith, January 5, 1982.

23. George Alan Hill, Transcribed Statement, District Attorney's Office, January 4, 1982.

24. Debra Lynn Blevins, Transcribed Statement, District Attorney's Office, January 5, 1982.

25. George Alan Hill, Transcribed Statement, District Attorney's Office, January 4, 1982.

26. Smith, Michelle R. "Pro Football Player Charged with Murder." Associated Press 26 June 2013. Accessed 06-26-2013 at http://bigstory.ap.org/article/pats-player-hernandez-taken-home-handcuffs.

27. Montgomery, Bill. "Defendant Acquitted of Savannah Slaying in Fourth Jury Trial." *The Atlanta Constitution* 13 May 1989: State News, A-1.

28. Supplemental Report of M.J. Anderson, 05-02-81, CRN-81-0500398.

29. Ibid.

30. Joseph E. Goodman, Transcribed Statement, District Attorney's Office, October 12, 1981.

31. Scardino, Albert. "Williams' Exclusive Interview." *The Georgia Gazette* 6 May 1981: 1A.

32. Ibid.

33. Report of M.J. Anderson, 4-3-81, 81-040051[X], Incident Report, Continuation and Supplemental (4 pgs.).

34. Ibid.

35. Ibid.

36. Joseph E. Goodman, Transcribed Statement, District Attorney's Office, October 12, 1981.

37. Lowrey, D. "Williams Cites Self-Defense." *Savannah News-Press* 3 May 1981: 1A.

38. Scardino, Albert. "Williams' Exclusive Interview." *The Georgia Gazette* 6 May 1981: 1A.

39. Ibid.

40. Ibid.

41. Joseph E. Goodman, Transcribed Statement, District Attorney's Office, October 12, 1981.

42. For the trivia buff, in 1988, Del Taco merged with the Naugles chain and went to 24/7 service.

43. Lowrey, D. "Williams Cites Self-Defense." *Savannah News-Press* 3 May 1981: 1A.

44. Curriden, Mark. "Lions of the Trial Bar: Bobby Lee Cook." *ABA Journal,* 2 March 2009. 25 June 2015. Accessed at http://www.abajournal.com/magazine/article/bobby_lee_cook/.

45. Ibid.

46. Sulzberger, A.G. "Town Mute for 30 Years About a Bully's Killing." *New York Times* 15 Dec. 2010. Accessed at http://www.nytimes.com/2010/12/16/us/ 16bully.html.

47. Joseph E. Goodman, Transcribed Statement, District Attorney's Office, October 12, 1981.

48. Ibid.

49. Oral Statement of Joseph Goodman to SPD Det. D.E. Ragan, May 2, 1981, per written notes of Det. Ragan.

50. Ibid.

51. Ibid.

52. Ibid.

53. Written, signed statement of Joseph E. Goodman, 05-02-81, 10:30 a.m., Witnessed by D.E. Ragan.

54. Reference: https://goo.gl/maps/gxdWN. Goodman's address was 2011 Linnhurst Drive and the route he took was west to Reynolds, Reynolds to Victory Drive, Victory to Drayton, Drayton to Gaston, Gaston to Bull, north on Bull, to and around Monterey Square, to Mercer House at 429 Bull Street. The distance is 4.4 miles. Travel time, with no traffic, estimated at 14 minutes.

55. Joseph E. Goodman, Transcribed Statement, District Attorney's Office, October 12, 1981..

56. Written, signed statement of Joseph E. Goodman, 05-02-81, 10:30 a.m., Witnessed by D.E. Ragan.

57. *Williams I*, Transcript, p. 162.

58. Aristotle, *Posterior Analytics*, transl. McKeon (1963), p. 150. [Publication information no available.]

59. Official Report, Georgia Bureau of Investigation, Division of Forensic Services, S81-01741, October 21, 1981. "BYF" is a WWII German ordnance code assigned to Mauser-Werke, Oberndorf am Neckar.

60. Erfurt Lugers were manufactured by a government arsenal in the town of Erfurt, Germany.

61. Official Report, Georgia Bureau of Investigation, Division of Forensic Services, S81-01741, October 21, 1981.

62. Fitzsimons, Bernard, ed. *The Illustrated Encyclopedia of Weapons and Warfare* (London: Phoebus, 1977), Volume 16, p. 1778, "Luger."

63. Candler General Hospital, Pathology Report, Autopsy CA-27-81, Performed 5-2-81, Danny L. Hansford.

64. Official Report, Georgia Bureau of Investigation, Division of Forensic Services, S81-01741, October 21, 1981 (Item 27).

65. Ibid.

66. Roderick A. Hardy, Hardy Halperin, Inc., Atlanta & Palm Springs.

67. Hsien-Hui Meng, Hsei-Chang Lee, "Elemental analysis of primer mixtures [...]," *Forensic Science Journal*, 2007, Vol. 6, No. 1., pp.39-55.

68. Official Report, Georgia Bureau of Investigation, Division of Forensic Services, S81-01741, October 21, 1981.

69. Supplemental Report of Det. D.E. Ragan, 05-05-81.

70. Hendricks, Gary. "Medical Examiner in Five Counties Says He'll Try to Handle Workload." *Atlanta Constitution* 11 Oct. 1988. Hard copy clipping.

71. McDonald, R. Robin. "Controversial Medical Examiner Goes Private." *Fulton County Daily Report* 29 Feb. 2000: 5.

72. Scardino, Albert. "Williams' Exclusive Interview." *The Georgia Gazette* 6 May 1981: 4A.

73. Joseph E. Goodman, Transcribed Statement, District Attorney's Office, October 12, 1981.

74. Supplemental Report of Det. D.E. Ragan, 05-05-81.

75. Scardino, Albert. "Williams' Exclusive Interview." *The Georgia Gazette* 6 May 1981: 4A.

76. Supplemental Report of M.J. Anderson, 05-02-81, CRN-81-0500398.

77. Georgia Regional Hospital, Danny Hansford Record, June 1979 Admission.

78. Supplemental Report of M.J. Anderson, 05-02-81, CRN-81-0500398.

79. This was erroneously referenced in *Midnight in the Garden of Good and Evil* by John Berendt.

80. Motion for New Trial, February 2, 1982; Amendment to Motion for a New Trial, filed April 12, 1982.

81. Transcript, Hearing on Motion for New Trial [As Amended], April 23, 1982.

82. Murder is designated a capital offense, and as such, appeals are taken directly to the supreme court.

83. *Williams v. State*, 250 Ga. 463 at 465 (1983).

84. Ibid.

85. *Williams v. State*, 258 Ga. 305 at 308 (1988).

86. *Williams v. State,* Brief on Behalf of the Appellant, June 30, 1982, at p. 29.

87. Id. at 46.

88. Id. at 47.

89. Id. at 48.

90. Id. at 51.

91. Bugliosi, Vincent. *Outrage: The Five Reasons Why O. J. Simpson Got Away with Murder* (Norton Kindle Edition, 2008), Kindle location 60.

92. The most recent firm name was Garland, Samuel & Loeb, P.C. Mr. Catts, at last check, was practicing in the Brunswick, Georgia, area under the firm name Catts & Brooks. I do not vouch for how current this information is. The State Bar of Georgia phone number is 404-527-8700.

93. May she rest in peace. Kathy Aldridge was one damned fine lawyer—and as tough as any nail ever made.

94. Joseph E. Goodman, Transcribed Statement, District Attorney's Office, October 12, 1981.

95. Now Armstrong Atlantic State University.

96. Fed. R. Evid. 611(c).

97. Official Report, Georgia Bureau of Investigation, Division of Forensic Services, S81-01741, October 21, 1981.

98. Fuhrman, Mark. *Murder in Brentwood*. (New York: Kensington, 1997).

99. Candler General Hospital, Pathology Report, Autopsy CA-27-81, Performed 5-2-81, Danny L. Hansford.

100. Williams, BJ, et. al. "Incidence of unintended durotomy in spine surgery based on 108,478 cases." *Neurosurgery* 2011 Jan, Vol. 68, No. 1: 117–23; discussion 123-4. http://www.ncbi.nlm.nih.gov/pubmed/21150757

101. Stolke D, Sollmann W, Seifert V. "Intra- and Postoperative Complications in Lumbar Disc Surgery," *Spine* 1989, No. 14: 56–9.

102. Georgia Regional Hospital, Danny Hansford Record, June 1979 Admission.

103. Motion for New Trial, October 21, 1983, filed October 31, 1983, as amended May 7, 1984, June 13, 1984, June 20, 1984, July 17, 1984, and July 25, 1984.

104. Affidavit of Timothy Wayne DeLoach dated June 2, 1984, and filed under cover of *Defendant's Amendment to Motion for New Trial - Rebuttal Affidavits*, filed June 13, 1984, Case No. 81-34982.

105. Affidavit of Walter Mitchell, Jr., Sheriff of Superior Court, Chatham County, sworn July 16, 1984.

106. Handwritten letter of James Williams dated August 11, 1984.

107. Memorandum of Chief Investigator J.D. Smith to District Attorney Spencer Lawton Jr., May 22, 1987.

108. *Knox v. Hayes*, 933 F. Supp. 1574, at 1586 (1995).

109. Id. at 1584.

110. *Williams v. State*, 254 Ga. 508 at 512 (1985).

111. Affidavit in Response to Supplemental Motion, filed November 11, 1987, Superior Court of Chatham County, Eastern Judicial Circuit; *Defendant James A. Williams' Motion to Strike as Scandalous, Impertinent and Immaterial Matters Improvidently Brought to the Supreme Court of Georgia* (Exhibit B), filed December 7, 1987, Supreme Court of Georgia.

112. Kathy Hogan Trocheck and David Corvette. "Murder Case Now Lawyers' Grudge Fight." *The Atlanta Constitution* 9 Dec. 1987: 23-A.

113. Transcript of Hearing on Motion to Suppress, August 12, 1986: 16.

114. Id. at 33.

115. Id. at 34.

116. Id. at 33, 34.

117. Id. at 47.

118. Daniell, R. "The Scandal That Shook Savannah." *US* 5 May 1986: 50.

119. Id. at 51.

120. District Attorney's Office, Interview with Rosemary Daniell, transcribed February

20, 1986.

121. Joseph E. Goodman, Transcribed Statement, District Attorney's Office, October 12, 1981, p. 6.

122. Candler General Hospital, Pathology Report, Autopsy CA-27-81, Performed 5-2-81, Danny L. Hansford.

123. *Final Report on Particle Analysis for Gunshot Residue Detection*, Law Enforcement Development Group, NILECJ, Law Enforcement Assistance Administration, US Department of Justice, September 1977. p. 52.

124. Candler General Hospital Admission Form, Danny Lewis Hansford, May 2, 1981.

125. Affidavit of James C. Metts Jr. filed by the defense August 14, 1987, p. 5.

126. Ibid.

127. Bynum, Russ. "Savannah Coroner of 40 Years Exits Under Suspicion." Associated Press 15 May 2013. Accessed 08-08-2013 at http://bigstory.ap.org/article/savannah-coroner-40-years-exits-under-suspicion.

128. Supplemental Report of Det. J. P. Jordan, 5-19-81, CRN-81-0500398.

129. Marilyn Case, Transcribed Statement, District Attorney's Office, October 5, 1987.

130. *Official Report*, GBI Division of Forensic Services Division, Case No. 87-20585, October 2, 1987, K.D. Ehret, Document Examiner.

131. Joseph Kelvin Williamson, Transcribed Statement, Special Agent R.S. Stone, Georgia Bureau of Investigation, May 9, 1984.

132. Bugliosi, Vincent. *Outrage: The Five Reasons Why O. J. Simpson Got Away with Murder* (Norton Kindle Edition, 2008), Kindle location 60.

133. Hendricks, Gary. "Medical Examiner in Five Counties Says He'll Try to Handle Workload." *Atlanta Constitution* 11 Oct. 1988. Hard copy clipping.

134. M. Trimpe. "The Current Status of GSR Examinations." FBI Law Enforcement Bulletin, May 2011. Accessed at http://www.fbi.gov/stats-services/publications/law-enforcement-bulletin/may_2011/

135. Candler General Hospital, Pathology Report, Autopsy CA-27-81, Performed 5-2-81, Danny L. Hansford.

136. In-Chambers Conference, *State of Georgia vs. James A. Williams*, June 9, 1987, p. 12.

137. Trocheck, Kathy Hogan. "Antiques Dealer Murder Case Threatens Savannah Veneer." *The Atlanta Journal and Constitution* 12 July 1987: 1A.

138. Skutch, Jan. "Foreperson: Prejudice Not Factor in Williams Trial Deliberations." *Savannah Morning News* 19 June 1987, photocopy w/o page number.

139. Barry Thomas, Transcribed Statement, District Attorney's Office, September 30, 1987.

140. Ibid.

141. Chief Investigator J.D. Smith, Confidential Memo to File, *State v. James A. Williams*, September 24, 1987.

142. Aleph Kamal, Transcribed Statement, New Scotland Yard (Metropolitan Police Service), Det. Sgt. P. Smith, 23rd September 1987, and Supplemental Statement thereto.

143. Ibid.

144. Ibid.

145. Allen Brock, Transcribed Statement, District Attorney's Office, March 28, 1989.

146. Id. at 3.

147. Id. at 9.

148. Id. at 16.

149. Id. at 17.

150. Television News Reports; *See*, Brief in Support of Motion to Disqualify District Attorney and His Assistants, August 13, 1987, 33; Transcript, September 17, 1987, 12, 18.

151. *Williams v. State*, 258 Ga. 305, 308 (1988).

152. Order on Defendant's Motion for Change of Venue, *State of Georgia vs. James A. Williams*, Case No. 081-34982, Hon. James W. Head, March 21, 1989.

153. Order on Defendant's Motions as to Double Jeopardy and Disqualification of District Attorney, *State of Georgia vs. James A. Williams*, Case No. 81-34982-H, November 2, 1987.

154. *Skilling v. United States*, 130 S.Ct. 2896, fn. 35 (2010).

155. *Rideau v. Louisiana*, 373 U.S. 723, 83 S.Ct. 1417, 10 L.Ed.2d 663 (1963).

156. *Skilling*, 130 S.Ct., at 2915.

157. Order on Defendant's Motions as to Double Jeopardy and Disqualification of District Attorney, Hon. James W. Head, November 2, 1987, p. 8.

158. Id., p. 7.

159. Skutch, Jan. "4th Jury Acquits Williams." *Savannah Morning News* 13 May 1989: 1-A.

160. Order on Defendant's Motions as to Double Jeopardy and Disqualification of District Attorney, Hon. James W. Head, November 2, 1987, Ibid.

161. *Coleman v. The State*, 257 Ga. 313, 357 SE2d 566 (1987).

162. Ibid.

163. Spencer Lawton Confidential Memorandum, March 12, 1997.

164. Cote, Joseph G. "Canada to Extradite One Suspect in 1988 Nashua Murder; Other Man Won't Face Fourth Trial." *The Telegraph* 8 Aug. 2013: 1. Accessed at http://www.nashuatelegraph.com/news.

165. Montgomery, Bill. "Defendant Acquitted of Savannah Slaying in Fourth Jury Trial." *The Atlanta Journal Constitution* 13 May 1989: State News, A-1.

166. E-mail from Barbara Wright, May 27, 2013.

167. Transcript, *Williams II*, 897.

168. Notes on reverse side of signed sketch by Danny Hansford.

169. Joseph Kelvin Williamson, Transcribed Statement, Special Agent R.S. Stone, Georgia Bureau of Investigation, May 9, 1984.

170. Debra Lynn Blevins, Transcribed Statement, District Attorney's Office, January 5, 1982.

171. O'Brien, Darcy. *The Hillside Stranglers* (Premier Digital Publishing Kindle Edition, 2013), Kindle location 6668.

172. Shakespeare, William. *Hamlet.* I.i.58–60.

173. Dufresne, Marcel. "'Midnight' in the Garden of Fact and Fiction." *Fulton County Daily Report* 21 Aug. 1998: 1.

174. The statue was originally sculpted by Sylvia Shaw Judson in 1936. Only four originals were cast. The "Bird Girl" is a 50" bronze. The statue was removed from Bonaventure Cemetery because of concerns for its safety and was given to the Telfair Museum of Art in Savannah.

CPSIA information can be obtained
at www.ICGtesting.com
Printed in the USA
FFOW01n1440140716
25814FF